Identity and Diversity:
Gender and the Experience of Education

Identity and Diversity: Gender and the Experience of Education

This Reader is part of an Open University Course (E826) Gender Issues in Education: Equality and Difference, forming one module in the MA in Education programme. The selection is related to other material available to students. Opinions expressed in individual articles are not necessarily those of the course team or of the University.

Other volumes published as part of this course by Multilingual Matters Ltd in association with The Open University:

Debates and Issues in Feminist Research and Pedagogy
    J. HOLLAND and M. BLAIR with S. SHELDON (eds)
Equality and Inequality in Education Policy
    L. DAWTREY, J. HOLLAND and M. HAMMER with S. SHELDON (eds)

Please information about books of related interest, please contact:
Multilingual Matters Ltd,
Frankfurt Lodge, Clevedon Hall, Victoria Road,
Clevedon, Avon BS21 7SJ, England

Gender Issues in Education: Equality and Difference

Identity and Diversity: Gender and the Experience of Education

A Reader edited by
Maud Blair and Janet Holland,
with Sue Sheldon

at The Open University

MULTILINGUAL MATTERS LTD
Clevedon • Philadelphia • Adelaide
in association with
THE OPEN UNIVERSITY

Library of Congress Cataloging in Publication Data

Identity and Diversity: Gender and the Experience of Education: A Reader/
Edited by Maud Blair and Janet Holland with Sue Sheldon.
(Equality and Difference)
Includes bibliographical references and index.
1. Sex differences in education. 2. Feminism and education. 3. Identity
(Psychology). 4. Masculinity (Psychology). 5. Educational sociology.
I. Blair, Maud. II. Holland, Janet. III. Sheldon, Sue. IV. Series.
LC212.9.I34   1995
370.19'345–dc20   94-27881

British Library Cataloguing in Publication Data

A CIP catalogue record for this book is available from the British Library.

ISBN 1-85359-248-X (hbk)
ISBN 1-85359-247-1 (pbk)

Multilingual Matters Ltd

UK: Frankfurt Lodge, Clevedon Hall, Victoria Road, Clevedon, Avon BS21 7SJ.
USA: 1900 Frost Road, Suite 101, Bristol, PA 19007, USA.
Australia: P.O. Box 6025, 83 Gilles Street, Adelaide, SA 5000, Australia.

Selection, editorial matter and commissioned items (Articles 4 and 15)
copyright © 1995 The Open University.

Cover design by Bob Jones Associates.
Index by Meg Davies (Society of Indexers).
Typeset by Action Typesetting, Gloucester.
Printed and bound in Great Britain by WBC Ltd, Bridgend.

CONTENTS

PREFACE

This Reader is the first of a set of three which have been prepared for the course E826, *Gender Issues in Education: Equality and Difference*, a module in the Open University's taught MA in Education. The course also includes two companion Readers, *Equality and Inequality in Education Policy* and *Debates and Issues in Feminist Research and Pedagogy*, as well as a Study Guide and audio-cassette materials.

In this Reader we introduce the notion of diversity and difference in education, first through a series of auto/biographical and life history accounts of educational experience, and secondly through articles demonstrating the theoretical diversity in explanations for gender difference. A further group of articles highlights the construction of different social identities. A wide range of perspectives are covered within this volume, and the opinions expressed are not necessarily those of the course writers nor of The Open University. The Reader should be of interest to anyone with a concern for equality in education.

Further information about the course can be obtained by writing to: Central Enquiry Service, PO Box 200, The Open University, Milton Keynes MK7 6YZ.

SOURCES

We would like to thank the authors and publishers concerned for kindly granting permission to reproduce copyright material in this Reader. Every effort has been made to trace the correct copyright owners, both authors and publishers, as listed by article below.

1. **b. hooks** Writing Autobiography
   From: hooks, b. (1989) *Talking Back: Thinking Feminist—Thinking Black* (pp. 155–159). London: Sheba Feminist Press.
2. **C. Steedman** Death of a Good Women
   From: Steedman, C. (1986) *Landscape for a Good Woman* (Chapter 2, pp. 1–24). London: Virago.
3. **F. Fever** Who Cares? Memories of a Childhood in Care
   From: Fever, F. (1984) *Who Cares? Memories of a Childhood in Barnardos.* London: Warner Books.
4. **U. Maylor** Identity, Migration and Education
   Commissioned article.
5. **L. Hills** The Senga Syndrome: Reflections on Twenty-one Years in Scottish Education
   From: Fewell, J. and Paterson, F. (eds) (1990) *Girls in Their Prime* (pp. 148–165). Edinburgh: Scottish Academic Press.
6. **M. Evans** Culture and Class
   From: Evans, M. (1991) *A Good School: Life at a Girls' Grammar School in the 1960s* (pp. 24–101). London: Women's Press (34 Great Sutton Street, London EV1V 0DX).
7. **Ngahuia Te Awekotuku** He Whare Tangata; He Whare Kura? What's Happening to our Maori Girls?
   From: Middleton, S. (ed.) (1988) *Women and Education in Aotearoa* (pp. 89–96). Wellington: Bridget Williams Books.
8. **M. Wetherell and C. Griffin** Feminist Psychology and the Study of Men and Masculinity: Assumptions and Perspectives
   From: *Feminism and Psychology*, Vol. 1 (3), pp. 361–91 (1991). London: Sage.
9. **J. Lown** Feminist Perspectives
   From: U207 *Issues in Womens Studies, Course Introduction* (pp. 53–62). Milton Keynes: Open University.
10. **J. Kenway** Feminist Theories of the State: To Be Or Not To Be?
    From: Muetzelfeldt, M. (ed.) (1992) *Society, State and Politics in Australia* (pp. 108–44). Annandale: Pluto Press.
11. **J. Flax** Postmodernism and Gender Relations in Feminist Theory
    From: Nicholson, L. (ed.) (1990) *Feminism/Postmodernism* (pp. 39–62). London: Routledge.
12. **R. Aziz** Feminism and the Challenge of Racism: Deviance or Difference?
    From: Crowley, H. and Himmelweit, S. (1992) *Knowing Women: Feminism and Knowledge* (pp. 291–305). Milton Keynes: The Open University.
13. **J. Hearn and D.H.J. Morgan** Contested Discourses on Men and Masculinities
    From: Hearn, J. and Morgan, D.H.J. (eds) (1990) *Men, Masculinities and Social Theory* (pp. 4–17). London: Unwin Hyman.
14. **K. Mercer and I. Julien** True Confessions: A Discourse on Images of Black Male Sexuality
    From: Chapman, R. and Rutherford, J. (eds) (1988) *Male Order: Unwrapping Masculinity* (pp. 131–141). London: Lawrence and Wishart.

INTRODUCTION

The recognition of diversity and difference has been a significant development in feminist theory in recent years. In this volume we attempt to approach and demonstrate these developments in a number of ways. First by drawing on women's and men's own experiences in auto/biographical and life history accounts, second by providing a range of theoretical explanations for gender and difference, and third by examining perspectives on the construction of social identities. We try in our selection of articles to illustrate the *major* axes around which difference coalesces into identities – gender, race and class – and provide studies and research which have illuminated these social processes.

One of the features of the feminist use of autobiography as research method and technique is that it can give a voice to those who would have traditionally remained silenced. However, as some of the contributors to Part 1 of the book show, finding a voice through autobiography is not a straightforward task. Hooks describes the psychological and cultural barriers to producing an autobiography, and in her short article she captures the tension between the autobiographical 'I' and the distortions of memory in constructing personal histories.

Steedman suggests a form of subversion of central cultural norms. She describes how working class auto/biography has been placed in cultural, historical and class analysis so as to render invisible some, particularly women's lives. She is intent in her article to show how autobiography can be used to question central cultural narratives, and to provide disruption and counterpoint. Elements of her own and her mother's biography are woven into the argument. Steedman's article provides a demonstration of recent developments in sociology in which the divisions between autobiography and biography are rejected since the two are seen as inextricably intermeshed and so cannot be considered separately – hence the term auto/biography.

Fred Fever's article is a personal account of the devastating impact of neglect and child abuse. It is a story of the adult abuse of power over children and the destructive effect this has on children's educational and life chances. The tone of the writing is itself a testimony to Fever's moving statement that the abuse had left him 'emotionally dead'.

Maylor in her article moves between the broad context of the interrelationship between her own and her father's biographies, and the tensions and contradictions of their personal relationship. She explores the intersection of gender, race, and class, with education as a key component in this complex web.

Leslie Hills' educational autobiography starts as she enters university, and the experience of the Scottish education system, which she describes from the viewpoint of a teacher in schools, an advisory teacher, and in educational administration. Exercising a certain amount of autonomy as a classroom teacher, and feeling cushioned from the gendered power structure, it was a shock to experience the full force of male domination within the educational hierarchy, and the absence of women in the centres of power. She vividly documents this absence.

Mary Evans describes a girls' grammar school in the 1950s as a prime location of social and cultural reproduction of the English middle-class girl. These schools, despite internal contradictions, 'maintained a homogeneous world which could even absorb bright children from the working class and produce a standard grammar school child'. Evans interweaves description and analysis to provide a collective educational biography of herself and her compatriots, related to the broader social and political context.

In a compelling narrative, Te Awekotuku also deals with issues of gender, race and class – in her case in the context of the New Zealand education system. She describes her experiences of schooling, a history of displacement, cultural disruption and alienation and her attempts to retain her cultural identity in the face of this onslaught. Her resistance takes forms which at different times accommodate or reject the cultural impositions of the educational system.

Wetherall and Griffin provide academic and personal biographies of men in psychology and sociology who are currently studying men and masculinity, an area of investigation which has expanded rapidly since the mid 1980s. Drawing on interviews or written statements from a number of researchers, the authors indicate through the words of these men their personal routes into 'male' studies, and the theoretical and methodological choices they have made. In this way Wetherall and Griffin lay out the main assumptions and perspectives underlying the study of men and masculinity both in the UK and the USA, and highlight some of the questions and issues it raises for feminists. They conclude their discussion with contrasting feminist views on men studying men and masculinity.

The articles in Part 2 provide examples of the variety of ways in which gender and difference have been theorized. Lown sketches the history of second-wave feminism, identifying the image of feminisms which emerged – Socialist/Marxist, lesbian, psycho-analytical, revolutionary, radical, Black and liberal feminism. This allows the following articles on theorizing gender and difference to be seen in the context of the historical development of feminist theory and practice. Feminists have been struggling to formulate the relationship between feminism and postmodernism since the mid 1970s, and to draw some conclusions about the usefulness of postmodern philosophy for feminism. Some fear that to take on the implications of postmodernist thought will threaten the political project of feminism, others feel with

Flax that 'feminist theory reveals and contributes to the growing uncertainty within Western intellectual circles about the appropriate grounding and methods for explaining and interpreting human experience'. Kenway examines the implications of postmodernism and post-structuralism for feminist theory, particularly in relation to the state. In this useful article, she outlines basic feminist theories of the state, describes the theoretical underpinning for post-structuralist, and more generally postmodern feminism drawn from the work of Foucault, and outlines both the drawbacks and advantages offered to feminist theorising from this perspective. While she recognises the challenge that postmodernism and post-structuralism present to feminist theory, the practical necessity for feminist political action presents them in turn with a demanding political and theoretical task if they are to be of use to feminism. In the article which follows, Flax sees feminism as taking a postmodern stance in theorizing gender relations, arguing that feminist theories should encourage us to tolerate and interpret ambivalence, ambiguity and multiplicity. She sees the tasks of feminist theorists as fourfold: (i) to articulate feminist viewpoints of/within the social worlds in which we live; (ii) to think about how we are affected by these worlds; (iii) to consider the ways in which how we think about them may be implicated in existing power/ knowledge relationships; and (iv) to imagine ways in which these worlds can be transformed.

The black feminist attempt to shift the ground of white feminist discourse, throws these requirements into sharp relief. Aziz argues that the adversary is not white feminists, but a feminism which comes from a universalizing white perspective. She outlines the black feminist critique, and sees the relationship between feminism and its critics as 'stormy', 'a schism', but potentially productive in suggesting new forms of alliance between women, and the creation of new forms of struggle, leading to what she calls a feminism of difference.

Hearn and Morgan bring together a range of perspectives on the theory and theorizing of men and masculinities within the social sciences. They contend that such studies owe much to feminist critiques and analyses of gender. However, the specific focus on men and masculinities is relatively recent and raises important questions about the structures and practices of the social sciences themselves and the role of studies of men and masculinities within the discipline. What criteria should govern the naming of such studies? What should be their focus? What is their role in relation to feminist theories of gender? What are the political and social implications of such studies? How is the complex interplay between axes such as class, race and sexuality to be addressed in the study of men and masculinities?

Mercer and Julien illustrate this latter point in the representation of black men. They are critical of the lack of political awareness of issues of 'race' within the white gay men's movement. This lack of awareness not only renders Black gay men invisible within the gay movement, but allows for the active construction and reproduction of hegemonic images of Black masculinity as evidenced in the representations of Black male sexuality in the photographic work of Robert Maplethorpe. This places the gay movement in a contradictory position in relation to its own politics, a contradiction which according to the authors, remains unrecognized.

Gilligan develops a psychological theory of gender difference, arguing that whilst early childhood might be a crucial period for masculine development, adolescence is critical for women. She argues that a relational crisis — a moment when vulnerability becomes unbearably heightened, occurs at different times for boys and girls living in patriarchy. Initiation into patriarchy involves the dissociation of self and voice from women, and a loss of relationship with self in order to form external 'relationships' appropriate to masculinity and femininity. For boys this crisis, occurring in early childhood, tends to be inchoate and laced with early loss and terror; girls in adolescence can articulate their relational crisis, but in separating from women they must also make a split within themselves which some attempt to resist. Gilligan concludes hopefully: 'The importance of girls' resistance to making these splits lies in the fact that if listened to it challenges us to think of alternatives.'

In Part 3 the discussion covers the construction of a range of social identities. Lloyd argues that disabled women are marginalized and disempowered, even in movements which might be seen as supportive. The women's movement is oriented towards non-disabled women and the disability movement is oriented towards disabled men. She sees their position as similar to Black women, who disappear from the dominant discourses of feminism (concerned with white women) and the Black movement (concerned with Black men). Drawing on the experience of Black feminists, Lloyd develops a feminist model of disability which can retrieve disabled women from invisibility. Vicinus traces the development of lesbian identities, demonstrating that such identities are both historically and culturally contingent. She traces the diversity of lesbian experiences and the changing modes of lesbian representation through the centuries.

The theme of invisibility, negative representations and constructions of sexuality is continued in Mac an Ghaill's discussion of Black gays in the school context. Here class, 'race' and gender interlink in the contradictory discourses of teachers and students to, on the one hand, undermine the validity of a gay identity, and on the other to deny the existence of Black gays through the construction of racialised Black masculinities.

Young women in search of a positive sexual identity have many hurdles to overcome, not least of which is pressure from peers, family, community and men to be and to behave in a particular way in relation to their sexuality. Often these messages and pressures are contradictory. Holland *et al.* develop a framework for analysis of the personal, social and male pressures which young women experience in the process of the construction of their sexual identity, and discuss the possibilities for empowerment, using the interrelated concepts of intellectual and experiential empowerment. They draw on empirical data from 150 in-depth interviews with young women (16–21 years old) and argue radically that: 'If women are to be able to negotiate the boundaries of sexual encounters so as to ensure both their safety and their satisfaction, the way in which both men and women are constituted as sexual subjects must change.'

Separate schooling has remained a theme in feminist discussions of girls' achievement in education. Khanum picks up this theme in relation to separate Muslim schools where the struggle to preserve the religious and cultural identities of Muslim girls, can sometimes occur at the expense of their academic achievement. She exposes the complexities and political contradictions which accompany campaigns for recognition and funding of Muslim schools in a context in which religion is racialized and religious schools are differentially treated. It is interesting, for example, that the funding of Muslim schools should be a matter of controversy when it is considered normal to fund Church of England and Roman Catholic schools.

In this collection of articles we bring together a range of theoretical perspectives on the central themes of identity and difference, with a particular focus on marginalized identities. The collection illustrates different ways of accessing the experience of diversity within the framework of current theoretical concerns about gender, and with attention paid to the place of education in these processes.

Note

1. The articles in this book have been edited: significant wording additions are shown in square brackets, and substantive deletions of text are indicated by ellipses (three points); however, minor changes are not flagged.

Part 1 Retrieving Personal Experiences: Auto/Biography

1 WRITING AUTOBIOGRAPHY

BEL HOOKS

To me, telling the story of my growing up years was intimately connnected with the longing to kill the self I was without really having to die. I wanted to kill that self in writing. Once that self was gone—out of my life forever—I could more easily become the me of me. It was clearly the Gloria Jean of my tormented and anguished childhood that I wanted to be rid of, the girl who was always wrong, always punished, always subjected to some humiliation or other, always crying, the girl who was to end up in a mental institution because she could not be anything but crazy, or so they told her. She was the girl who sat a hot iron on her arm pleading with them to leave her alone, the girl who wore her scar as a brand marking her madness. Even now I can hear the voices of my sisters saying 'mama make Gloria stop crying.' By writing the autobiography, it was not just this Gloria I would be rid of, but the past that had a hold on me, that kept me from the present. I wanted not to forget the past but to break its hold. This death in writing was to be liberatory.

Until I began to try and write an autobiography, I thought that it would be a simple task this telling of one's story. And yet I tried year after year, never writing more than a few pages. My inability to write out the story I interpreted as an indication that I was not ready to let go of the past, that I was not ready to be fully in the present. Psychologically, I considered the possibility that I had become attached to the wounds and sorrows of my childhood, that I held to them in a manner that blocked my efforts to be self-realized, whole, to be healed. A key message in Toni Cade Bambara's novel *The Salteaters*, which tells the story of Velma's suicide attempt, her breakdown, is expressed when the healer asks her 'are you sure sweetheart, that you want to be well?'

There was very clearly something blocking my ability to tell my story. Perhaps it was remembered scoldings and punishments when mama heard me saying something to a friend or stranger that she did not think should be said. Secrecy and silence—these were central issues. Secrecy about family, about what went on in the domestic household was a bond between us—was part of what made us family. There was a dread one felt about breaking that bond. And yet I could not grow inside the atmosphere of secrecy that had pervaded our lives and the lives of other families about us. Strange that I had always challenged the secrecy, always let something slip that should not

Source: hooks, b. (1989) *Talking Back: Thinking Feminist—Thinking Black* (pp. 155–9). London: Sheba Feminist Press.

be known growing up, yet as a writer staring into the solitary space of paper, I was bound, trapped in the fear that a bond is lost or broken in the telling. I did not want to be the traitor, the teller of family secrets—and yet I wanted to be a writer. Surely, I told myself, I could write a purely imaginative work—a work that would not hint at personal private realities. And so I tried. But always there were the intruding traces, those elements of real life however disguised. Claiming the freedom to grow as an imaginative writer was connected for me with having the courage to be open, to be able to tell the truth of one's life as I had experienced it in writing. To talk about one's life—that I could do. To write about it, to leave a trace—that was frightening.

The longer it took me to begin the process of writing autobiography, the further removed from those memories I was becoming. Each year, a memory seemed less and less clear. I wanted not to lose the vividness, the recall and felt an urgent need to begin the work and complete it. Yet I could not begin even though I had begun to confront some of the reasons I was blocked, as I am blocked just now in writing this piece because I am afraid to express in writing the experience that served as a catalyst for that block to move.

I had met a young black man. We were having an affair. It is important that he was black. He was in some mysterious way a link to this past that I had been struggling to grapple with, to name in writing. With him I remembered incidents, moments of the past that I had completely suppressed. It was as though there was something about the passion of contact that was hypnotic, that enabled me to drop barriers and thus enter fully, rather re-enter those past experiences. A key aspect seemed to be the way he smelled, the combined odors of cigarettes, occasionally alcohol, and his body smells. I thought often of the phrase 'scent of memory,' for it was those smells that carried me back. And there were specific occasions when it was very evident that the experience of being in his company was the catalyst for this remembering.

Two specific incidents come to mind. One day in the middle of the afternoon we met at his place. We were drinking cognac and dancing to music from the radio. He was smoking cigarettes (not only do I not smoke, but I usually make an effort to avoid smoke). As we held each other dancing those mingled odors of alcohol, sweat, and cigarettes led me to say, quite without thinking about it, 'Uncle Pete.' It was not that I had forgotten Uncle Pete. It was more that I had forgotten the childhood experience of meeting him. He drank often, smoked cigarettes, and always on the few occasions that we met him, he held us children in tight embraces. It was the memory of those embraces—of the way I hated and longed to resist them—that I recalled.

Another day we went to a favorite park to feed ducks and parked the car in front of tall bushes. As we were sitting there,we suddenly heard the sound of an oncoming train—a sound which startled me so that it evoked another long-suppressed memory: that of crossing the train tracks in my father's car. I recalled an incident where the car stopped on the tracks and my father left us sitting there while he raised the hood of the car and worked to repair it. This is an incident that I am not certain actually happened. As a child, I had been terrified of just such an incident occurring, perhaps so terrified that it played itself out in my mind as though it had happened. These are just two ways this encounter acted as a catalyst breaking down barriers enabling me to finally write this long-desired autobiography of my childhood.

Each day I sat at the typewriter and different memories were written about in short vignettes. They came in a rush, as though they were a sudden thunderstorm. They came in a surreal, dreamlike style which made me cease to think of them as strictly autobiographical because it seemed that myth, dream, and reality had merged. There were many incidents that I would talk about with my siblings to see if they recalled them. Often we remembered together a general outline of an incident but the details were different for us. This fact was a constant reminder of the limitations of autobiography, of the extent to which autobiography is a very personal story telling—a unique recounting of events not so much as they have happened but as we remember and invent them. One memory that I would have sworn was 'the truth and nothing but the truth' concerned a wagon that my brother and I shared as a child. I remembered that we played with this toy only at my grandfather's house, that we shared it, that I would ride it and my brother would push me. Yet one facet of the memory was puzzling, I remembered always returning home with bruises or scratches from this toy. When I called my mother, she said there had never been any wagon, that we had shared a red wheelbarrow, that it had always been at my grandfather's house because there were sidewalks on that part of town. We lived in the hills where there were no sidewalks. Again I was compelled to face the fiction that is a part of all retelling, remembering. I began to think of the work I was doing as both fiction and autobiography. It seemed to fall in the category of writing that Audre Lorde, in her autobiographically based work *Zami*, calls bio-mythography. As I wrote, I felt that I was not as concerned with accuracy of details as I was with evoking in writing the state of mind, the spirit of a particular moment.

The longing to tell one's story and the process of telling is symbolically a gesture of longing to recover the past in such a way that one experiences both a sense of reunion and a sense of release. It was the longing for release that compelled the writing but concurrently it was the joy of reunion that enabled me to see that the act of writing one's autobiography is a way to find again that aspect of self and experience that may no longer be an actual part of one's life but is a living memory shaping and informing the present. Autobiographical writing was a way for me to evoke the particular experience of growing up southern and black in segregated communities. It was a way to recapture the richness of southern black culture. The need to remember and hold to the legacy of that experience and what it taught me has been all the more important since I have since lived in predominately white communities

and taught at predominately white colleges. Black southern folk ·experience
was the foundation of the life around me when I was a child; that experience
no longer exists in many places where it was once all of life that we knew.
Capitalism, upward mobility, assimilation of other values have all led to rapid
disintegration of black folk experience or in some cases the gradual wearing
away of that experience.

Within the world of my childhood, we held onto the legacy of a distinct
black culture by listening to the elders tell their stories. Autobiography was
experienced most actively in the art of telling one's story. I can recall sitting at
Baba's (my grandmother on my mother's side) at 1200 Broad Street—listening
to people come and recount their life experience. In those days, whenever I
brought a playmate to my grandmother's house, Baba would want a brief
outline of their autobiography before we would begin playing. She wanted
not only to know who their people were but what their values were. It was
sometimes an awesome and terrifying experience to stand answering these
questions or witness another playmate being subjected to the process and yet
this was the way we would come to know our own and one another's family
history. It is the absence of such a tradition in my adult life that makes the
written narrative of my girlhood all the more important. As the years pass
and these glorious memories grow much more vague, there will remain the
clarity contained within the written words.

Conceptually, the autobiography was framed in the manner of a hope chest.
I remembered my mother's hope chest, with its wonderful odor of cedar and
thought about her taking the most precious items and placing them there for
safekeeping. Certain memories were for me a similar treasure. I wanted to
place them somewhere for safekeeping. An autobiographical narrative seemed
an appropriate place. Each particular incident, encounter, experience had its
own story, sometimes told from the first person, sometimes told from the
third person. Often I felt as though I was in a trance at my typewriter, that
the shape of a particular memory was decided not by my conscious mind but
by all that is dark and deep within me, unconscious but present. It was the
act of making it present, bringing it into the open, so to speak, that was
liberating.

From the perspective of trying to understand my psyche, it was also interesting to read the narrative in its entirety after I had completed the work.
It had not occurred to me that bringing one's past, one's memories together
in a complete narrative would allow one to view them from a different perspective, not as singular isolated events but as part of a continuum. Reading
the completed manuscript, I felt as though I had an overview not so much of
my childhood but of those experiences that were deeply imprinted in my consciousness. Significantly, that which was absent, left out, not included also was
important. I was shocked to find at the end of my narrative that there were
few incidents I recalled that involved my five sisters. Most of the incidents
with siblings were with me and my brother. There was a sense of alienation

from my sisters present in childhood, a sense of estrangement. This was reflected in the narrative. Another aspect of the completed manuscript that is interesting to me is the way in which the incidents describing adult men suggest that I feared them intensely, with the exception of my grandfather and a few old men. Writing the autobiographical narrative enabled me to look at my past from a different perspective and to use this knowledge as a means of self-growth and change in a practical way.

In the end I did not feel as though I had killed the Gloria of my childhood. Instead I had rescued her. She was no longer the enemy within, the little girl who had to be annihilated for the woman to come into being. In writing about her, I reclaimed that part of myself I had long ago rejected, left uncared for, just as she had often felt alone and uncared for as a child. Remembering was part of a cycle of reunion, a joining of fragments, 'the bits and pieces of my heart' that the narrative made whole again.

2 DEATH OF A GOOD WOMAN

CAROLYN STEEDMAN

Editors' note:

The following article is the introduction to Carolyn Steedman's *Landscape for a Good Woman*. In describing the book and her intentions for it, the author provides a beautifully written example of one of the ways in which auto/biography can be used. Any references to 'the book' made in this article are, of course, to *Landscape for a Good Woman*.

She died like this. I didn't witness it. My niece told me this. She'd moved everything down into the kitchen: a single bed, the television, the calor-gas heater. She said it was to save fuel. The rest of the house was dark and shrouded. Through the window was only the fence and the kitchen wall of the house next door. Her quilt was sewn into a piece of pink flannelette. Afterwards, there were bags and bags of washing to do. She had cancer, had gone back to Food Reform, talked to me about curing it when I paid my first visit in nine years, two weeks before her death: my last visit. She asked me if I remembered the woman in the health-food shop, when I was about eight or nine, pointing out a man who'd cured cancer by eating watercress. She complained of pains, but wouldn't take the morphine tablets. It was pains everywhere, not in the lungs where the cancer was. It wasn't the cancer that killed: a blood clot travelled from her leg and stopped her heart. Afterwards, the doctor said she'd been out of touch with reality.

We'd known all our childhood that she was a good mother: she'd told us so: we'd never gone hungry; she went out to work for us; we had warm beds to lie in at night. She had conducted a small and ineffective war against the body's fate by eating brown bread, by not drinking, by giving up smoking years ago. To have cancer was the final unfairness in a life measured out by it. She'd been good; it hadn't worked.

Upstairs, a long time ago, she had cried, standing on the bare floorboards in the front bedroom just after we moved to this house in Streatham Hill in 1951, my baby sister in her carry-cot. We both watched the dumpy retreating figure of the health visitor through the curtainless windows. The woman had said: 'This house isn't fit for a baby.' And then she stopped crying, my mother, got by, the phrase that picks up after all difficulty (it says: it's like this; it shouldn't be like this; it's unfair; I'll manage): 'Hard lines, eh Kay?'

Source: Steedman, C. (1986) *Landscape for a Good Woman* (chapter 2, pp. 1–24). London: Virago.

(Kay was the name I was called at home, my middle name, one of my father's names).

And I? I will do everything and anything until the end of my days to stop anyone ever talking to me like that woman talked to my mother. It is in this place, this bare, curtainless bedroom that lies my secret and shameful defiance. I read a woman's book, meet such a woman at a party (a woman now, like me) and think quite deliberately as we talk: we are divided: a hundred years ago I'd have been cleaning your shoes. I know this and you don't.

Simone de Beauvoir wrote of her mother's death, said that in spite of the pain it was an easy one: an upper-class death. Outside, for the poor, dying is a different matter:

> And then in the public wards when the last hour is coming near, they put a screen round a dying man's bed: he has seen this screen round other beds that were empty the next day: he knows. I pictured Maman, blinded for hours by the black sun that no one can look at directly: the horror of her staring eyes with their dilated pupils. (de Beauvoir, 1964)

Like this: she flung up her left arm over her head, pulled her knees up, looked out with an extraordinary surprise. She lived alone, she died alone: a working-class life, a working-class death.

STORIES

This book is about lives lived out on the borderlands, lives for which the central interpretative devices of the culture don't quite work. It has a childhood at its centre—my childhood, a personal past—and it is about the disruption of that fifties' childhood by the one my mother had lived out before me, and the stories she told about it. Now, the narrative of both these childhoods can be elaborated by the marginal and secret stories that other working-class girls and women from a recent historical past have to tell.

This book, then, is about interpretations, about the places where we rework what has already happened to give current events meaning. It is about the stories we make for ourselves, and the social specificity of our understanding of those stories. The childhood dreams recounted in this book, the fantasies, the particular and remembered events of a South London fifties' childhood do not, by themselves, constitute its point. We all return to memories and dreams like this, again and again; the story we tell of our own life is reshaped around them. But the point doesn't lie there, back in the past, back in the lost time at which they happened; the only point lies in interpretation. The past is re-used through the agency of social information, and that interpretation of it can only be made with what people know of a social world and their place within it. It matters then, whether one reshapes past time, re-uses the ordinary exigencies and crises of all childhoods whilst looking down from the curtainless windows of a terraced house like my mother did, or sees at that moment the long view stretching away from the big house in some richer and more detailed landscape. All children experience a first loss, a first exclusion; lives shape themselves around this sense of being cut off and denied. The health visitor repeated the exclusion in the disdainful language of class, told my mother exactly what it was she stood outside. It is a proposition of this book that specificity of place and politics has to be reckoned with in making an account of anybody's life, and their use of their own past.

My mother's longing shaped my own childhood. From a Lancashire mill town and a working-class twenties' childhood she came away wanting: fine clothes, glamour, money; to be what she wasn't. However that longing was produced in her distant childhood, what she actually wanted were real things, real entities, things she materially lacked, things that a culture and a social system withheld from her. The story she told was about this wanting, and it remained a resolutely social story. When the world didn't deliver the goods, she held the world to blame. In this way, the story she told was a form of political analysis, that allows a political interpretation to be made of her life.

Personal interpretations of past time—the stories that people tell themselves in order to explain how they got to the place they currently inhabit—are often in deep and ambiguous conflict with the official interpretative devices of a culture. This book is organized around a conflict like this, taking as a starting point the structures of class analysis and schools of cultural criticism that cannot deal with everything there is to say about my mother's life. My mother was a single parent for most of her adulthood, who had children, but who also, in a quite particular way, didn't want them. She was a woman who finds no place in the iconography of working-class motherhood that Jeremy Seabrook (1982) presents in *Working Class Childhood*, and who is not to be found in Richard Hoggart's (1959) landscape. She ran a working-class household far away from the traditional communities of class, in exile and isolation, and in which a man was not a master, nor even there very much. Surrounded as a child by the articulated politics of class-consciousness, she became a working-class Conservative, the only political form that allowed her to reveal the politics of envy.

Many of these ambiguities raise central questions about gender as well as class, and the development of gender in particular social and class circumstances. So the usefulness of the biographical and autobiographical core of the book lies in the challenge it may offer to much of our conventional understanding of childhood, working-class childhood, and little-girlhood. In particular, it challenges the tradition of cultural criticism in this country, which has celebrated a kind of psychological simplicity in the lives lived out in Hoggart's endless streets of little houses. It can help reverse a central question within feminism and psychoanalysis, about the reproduction of the desire to mother in little girls, and replace it with a consideration of women who, by refusing to mother, have refused to reproduce themselves or the circumstances of their exile. The personal past that this book deals with can also serve to raise the question of what happens to theories of patriarchy in households where a father's position is not confirmed by the social world outside the front door. And the story of two lives that follows points finally to a consideration of what people—particularly working-class children of the recent past—come to understand of themselves when all they possess is their labour, and what becomes of the notion of class-consciousness when it is seen as a structure of feeling that can be learned in childhood, with one of its components a proper envy, the desire of people for the things of the earth. Class and gender, and their articulations, are the bits and pieces from which psychological selfhood is made.

I grew up in the 1950s, the place and time now located as the first scene of Labour's failure to grasp the political consciousness of its constituency and its eschewal of socialism in favour of welfare philanthropism.[1] But the left had failed with my mother long before the 1950s. A working-class Conservative from a traditional Labour background, she shaped my childhood by the stories she carried from her own, and from an earlier family history. They were stories designed to show me the terrible unfairness of things, the subterranean culture of longing for that which one can never have. These stories can be used now to show my mother's dogged search, using what politics came to hand, for a public form to embody such longing.

Her envy, her sense of the unfairness of things, could not be directly translated into political understanding, and certainly could not be used by the left to shape an articulated politics of class. What follows offers no account of that particular political failure. It is rather an attempt to use that failure, which has been delineated by historians writing from quite different perspectives and for quite different purposes, as a device that may help to explain a particular childhood, and out of that childhood explain an individual life lived in historical time. This is not to say that this book involves a search for a past, or for what really happened.[2] It is about how people use the past to tell the stories of their life. So the evidence presented here is of a different order from the biographical; it is about the experience of my own childhood, and the way in which my mother re-asserted, reversed and restructured her own within mine.

Envy as a political motive has always been condemned: a fierce morality pervades what little writing there is on the subject. Fiercely moral as well, the tradition of cultural criticism in this country has, by ignoring feelings like these, given us the map of an upright and decent country. Out of this tradition has come Jeremy Seabrook's (1982) *Working Class Childhood* and its nostalgia for a time when people who were 'united against cruel material privations ... discovered the possibilities of the human consolations they could offer each other' (pp. 23–7), and its celebration of the upbringing that produced the psychic structure of 'the old working class' (p. 33). I take a defiant pleasure in the way that my mother's story can be used to subvert this account. Born into 'the old working class', she wanted: a New Look skirt, a timbered country cottage, to marry a prince.

The very devices that are intended to give expression to childhoods like mine and my mother's actually deny their expression. The problem with most childhoods lived out in households maintained by social class III (manual), IV and V parents is that they simply are not bad enough to be worthy of attention. The literary form that allows presentation of working-class childhood, the working-class autobiography, reveals its mainspring in the title of books like *Born to Struggle*; *Poverty, Hardship, But Happiness*; *Growing Up Poor in East London*; *Coronation Cups and Jam Jars*—and I am deeply aware of the ambiguities that attach to the childhood I am about to recount. Not only was it not very bad, or only bad in a way that working-class autobiography doesn't deal in, but also a particular set of emotional and psychological circumstances ensured that at the time, and for many years after it was over and I had escaped, I thought of it as *ordinary*, a period of relative material ease, just like everybody else's childhood.

I read female working-class autobiography obsessively when I was in my twenties and early thirties (a reading that involved much repetition: it's a small corpus), and whilst I wept over Catherine Cookson's (1969) *Our Kate* I felt a simultaneous distance from the Edwardian child who fetched beer bare-footed for an alcoholic mother, the Kate of the title (I have to make it very clear that my childhood was really *not* like that). But it bore a relationship to a personal reality that I did not yet know about: what I now see in the book is its fine delineation of the feeling of being on the outside, outside the law; for Catherine Cookson was illegitimate.

In 1928, when Kathleen Woodward, who had grown up in not-too-bad Peckham, South London, wrote *Jipping Street*, she set her childhood in Bermondsey, in a place of abject and abandoned poverty, 'practically off the map, derelict', and in this manner found a way, within an established literary form, of expressing a complexity of feeling about her personal past that the form itself did not allow.

The tradition of cultural criticism that has employed working-class lives, and their rare expression in literature, had made solid and concrete the absence of psychological individuality—of subjectivity—that Kathleen Woodward struggled against in *Jipping Street*. 'In poor societies,' writes Jeremy Seabrook (1982, p. 140) in *Working Class Childhood*, 'where survival is more important than elaboration of relationships, the kind of ferocious personal struggles that lock people together in our own more leisured society are less known.' But by making this distinction, the very testimony to the continuing reverberation of pain and loss, absence and desire in childhood, which is made manifest in the words of 'the old working-class' people that makes up much of *Working Class Childhood*, is actually denied.

It would not be possible, in fact, to write a book called 'Middle Class Childhood' (this in spite of the fact that the shelves groan with psychoanalytic, developmental and literary accounts of such childhoods) and get the same kind of response from readers. It's a faintly titillating title, carrying the promise that some kind of pathology is about to be investigated. What is more, in *Working Class Childhood* the discussion of childhood and what our society has done to the idea of childhood becomes the vehicle for an anguished rejection of post-War materialism, the metaphor for all that has gone wrong with the old politics of class and the stance of the labour movement towards the desires that capitalism has inculcated in those who are seen as the passive poor. An analysis like this denies its subjects a particular story, a personal history, except when that story illustrates a general thesis; and it denies the child, and the child who continues to live in the adult it becomes, both an unconscious life, and a particular and developing consciousness of the meanings presented by the social world.

Twenty years before *Working Class Childhood* was written, Richard Hoggart (1959) explored a similar passivity of emotional life in working-class communities, what in *The Uses of Literacy* he revealingly called 'Landscape with Figures: A Setting'—a place where in his own memories of the 1920s and 1930s and in his description of similar communities of the 1950s, most people lacked 'any feeling that some change can, or indeed ought to be made in the general pattern of life (p. 91). All of Seabrook's corpus deals in the same way with what he sees as 'the falling into decay of a life once believed by those who shared it to be the only admissible form that life could take' (Seabrook, 1967). I want to open the door of one of the terraced houses, in a mill town in the 1920s, show Seabrook my mother and her longing, make him see the child of my imagination sitting by an empty grate, reading a tale that tells her a goose-girl can marry a king.

Heaviness of time lies on the pages of *The Uses of Literacy* (Hoggart, 1959). The streets are all the same; nothing changes. Writing about the structure of a child's life, Seabrook (1967, pp. 202–3) notes that as recently as thirty years ago (that is in the 1950s, the time of my own childhood) the week was measured out by each day's function—wash-day, market-day, the day for ironing and the day itself timed by 'cradling and comforting' ritual. This extraordinary attribution of sameness and the acceptance of sameness to generations of lives arises from several sources. First of all, delineation of emotional and psychological selfhood has been made by and through the testimony of people in a central relationship to the dominant culture, that is to say by and through people who are not working class. This is an obvious point, but it measures out an immensely complicated and contradictory area of historical development that has scarcely yet been investigated. Superficially, it might be said that historians, failing to find evidence of most people's emotional or psycho-sexual existence, have simply assumed that there can't have been much there to find. Such an assumption ignores the structuring of late nineteenth and early twentieth-century psychology and psychoanalysis, and the way in which the lived experience of the majority of people in a class society has been pathologized and marginalized. When the sons of the working class, who have made their earlier escape from this landscape of psychological simplicity, put so much effort into accepting and celebrating it, into delineating a background of uniformity and passivity, in which pain, loss, love, anxiety and desire are washed over with a patina of stolid emotional sameness, then something important, and odd, and possibly promising of startling revelation, is actually going on. This refusal of a complicated psychology to those living in conditions of material distress is a central theme of this book.

The attribution of psychological simplicity to working-class people also derives from the positioning of mental life within Marxism:

> Mental life flows from material conditions. Social being is determined above all by class position—location within the realm of production. Consciousness and politics, all mental conceptions spring from material forces and the relations of production and so reflect these class origins. (Alexander, 1984)

This description is Sally Alexander's summary of Marx's Preface to *A Contribution to the Critique of Political Economy* (Marx, 1859: Preface), and his thesis, expressed here and elsewhere, that 'the mode of production of material life conditions the general process of social, political and mental life'. The attribution of simplicity to the mental life of working people is not, of course, made either in the original, nor in this particular critique of it. But like any theory developed in a social world, the notion of consciousness as located within the realm of production draws on the reality of that world. It is in the Preface itself that Marx mentions his move to London in the 1850s as offering among other advantages 'a convenient vantage point for the observation of bourgeois society', and which indeed he did observe, and live within, in the novels he and his family read, in family theatricals, in dinner-table talk: a mental life apparently much richer than that of the subjects of his theories. Lacking such possessions of culture, working-class people have come to be seen, within the field of cultural criticism, as bearing the elemental simplicity of class-consciousness and little more.

Technically, class-consciousness has not been conceived of as *psychological* consciousness. It has been separated from 'the empirically given, and from the psychologically describable and explicable ideas that men form about their situation in life', and has been seen rather as a possible set of reactions people might have to discovering the implications of the position they occupy within the realm of production (Lukas, 1968, pp. 46–82, esp. pp. 50–5; see also Hobsbawm, 1984). Theoretical propositions apart though, in the everyday world, the term *is* used in its psychological sense, is generally and casually used to describe what people have 'thought, felt and wanted at any moment in history and from any point in the class structure' (Lukas, 1968, p. 51). Working-class autobiography and people's history have been developed as forms that allow the individual and collective expression of these thoughts, feelings and desires about class societies and the effect of class struc-tures on individuals and communities. But as forms of analysis and writing, people's history and working-class autobiography are relatively innocent of psychological theory, and there has been little space within them to discuss the *development* of class-consciousness (as opposed to its expression), nor for understanding of it as a *learned* position, learned in childhood, and often through the exigencies of difficult and lonely lives.

Children present a particular problem here, for whilst some women may learn the official dimensions of class-consciousness by virtue of their entry into the labour market and by adopting forms of struggle and under-standing evolved by men (Hunt, 1980),[3] children, who are not located directly within the realm of production, still reach understandings of social position, exclusion and difference. At all levels, class-consciousness must be learned in some way, and we need a model of such a process to explain the social and psychological development of working-class children (indeed, of all children).

When the mental life of working-class women is entered into the realm of production, and their narrative is allowed to disrupt the monolithic story of wage-labour and capital and when childhood and childhood learning are reckoned with, then what makes the old story unsatisfactory is not so much its granite-like *plot*, built around exploiter and exploited, capital and prolet-ariat, but rather its *timing*: the precise how and why of the development of class-consciousness. But if we do allow an unconscious life to working-class children, then we can perhaps see the first loss, the earliest exclusion (known most familiarly to us as the oedipal crisis) brought forward later, and articu-lated through an adult experience of class and class relations.

An adult experience of class does not in any case, as Sally Alexander (1984, p. 131) has pointed out, 'produce a shared and even consciousness', even if it is fully registered and articulated. This uneven and problematic consciousness (which my mother's life and political conviction represents so clearly) is one of the subjects of this book. A perception of childhood experience and under-standing used as the lineaments of adult political analysis, may also help us see under the language and conflicts of class, historically much older articula-tions—the subjective and political expressions of radicalism—which may still serve to give a voice to people who know that they do not have what they want, who know that they have been cut off from the earth in some way. (See Steedman, 1986, pp. 119–21; see also Stedman-Jones, 1983b, pp. 90–178.)

The attribution of psychological sameness to the figures in the working-class landscape has been made by men, for whom the transitions of class are at once more ritualized than they are for women, and much harder to make. Hoggart's (1959, p. 293) description of the plight of the 'scholarship boy' of the thirties and forties, and the particular anxiety afflicting those in the working class 'who have been pulled one stage away from their original culture and have not the intellectual equipment which would then cause them to move on to join the "declassed" professionals and experts' makes nostalgic reading now in a post-War situation where a whole generation of escapees occupies professional positions that allow them to speak of their working-class origins with authority, to use them, in Seabrook's (1978, pp. 260–1) words 'as a kind of accomplishment'. By the 1950s the divisions of the educational establishment that produced Hoggart's description were much altered and I, a grammar-school girl of the 1960s, was sent to university with a reasonably full equipment of culture and a relative degree of intellectual self-awareness. Jeremy Seabrook, some eight years older than me and at Cambridge in the late fifties, sat with his fellow travellers from working-class backgrounds 'telling each other escape stories in which we were all picaresque heroes of our own lives' (Seabrook, 1978, p. 262).

But at the University of Sussex in 1965, there were no other women to talk to like this, at least there were none that I met (though as proletarianism was fashionable at the time, there were several men with romantic and slightly untruthful tales to tell). And should I have met a woman like me (there must have been some: we were all children of the Robbins generation), we could not have talked of escape except within a literary framework that we had learned from the working-class novels of the early sixties (some of which, like *Room at the Top*, were set books on certain courses); and that framework was itself ignorant of the material stepping-stones of our escape: clothes, shoes, make-up. We could not be heroines of the conventional narratives of escape. Women are, in the sense that Hoggart and Seabrook present in their pictures of transition, without class, because the cut and fall of a skirt and good leather shoes can take you across the river and to the other side: the fairy-tales tell you that goose-girls may marry kings.

The fixed townscapes of Northampton and Leeds that Hoggart and Seabrook have described show endless streets of houses, where mothers who don't go out to work order the domestic day, where men are masters, and children, when they grow older, express gratitude for the harsh discipline meted out to them. The first task is to particularize this profoundly a-historical landscape (and so this book details a mother who was a working woman and a single parent, and a father who wasn't a patriarch). And once the landscape is detailed and historicized in this way, the urgent need becomes to find a way of theorizing the result of such difference and particularity, not in order to find a description that can be universally applied (the point is *not* to say that all working-class childhoods are the same, nor that experience of them produces unique psychic structures) but so that the people in exile, the inhabitants of the long streets, may start to use the autobiographical 'I', and tell the stories of their life.

There are other interpretative devices for my mother which, like working-class autobiographies of childhood, make her no easier to see. Nearly everything that has been written on the subject of mothering (except the literature of pathology, of battering and violence) assumes the desire to mother; and there are feminisms now that ask me to return Persephone-like to my own mother, and find new histories of my strength. When I first came across Kathleen Woodward's (1928) *Jipping Street*, I read it with the shocked astonishment of one who had never seen what she knows written down before. Kathleen Woodward's mother of the 1890s was the one I knew: mothers were those who told you how hard it was to have you, how long they were in labour with you ('twenty hours with you', my mother frequently reminded me) and who told you to accept the impossible contradiction of being both desired and a burden; and not to complain.[4] This ungiving endurance is admired by working-class boys who grow up to write about their mother's flinty courage. But the daughter's silence on the matter is a measure of the price you pay for survival. I don't think the baggage will ever lighten, for me or my sister. We were born, and had no choice in the matter; but we were burdens, expensive, never grateful enough. There was nothing we could do to pay back the debt of our existence. 'Never have children dear,' she said; 'they ruin your life.' Shock moves swiftly across the faces of women to whom I tell this story. But it is *ordinary* not to want your children, I silently assert; normal to find them a nuisance.

I read the collection *Fathers: Reflections by Daughters* (Owen, 1983), or Ann Oakley's (1984) *Taking It Like a Woman* and feel the painful and familiar sense of exclusion from these autobiographies of middle-class little-girlhood and womanhood, envy of those who belong, who can, like Ann Oakley, use the outlines of conventional romantic fiction to tell a life story. And women like this, friends, say: but it was like that for me too, my childhood was like yours; my father was like that, my mother didn't want me. What they cannot bear, I think, is that there exists a poverty and marginality of experience to which they have no access, structures of feeling that they have not lived within (and would not want to live within: for these are the structures of deprivation). They are caught then in a terrible exclusion, an exclusion from the experience of others that measures out their own central relationship to the culture. The myths tell their story, the fairy-tales show the topography of the houses they once inhabited. The psychoanalytic drama, which uses the spatial and temporal structures of all these old tales, permits the entry of such women to the drama itself. Indeed, the psychoanalytic drama was constructed to describe that of middle-class women (and as drama it does of course describe all such a woman's exclusions, as well as her relationship to those exclusions, with her absence and all she lacks lying at the very heart of the theory). The woman whose drama psychoanalytic case-study describes in this way never does stand to one side, and watch, and know she doesn't belong.

[. . .]The sense of exclusion, of being cut off from what others enjoy, was a dominant sense of both childhoods, but expressed and used differently in two different historical settings. This detailing of social context to psychological development reveals not only difference, but also certain continuities of experience in working-class childhood. For instance, many recent accounts of

psychological development and the development of gender, treat our current
social situation as astonishingly new and strange:

> On the social/historical level ... we are living in a period in which
> mothers are increasingly living alone with their children, offering oppor-
> tunities for new psychic patterns to emerge. Single mothers are forced to
> make themselves subject to their children; they are forced to invent new
> symbolic roles ... The child cannot position the mother as object to the
> father's law, since in single parent households her desire sets things in
> motion. (Kaplan, 1984, p. 335)

But the evidence of some nineteenth- and twentieth-century children used
in this book shows that in their own reckoning their households were often
those of a single female parent, sometimes because of the passivity of a father's
presence, sometimes because of his physical absence. Recent feminisms have
often, as Jane Gallop points out in *The Daughter's Seduction*, endowed men
with 'the sort of unified phallic sovereignty that characterises an absolute
monarch, and which little resembles actual power in our social, economic
structure' (p. xv). We need a reading of history that reveals fathers mattering
in a different way from the way they matter in the corpus of traditional
psychoanalysis, the novels that depict the same familial settings and in the
bourgeois households of the fairy-tales.

A father like mine dictated each day's existence; our lives would have been
quite different had he not been there. But he didn't *matter*, and his singular
unimportance needs explaining. His not mattering has an effect like this: I
don't quite believe in male power; somehow the iron of patriarchy didn't
enter into my soul. I accept the idea of male power intellectually, of course
(and I will eat my words the day I am raped, or the knife is slipped between
my ribs; though I know that will not be the case: in the dreams it is a woman
who holds the knife, and only a woman can kill).

Fixing my father, and my mother's mothering, in time and politics can
help show the creation of gender in particular households and in particular
familial situations at the same time as it demonstrates the position of men
and the social reality represented by them in particular households. We need
historical accounts of such relationships, not just a longing that they might
be different.[5] Above all, perhaps, we need a sense of people's complexity of
relationship to the historical situations they inherit. In *Family and Kinship in
East London* (Young and Willmott, 1962), the authors found that over half the
married women they interviewed had seen their mothers within the preceding
24 hours, and that 80% had seen them within the previous week. Young and
Willmott assumed that the daughters wanted to do this, and interpreted four
visits a week on average as an expression of attachment and devotion. There
exists a letter that I wrote to a friend one vacation from Sussex, either in 1966
or in 1967, in which I described my sitting in the evenings with my mother,
refusing to go out, holding tight to my guilt and duty, knowing that I *was*

her, and that I must keep her company; and we were certainly not Demeter and Persephone to each other, nor ever could be, but two women caught by a web of sexual and psychological relationships in the front room of a council house, the South London streets stretching away outside like the railway lines that brought us and our history to that desperate and silent scene in front of the flickering television screen.

Raymond Williams (1979) has written about the difficulty of linking past and present in writing about working-class life, and the result of this difficulty in novels that either shows the past to be a regional zone of experience in which the narrator cancels her present from the situation she is describing, or which are solely about the experience of flight. Writing like this, comments Williams (1979), has lacked 'any sense of the continuity of working class life, which does not cease just because the individual [the writer] moves out of it, but which also itself changes internally'.[6]

This kind of cancellation of a writer's present from the past may take place because novels—stories—work by a process of temporal revelation: they move forward in time in order to demonstrate a state of affairs. The novel that works in this way employs contingency, that is, it works towards the revelation of something not quite certain, but *there* nevertheless, waiting to be shown by the story (Chatman, 1978, pp. 45–8), and the story gets told without revealing the shaping force of the writer's current situation.

The highlighting not just of the subject matter of this book, but also of the possibilities of written form it involves, is important, because the construction of the account that follows has something to say about the question that Raymond Williams has raised, and which is largely to do with the writing of stories that aren't central to a dominant culture. My mother cut herself off from the old working class by the process of migration, by retreat from the North to a southern country with my father, hiding secrets in South London's long streets. But she carried with her her childhood, as I have carried mine along the lines of embourgeoisement and state education. In order to outline these childhoods and the uses we put them to, the structure of psychoanalytic case-study—the narrative form that Freud is described as inventing—is used in this book.[7] The written case-study allows the writer to enter the present into the past, allows the dream, the wish or the fantasy of the past to shape current time, and treats them as evidence in their own right. In this way, the narrative form of case-study shows what went into its writing, shows the bits and pieces from which it is made up, in the way that history refuses to do, and that fiction can't.[8] Case-study presents the ebb and flow of memory, the structure of dreams, the stories that people tell to explain themselves to others. The autobiographical section of this book, the second part, is constructed on such a model.

But something else has to be done with these bits and pieces, with all the tales that are told, in order to take them beyond the point of anecdote and into history. To begin to construct history, the writer has to do two things,

make two movements through time. First of all, we need to search backwards from the vantage point of the present in order to appraise things in
the past and attribute meaning to them. When events and entities in the past
have been given their meaning in this way, then we can trace forward what
we have already traced backwards, and make a history (Ricoeur, 1984, pp. 118,
157). When a history is finally written, events are explained by putting them
in causal order and establishing causal connections between them. But what
follows in this book does not make a history (even though a great deal of historical material is presented). For a start, I simply do not know enough about
many of the incidents described to explain the connections between them. I
am unable to perform an act of historical explanation in this way.

This tension between the stories told to me as a child, the diffuse and
timeless structure of the case-study with which they are presented, and the
compulsions of historical explanation, is not mere rhetorical device. There
is a real problem, a real tension here that I cannot resolve (my inability to
resolve it is part of the story). All the stories that follow, told as this book tells
them, aren't stories in their own right: they exist in tension with other more
central ones. In the same way, the processes of working-class autobiography,
of people's history and of the working-class novel cannot show a proper and
valid culture existing in its own right, underneath the official forms, waiting
for revelation. Accounts of working-class life are told by tension and ambiguity, out on the borderlands. The story—my mother's story, a hundred
thousand others—cannot be absorbed into the central one: it is both its disruption and its essential counterpoint: this is a drama of *class*.

But visions change, once any story is told; ways of seeing are altered. The
point of a story is to present itself momentarily as complete, so that it can
be said: it does for now, it will do; it is an account that will last a while.
Its point is briefly to make an audience connive in the telling, so that they
might say: yes, that's how it was; or, that's how it could have been. So now,
the words written down, the world is suddenly full of women waiting, as in
Ann Oakley's extraordinary delineation of

> the curiously impressive image of women as always waiting for someone
> or something, in shopping queues, in antenatal clinics, in bed, for men to
> come home, at the school gates, by the playground swing, for birth or the
> growing up of children, in hope of love or freedom or re-employment,
> waiting for the future to liberate or burden them and the past to catch
> up with them. (Oakley, 1981, p. 11)

The other side of waiting is wanting. The faces of the women in the queues
are the faces of unfulfilled desire; if we look, there are many women driven
mad in this way, as my mother was. This is a sad and secret story, but it
isn't just hers alone.

What historically conscious readers may do with this book is read it as a
Lancashire story, see here evidence of a political culture of 1890–1930 carried

from the north-west, to shape another childhood in another place and time. They will perhaps read it as part of an existing history, seeing here a culture shaped by working women, and their consciousness of themselves as workers. They may see the indefatigable capacity for work that has been described in many other places, the terrifying ability to *get by*, to cope, against all odds. Some historically conscious readers may even find here the irony that this specific social and cultural experience imparted to its women: 'No one gives you anything,' said my mother, as if reading the part of 'our mam' handed to her by the tradition of working-class autobiography. 'If you want things, you have to go out and work for them.' But out of that tradition I can make the dislocation that the irony actually permits, and say: 'If no one will write my story, then I shall have to go out and write it myself.'

The point of being a Lancashire weaver's daughter, as my mother was, is that it is *classy*: what my mother knew was that if you were going to be working class, then you might as well be the best that's going, and for women, Lancashire and weaving provided that elegance, that edge of difference and distinction. I'm sure that she told the titled women whose hands she did when she became a manicurist in the 1960s where it was she came from, proud, defiant: look at me. (Beatrix Campbell had made what I think is a similar point about the classiness of being a miner, for working-class men (Campbell, 1984, pp. 97–115).)

This is a book about stories; and it is a book about *things* (objects, entities, relationships, people), and the way in which we talk and write about them: about the difficulties of metaphor. Above all, it is about people wanting those things, and the structures of political thought that have labelled this wanting as wrong. Suggestions are also made about a relatively old structure of political thought in this country, that of radicalism, and its possible entry into the political dialogue of the north-west; and how perhaps it allowed people to feel desire, anger and envy—for the things they did not have.

The things though, will remain a problem. The connection between women and clothes surfaces often in these pages, particularly in the unacknowledged testimony of many nineteenth- and twentieth-century women and girls; and it was with the image of a New Look coat that, in 1950, I made my first attempt to understand and symbolize the content of my mother's desire. I think now of all the stories, all the reading, all the dreams that help us to see ourselves in the landscape, and see ourselves watching as well. 'As woman must continually watch herself,' remarked John Berger some years ago.

> She is almost continually accompanied by her own image of herself. Whilst she is walking across a room or whilst she is weeping at the death of her father, she can scarcely avoid envisioning herself walking and weeping. (Berger, 1972, p. 46)

This book is intended to specify, in historical terms, some of the processes by which we come to step into the landscape, and see ourselves.

But the *clothes* we wear there remain a question. Donald Winnicott (1974, p. 6) wrote about the transitional object (those battered teddies and bits of blanket that babies use in the early stages of distinguishing themselves from the world around them) and its usefulness to the young children who adopt it. The transitional object, he wrote, 'must seem to the infant to give warmth, or to move, or to have texture, or to do something that seems to show it has vitality or reality of its own. Like clothes: that we may see ourself better as we stand there and watch; and for our protection.

Notes

1. See Stedman-Jones (1983a). Beatrix Campbell (1984, pp. 217—34) surveys critiques of the 1950s in *Wigan Pier Revisited*. See also Hinton (1983, pp. 182—7).
2. 'What actually happened is less important than what is felt to have happened. Is that right?' says Ronald Fraser to his analyst, and his analyst agrees. Fraser (1984, p. 95)
3. Pauline Hunt (1980, pp. 171—9). A direct and simple learning isn't posited here; but it is the workplace and an existing backdrop of trade-union organization that provides for the expression of women's class consciousness.
4. To be told how difficult it was to give birth to you is an extremely common experience for all little girls, and as John and Elizabeth Newson (1976, pp. 186—7) point out in *Seven Years Old in the Home Environment*, pp. 186—7, chaperonage, and the consequent amount of time girls spend in adult company, is likely to make such topics of conversation accessible to them. But the punishment and the warning involved in telling girl children about the difficulties their birth presented to their mother is rarely written about. But see Carolyn Steedman (1982, pp. 34—5, 145—7).
5. For recent arguments concerning the necessity of historicization, see Jane Lewis (1985).
6. See also Seabrook (1978, p. 261) where the same process is described: a working-class life, ossified by time, enacted in 'symbolic institutional ways, by those who teach in poor schools, or who write novels and memoirs about a way of life which they have not directly experienced since childhood'.
7. See Steven Marcus for the argument that Freud invented a new narrative form in his writing of the 'Dora' case.
8. For a brief discussion of the way in which historical writing masks the processes that brought it into being, see Timothy Ashplant (1981), and Hayden White (1980).

References

Alexander, Sally (1984) Women, class and sexual difference. *History Workshop Journal* 17, 125—49.
Ashplant, Timothy (1981) The new social function of cinema. *Journal of the British Film Institute* 79/80, 107—9.
de Beauvoir, Simone (1964) *A Very Easy Death*. London: Penguin.
Berger, John (1972) *Ways of Seeing*. London: BBC/Penguin.
Campbell, Beatrix (1984) *Wigan Pier Revisited*. London: Virago.
Chatman, Seymour (1978) *Story and Discourse: Narrative Structure in Fiction and Film*. London: Cornell University Press.
Cookson, Catherine (1969). *Our Kate*. London: Macdonald.
Fraser, Ronald (1984) *In Search of a Past*. London: Verso.

Gallop, Jane (1982) *Feminism and Psychoanalysis: The Daughter's Seduction*. London: Macmillan.

Hinton, James (1983) *Labour and Socialism: A History of the British Labour Movement, 1867–1974*. Brighton: Wheatsheaf.

Hobsbawm, Eric (1984) Notes on class consciousness. In Eric Hobsbawm, *Worlds of Labour* (pp. 15–32). London: Weidenfeld & Nicolson.

Hoggart, Richard (1959) *The Uses of Literacy*. London: Penguin.

Hunt, Pauline (1980) *Gender and Class Consciousness*. London: Macmillan.

Kaplan, E. Ann (1984) Is the gaze male? In Ann Snitow *et al.* (eds) *Desire: The Politics of Female Sexuality*. London: Virago.

Lewis, Jane (1985) The debate on sex and class. *New Left Review* 149, 108–20.

Lukas, George (1968) *History and Class Consciousness*. London: Merlin Press.

Marcus, Steven (1976) Freud and Dora: Story, history, case-history. In Steven Marcus, *Representations* (pp. 247–310). New York: Random House.

Marx, Karl (1859) *A Contribution to the Critique of Political Economy*. In *Early Writings*, the Pelican Marx Library. London: Penguin (1975).

Newson, John and Newson, Elizabeth (1976) *Seven Years Old in the Home Environment*. London: Allen & Unwin.

Oakley, Ann (1981) *From Here to Maternity: Becoming a Mother*. London: Penguin.

— (1984) *Taking It Like a Woman*. London: Cape.

Owen, Ursula (ed.) (1983) *Fathers: Reflections by Daughters*. London: Virago.

Ricoeur, Paul (1984) *Time and Narrative*. Chicago: University of Chicago Press.

Seabrook, Jeremy (1967) *The Unprivileged*. London: Penguin (1973).

— (1978) *What Went Wrong?* London: Gollancz.

— (1982) *Working Class Childhood*. London: Gollancz.

Stedman-Jones, Gareth (1983a) Why is the Labour Party in a mess? In Gareth Stedman-Jones, *Languages of Class: Studies in English Working Class History, 1832–1982* (pp. 239–56). Cambridge: Cambridge University Press.

— (1983b) Rethinking Chartism. In Gareth Stedman-Jones, *Languages of Class: Studies in English Working Class History, 1832–1982* (pp. 90–178). Cambridge: Cambridge University Press.

Steedman, Carolyn (1982) *The Tidy House: Little Girls Writing*. London: Virago.

— (1986) *Landscape for a Good Woman*. London: Virago.

White, Hayden (1980) The value of narrativity in the representation of reality. *Critical Inquiry* 7, 1, 5–27.

Williams, Raymond (1979) *Politics and Letters*. London: NLB/Verso.

Winnicott, Donald (1974) *Playing and Reality*. London: Penguin.

Woodward, Kathleen (1928) *Jipping Street*. London: Virago (1983).

Young, Michael and Willmott, Peter (1962) *Family and Kinship in East London*. London: Penguin.

3 WHO CARES? MEMORIES OF CHILDHOOD IN CARE

FRED FEVER

IN THE BEGINNING

(I was three months old when I was placed in the care of Dr Barnardo's in Tunbridge Wells.) My early years were happy and secure. St Christopher's children's home offered a new approach to child care back in the 1960s. It was completely different from the big old institutions which had lots of children in one large house, and were run like something out of a Dickens novel.

The house parents up to 1971 were Jenny and Peter Cole. Jenny had herself been in Dr Barnardo's as a child. She had a warm, friendly face and a lovely smile. She always had, or made, time for us children; she gave me love and was a very wonderful mother to me. She had many outstanding qualities: she was generous, fair, approachable and very caring, and she also had a wonderful sense of humour. On the whole, life at St Christopher's with Jenny was a very happy one indeed.

I have fond memories of nursery school. I enjoyed painting and loved the bright colours. Being very shy, I preferred my own company at school.

I have no recollection of my first day at St Peter's Primary School, although I do remember my early years there with some affection.

When I was about six and a half years old I learnt that Jenny and Peter were leaving St Christopher's to start a family of their own. I would have given anything for them to have taken me with them (especially as it was soon after my best friends Clare and John had left).

I missed Clare and John badly but this was really serious. Jenny and Peter leaving! I was devastated. My whole world had been destroyed.

An hour or two after Jenny and Peter left the new house parents, Patrick and Vivienne Mitchell, were on their way to St Christopher's.

THE END OF MY CHILDHOOD

Within days of the Mitchell's arrival the situation between us had become an 'us and them' confrontation.

Patrick found every opportunity he could to humiliate me.

When it was felt by a member of staff that I had done something wrong, Patrick would punish me. One of his favourite punishments was to make

Source: Fever, F. (1994) *Who Cares? Memories of a Childhood in Barnados.* London: Warner Books. This article has been extracted from the whole book. In the interests of readability, the use of ellipses has been omitted.

make me stand and stare at a wall for hours on end. This penance was dealt out to me many times and I always hated it, no matter how long or short its duration.

Staring at walls wasn't the only punishment Patrick dealt out to me. He also smacked me. The smacks came in various degrees of severity from hard, to very hard, to extremely hard. I was hit fairly often.

I cannot remember precisely when or in what order all these events took place, but they are so heavily ingrained on my mind that they still haunt me day and night. It all happened during the time I spent with the Mitchells, from 1971 to 1974, when I was between seven and ten.

During this time I moved from the small bedroom I had had to myself to sharing one with David who was older than me and stood over six feet tall.

From the outset I felt uneasy about sharing a bedroom with someone I didn't know, especially someone who was almost grown up, but being a mere child I had no say in such matters.

David put me through horrendous sexual abuse, and then made me fear for my life. Although at the time I didn't understand what was happening, I was afraid of going to bed at night, and of the inside light going on, for this signalled terror.

He made me fear for my life by threatening me with castration.

Each night I would hope and pray that an adult might come in and catch him, but they never did.

I was enormously relieved to be moved out of the double bedroom and put once again into a small bedroom of my own. Yet my nights free from sexual abuse were numbered. Soon, David was invading my room, but this time he didn't turn on the light for fear of detection, so instead of being scared when the light went on I was scared of the dark. The abuse went on relentlessly as before.

It is difficult to describe my feelings at that point. I was terrified that I would never be free of this living hell and that I would always be living in fear of David. There are no words in the English language that are capable of conveying the feelings of being a rape/sexual abuse victim, and it is impossible to truly express what my feelings were. The pain of rape/sexual abuse goes not only through your body and mind but reaches down into the depths of your soul.

Life had now become a never-ending, painfully harrowing assault course.

From about the age of seven I was sent out of various classes for talking, shouting, messing around or not paying attention. The twenty-minute walk between home and school was about the only time I was free from abuse, trouble, aggravation or punishment. I never wanted to arrive at either destination, so I always took my time. The walk back to St Christopher's from school never failed to be a most horrendous journey. I knew that every step I took was a step closer to many painful hours of ill treatment in one form or another. I cannot put my innermost feelings about that treacherous walk into words, because the pain of those journeys went far beyond any words that can be written or spoken.

A GLIMMER OF HAPPINESS

In 1974, it was decided that I should be fostered by Betty and Bernard Simons. On Christmas Eve, 1974, I left institutionalized care.

After the Christmas holidays I started at my new junior school. It was called Barrow Grove. Not long after starting at Barrow Grove I began to make many new friends, both boys and girls. Some of them weren't even in my class—I would get to know other children in the playground. All the children were very friendly and this helped me to settle down with my new teacher. My new friends didn't make fun of my reading and writing difficulties. Instead they tried to help me. I also made friends on the Manor Grove Estate.

I looked forward to starting senior school with great anticipation because it made me feel grown up. Many of the kids I knew at Barrow Grove were starting senior school at the same time. It made a big difference, because it meant I would have friends before I even arrived. Most of my new friends on the Manor Grove Estate also attended or were soon to attend Westlands High School.

Once I got used to my new school and settled down, I began to take an interest in my school work. I always tried my best. I wanted to do well and enjoyed the work and I was also desperate to impress the Simons. I thought that if I got a good school report, Betty would be happy and pleased with me. I liked going to Westlands very much; I liked the lessons, the school and the teachers. I never dreaded going to school; in fact I looked forward to it. I was never sent out of a class or kept in detention, although I daresay I was probably told off a couple of times. I have only happy memories of Westlands High.

My circle of friends was growing even larger. To add to those I had on the estate and from Barrow Grove, I also made new friends at Westlands, children in my form and some from other classes, and I was never short of company. Sometimes I felt some of them were more intelligent than me, but this didn't pose any problems. None of them ever suggested that I was less able than them at school work. Much has happened since those days, and it is many years since I last saw any of them—I can't even remember some of their names—but I have always been grateful to have known such friendly and caring people.

My school reports from Westlands High School show that (Figure 3.1), the effort I put into my school work was clearly evident from the teacher's comments.

Then one day Jim (Johnson, my social worker) came to see me for a chat.

He dropped a bombshell on me that blew up my whole world. He said: 'Fred, you won't be going back to your foster parents after this holiday. You're going to Highbroom.'

I was totally shocked by this devastating news. I just couldn't speak.

'Mrs Simons says she can't cope and is ill, so you have to go back into a children's home,' Jim went on.

I thought, this isn't real, it's not happening, surely this is a mistake. I am not going back to a children's home . . .

It wasn't a nightmare, it really *was* happening. I couldn't take it all in properly, nor could I think clearly of the full implications.

FIGHTING HARD TO SURVIVE

In the short space of time it took to bump up the drive of Highbroom I think a major transformation took place within me. Until then I had had respect for most adults and authority. That isn't to say I respected all adults: in some cases, I held little regard for them. During my transformation all this was to change—that respect was now a thing of the past. On entering Highbroom I looked upon adults and authority as the vile enemy. I had been utterly betrayed. I felt nothing but anger and contempt for the people that I was supposed to look up to. Adults, I'd been led to believe when I was younger, were people to be emulated. But adults were untrustworthy, unreliable and undesirable people and I wanted nothing to do with any of them. Their words were meaningless. The 'us and them' had been triggered off. The fight had now begun.

Highbroom, built before the 1900s, was dark, cold and institutional, a world away from the modern, family-house atmosphere of (St Christopher's).

Mr Jenton (the head of the home), and his wife were not a young couple. They were probably in their fifties and looked every day of it.

The new school where I started only a week or so after arriving at Highbroom was called Beacon Comprehensive. Beacon School was very large, with over 1,000 pupils, because it served a very wide area encompassing many of the small villages and farms. I didn't want to start another new school and I didn't want to go to school in Crowborough. I had done well at Westlands, and had I gone back there for the second year I would have been moved up a class; I had been told that before breaking up for the summer holidays. I had been pleased that my hard work had been rewarded. At the beginning of the summer holidays I had looked forward to starting back at Westlands in the new higher class. The thought of starting at yet another school liter-ally made me feel ill. As if it wasn't bad enough moving to a new area, and being put back into care like some piece of electrical goods being taken back to the shop while still under warranty for being faulty.

KENT COUNTY COUNCIL   EDUCATION DEPARTMENT

WESTLANDS HIGH SCHOOL SITTINGBOURNE

NAME __A..FRED FEVER__................................   FORM ....__IB1__...............

REPORT FOR HALF YEAR ENDING __19th FEBRUARY 1976__....................

No. of half-day absences ....__0__...................   No. of detentions ....

Position of responsibility ....

Subject	Term	Exam	Teachers' Comments
ENGLISH	C+		Alfred tries hard and produces some good work.
MATHEMATICS	C+		Alfred tries very hard and has achieved some pleasing results
GEOGRAPHY	C		Alfred tries hard
RELIGIOUS EDUCATION	C-		Alfred tries very hard
~~FRENCH~~ READING	B-		Alfred tries hard
HISTORY	C+		Alfred's work is satisfactory
BIOLOGY	C		Alfred's work is satisfactory. He will work hard. He has a pleasant, extrovert character which enables him to
CHEMISTRY			communicate well orally.
PHYSICS			
INTEGRATED SCIENCE	C-		Alfred tries hard. His work has improved lately
RURAL SCIENCE	C+		Alfred tries very hard. Shows an interest
MUSIC	C		Some good work
DRAMA	C		Has made a good start in drama, lacks confidence
ART/DESIGN	C+		Alfred always works well
DOMESTIC SCIENCE			
NEEDLEWORK			
METALWORK			
WOODWORK			
TECHNICAL DRAWING			
PHYSICAL EDUCATION	C+		Quite good

GRADES: A = Very Good   B = Good   C= Average   D = Below Average   E = Unsatisfactory

Form Teacher's Comments ...__Fred tries hard and is a helpful member of the form. He needs to overcome his fear of being behind the other children in the class with his work__ Signature __E. Newman__

Head of Lower/~~Middle~~ School's Comments ...__A very pleasant personality and I am pleased to see that he is working so well.__

Signature __L.N. Foster__

...........__b.a. Jewett__...........Signature of Headmaster

0008168

FIGURE 3.1

KENT COUNTY COUNCIL   EDUCATION DEPARTMENT

WESTLANDS HIGH SCHOOL SITTINGBOURNE

NAME ...... ALFRED FEVER ......   FORM ...... IB1 ......

REPORT FOR HALF YEAR ENDING ...... 21st JULY 1976 ......

No. of half-day absences ...... 0 ......   No. of detentions ......

Position of responsibility ...... FORM CAPTAIN ......

Subject	Term	Exam	Teachers' Comments
ENGLISH	B	74%	Fred tries very hard and obtains satisfactory results
MATHEMATICS	C+	54%	Fred perseveres with his maths, but sometimes has difficulties
GEOGRAPHY	C+	47½	Fred tries hard and works enthusiastically
RELIGIOUS EDUCATION	C+	73	Fred has gained confidence and done well
~~FRENCH~~ READING	B		Fred has made excellent progress
HISTORY	B-	62%	Fred has made very good progress
BIOLOGY	B-	B+	A good enthusiastic worker who is making excellent progress. Well done Fred.
CHEMISTRY			
PHYSICS			
INTEGRATED SCIENCE	C	54%	Fred takes an interest in his work
RURAL SCIENCE	C+	20/30	Tries hard and is gaining confidence
MUSIC	C+		Fred always tries hard
DRAMA	C+	34%	Fred has worked hard all year, well done
ART/DESIGN	C+		Always works well
DOMESTIC SCIENCE			
NEEDLEWORK			
METALWORK			
WOODWORK			
TECHNICAL DRAWING			
PHYSICAL EDUCATION	C		Good effort made

GRADES: A = Very Good   B = Good   C= Average   D = Below Average   E = Unsatisfactory

Form Teacher's Comments ...... Fred is a pleasant helpful boy. He has made good progress and this should continue if he tries hard. He is also outgrowing his immaturity.   Signature ...... E Newman

Head of Lower/~~Middle~~ School's Comments ...... Fred is really keen to give satisfaction in his work and anxious to learn. Signature ...... J Rossiter

...... b.a. Jarrett ...... Signature of Headmaster

0008158

As soon as I got to the school teachers started passing judgement on me and labelling me as a Dr Barnardo's child. The in-care factor put me in a special category straight away— many children in care were, and still are, discriminated against in this way. Not long after the basic formalities were over, the teacher got me to do an IQ test. Before I even put pen to paper I knew where my destiny lay; the bottom class. Lo and behold I was correct. The bastards had done it! I was exiled to the bottom class yet again. The bastards! Although I knew it was going to happen long before it did, deep down I nursed a small hope that somehow I wouldn't have to suffer that dreadful fate. Putting me into the bottom class was the last act of their despicable play. They could do no more damage to me now, they had taken my home from me, they had taken my friends from me and now, finally, they had taken my chance of an education from me. From the moment I started at Beacon School I realised that it wasn't a place where my education would flourish. I had been taken away from the school in which I would have flourished.

After being placed in the bottom class I could see no point in trying hard at school. Once you were put in the bottom class you knew there was no way out, and that no matter how hard you worked you would always be there. Because of this I adopted an attitude that it didn't really matter what I did, because the teachers would always see me as unintelligent. Yet I did still try at school until my second year, but after that I gave up. My life was so horrible that I really didn't give a shit about anything. I hated authoritarian people, and during my short life I had had a great deal of contact with such people. I saw teachers as oppressive adults who were part of the system, and who were in collusion with Barnardo's. I hated the teachers at Beacon School, but I hated Barnardo's staff even more. The teachers, although strict, didn't have the power to punish me like the staff at Barnardo's did, so their ability to frighten me was much reduced. Unlike other children in the class, I was very familiar with constant confrontation with authoritarian adults. As time went on I had more and more problems outside school, and so my behaviour and school work deteriorated to the extent that there was little or no point in me even attending.

For some children doing well at school meant that they would one day get a decent job. I knew that even if I'd tried and had done well at school there would be no way I would get a decent job. After all, what use were CSEs when other children were taking O-Levels from the beginning? I realised that it was all a waste of time. The carrot and the stick didn't work for me. I was used to the stick and the carrot wasn't worth having.

In a matter of months after arriving I began to get into trouble with the police. It wasn't exactly the crime of the century, but two other boys and I got into trouble for stealing. We hadn't nicked much, but enough in the eyes of the law to warrant a caution at the local police station.

We received our pocket-money on Saturdays, and in the afternoon we would go into Crowborough to spend it. It wasn't very much and it didn't last long. So (my friends) Gary, Tim and I eked it out by stealing what was fairly easy to take and using the money for things that were difficult to nick, such as cigarettes.

The gaining of material wealth from crime wasn't what gave the most pleasure, it was 'getting one over on society'. In some strange way I felt I was beating the system; I was conning them, they weren't conning me. I never looked upon stealing from shops as dishonest, more as a bit of harmless fun.

Gary, Tim and I even pinched a tape-recorder from Beacon School. It was kept under lock and key in one of the stationery cupboards.

That evening the police came to Highbroom.

The questioning began, first about school, then about home, and then about stealing from shops. Yes, I said I had done some thieving at school but I admitted nothing else. Time went on and I was still not saying what they wanted to hear.

The next thing I knew I felt a punch in my stomach. A hand hit my face and I lost my balance as I was shoved, hard, across the room. I fell against the wall, winded and shocked. I recovered quickly from the shock but the bastard was still pushing me against the wall and punching and slapping me. After a few minutes the beating stopped and I was given a seat.

I sat down. I was astounded at what had just occurred. I was completely out of my depth. I didn't know the script for this scene and had no idea what would happen next. I had never felt so vulnerable in my whole life. Mr Jenton, the head of the home, had just sat and watched me take a beating from a policeman and had raised neither voice nor hand to protect me. No one gave a shit about me, the coppers could do what they liked. Frightened, crying and shaking I then, at last, answered their bloody questions. Mr Jenton had sat there with that self-satisfied smug look on his face while I'd been beaten. It was as if he enjoyed watching me being knocked about.

NO ESCAPE

That same year I asked my social worker about my parents. I wanted to know about them and to visit them.

It was more than a natural curiosity. I was more desperate than ever before to find my parents. They were my last and only hope, for I knew that if I didn't find them I would never escape institutional life. It never occurred to me that my mum and dad might have been unsuitable parents. I suppose this was because they were my dream, the dream that kept me alive when things got bad. I never thought ill of them except for having put me into care. I had a picture in my mind of roses around a door and a warm, homely house inside, and a perpetual hope that one day I would go there to the loving arms of my mother and father. That dream was still with me in 1977, and because of it I kept on at my social worker to take me to see them.

Jim was against it, but eventually he relented.

He advised me not to expect too much, and warned me that I might be a bit shocked by what I found.

We approached the front door. I was almost shitting myself for I knew that behind that door were my mother and father. The parents I had dreamed of seeing for thirteen long years were now only seconds away. There was no turning back. My social worker knocked on the door.

A few seconds later the door opened. There in front of me stood a short, poorly dressed old woman who bore no resemblance to me. My first sight of my mother was to be one of the biggest shocks of my life.

We entered the house, and my mother started to talk. I couldn't believe my ears. She spoke like a retarded child. Immediately I knew she was mentally subnormal. It was too much to take in. I was in a state of severe shock. The house looked as if nothing much had changed since the 1920s.

My social worker said something to my mother about some papers my dad had to sign. 'Oh, I will have to sign them—Mr Fever can't write,' she replied. I thought to myself, my father can't write his own name? This isn't really happening, it's all a horrible nightmare. After only minutes in my parents' house thirteen years of hopes and dreams had started to disintegrate. I knew it would never be my home or sanctuary from institutional life.

I felt physically ill and emotionally devastated. I had been conned. The bastards. This wasn't my mother, this wasn't my parents' home. They had done this deliberately so that I wouldn't get any ideas about leaving care. The bastards!

My father had not even bothered to take the day off work so I never saw him that fateful day. It was probably just as well—I had had more than enough shocks for one day.

Soon after starting at Beacon School I began to get thrown out of classes. I was expelled from lessons with such regularity that I didn't need to bunk off. For some classes, I saw no point in turning up in the first place because it was so unlikely that I would complete the whole lesson without being sent out. I don't know what the teachers were trying to achieve by throwing me out. If it was meant as a punishment it didn't work. I didn't mind being ejected—it only reinforced my belief that school was a waste of time and that I could never get anything out of it except more aggravation. Being thrown out of the bottom class meant that there was nothing more the teachers could do to you, except, of course, expel you from the school. I suppose I did feel a bit rejected after a while, but I had come to expect rejection by the authorities as normal: nobody wanted me, that was the way it was. Two could play at that game: I was rejecting them as surely as they rejected me. I finished up not giving a shit whether I was in a lesson or not.

By the time I was in the fourth year the teachers had given up on me. It no longer mattered what I did or how much I achieved, they weren't really interested in me. All they wanted was a quiet life and this was easy to achieve by sending me out of the class. I didn't want to be there, the teachers didn't want me there, I didn't want the lessons, they didn't want to teach me. It was a recipe for confrontation. I didn't loathe all the teachers at Beacon School—there were about two or three whom I respected. Those few individuals treated me as a human being with feelings and not as an object to ridicule and discard.

At Highbroom the staff were very strict as regards school attendance. They even made us go to school when we were ill. The staff's attitude seems even more perverse when I consider it more thoroughly. No one seemed bothered about what you did at school or whether you achieved good results, all you had to do was simply go there. So it would appear that the staff just wanted to get us off their hands for a few hours and were keener to shift responsibility for us than to show a genuine concern about our education.

Throughout my time at Highbroom I witnessed and experienced a great deal of staff violence. Ninety-nine per cent of the violent attacks on the children were carried out by the male staff, although Mrs Jenton was known to lash out occasionally. The staff saw it as a means of control and punishment, but in fact it was blatant aggression and violence. In general the sort of violence I experienced was being slapped about and punched, usually in the head, legs and buttocks. Before, during and after an assault you would more often than not be pushed around, sometimes into walls or sharp objects. Often we were beaten with objects, such as rulers, pieces of wood or a belt.

A LIVING HELL

In the summer of 1978 I was walking alone along a country lane near Highbroom when a man pulled up in a van and asked if I would like a lift. I had never seen the man before, I didn't know him and I certainly wasn't going to get into his van. He asked me a second time if I wanted a lift as he was going the same way. I insisted that I would walk. After that he drove off. I was quite frightened by the experience and was relieved when he left me alone. I thought it was an isolated incident and that I had seen the last of the man. But a few days later I saw him again, and again he asked me if I wanted a lift. Again I said no. This time, however, he tried to strike up a conversation. I walked away from the van but he drove up alongside me and started talking to me. By this stage I was very frightened. I wasn't sure what he might do next. Eventually he drove off, after offering me money and cigarettes, both of which I refused. The man went by the name of Billy Bulldog.

Throughout that summer I was constantly harassed by Billy Bulldog. I had by now a long-standing fear and mistrust of men, especially middle-ged men. Over the years I had been subjected to a great deal of physical, emotional and sexual abuse by men, and their sheer presence was enough to make me feel uneasy. The quiet and secluded country lanes served only to heighten my feelings of fear and danger. Anyone who has been in a similar situation will understand that to be approached in such an environment by an intimidating man in a vehicle is very frightening. Billy ignored my refusals and pursued me relentlessly. It was as if the more I said no the more he harassed me. Unfortunately I had no alternative but to walk the long and winding country lanes. There were no buses which came anywhere near the home.

Because of Highbroom's isolated location the children had to walk everywhere. The school was a two-mile walk; the town centre was a little bit further than the school. Even the nearest shops were about ten minutes' walk from the home. So, from the early summer of 1978. I had little respite from persecution by somebody or other every hour of the day. At school I would be in trouble with the teaching staff and thrown out of classes; on my way home from school I would regularly be hounded by Billy Bulldog in the van. When I got back to the home the staff would give me a hard time by physically or emotionally abusing me, and often both. The abuse sometimes would go on into the evening, for example, when I was put on punishment. Then would come the peeling of tons of potatoes or staring at walls, both of which would last for some time. Before the punishments even started, Mr Jenton would tell me off and physically assault me. Even when I was not punished or otherwise abused I would often have nightmares. So I lived with different forms of abuse twenty-four hours of the day.

The pressure of Billy Bulldog's ever-increasing harassment became a terrible ordeal. I was now at breaking-point. I was literally frightened for my life. I had just started my fourth-year studies at school, and the next two years were the important years in which you were supposed to work hard for your final exams. (It was at this point that Billy Bulldog began to subject me to sexual abuse.)

After the first assault, I scrubbed and scrubbed (myself in the bath) using tons of soap. I desperately tried to cleanse myself. No matter how much bathing and scrubbing I did, I still felt filthy dirty. The full horror of what had happened was sinking in. Billy Bulldog had sexually assaulted me. He had sucked my penis. I wanted to throw up. I hated myself. I thought I was disgusting and dirty. I couldn't stop thinking about what had happened and how dirty I was.

I hated myself. I considered myself the lowest form of life for having given in to that dirty pervert.

I thought long and hard about who I could possibly tell, for I was going out of my mind and desperately wanted to talk to someone who could sort the matter out. The police were my first option, but I thought they would blame me. I had terrible memories of the unexpected beating they had given me before and couldn't be sure they wouldn't do it again. I just couldn't bring myself to trust the staff; also I felt that they didn't care about me anyway, so what was the point? I didn't even consider approaching my teachers at school. In most of their eyes I was nothing more than a trouble-maker. In last-ditch desperation, I thought about telling my mates at school. I soon abandoned that idea, because of the thought of being misunderstood and labelled as dirty, or a 'poof' or pervert.

I soon realised I could tell no one. I was in this alone, with no one to help me. The full enormity hit me: I could rely on nobody for help. I was at the mercy of all adults and those in authority. I had now been completely crushed by the system. I had no more fight to give, they had broken me. I had no power, no dignity, no pride, no self-respect. I had nothing more to give and they could take no more from me. They had already taken everything.

By January 1979 I was being sexually abused on a regular basis, some-times once or twice a week and sometimes more. The circumstances I was in—not being able to talk or to get help from anyone—put the abuser in a position of immense power.

As time went by I began to lose all hope and could see no end to the misery. My life was a living hell. I hated every hour of every day. Each day was a huge struggle from beginning to end. I seemed to be constantly in trouble. At school I couldn't concentrate and the teachers were always telling me off. On the way to and from school I was harassed by Billy Bulldog, and at Highbroom the staff would regularly hit and punish me. Over the years I had always fought back no matter what, but now I felt the fight seep out of me. All those years had taken their toll. I was fourteen and life had gone from bad to worse. My parents had been a great let-down, and I knew they could never save me from my desperate plight.

I had always fought back because I had always had hope of a better life. Having gone through so much and having seen no improvement I was now watching my life go down to the lowest depths imaginable, and I lost that hope. When I was in trouble at school, being punished at the home, or being sexually assaulted I was overcome by a sense of numbness. Only after the events had happened would I feel anger and loathing towards the adults who had committed these acts. After a while I felt nothing during or afterwards: not hope, not anger, not hatred, not happiness, not sadness, nothing. Emp-tiness. I was no longer alive. I was no longer capable of feeling. I was an object. I could see no way out, no hope, no future. I was emotionally dead.

In March 1979 I wrote a letter to my mother and father suggesting the idea of spending my half-term with them. It was not a plan I particularly relished but I had to believe it could work—it was my last chance.

A few days after I spoke to my social worker, arrangements were made for us to go and see my parents one evening after school.

When we arrived at my parents' house in Kent, it was still light. We went up the path and knocked on the door. There was no answer. We knew my parents were in so we just carried on knocking. After a very long five minutes my father opened the door a crack, just enough to put his head round. He looked very upset and I think he was almost in tears. Denis and I asked if we could come in but my father said we couldn't He (said that) my mother didn't want to see me and didn't want to talk to me.

My heart sank like a stone. I wanted to cry and scream for my mother. I couldn't believe that she could reject me like that. I didn't know what to say or do. It was one of the saddest and most profoundly disturbing moments of my life. I had longed all my life to have a real mother and father and now here I was, standing on the front step of my parents' house, being totally rejected by my mother. I wanted to die there and then. I had kept myself going all those years by dreaming of the happy day when I would return to my loving parents. Even the discovery of what poor parents they were had not completely destroyed that dream, but now it was smashed into tiny fragments which poured from my heart. I could take being rejected by the rest of society, but not by my own mother.

After the traumatic episode at my parents' house, life at Highbroom deteriorated steadily. Not surprisingly, the disintegration of my life made my behaviour at school worse, and I was often sent to see the headmaster (or my head of house, or the deputy headmaster). I also discovered that I was only one of Billy Bulldog's victims. He sexually abused many young boys in the Crowborough area and by the summer of 1979 he was regularly assaulting several young boys from Dr Barnardo's at Highbroom I cannot comment on what other victims' feelings were at the time, as sexual abuse can affect people in different ways. At the time the abuser's conspiracy of silence condemned each of us to our own lonely misery.

One Saturday lunchtime in the autumn of 1979, I and some of the other children who were victims of sexual abuse were queuing up for our dinner. I was in the front of the queue, and went into the kitchen first to receive my lunch, closely followed by the others. Mrs Jenton looked up at us and said in a loud and threatening voice: 'I see we have a load of nancy boys in the home!'

I couldn't believe what I was hearing. Mrs Jenton calling us nancy boys. The staff *knew* that the children in their care were being sexually abused by a pervert and were doing nothing about it, and even worse than doing nothing, were ridiculing us by calling us nancy boys? I was mortified. Until Mrs Jenton had said that I hadn't dreamt that the staff knew what was happening. My worst fears were now confirmed. The staff at Highbroom didn't give a shit what happened to the children. I was fifteen at the time and now faced the full horror of the knowledge that staff at Highbroom would actually stand by and let me and others be assaulted sexually by a paedophile. I knew with cold certainty that I would never get out of this systematic cycle of abuse while I remained in Crowborough.

At that stage in my life I am not sure who I hated most, the staff at Highbroom or Billy Bulldog. I knew the staff were bastards but this was too much to cope with. The fucking bastards knew and did nothing.

After I left school I asked if I could have my old school reports from my file. Somehow there was a mix-up and what (I got) were some unofficial school reports that I was never intended to see. These unofficial reports had been written yearly and sent direct to the home and the authors remained anonymous. I kept them and (also) asked for my official school reports.

My first reaction to the unoffical reports was shock. I was astounded to read what my teachers secretly thought of me, and how badly they judged me. But then I realized this was yet another example of the lack of any real communication between those supposedly looking after my welfare and education and myself. The unofficial reports, and my ordinary school reports for that matter, were yet another example of how adults in powerful positions were labelling me and writing me off.

When I lived in Crowborough there were very few, if any, job opportunities. If you had poor or no qualifications then the only job available in the Crowborough area was in Buxted chicken factory. The chicken factory was predicted for me—if I played my cards right. The teachers would constantly sneer that I would end up in a detention centre, borstal and prison. I hated these speculations. I had already spent a lifetime in institutions and didn't relish the idea that I would never be free from institutional life.

The teachers' continual prejudiced insinuations that I would be going to a detention centre, borstal and then prison didn't in any way change my behaviour or attitude towards people in authority, or towards the system itself. When they made these remarks I knew they were talking a load of shit and knew bugger all and it wouldn't be long before I proved them all wrong.

The teachers at Beacon School also said I would never pass any exams. I didn't want to take my CSE examinations because I knew long before leaving school that CSEs were not worth the paper they were written on. However, I decided to sit them purely to prove a point. I passed all my five CSE exams. I didn't exactly get brilliant grades, but I passed, which was the object of the exercise. Thus I showed that some teachers at Beacon School really talked a load of shit.

From the beginning of 1980, children started to leave Highbroom (which was being closed down), and weren't replaced. Many of the children who left at this time went home to live with their parents, while others were found foster parents, some of whom lived in the local community. I, however, wasn't to be fostered and neither was I going home to my parents. I was being sent to a hostel. For the last two months of my time there, there was only me.

Mr Jenton and the staff had, over the years, put me through some awful punishments, but this was by far the worst—two months of psychological torture. I felt very insecure and even more vulnerable being there alone. There were no other children to offer comfort and solidarity—it was just me and them now. At times I didn't know if my nerves could stand it, but I managed to hang in there to the end. The worst thing about watching others leave to go home was knowing that that day would never be mine. I could never go home. I had no home.

I left Beacon School [and Highbroom] in May 1980. I was to spend another four unhappy years in a Barnardos hostel.

At the end of May 1984 I left Kingston hostel, and left care. A friend of mine from the hostel and I moved to a flat in Surbiton. I could hardly believe it when it happened. I was now free. My twentieth birthday was less than three weeks away but I kidded myself that at least I had got out as a teenager.

September 1964 to May 1984.

Twenty years in care for a crime I didn't commit.

4 IDENTITY, MIGRATION AND EDUCATION

UVANNEY MAYLOR

Writing an autobiography can be a very painful and traumatic experience. Lewis (1992, p. 5) questions whether autobiography is a 'legitimate educational task' or 'a form of pedagogic terrorism'. In many ways it is a form of 'terrorism', a 'literary striptease' (Lewis, 1992, p. 5). I have bared my soul. I have died many deaths.

> Telling the truth about one's life is not simply about naming the 'bad' things, exposing horrors. It is also about being able to speak openly and honestly about feelings, about a variety of experiences. (hooks, 1993, p. 27)

My baptism into autobiography came whilst researching life histories of black women student teachers in initial teacher education. I asked the participants if they would consider writing their own educational autobiography—using a questionnaire to help them frame their ideas. This was a way of eliciting whether the lives they wrote about differed from their spoken text. With time and further reflection would they see themselves differently? The lack of response seemed to imply that this was an inappropriate task. What was it about the written task that created silence? I reacted to their muteness by attempting to construct my own autobiography.

Involving myself in the research process was an important learning experience. It helped shape my own understanding of the participants, in my research on their life histories. Until I had actually begun to explore my own life I had underestimated the difficulty that some of my subjects faced in attempting such a task. hooks (1989) revealed that her attempt at autobiographical writing took years to complete. If I was prepared to ask students to throw off their masks and expose themselves to me, then I needed to know what this entailed for them. 'We must explore such experiences from the inside ... not just as 'researchers' leeching on the experiences of others but unwilling to use our experiences as we do those of other people' (Stanley, 1990, p. 122). I found that it was much more than revealing snippets in interviews. I understood better the delicate balance between detached researcher, counsellor and friend that had been demanded of me by some of my research participants.

The autobiography outlined below is my version of events. A mere fraction of my whole life, it is what I could safely allow the public to know

Source: This article has been specially commissioned for this Reader.

without knowing all of me. However, this does not constitute grounds
for the dismissal of autobiography as a viable research method. It is after
all a story,

> written or told to explain, to make sense of, some problematic event
> or experience. The value of educational autobiography is that it is a
> story that can tell us about an individual's inquiry into what it means
> to become an educated self. (Franzosa, 1992, p. 412)

This article is part of the journey I took to becoming an 'educated self'. It
explores my relationship with my father and outlines the social and political
factors which shaped and determined my relationship. In writing it I came
to understand my father better and to realize that I too was an agent in my
own destiny and not, as I had thought, the victim of a relentless patriarchy.

THE RELATIONSHIP WITH MY FATHER

> I was thinking, you know mother, that I wish I'd found you while you
> were living. We could have exchanged views. I could have told you what
> I've been doing and we could have got to know each other and you could
> have told me who I am—that's important to me, to know who I am.
> (cited by Feuchtwang (1992, p. 155) from *Lost Children of the Empire*)

My mother died when I was three years old. Since that day my father has
been mother and father to me. He seemed to me to be at once all knowing
and frightening. In one breath he could shout loudly in anger and in another
he would quietly reveal the wealth of historical data he had acquired as a
child and as an adult. He expected obedience at all times, and adhered to
the philosophy of 'spare the rod and spoil the child'. But although some
might consider this a violent philosophy, I never thought of my father as
a violent man.

He seemed to me to be kind, generous and thoughtful. Materially, I wanted
for nothing, but I did crave a more open demonstration of the love he had
for me. I suppose the love that might have been there for me died when my
mother passed away. I had never considered my father unloving until I was
about ten years old when I began to notice that he did not return my kiss as
he left for work. I was always the demonstrative one—I liked to be loved.
My friends' parents hugged their children and hugged me too. What held my
father back? What kind of relationship had he had with his parents? Were
they distant? Did he think I would think any less of him as a man? Would
my father reveal himself as vulnerable if he expressed his love? Had he forgotten how to show love? Although I hurt deep inside I never asked.

> Many black people, and black women in particular, have become so
> accustomed to not being loved that we protect ourselves from having to
> acknowledge the pain that such deprivation brings. (hooks, 1993, p. 145)

I only knew that I was a child who longed for the hugs and kisses that fairytales were filled with.

I thought then that 'real' men were devoid of feelings. Now I understand what my father meant when he asked me if I thought that 'so so' love could feed me. When you have finished loving you still have to eat. Love was a luxury he could ill afford. It did not pay the rent. hooks' (1993) depiction of her American childhood in many ways mirrors my British (Caribbean) upbringing. Her reflections partly reassure me that 'struggling to survive, to make ends meet, was more important than loving' (p. 134). Struggling to survive was undoubtedly a feature of black immigrant life in Britain, but it did not to me warrant repression of feelings. It was not an equal exchange. I was a child who did not understand the intricacies of life as my father perceived them. I saw only two worlds—the loving and the unloved.

In patriarchal societies gender roles are differentiated between the private world of the home and the public world of paid labour. Women are subordinated to the former sphere. As carers and nurturers they are expected to reproduce, rear children, provide emotional support, satisfy sexual needs and take responsibility for household chores (Walby, 1990). The husband/father as head of the household regards it as his duty to maintain authority and to protect and provide economic support for his family by engaging in paid labour. My father's philosophies about the world and relationships pertained to a patriarchal framework. With mother's last breath he found himself struggling with contradictory gender roles. He coped well in combining his private and public roles. However, hugs and kisses did not fit into his newly acquired role.

Father was 'a man's man', an authoritarian. In his relations with women and children he considered himself always to be right, never wrong. This was a particularly difficult trait of his personality. It did not matter how plausible your explanation was, if it did not coincide with his it was automatically deemed wrong. Stanley's (1990) account of her mother's oppression at the hands of her father, is just one of the many examples of the way patriarchal society legitimates and accords rights to men, to exert 'a necessary and proper control over "bossy" (all) women' (p. 117).

It is difficult to assess whether my father's assumed power would have gone unchallenged had my mother lived. However, such dominance needs to be understood in the light not only of a patriarchal culture, but the social context in which my father found himself after my mother's death. On reflection, I associate his need to be respected, to be obeyed, to have status, with his status in Britain. When he arrived in Britain, the difficulties in settling in a foreign land were compounded by the denial and rejection of his skills as a tailor, of him as a man. He was vilified because of the colour of his skin. Carter and Joshi (1984) cited in Clarke (1992) suggest that the 'civilizing mission discourse of high colonialism', led to perceptions of blacks as 'uncivilizable' (p. 19). Coming from a country where his family name commanded respect, father found his treatment difficult to comprehend. His family were considered wealthy. They owned land, bakeries and had business interests in a well-known beverage factory. They were major employers. Contrary to stereotypes which attribute migration to the push–pull factors associated with poverty, and which were associated with the new arrivals to Britain in the late 1950s, father was quite well off. Unfortunately, my mother's illness together with the difficulty in securing employment and accommodation helped to erode much of that income.

Father was a proud man, who had assumed that his British passport afforded him the rights that fellow citizens took for granted. He found it difficult to acknowledge the alien and lowly status accorded to him. With these denials it is possible to understand why father proceeded on the track that he did. He sought to regain his pride through the achievements of his children, and with my brother and sister still in Jamaica, I bore the brunt of his ambitions. Father's belief in Britain as a meritocratic society created several problems for me.

EDUCATION

I was neither spoilt nor physically abused, but I suffered mentally. Father expected me to be successful and brooked no argument on the matter. This success was to come through education. 'Our parents, anxious that we should escape the menial, low-paid work they had been forced to accept, urged us to seize any educational opportunity which came our way' (Bryan, Dadzie and Scafe, 1985, p. 68). Father believed implicitly in the power of education. He lived by such maxims as: 'if at first you don't succeed, try and try again'; 'never let them use your colour as an excuse not to employ you, let it be for lack of qualification'. Dad's obsession with education was both the source of my subordination at home and the key to my freedom.

He believed that with education came a good job, a decent income, decent housing, better economic and social opportunities and more importantly the ability to choose. Because of family circumstances, my father had learned a trade and became a skilled tailor. But even these qualifications were later rejected by British companies who wanted him to return to college to gain a 'proper' British qualification—an impossibility with a family to support. Unlike Jamaica, where if it became necessary he could live off the land, he had to undertake waged work to eat. It took many years for father to acknowledge the real reason for his rejection.

As I reflect I realise that education became the substance of my father's life. The 'mother country' had stripped him of his status, his standing in the community. I represented the opportunity to regain that lost status. In raising my class position he would raise his own. My education became a personal crusade for my father, a crusade motivated by guilt at his own loss. The irony is that while my childhood and youth were being sacrificed on the altar of achievement, in search of a new identity for my father (although he would argue that it was for my benefit), he was at the same time subverting the notion that a 'woman's place is in the home'. I had to move from the boundaries imposed by my working-class position, and higher education would show me the way. Unfortunately, father did not realize that the very education system in which he placed so much faith, was built upon and perpetuated the social divisions of class and 'race' now responsible for his diminished self-image (Sarup, 1991; Welch, 1993). Like Martin Luther King, father had a dream, but it was a dream of social mobility. A dream thwarted in a world where skin colour persisted as a marker of exclusion. A fact which father would not acknowledge.

SCHOOL

From the age of seven life at school was a constant struggle. At that point in time I became more aware of my racial identity. As one of a small minority of black pupils, I was subjected to continuous racial abuse. I wore my hair in plaits to school—it was both convenient and made my hair easier to manage. The partings in my hair led the children to invent the nickname of 'square head'. I longed for the day when I could wear my hair in one as the other girls did. I was 'affectionately' known as, 'blackie/darkie'. At secondary school 'square head' was replaced by 'monkey'. The contrast between my dark skin and white teeth provided a source of derision for one of my teachers: if we turn the lights out we will be able to see Uvanney's teeth.

It was not the name calling which bothered me so much—it was the malicious intent that I found painful (see Essed, 1991). These were children with whom I shared 35 hours of the week. I considered them to be my friends. Behind their surface smiles seemed to lurk a mountain of hostility. Who taught them to hate me? And why did racial forms of abuse hurt me so much more than any other forms? Although I did not understand it at the time, I realise now that this kind of abuse did not make me feel less of a person, less human, but I must have known at some level that they also referred to my father, my friends and all the other black people in the world. Perhaps at some unconscious level, I was already making connections between my father's subordinate status and his skin colour. As Marable states:

> Race only becomes 'real' as a social force when individuals or groups behave towards each other in ways which either reflect or perpetuate the hegemonic ideology of subordination and the patterns of inequality in daily life. These are, in turn, justified and explained by assumed differences in physical and biological characteristics. (Marable, 1993, p. 114)

Thus, feeling isolated and excluded, but unable to retaliate at the same level, and unsupported by teachers, I resorted to fighting physically as my only defence.

McElroy-Johnson (1993, p. 94) contends that, 'a good teacher would have seized the day, would have talked about "good" hair versus "bad", dark skin versus light skin'. I would add that a 'good' teacher is anyone who is able to take differences between black and white children as well as within each group and discuss them openly and positively. Such differences can be used in the understanding of how student identities and subjectivities are constructed in multiple and contradictory ways (Giroux, 1992). A 'good' teacher is one who, regardless of colour or creed, is able to create an environment in which all children can grow and develop (see Ladson-Billings, 1990; McElroy-Johnson, 1993).

None of my school teachers seemed to understand my emotional needs. One or two encouraged me academically; the rest were caught up in their own prejudices, unable to provide the kind of environment in which a black child could grow with a positive sense of self. The one black teacher I encountered in primary school showed little support. As I reflect I wonder if he was aware, or if he was just powerless. Mirza's (1992) research shows that many teachers do not consider finding out about black children, or educating the school community, as part of their practice. Many take a colour-blind approach to their teaching. 'Race' was not a relevant factor for the quality of their teaching or ability to communicate.

> Sometimes educational institutions in the effort to assimilate minority students, follow a norm of promoting sameness, thus ignoring differences. This posture may encourage students (and staff)—to reject their ethnic identity and the unique qualities of being black. (Ward, 1990, p. 228)

I was growing up in a world where my isolation was compounded by the many difficulties associated with adolescence, and my inability to share my thoughts with the closest person to me, my father. Where I needed and hoped to get support I received chastisement for reacting angrily to the constant abuse. Father considered that derogatory remarks and racist name calling were but minor irritants. If I ignored them, he contended, they would die for lack of response. On numerous occasions he informed me that the purpose of sending me to school was to learn. When I had attained a significant position then I would be free to react as the need arose, with words not fists. But what I needed most was his understanding of my pain and my feelings of vulnerability. Even if I could accept that he was right at some level, I needed him to see me for the little girl that I was and not treat me as though I were an automaton, only programmed to take in information and pass examinations.

CULTURE AND IMPERIALISM

Mackenzie (1993, p. 52) cites Michael Manley, former Prime Minister of Jamaica, who suggests that education under colonial rule 'reflected the realities of power within the system'. Children were offered 'a very elementary form of the three R's', similar to that provided to the very poor in Britain in the late nineteenth century. Colonial education 'alienated the local people from their environment, denigrated local culture, traditional values and norms' (Ellis, 1988, p. 91). In Jamaica African-Caribbeans were taught that the 'key to survival was to carry a higher regard for things European than for things African' (Nicholas, cited by Mackenzie, 1993, p. 52). After independence the ruling echelon in Jamaica remained white (Henriques, 1976). 'If anything, blacks were taught (more intensely) to despise and fear everything reminiscent of their African heritage' (Nicholas, cited by Mackenzie, 1993, p. 52).

In common with many African-Caribbeans father denied his African heritage. He would not acknowledge the significance of the insignia on the Jamaican coat of arms—'out of many, one people'. Slavery was something he did not discuss. In his view no one in his family had ever been slaves. It was not in his power to change history so he preferred to let sleeping dogs lie; he expressed ignorance of racial imperialism while proudly demonstrating his detailed knowledge of English history.

The pathological acceptance of things European, of placing European culture at the centre of civilisation, enabled my father to reject his heritage and become a subjected individual. He failed to make the connection between imperialism, past and present, with what was happening to him in Britain. Colonialism had not only suppressed his heritage but had consciously muted and stifled his voice, his very existence. Father passionately believed that living in the past would not secure success in the present. A denial of his self, his history and the history of racism, had so far been the key to his survival. He encouraged me not to rock the boat, not to search for my voice. Like fighting, these were considered distractions from my main goal. He encouraged me to put negative experiences out of my mind. I was black, yes, but my skin colour was not as important as succeeding within the education system. Class overrode any considerations of 'race' and gender. But whilst he exhorted me to be proud of my colour he was unable to see the contradictions of pushing me in a direction which could have ultimately led to a rejection of my black identity. 'One of the tragic ironies of contemporary black life is that individuals succeed in acquiring material privilege often by sacrificing their positive connection to black culture and black experience' (hooks, 1992, p. 19).

I received and interpreted these contradictory messages. I was to speak English at home and reject patois. Father spoke patois at home, English outside, but it was not appropriate for me to do both. He associated patois with underachievement; I rebelled by conversing and writing in patois at home. Father felt that he could not be African since he did not speak any of the African languages. He did not seem to realize that slavery muted many languages, and that patois is just one of the languages of resistance that emerged from this imposed silence (Dalphinis, 1985; Devonish, 1986). For me, the use of patois represented my awareness of a separate black identity. Father saw language in instrumental terms and patois as an obstacle to his ambitions for me. He could not accept that it was possible for me to communicate in both languages and still be successful. Success could only be achieved through total assimilation into English culture. And so, whilst colonialism denied my father his heritage, he denied me access to mine. But total assimilation, even had I wished it, was not the answer. My experiences taught me that I would not be accepted as English by the 'host' community. As Enoch Powell reminded us: 'The West Indian does not by being born in England, become an Englishman. In law, he [sic] becomes a United Kingdom citizen by birth; in fact he is a West Indian ... still' (cited by Sarup, 1991, p. 89).

At my Catholic school, my skin colour marked me as an outsider. The older pupils questioned my origins—it was assumed that culturally, black children could not be English. Shamrock signified the Irish children as Irish. The rest of us had no recognized affiliations. I did not know of any black saints. The feeling of rejection made it difficult to empathize and share in patriotic celebrations on special occasions. Only during mass were we one—our 'alien' status was hidden in the ritual of prayer and communion. Yet outside this context our black skins were markers of exclusion, symbols of unbelonging.

I yearned to belong, to be part of a community which would willingly accept me for who I was. My tough exterior suggested otherwise. It was impossible for me to reveal this tension that I felt. I was a displaced child of the diaspora trying to find my way home. It did not matter then that the community from which I sought solace was white, I had experienced no other. Ironically, it was in higher education, the very system into which I had been pressurised, that presented me with the opportunity to learn about myself and my black identity. I attached myself to a group of black women who had a sense of themselves and their history. I immersed myself in 'blackness'. This signalled the beginning of my transformation, from a lost and confused child to a positive sense of who and what I was, a proud black woman.

With hindsight I understand that my father's educational experiences denied him the possibility of preparing me for the onslaught of negation I was to endure at school. Unfortunately, colonialism had whipped him into a sense of unimportance. I had a positive self-concept but had been denied the ability to reinforce my black identity.

> So institutionalized is the ignorance of our history, our culture, our everyday existence, that often, we do not even know ourselves. (Njeri, cited by hooks, 1992, p. 172)

THE PROCESS OF SELF-RECOVERY

This is the process by which the dominated and exploited individual would experience a new and different relationship to the world. (hooks, 1989, p. 33)

Mukai (1989) describes the trauma and silencing effects of anorexia nervosa:

When I was anorexic, I was silenced. My whole body was silenced not because I/we were wordless, but because our voices got tangled up with each other and did not flow out. However, once the knot was disentangled, once the boundary was dissolved, and once the membranes became permeable, then . . .(Mukai, 1989, p. 636)

Similarly, I found my voice after a year-long battle with the excruciating pain of an abscessed tooth. I was eager to speak, but I was held back by fear—fear of my self. Who was Uvanney? Who wanted to know? I did. I spent hundreds of hours contemplating betrayal. Could I betray the hand that fed me? If I spoke I betrayed my father, my upbringing, my identity, my (our) struggles. This was no easy option for me—I had to speak. If I remained silent I too like my father would exist in an enslaved state. The process of 'disentangling the knot' allowed me space to reflect, and brought me to a new realization of my father's influence and ultimate hold over my life. Rich (1976) described coming to terms with her father as a 'painful experience'—the events which led to my own self-realization were painful indeed.

Despite the realization that the pursuit of more education was imposed on me, I continued to study. But why? What more did I have to prove? Did I continue because I was thirsty for knowledge or because my father demanded it? Eventually I found the courage to challenge my father, thereby transgressing my role as the obedient silent female. I hinted that there was more to life than studying, that there was no age limit on studying. He was hurt, accused me of being ungrateful, of throwing away all his years of hard work. He had guided me to goals outside his personal experience. Now I was about to throw it all away.

Father's response was more painful than all the hateful comments I had endured at school. My own contribution to my educational uplift was neither mentioned nor recognized. I was merely a pawn, expected to play the role of the dutiful daughter who fulfilled his every expectation. It was I who had submerged my experiences of racism and sexism in order to allow his class aspirations to bear fruit. But he took the credit. It seemed as though it was he who had achieved in the face of the odds against which he found himself, not I.

Yet this seeming self-centredness was itself an example of the contradiction which ruled his life. On the one hand, he was motivated by a desire to provide only the best for me, in order that my life would be easier than his, that I would want for nothing. He wanted me to become economically independent, to ensure that no man 'could take steps with me'. My place was not in the home. I was 'much better than that'. On the other hand, I was a 'lady' and my place was to listen and obey. 'Being a girl meant learning to obey, to be quiet, to clean, to recognize that you had no ground to stand on' (hooks, 1992, p. 87).

As I grew older I resented my father for his gender impositions: his insistence on a lady-like dress code which excluded the wearing of trousers or jeans; forcing me to live by his own definition of what constituted 'high moral standards'; for disapproving of 'low dive' people, my friends, and 'low class' music, reggae. Father had a tendency to designate anyone as 'low dive' and 'low class' if he considered them to be unambitious. My friends became 'low class' because their parents allowed them to go to discos, stay out late and wear jeans. It did not matter that they too were studying—they were never good enough for me to associate with. 'Black people', he would say, 'never look up, they always look down. It's far easier to go down than it is to come up.' 'Up' for father meant as far away from one's black or African heritage as possible. This extended to the music I listened to. Reggae was undoubtedly a downward move and Bob Marley and all Rastafarians were subversive elements. His world was full of witticisms, proverbs, riddles and stories to illustrate his beliefs and values, whilst his advice was continually laced with criticisms about ingratitude and wasted opportunities. Was he blaming me for thwarting his dreams and frustrating his ambitions? Was he determined that I should regenerate his crushed manhood? Was I an easier target than the system which had so dehumanized him?

In Brackenbury's (1993) autobiography I find solace that I am not alone in the arguments I had with my father over the years. Through her story I realise that I was not always at fault—in a patriarchal society women often live their lives in the shadow of men (Heilbrun, 1988). His 'longing shaped my child/adulthood' (Steedman, 1989, p. 6). He lived his life through me. I bore the brunt of patriarchal socialisation in the first instance and unfulfilled ambitions in the second.

CONCLUSION

Boyce-Davies and Savory-Fido (1990) refer to Patricia McFadden's redefinition of feminism in a third-world context, a feminism in which women are engaged in the anti-colonial and anti-racist struggles in Namibia and South Africa. Feminism for African women thus moves beyond a focus on patriarchal relations alone to 'the woman's right to life as a free woman and as a complete social being' (Boyce-Davies and Savory-Fido, 1990, p. xiii). In examining aspects of my own life, I have come to understand the racialized, gendered and classed context of my relationship with my father. Confronting this relationship and writing about it has been an empowering process for me. But it has also been costly. I have criticized my father, questioned and rebuked him. Above all I have exposed my inner self. But through self-reflection I have discovered that the real motive behind my interest in the life histories of black women is rooted in my own life, as daughter, student, as a black woman.

If there is an end point to my autobiography it is that I have learnt a significant lesson. That:

we all bring almost unnameable information from childhood. We are unable to shuffle all that particular mortal coil. If we are lucky, we make transitions, and don't live in that time of pain and rejection and loneliness and desolation. But there will understandably be bits of it which adhere to us and will not be pulled off by love nor money. (Angelou 1988, p. 6)

References

Angelou, M. (1988) in conversation with Rosa Guy. In M. Chamberlain (ed.) extracts from *Writing Lives—Conversations Between Women Writers* (pp. 3–23). London: Virago.

Bean, P. and Melville, J. (1989) *Lost Children of the Empire: The Untold Story of Britain's Child Migrants*. London: Unwin Hyman.

Boyce-Davies, C. and Savory-Fido, E. (1990) *Out of the Kumbla*. Trenton, NJ: Africa World Press.

Brackenbury, R. (1993) Fathers and daughters. *Resurgence* 154, 38–9.

Bryan, B., Dadzie, S. and Scafe, S. (1985) *Heart of the Race*. London: Virago.

Clarke, J. (1992) National exclusions. In A.X. Cambridge and S. Feuchtwang (eds) *Where you Belong* (pp. 14–32). Aldershot; Brookfield, VT: Avebury Ashgate Publishing Ltd.

Dalphinis, M. (1985) *Caribbean and African Languages: Social History, Language, Literature and Education*. London: Karia Press.

Devonish, H. (1986) *Language and Liberation: Creole Language, Politics in the Caribbean*. London: Karia Press.

Ellis, P. (1988) Education and women's place in Caribbean society. In P. Ellis (ed.) *Women of the Caribbean* (pp. 91–100). London; NJ (2nd Edition): Zed Books Ltd.

Essed, P. (1991) *Understanding Everyday Racism*. London; Thousand Oaks: Sage.

Feuchtwang, S. (1992) Where you belong. In A.X. Cambridge and S. Feuchtwang, (eds) *Where you Belong* (pp. 1–13). Aldershot; Brookfield, VT: Avebury Ashgate Publishing Ltd.

Franzosa, S.D. (1992) Authoring the educated self educational autobiography and resistance. *Educational Theory* Fall 42, 395–412.

Giroux, H. (1992) *Border Crossings*. London: Routledge.

Heilbrun, C. (1989) *Writing a Woman's Life*. London: The Women's Press.

Henriques, F. (1976) *Family and Colour in Jamaica*. St. Albans: Granada Publishing. (In association with Sangster's Book Store.)

hooks, b. (1989) *Talking Back: Thinking Feminist—Thinking Black*. Boston: South End Press.

— (1992) *Black Looks: Race and Representation*. London: Turnaround.

— (1993) *Sisters of the Yam: Black Women and Self Recovery*. London: Turnaround

Joshi, S. and Carter, B. (1984) The role of labour in creating in creating a racist Britain. *Race and Class*, 25 March 1984.

Ladson-Billings, G. (1990) Like lightning in a bottle: attempting to capture the pedagogical excellence of successful teachers of black students. *Qualitative Studies in Education* 13, 4, 335–44.

Lewis, R. (1992) Autobiography and biography as legitimate educational tasks or pedagogic terrorism. Working paper presented at the 'Teachers' Stories of Life and Work' Conference, Chester, April 1992.

McElroy-Johnson, B. (1993) Teaching and practice: giving voice to the voiceless. *Harvard Educational Review* 63, 1, Spring, 85–104.

MacKenzie, C.G. (1993) Demythologising the missionaries: a reassessment of the functions and relationships of Christian missionary education under colonialism. *Comparative Education* 29, 1, 45–66.

Manley, M. (1974) *The Politics of Change: A Jamaican Testament.* London: Andre Deutsch.

Marable, M. (1993) Beyond racial identity politics: towards a liberation theory for multicultural democracy. *Race and Class*, 35, 1, 113–30.

Mirza, H.S. (1992) *Young Black and Female.* London: Routledge.

Mukai, T. (1989) A call for our language: anorexia from within. *Women's Studies International Forum* 12, 6, 613–38.

Nicholas, T. (1979) *Rastafari: A Way of Life.* New York: Anchor Books.

Njeri, I. (1991) *Every Goodbye Ain't Gone.* New York: Random House.

Rich, A. (1976) *Of Women Born: Motherhood as Experience and Institution.* Norton.

Sarup, M. (1991) *Education and the Ideologies of Racism.* Stoke-on-Trent: Trentham Books.

Stanley, L. (1990) 'A referral was made': behind the scenes during the creation of a social services department 'elderly' statistic. In L. Stanley (ed.) *Feminist Praxis.* London and NY: Routledge.

Steedman, C. (1986) *Landscape for a Good Woman.* London: Virago.

Walby, S. (1990) From the private to public patriarchy: the periodisation of British history. *Women's Studies International Forum* 13, 1/2, 91–104.

Ward, J.V. (1990) Racial identity formation and transformation. In C. Gilligan, N.P. Lyons and T.J. Hanmer (eds) *Making Connections: The Relational Worlds of Adolescent Girls at Emma Willard School* (pp. 215–32). Cambridge, MA and London: Harvard University Press.

Welch, A.R. (1993) Class, culture and the state in comparative education: problems, perspectives and prospects. *Comparative Education* 29, 1, 7–27.

5 THE SENGA SYNDROME: REFLECTIONS ON TWENTY-ONE YEARS IN SCOTTISH EDUCATION

LESLIE HILLS

I am a child of the land of the Democratic Intellect; the land of the lad o' pairts. A land famed for its excellent egalitarian education system. This is a strong male myth which has served the women of Scotland ill. Since women have been largely invisible there is a habit of silence. When women seek to break the silence there is no precedent and they are isolated and vulnerable. Gender codes and behaviours are so institutionalized as to go unnoticed. My professional education and working life spans the years of equal opportunities legislation in Westminster and, at local level, the introduction of codes of practice designed to eliminate discrimination. My experience leads me to believe that legislation and codes of practice have made little difference to the ability of women to influence and shape policy and thus the future. Neither have been applied to significant effect on the system of patronage and appointment which systematically excludes women. There was a smaller proportion of women in positions of power and influence in Scotland in 1988 than there was in 1966 when, armed with a belief in the eventual triumph of natural justice, I took up my first teaching post.[1]

My very first job was in a Clyde coast boarding house. I was a skivvy, worked 7.30 until 4.00 and was paid two guineas a week. This was in 1959. I was lucky in that after the Glasgow school holiday I could leave and return to school—and a Saturday morning job in a city centre store which paid me ten shillings and sixpence for three and a half hours' work. My subsequent jobs, during evenings and holidays until I finally started teaching were little better, although the worst must have been the hell-kitchen in Rutherglen where we boiled shortbread tins and where through an open window my mother told me I'd been accepted for university. All but two of my methods of financing myself were characterized by long hours and very low pay. They were women's work. Physically hard, grindingly boring, in many cases demanding servility, unquestioning obedience and an ability to ignore lewd and suggestive remarks. In every case the person in authority was a man. I went to university believing that a professional job would be different. In the event being a woman in education proved less hard physically

Source: Abridged from Fewell, J. and Paterson, F. (eds) (1990) *Girls in their Prime*. Edinburgh: Scottish Academic Press.

and was never boring. In other respects there was often little difference. While I skivvied a fellow student worked as a docker earning literally ten times my wage. He worked hard but in those days of the ascendency of the National Dock Labour Board was not required to be subservient, nor asked to do ridiculous things and could have self respect and enjoyment in his work. This was men's work. And thus it was for most in the fifties and early sixties. Men, on the whole, were adequately if not generously paid. Women, save for a very few, found it difficult to make a living wage and often had to resort to demeaning toil so to do.

I went to university in 1962 some two months after my seventeenth birthday. I found myself sitting in a row of six women in front of the Director of Studies (Women) whose job was to assign us to courses. I had four highers including Mathematics and Science, and sundry O grades taken at one sitting. The director assigned us all to English, History and French, these being, and I quote, suitable courses for young women. We were from different scruffy state schools and no one said a word. I barely said a word within the walls of the university for the next two years. All my lecturers were male. The professor of English refused to lecture to mixed classes. Lecturing to us he would sneer his lectures from the podium and on one occasion threw out a woman who spoke. Among the men he was known as a fine lecturer and wit, and indeed as we sat below at our alternate lecture we could hear howls of laughter and the stamping of feet as the men were regaled. It seems incredible now that there was not a revolt. In common with my friends I felt irredeemably, genetically, inferior and most definitely there on sufferance. It was a male world governed by male rules and mores. There were no positive female role models and no articulation of our numbing sense of impotence. There was a complicit silence. To admit and discuss our predicament would have been totally against our upbringing and training. Who would be first to confront the pain and indignity? Not I.

I was also, for most of the time, bored and frustrated. The work was not hard but I was able to engage with little of it. I assumed it was my fault.

I graduated and for no good reason went to training college and concurrently attended post-graduate courses in education at university. Many of my contemporaries also went into teaching for want of something better to do. Years later I heard my experience summed up by a very senior official in Lothian Region. The Senga Syndrome he called it and when pressed for an explanation by his male east-coast audience, explained that Senga, a name found only among the working classes in the West, was Agnes backwards and Senga was the typical Glasgow working class girl from a state school, who goes to Glasgow University, does an Ordinary degree, goes to Jordanhill College and returns, if she has ever left, to live near and teach in her old school or very close to it. Unfortunately this cruel description was largely accurate.

Two of us attended the university courses because it felt like a lifeline,

although I doubt we would have said so at the time. All my lecturers were
male except for the 'speech ladies'. By the time I became a teacher I knew
only two women lecturers and had met only two women who were head
of departments of academic study. However, I had discovered an unexpected
area of competence. Sent on teaching practice to three schools in peripheral
housing estates in Glasgow, I found I could teach the most 'difficult' of classes.
Through the inarticulate fog that was my consciousness penetrated the realization that the reason I was prepared to expend so much energy and time
on making lessons work was a strong fellow feeling for these unfortunates at
the bottom of the pecking order in a rigidly organized hierarchical system. The
writings of women contributors to the then *Guardian* Women's page began
to make an impact and enabled me to reflect upon my situation as a woman
in a very male world. The dawning realization of the root cause of my sense
of incompetence throughout my education made me very uneasy.

In 1966 immediately upon qualifying I married. All of my friends did. It
now seems extraordinary but we had been taught a limited set of expectations and it was what one did then. And in common with my friends I got
a teaching job and supported my husband through a second degree. That was
also what one did. Second degrees, with few exceptions, were for men. Their
careers were more important and therefore to be nurtured.

My first teaching job involved moving from Glasgow to Edinburgh. I was
interviewed by two men. In 21 years and six interviews in Edinburgh and
subsequently Lothian I have never been interviewed by a woman. My initial
interview was perfunctory. Certainly no one was concerned with what sort
of career I envisaged. The impression given was that I was definintely a short-
term proposition with a shelf-life of only a few years before immersing myself
in domesticity. In fact there were fewer male than female staff in my first
school and more of the latter were over forty than in their twenties and
thirties. Several had families and none, save the lady adviser and the head of
Domestic Science, were promoted. The interviewers commented favourably
on the fact that I had a prestigious award from the Girl Guides and had sung
in a well-known girls choir. I was asked if I intended to get married and was
appointed to a junior secondary school. I knew few people in the city and
no teachers.

On my first day I was given a timetable and shown a room by the head of
English. I saw him once more in the next twelve months. I could not meet
him informally because the staffrooms were segregated. The male staffroom
was strictly out of bounds. A man who invited me in was censured and I
put out. If I wanted to talk with a male teacher I must do so in the corridor. Even this must be arranged as the allocation of rooms was such that,
male and female, we went to and from our rooms and staffrooms without
ever crossing each others' paths. The female staffrooms were also segregated.
There was a Lower Ladies on the ground floor and the Upper Women
upstairs. I was led to the Lower Ladies and was given to understand that

the Upper Women were distinctly *déclassée*. In truth they were different. They were younger, taught such subjects as Art and Music; one had a son and yet was single—and one was even English. They conformed less and had no part in the power structure of the school. The Lower Ladies was presided over by the lady adviser. Lady advisers were with practically no exceptions the only women with any position of power in schools. They were a special breed who had adopted the *modus operandi* assigned them by the male establishment—who of course appointed them. They were necessary to deal with practical problems like menstruation and to inflict punishment on girls.

The men belted regularly and appeared amazed when I protested when they dragged a child from my poetry lesson to beat him. They did not beat girls. On the whole they did not teach them and were uneasy if forced to confront them. The senior men were for the most part awaiting retirement. They attempted no contact, professional or otherwise. Some of them may well have been good and caring teachers. I had no way of knowing and until a new head of English was appointed all my experience of them was negative. I learnt what little I could about teaching from a small number of tough, hard-working women who accepted the laziness and caprice of their male superiors wryly and with humour. That was the way things were and nothing was going to change.

There was no attempt to discuss the teaching I inflicted on my pupils. I was given to understand that I was doing well and that the measure of this was that I bothered no one with my problems. Nobody asked me what I taught as since I was a very new and female teacher I had the classes no one else wanted—the girls, and the boys who were following modified courses.

Had I been aware of the issue I would have had few problems with sexist materials. There was one novel, *Shane*, and the oldest set of poetry books in the world. I used neither and put together my own texts with great labour and little system although when I survey them now I find a good measure of women's writing especially poetry. What my 'modified boys' really thought of Sylvia Plath I shall never know for they were a patient and kindly bunch.

The extraordinary thing was that I was delighted with this job. I worked hard and long hours but was in charge in my own space and earned what seemed then good money. Physically it was nowhere near as demanding as most 'women's' work and it was anything but boring. In relation to other men's work teaching compared badly. Compared with other women's work it was well paid and offered excellent conditions. It took me a long time to come to the sad conclusion that teaching in Scotland is not in fact the best of jobs for women.

I was very young—barely 21—when I was appointed and seemed to progress very quickly. By the time I was 24 I was in charge of a centre preparing to deal with pupils required to remain at school after the raising of the leaving age. We saw the alienated products of all the junior secondary schools in

Edinburgh. It was a tough, lonely job. I was responsible for the day-to-day running of an old and leaky establishment housing janitor, technician, five teachers and a threatre-in-education team and for after-hours activities and in-service training. I had no idea apart from a vague belief in democracy and non-authoritarian procedures how to manage a staff and an establishment and was given no training. I was responsible to two advisers, both men, but they were rarely around. It was my first taste of what became a recurring theme—lots of responsibility without power: my authority was entirely personal. At the time I was grateful for the chance to do something innovative in curriculum and in-service and to be called Teacher-in-Charge. The staff were mostly women. Men with a few notable exceptions did not stay long. It was not a road to promotion and therefore unacceptable to men. I wasn't officially promoted, and thus paid a responsibility allowance, for five years. There were few comparable jobs at the time but where they existed they were held by men and the responsibility properly recognized and paid. It was a feature of the times and an illustration of the fact that women were not perceived as proper professionals to be treated as such.

I remained in the job for ten years during which I twice took maternity leave. When I was ready to move on I was well into my thirties. At the time, continuing to work with short breaks for child bearing was fairly unusual. However, those of us who did were little better off in terms of advancement than those who left and returned in their mid thirties. Careers in teaching accelerate in the late twenties and early thirties when women are disadvantaged by bearing or looking after children. Men on the promotion ladder are not, on the whole, similarly disadvantaged by their young children. Promoted posts in Scottish schools are overwhelmingly occupied by men. Although motherhood is not alone responsible for the scarcity of women in promoted posts it is a more visible and acceptable factor than many others which have to do with unstated expectations, perceptions, prejudices and powerful male informal and formal networks. [. . .]

In my position at the centre I was cushioned: out of the mainstream and almost autonomous in my own sphere. I was aware however that in a decade of contact with senior staff in all the Lothian high schools I dealt with two women. In these ten years I had a great deal of heartening and rewarding contact with men in education. A few were at senior level. Most taught in the schools. After my almost totally negative experience in my first school, it was a revelation to be associated with men who neither feared women nor regarded them as alien infantile creatures to be avoided or patronized. I found common cause with many.

During the last few years at the centre I wanted to move but there were very few jobs for which my unusual experience would count. The career pattern of smooth and continuous transition from classroom teacher to assistant principal teacher, principal teacher, assistant, deputy and headteacher, with few exceptions, prevailed.

Finally I was appointed advisory teacher, the lowest form of professional life, in a centre housing advisory staff. It was made clear to me, however, that I would be required to take on wider and more onerous responsibilities than the position normally implied. I completely acceded in this. The assumption of the handmaiden role, nurturing and propping up the system is fairly common among women in education. It was regretted that it was impossible to give me a position or salary commensurate with the demands of the role. The adviser with whom I worked was very ill. We did his job together. When he recovered I was given a wide-ranging brief involving a large amount of in-school in-service. In this time the salary differential, which was substantial, between advisory teachers and the advisers, increased considerably. This was because we were an anomaly. Neither advisers nor teachers, we were on no promotion ladder and existed to service the system. No one in the hierarchy made our case. The teaching union, Educational Institute of Scotland, advised patience.

The vast majority of advisers were men. A small but significant number resented women in their midst. It was necessary to tolerate repeated derogatory references to competent women and 'jokes' about the inability of women (and more disturbingly, of female pupils) to understand the technical and scientific. I heard myself described as forceful and articulate in tones which made it clear that it was not a compliment. I heard one senior official describe me to another as very intelligent and then beam at me, waiting for me to wag my tail. Worst of all, was unthinking, demeaning and insulting behaviour of senior officials who regarded treating a middle-aged professional colleague as though she were a naive, flighty and essentially frivolous slip of a girl as gallant. One offered at the top of his voice in a corridor, not to spank me this time, when I reported some trivial slip of memory. At the time I was 41. Attempts to counter such behaviour were seldom successful. Those who tried were labelled, contrary to all evidence, men-haters.

The structure of the division was the classic pyramid. There was a chief adviser, two principal advisers, three senior advisers, advisers, assistant advisers and finally four female advisory teachers. All but one of the senior positions were occupied by men. When she retired she was replaced by a man. Over the years I spent there the gender balance worsened. When I left, the only senior female was a primary adviser. Nine of 31 advisers were women and of these all save one were in traditional female subjects with low status. This pattern of promotion matters. It matters because it provides few role models for younger women and militates against female careers.

It also matters because it has a direct discriminatory effect on the experience of pupils in schools. Advisers in the Scottish education system are heavily involved in appointments and the structuring of the curriculum and the design of materials. They are predominantly male. This has two results. The first and more difficult to tackle is that the perspective on the world contained in course materials is not so much discriminatory as gender-blind, and the second is the occurrence of incidents which demonstrate often unconscious disregard and contempt for women and girls.

Over the last few years in Scotland, a vast amount of curriculum materials, bulletins and newsletters was produced. This provided ample evidence of institutionalized sexism and gender-blindness. In Lothian the professional editor, engaged on a freelance basis to edit materials for courses for 16+, automatically weeded out discrimination and bias. Other texts were not independently edited resulting in materials ranging from the trivially irritating to the offensive. I objected to a cartoon sent to all primary schools. It depicted a young teacher, saved from falling on her face due to huge breasts only by the counterbalancing effect of her pronounced rear. She was in a state of sweaty confusion caused by the crude sexual innuendo of a small boy. Were the innuendo not perceived, the implication and presumably the reason for amusement was incompetence in matters technical. Although my complaint was met with instant response at a senior level, I had no support at the subsequent meeting of the committee charged with the production of the newsletter, apart from the embarrassed concern and honest regret of the man responsible. Some days after the committee meeting at which were three other women, the most senior took me aside to say that she completely agreed with me but said nothing for fear of being thought prudish by the young men on the committee. Although very senior she felt unable to speak. Women perceiving discrimination and insult in male-dominated meetings are very vulnerable. Making the case in these circumstances is hard, lonely and wearisome. There is also the bleak recognition of the women who have intentionally or by default, joined the system and accepted its values and codes: the woman, in this case, who could see nothing wrong with the cartoon. It was of obscene intent and was insulting to women teachers both as women and as professionals and yet so institutionalized is this kind of humour that she, an intelligent woman, saw no fault. My request that a note dissociating my name from the cartoon be circulated to schools was ignored. The incident was capped when a male colleague proudly brought his mathematics newsletter to me. There was no sexism in his publication, he said. No portrayals of women in demeaning positions. There were, as I pointed out, no portrayals of women or girls at all and he rushed off to have the graphic artist (male) 'put a few bumps on'.

With a two year intermission when I was seconded to the Scottish Examination Board (SEB) I worked in the advisory division from its formation in 1972 until I resigned in 1987.

Leaving the education system let me step back and reflect upon my experiences with some detachment. For a long time I worked within the system and played the game. I knew the rules well even if I could never join the club. There came a time however when it just didn't seem like the kind of thing a responsible grown-up should be doing. I found it increasingly more difficult to accept the role of token woman, serving committees, covering up incompetence, working in isolation and nurturing and sustaining a system which neither recognized or met my needs and professionalism nor was helpful to other women and made little acknowledgement of their commitment.

Over these years I worked for and with most of the bodies and agencies which constitute centres of power and influence in Scottish education. I became an excellent minute-taker and secretary and, calling on skills acquired outside education in fields where women in responsible positions were tolerated, adroit at chairing meetings, albeit from the sidelines.

I was secretary to a Central Committee of the Consultative Council on the Curriculum (now SCCC), and worked on a Standard Grade Joint Working Party, numerous *ad hoc* curriculum and in-service committees, Scottish Education Department (SED) Advisory committees for research projects, a joint CCC and 16+ Curriculum and Advice Support Team (CAST) Working party, college of education committees and a variety of other official and semi-official bodies. In every case but one the group was chaired by a man. The exception was a group chaired by me where most of the members were from outside education and where the position of chair was elective. In all other cases the chair was appointed and systems of appointment and patronage do not work in favour of women. In Scotland our political and educational system works through appointment and patronage. It was described to me recently by a male colleague as a male membership system—only Rotarian church members with willies need apply. [...]

In my role as field officer for Creative and Aesthetic Studies it was often difficult to convey the experience of the teachers and pupils, often predominantly female, to members of staff and working party members, predominantly male. The position was further exacerbated by the fact that my discourse with many practitioners reflected their concept of teaching and of relationships and therefore was in many cases incomprehensible to the senior officials [...]. Mediation was necessary. If gender differences in perception were so obvious in Creative and Aesthetic Studies, one wonders what effect they had on the development of Health Studies which was marked by dissent about the relative importance of the scientific, biological and thus 'examinable' aspects and the personal affective and less easily quantifiable aspects.

To a great extent the content of the examination papers, and their marking, and the appointment of setters and markers is in the hands of the board subject panels which have, therefore, a formative influence on what is taught in schools and how it is taught. They are appointed by the examination's subcommittee. [...]

The criteria for judging suitability and choosing sources are not given. None of the staff or members I talked to mentioned gender or gender perspectives on judgments made about content and marking. It is extremely difficult to pin down the exact nature of the process. According to the chairman of whom I enquired explicitly on several occasions, the main source of new names is the panel itself. Again both institutionalized and customary practice militates against women. [...]

Women in Scottish education are disadvantaged by structural and systematic exclusion. The system of appointments is the management tool. Appointments are almost invariably made by men who appoint in their own image. However, when the teaching profession is allowed to elect to positions of power it nominates and elects women. The elective positions of the National Council of the Educational Institute of Scotland (EIS) and the General Teaching Council (GTC) are increasingly held by women. [...]

When I have commented on the discrepancy between the number of women elected and those appointed I have been given to understand that it should not be taken seriously because there are more female than male teachers and women vote for women. The implication that this somehow devalues an election is an example of real unthinking prejudice. The fact that men vote for men or Tories for Tories does not devalue a democratic election. Moreover, putting aside the question of the truth of the dubious assertion, is it not in some sense better that women elect women rather than men appoint men?

Regardless of how it happens it is clear that the membership of the Council by gender differs greatly from that which would obtain were the teaching profession allowed democratically to elect all the members of its self-regulating body. The appointments system ensures that women are excluded.

At Council level the system of appointing members to paid jobs and to committees militates against women because of the constituencies from which committee members are nominated. If a vacancy occurred tomorrow a committee of seven would be apppointed to it. It would, in theory, be possible for a maximum of three women to be on the committee. When I asked the registrar, who was extremely helpful, about training of members in interviewing and appointments procedures I was told there was none. However, the committee was 'carefully grounded in terms of procedure, structure of the session and questions to be asked', by the registrar. I asked if he had received any training and was told that he had long experience in local authorities. He had made many appointments and usually knew the right man for the job. [...]

Since the late 1960s the number of women in influential positions has decreased. There are few positive career models for women. Those who are appointed are mainly in low status areas traditionally reserved for women. When there are elected positions to be filled women do well but most positions are filled through the system of appointment and patronage which excludes women. The number of professional classroom teachers involved in policy and decision making has declined to practically nil. While there has been recognition of imbalance, there is institutional gender-blindness and discrimination. In a period of considerable revision of curriculum and assessment which will have long-term effects on the experience of Scottish schoolgirls and boys, the number of women on official working groups and panels is derisory.

The products of these self-replicating working groups and panels are likely to remain dominated by a particular male perception of the world, characterized at best by female stereotypes and at worst by disregard and contempt for women's history. These products influence directly the experience of girls and boys in schools.

In education we are not a special case. The position of women is a result of historical and social forces which affect most women and a large number of men who do not share the assumptions and background of the leadership. Along with many women of my generation I had a belief in gradual improvement and a hope for a future in which power relationships between the sexes could change. In education as in many fields our hopes are proved false.

There has been superficial change. There are carefully chosen token women, given the function of representing women. It is a very odd position in which to be put. Men on committees are not supposed to represent men. Token women are also extremely visible. When a woman is given a position of power and makes mistakes it is taken as an indication of the incompetence of the sex in general. If further appointment of men to leadership were to rest on the competence of their predecessors few men would ever again be appointed to anything.

Many of my male erstwhile colleagues are baffled by our angry despair. They really cannot see what we have to complain about. And indeed the position of women in Scottish education cannot be attributed to the beliefs, intentions and actions of these men. In the documented policy of the 1970s and 1980s there is little that is explicitly discriminatory. Rather, as in for example, the composition of the GTC, the issue of gender is not on the agenda. It is an option which is not on the agenda because it has never been consciously entertained; just as many of the senior men in Scottish education have never consciously entertained the thought that they might need some form of education about gender issues in order to do their jobs properly. At the time of writing, Strathclyde and Lothian Regional Councils have initiatives under way which could prove to have far reaching effects on women, and more importantly girls. These initiatives, certainly on paper at least, spring from the instructions of councils which have education committees which are listening to women's committees, to women-in-education groups and are demanding information upon which more equitable and saner policies can be based. [. . .]

But there is no obvious reason why those in power should address the issues. It is not in their vested interest so to do. Apart from anything else the level of veneration of tradition—a tradition which is almost entirely male—and complacency about our education system is staggering. The centenary of the highers was celebrated with due solemnity and the pronouncement made that the highers must have something going for them if they've lasted a hundred years. So did the Hundred Years' War.

6 CULTURE AND CLASS

MARY EVANS

Being a grammar school pupil has always had status in English society—any grammar school, however inferior or unsuccessful, has been able to make to the world the proud boast that its pupils have been 'selected'. [. . .] Passing the eleven plus was thus a major event in a child's life: if you passed you had access to the school where pupils wear uniform, take publicly recognized examinations and stay on at school until late adolescence. Not passing—at least in the 1950s—meant going to the school with no uniform, no examinations and a short career. [. . .]

Inside the golden world of educational success the yellow brick road led from the eleven plus to GCE O and A level. Being good at exams, and being able to summon up the wit to perform well on these occasions, was a skill which the school fostered and rewarded. In this article I want to explore the ways that we learnt, not just the serious contradictions and paradoxes in the process of learning, being taught and taking examinations, but also the language and culture of the divisions of the English class system.

For the great majority of English children in the 1950s and the 1960s the eleven plus was the first (and in many cases the last) public examination that they took. On one single day in the January of our last year in primary school we were marshalled into the gymnasium of a local secondary school and asked (no, told) to take three papers: in Mathematics, English Language and something called General Intelligence. The mathematics paper (and this was at least a decade before any sign of a 'new' mathematics) involved simple addition, subtraction and so on. My recollection is that this paper was simply dull. English language on the other hand involved greater creative possibilities: we were invited to write about a recent outing (bad luck if you had the misfortune not to go on them) and describe the happiest day of our holidays. These two exercises in the recollection of middle-class social life were accompanied by tests of word comprehension. (For readers born after these days this involved demonstrating that we knew what a dog was by underlining the word animal from a choice of flower, person and tea cup, or some other random collection of nouns. General Intelligence was about the recognition of order in the symbolic world: numbers and patterns in sequence was the test here and a mania for the orderly classification of the universe was a valuable skill.) All these papers lasted about half an hour, and so after one

Source: Abridged from Evans, M. (1991) *A Good School: Life at a Girls' Grammar School in the 1960s* (pp. 24–101). London: Women's Press.

and a half hours the die was cast, our educational fate was sealed. In those days there was no assessment element in this testing; it was make or break on one day.

Passing or failing these tests was announced some three months later. I remember that summer had almost come when a bleak postcard arrived which stated that I had passed the 'selective examination'. Bureaucrats did not use the term 'eleven plus' and so the education segregation of the ten-year-old population was given the kind of ideological gloss that the term 're-settlement' gave to the forced deportation of the Jews in Nazi Germany. Indeed, the very term 'selection' suggested a lengthy process of careful thought by the selectors, rather than a cursory, and limited, test which gave middle-class children considerable advantages. Indeed, unless middle-class children could not do the most simple mathematics I suspect that the eleven plus was almost impossible to fail—or put it another way, the eleven plus was almost impossible for working-class children to pass. The emphasis on the written word, and a particular kind of Janet and John, petit-bourgeois normality that the tests relied on, demanded a conceptual leap that many children clearly found impossible to make. Added to this, the examination had different implications in different parts of the country and for boys and girls: the numbers of grammar school places were, for example, traditionally higher in Wales than in other parts of the country and throughout England the numbers of places available in grammar schools for girls were lower than for boys. All these points have since been extensively documented, and only recently Birmingham's education authority was found guilty of maintaining discriminatory practices by allocating more 'selective' places to boys than to girls.

So those of us 'selected' at the tender age of ten for admission to grammar schools could, with some justification, think of ourselves as particularly blessed. And how homogeneous we were. Arriving at grammar school on the first day of the first term, the most striking characteristic of the other new pupils was that they too arrived in cars, from detached homes and with standard English voices. Everybody was fully equipped with the expensive uniform, and everyone could be reliably expected to own books and pens. The sheer cost of passing the eleven plus was identified, rightly, in the 1950s as a disincentive to working-class children and their parents. The emotional and social cost of being plunged into a middle-class world was doubtless considerable, but equally significant for many homes must have been the capital outlay necessary to take part in this new educational experience. It is no exaggeration to say that we needed an entire new wardrobe: from socks to vests and knickers to skirts, hats (one for summer, one for winter), shoes (three pairs minimum, one for summer, one for winter and one for indoors), coat, scarf and gloves. The whole outfit was completed by that symbol of masculine, white-collar order: the tie. We were expected to be clad in entirely uniform navy blue, to be purchased at an eminently respectable department store in London. Since the school was some 40 miles from central London, just going to buy the clothes entailed expense. Nor was this list of everyday clothes the only list that our parents were presented with. In addition there was also the sports list (two pairs of shorts, an aertex shirt, plimsolls, hockey boots and a sporting sweater) and the list of semi-industrial training wear—that is, the overall for science, the pinafore for domestic science and the totally encompassing shroud for arts and crafts. This list is still incomplete: I have omitted the swimming costume, the swimming hat and the bags for shoes and books. When our mothers took out their cheque books to pay for this mountain of clothes they were buying into an educational world which was clearly going to differentiate between those who passed the eleven plus (and wore uniform) and those who did not. Inevitably, bright working-class children were excluded from a world which was expensive even before they had entered it.

Nevertheless, one or two working-class pupils did enter this select, and selected, world. Yet how they were expected to survive it, and not commit suicide in the playground, is a vivid, if retrospective question. Two practices of the school made class divisions and distinctions immediately apparent. During the first week at school we all had to complete forms giving our father's occupation (such were those days that: (a) fathers automatically had occupations, (b) children automatically had resident fathers, and (c) mothers were full-time mothers) and submit to a shoe inspection. The exercise of completing the form about our personal circumstances produced the inevitable parade of middle-class occupations: as doctor followed architect, solicitor, bank manager, teacher, civil servant, university teacher and so endlessly on and on, it was really bad luck, almost bad form, to interrupt this panorama of suburban life with a lone voice saying factory worker or merchant seaman. Those two occupations struck me at the time as part of a foreign and bizarre world. Where did those fathers work, we wondered? Since we were used to coming to school and passing the schools, the banks, the surgeries and the offices where our fathers worked—and which we assumed represented the world of work—it was something of a problem to find a physical location for a factory worker or a seaman. The town in which our grammar school was located was devoid of industry, light or heavy, and so it was immediately apparent that here, in our midst, were people from hitherto unexplored territories.

But if occupational uniformity was demonstrated by the answers to this form so too was domestic uniformity. In my year at school we did not have one child from anything approaching a 'broken' home: divorce had made no impact on the English middle classes (or for that matter any class) in the 1950s. What did constitute social deviance and marginality in those far-off days was largely constituted by two factors—having a mother with a job, and belonging to a religion other than Church of England. Anglicanism, in the 1950s, was not a form of social radicalism. Nor did two-career families constitute a sub-urban norm. Yet even these two factors were limited to a tiny number of pupils: one or two girls in each class had mothers who had jobs, and about a dozen in each year were either Roman Catholic or Jewish. Of these deviants the Jewish girls were the most immediately visible, since they had to stand outside the school hall each morning while the rest of us trooped in to share a Bible reading, a hymn (Songs of Praise version) and prayers. [. . .]

The school endorsed the view—later taken up by feminists and feminism—that every mother was a working mother. The responsibilities of the housewife and the mother were given full credit by the staff and 'making a home' was an ideal which was accorded full status by a staff that was largely unmarried. So having a 'working' mother was regarded as slightly peculiar, and rather eccentric, but not seriously threatening to the status quo as it was assumed that working mothers were simply women who chose to do a little bit more than others. They remained, therefore, part of the assumptive world of the school, as women who were primarily mothers but also had paid interests. When the school debated the issue that 'A Woman's Place is in the Home' the school decided that this was certainly the case. Women should be at home, waiting for us to come home and ready to ferry us about to dancing class or whatever else. If women did not do this, and accept this way of life, then their only alternative fate was to be an unmarried schoolmistress. In the late 1950s this career did not look attractive and the dichotomy between employed woman and wife and mother remained absolute.

So distinctions were made, and apparent, on the basis of our religions and our fathers' occupations. Distinctions were also made, and were equally rapidly apparent, on the basis of the shoes on our feet. At the beginning of our first term, and at the beginning of every subsequent term, we had to produce the regulation number of pairs of shoes and submit them to examination. To many readers this apparently trivial exercise may appear as precisely that, just an exercise in the endless pedantry that is possible when an institution decides on enforcing a uniform dress code. Equally, the exercise might sound like one of those very sensible nanny exercises that the English sometimes engage in. Making sure that we were wearing shoes that did not deform or harm our feet was, from the point of view of the health-conscious, a perfectly justifiable exercise. But this shoe inspection had another apsect to it which made it an immediate indicator of social class: 'good' shoes, made by Clarks and Start-Rite, were the shoes of the middle class (and immediately passed as acceptable) whereas 'bad' shoes, sold in shops such as Bata and Freeman, Hardy and Willis, were held up for condemnation and dismissal. [. . .]

Social distinctions were made between individuals on the basis of what they had on their feet. 'Good' shoes cost more than cheap shoes, and actually having the three pairs of shoes that the school demanded was in itself a significant capital expenditure. So what was being examined in this ostensibly harmless exercise was, first, the financial resources of our parents. But the second aspect of us, and our homes, that was on trial in the parade was a set of moral attitudes about appearance and vanity. 'Good' girls did not bother about whether or not their shoes were fashionable. They chose shoes that were functional, good for their feet and as inconspicuous as possible. 'Bad' girls chose shoes that were flimsy, fashionable and as conspicuously part of an attempt at chic as was possible within the extremely narrow boundaries of school uniform. To care about one's appearance was therefore part of an unacceptable attitude to the world. This did not mean that any kind of careless attire would do; on the contrary, it meant that as far as possible a 'good' girl did not have an appearance. What she had was a correct uniform, which gave the world the correct message about her—that is, that she was a well-behaved, sensible person who could be trusted not to wish to attract attention to herself by an unusual, let alone a fashionable appearance.

This training in how to dress is quite obviously still an extremely successful one. Although many grammar schools have not only been abolished as institutions but have abolished school uniform as part of their new existence as comprehensive schools, a glance at any gathering of the British middle and upper classes shows that uniformity in dress is still deeply ingrained. [. . .] Whatever the more bizarre choices of dress of younger members of the British Royal Family it remains consistently true that the wealthy, or even the comfortably off, like their clothes to suggest nothing other than a class uniform, in the way that our school uniforms once suggested a universal acceptance of a certain way of life and particular views of the world. Scorned by the values of this world were personal narcissism and an interest in style. These attitudes and inclinations were somehow vulgar and vaguely suggestive of an unhealthy preoccupation with self and sexual attraction.

So 'good' girls were expected to have little interest in clothes, no personal narcissism and no interest in self-expression in dress. In maintaining this expectation the school's position was similar to that of King Canute. [. . .] A complete lack of interest in dress was quite uncommon among my contemporaries; what was much more common was a studied and affected apparent lack of interest that masked either a complete or near complete obsession. Admitting to caring about the matter was about the same as saying that you were in favour of sin. [. . .]

Our complacent world had a Janus-like quality to it. On the one hand, the taken-for-granted assumption that there would always be food on the table, while on the other, the frequent reminder that 'all this' was not an inherited given, but an earned acquisition, an acquisition to be safe-guarded and valued. What this dualism was teaching us was the fragility of the social world, but in an essentially conservative sense. We were not being taught the radical lesson that 'men make their history', and that men (or these days, people) can make, unmake and re-make their social reality. On the contrary, we were being taught that what has been constructed must be valued. We were seldom invited to question what had been constructed; in a very real sense we were told that the world was there and it was our responsibility to value it. But alongside the contradiction of security/insecurity that we grew up with we were also being taught two other essential features of middle-class femininity: that we must accept the values of this world and that if we were to take part in employment (or the public world) then we must do so in class-appropriate ways. In one sense, of course, we were being encouraged in a lie. As middle-class girls it was highly unlikely that we would spend our adult lives in employment. Our mothers, in general, did not have paid jobs, and the school did not encourage the employment of married teachers. Despite this, we were encouraged to think about going to university, training for professional employment and generally being serious about passing examinations and acquiring qualifications. Such an attitude on the part of the teaching staff is nowadays sometimes interpreted as a fervent feminism, a determination to ensure that girls can gain access to higher education. That determination was undoubtedly there, but so too was the determination (and this was particularly true on the part of the parents) that middle-class girls should remain in a middle-class world. The surest way to do this was, in the 1950s and the 1960s, to go to university or training college or medical school or some other enclave of middle-class expectations and aspirations.

One incident that occurred in my school days illustrates this painful ambivalence towards education for girls. In a sixth form discussion about careers (organized and chaired by the Headmistress, since this was a Serious Subject) we were all asked, in turn, about our future plans. Most of us managed to come out with some appropriate and acceptable answer. Then one unfortunate girl replied that in her future career she hoped 'to meet people'. There was an awful silence. Then the Headmistress asked exactly what this girl meant. Without waiting for a reply, the Headmistress said in tones of icy dislike and contempt: 'I suppose you want to meet men. There is hardly any point in asking you serious questions about your future.' A hushed room waited for the next onslaught, but the moment—and the Headmistress's wrath—passed, and we turned to a discussion of the A levels most appropriate for gaining entry to a training college. But the conversation was not the same. Whatever ease there had been had vanished and we were left with the uneasy feeling that the Headmistress had denounced for all of us the mere possiblity of adult sexual relations with men. It was baffling. We were laughed at in our junior years in the school if we had romantic enthusiasms for the staff or the older girls, yet condemned if we displayed an interest in boys. At the same time we all (or virtually all) came from families constructed through the most orthodox mechanisms of conventional patriarchy: marriage and female economic dependence was the norm of our backgrounds. How were we going to achieve that? Had the poor unfortunate who wanted to meet people told one of those unacceptable public truths that no one wants to hear? We strongly suspected that such was the case, that a skeleton had been well and truly let out of a cupboard. The attempt to slam the door by the Headmistress merely emphasized the lengths to which the culture was prepared to go to deny and yet tacitly maintain conventional sexuality.

Denial of the realities of adult middle-class life was thus in a real sense a part of the culture of the school. We lived in a semi-fictional world in which education, and educational success, mattered more than anything else. If we chose to believe in this fiction then we could be assured of adult success, and we could also be assured of the approval and support of the school. But like all fictional worlds—or worlds constructed through strictly controlled and regulated values and beliefs—this world had to be thoroughly policed and thoroughly systematic. Hence the dislike of influences outside the school, the taste for uniform and the condemnation of those who raised the possibility of divergence and difference in this sealed world. [. . .]

The world of the traditional grammar school, with its social limitations and its single-minded pursuit of success in exams was a world which in Britain of the 1950s and the 1960s provided an apparently perfectly coherent and congruent training ground for the managers—and their wives—of the new Elizabethan world. We were told, repeatedly, that we lived in a 'modern' world, and that in this 'modern' world education was vitally important. At the same time as we were all citizens of a modern, and modernizing, Britain we were also citizens of a country with a proud history and a glorious recent past. We had, after all, recently defeated (yet again) the Germans. The peace of the world was, we were assured, safe in the hands of a responsible government. If only the Russians did not suddenly develop a particularly aggressive foreign policy, and if only the trade unions remained content to believe that they had 'never had it so good', then there seemed to be no reason why our future should not be safe. As we entered the sixth form, and as the world entered the 1960s, it did begin to look as if a more actively interventionist stance might be necessary in the economy. Words such as 'efficiency' and 'management' began to be part of our essays on the modern world and a certain politicization began to creep into our assumptions about the world. The middle class was, if only marginally and if only occasionally, being asked to consider its place in the world. Serious middle-class figures, from serious middle-class universities, started to make noises about the future of Britian and the need for radical reform. Some, although by no means all, of the debates that gave rise to the Robbins Report and subsequent reforming legislation of the late 1960s on moral issues began to be part of sixth form debates. Views about the role of women, the nature of the family and the role of higher education, which had had the status of certainties in the 1950s, began to look more ambiguous.

Our part in all this seemed to be at the time to receive the news of these changes and to continue taking our examinations. [. . .] Riddled with contradictions as the schools were—crucially over the matters of education for girls and the limits of the importance of education in, and to, the class structure—they nevertheless maintained a homogeneous world which could even absorb bright children from the working class and produce a standard grammar school child. The power of the institution, therefore, was that it

could apparently be relied upon to institutionalize and do for middle-class
children what the public schools so effectively did for upper-class children.
A reliable product, the grammar school child, emerged at the end of a seven-
year education, and the product was reliably well schooled in writing legibly,
writing grammatically, being punctual and having at least the appearance of
respect for authority. We knew, even if we sometimes forgot, that it was
polite to stand up when people older than ourselves came into a room, that
you did not hold your knife like a pen and that relations with adults involved
a litany of silence and gratitude. We knew, in short, how to behave ourselves
in public.

Unfortunately for the middle class, particularly for its more traditional sections, the public and the public world was beginning to change. The social
order—the world that would predictably evaluate us—was changing and losing
that single-minded absolutism that it had once had. By the mid-1960s it had
finally become apparent that quite respectable, married, middle-class women
did not always wear hats and gloves, sometimes they even wore trousers and
smoked cigarettes. Middle-class adolescents began to perceive that out there,
on the urban streets, were working-class boys and girls who were spending
time in the company of the opposite sex and who were buying and wearing
clothes of a positively subversive chic. [. . .]

But by the end of the 1950s the mould was beginning to crack. In one of
its editions in the late 1950s *The Young Elizabethan* instituted a problem page
and began to publish what it described as 'fashion hints'. The first question
put to the agony aunt behind the problem page was the appropriate age at
which girls might (a) wear high heels, (b) wear make-up, and (c) go out alone
with a member of the opposite sex. The first significance of these questions is
that anyone felt that they were worth asking. The second significance is the
assumption that anyone would take any notice of the answers. Inevitably,
the answers bordered on the conservative. Both high heels and make-up were
banned until the age of at least sixteen and going out with a member of the
opposite sex was not something that anyone could properly do until the age
of seventeen or eighteen. Reading this advice at the age of thirteen I reflected
that it would be a long time before the world would really begin, and that
since I already possessed a pair of shoes with (very low) stiletto heels I was
doomed to three years of illicit footwear. So great and so all-pervasive was
my internalization of these commandments that the shoes went completely
out of fashion long before I felt I was 'officially' old enough to wear them.
Along with my friends I lived a secret life of fascination with adult clothes.
The great *rite de passage* in our lives, universally longed for, was the prize-
giving that followed school-leaving. To this we could return wearing our
own clothes and it was the occasion of the most furious competition. [. . .]
The occasion was one at which the values of the school and the values of
the real world became transparent: we had accepted seven years of giving
education the primary importance in our lives, now we turned around and

said with some defiance that here, in this bold statement of fashion and the possibilities of sexual attraction, are other values and other priorities. [...]

The two unwritten prohibitions of the school—not loving each other and not thinking too much about ourselves as emotional beings—formed a powerful sanction against the consideration of human emotional reality and in favour of a conception of ourselves as individuals destined to carry out certain tasks. Too much introspection, too much emotional involvement (and certainly misplaced emotional involvement), and any recognition of the generality of sexual desire and human emotional complexity would have seriously threatened not only our health, but also the stability of the community in which we lived and worked. The health of that community was actually founded on the commitment of women staff to the education of women and to the establishment of educational opportunities for women. That this commitment involved a certain affection for women, if not love in the explicitly sexual sense, was not something that could be made apparent within the culture of normality and conventionality that the school endorsed and adopted as its *raison d'être*. To have loved each other would have challenged this culture, just as unbridled enthusiasm for academic work raised the spectre of the blue-stocking and a concomitant contempt for the ordinary skill of the ordinary world. Thus excellence as defined by the standards of the University of London's examining board was a convenient, institutional, measure of excellence. It was a measure that was entirely predictable (our teachers could, and did, predict our performance in public examinations with endless accuracy) and it was a measure that had all the hallmarks of total respectability and orthodoxy.

The powerful unwritten rules of the school—both of them essentially about not getting too 'involved' or too 'committed'— prepared us for adult life in middle-class England. Too much passion, either for another human being or for intellectual work, would have unbalanced the stability of ordinary life, which depended upon the individual performance of allocated tasks. Those endless sayings about 'if a job's worth doing it's worth doing well' and a 'fair day's pay for a fair day's work' were not actually engraved above the school's Honour Board but these values were enshrined in the institutional practices of the school, which put a great store on the fulfilment of allotted tasks, however mundane or however apparently pointless. A major part of our socialization was therefore learning about the order of bourgeois life. This did not involve an education in the mechanisms of the cash nexus, but it did involve, centrally, a gradual integration into the social mechanisms and social processes that made possible the orderly functioning of capitalism and the moral and social order of the market economy.

To supply this education the school provided three sets of exercises, all of them policed in various ways. The first was the education in the thankless task. The second was the education in obedience to rules and statements by authority and the third was the independent performance of allocated work.

The education in the thankless task began on the day when we arrived at school, and we learned that all of us, whatever our interests and inclinations, were going to spend a year's lessons in Domestic Science smocking a pinafore. This task was so utterly, wildly and absurdly redundant that it remains in my memory as the definitively ridiculous task. The pointlessness of the task lay, first, in the fact that after this first year very few of us were going to have any more lessons in Domestic Science, since after the first year we would begin to take additional courses in foreign languages. So here we were, attempting to learn this intricate art in order to make a garment that we would never use. We were not encouraged to view smocking as part of the great folk art tradition of English life, or some such worthy, liberal, interpretation. On the contrary we were quite explicitly told that our performance at this task would be taken as a measure of our 'patience' and our ability to do something called 'work steadily'.

So for over 40 weeks of my first year at grammar school I, and my 90 equally sausage-fingered contemporaries, sat in various degrees of mutiny attempting to make a couple of yards of green gingham into a garment worthy of William Morris. We nearly all failed and completed the year's work with pinafores that we were told to throw away when we arrived home—if we had not done so on the way home. The agony of the exercise was not so much that smocking was particularly boring or hard, but it was forced, and it was forced at a pace that frustrated all natural interest and inclination. One interpretation of the exercise could have been that the school was attempting to educate us in contempt for traditional female crafts. This argument was not, I think, the case, largely because the school did not see smocking or embroidery as a distinctly female art-form, as might be the case today. What was at stake in the exercise was educating us in doing something that we did not want to do. If we were too impatient in our attitude to the task, or mutinous, then it was assumed that there was quite a good chance that when faced with other, equally mundane and pointless, tasks we would simply walk away. It was an initiation, painless enough perhaps, into the hierarchy of a world that was essentially about the obedient learning of views about the world.

Our moral capacities assessed through the pinafore exercise, the first year was also the time of the moral evaluation of our physical selves. For first year girls at the school there was a peculiar on-going examination of our posture. This did not involve any specific allocation of time-tabled lessons, but it did involve the assessment throughout the year of our posture by the staff. At the end of the year the upright would be awarded with a posture stripe. This piece of blue bias binding could then be sewn on to our navy blue tunics and was supposed to indicate that we—with the blue stripes—walked like proper, upright human beings and not like the slouching chimpanzees who did not have these precious blue stripes. Again, the moral implications of the test are, in retrospect, transparent. The slouchers, the round-shouldered and the generally physically incompetent all turned out to correspond more or less exactly to the girls who had already been detected as (a) having the 'wrong' attitude, and/or (b) coming from the wrong kind of home. The most primitive kind of physical moralism was involved here: anyone who slouched about or who sat sprawled at her desk was clearly dissolute. With the enthusiasm of the most authoritarian military regime the school watched for the signs of sloppy behaviour and sloppy thinking that might be detected in a misplaced elbow or a lounging pose. Since we were girls we could not be told to take our hands out of our pockets, but we could be told to stand up straight, sit up straight and never, ever, sit with our head in our hands. Such a posture would mean goodbye to the posture stripe forever, or the sarcastic comment that perhaps our neck could not support our head unaided.

Standing up straight, looking people in the eye and sitting in a chair as if it was an ejector seat were all the marks of a well-behaved, sensible person. No wonder that James Dean and Elvis Presley were such threats to the physical standards of the English middle class. Not only did these men slouch about, and even positively sprawl, but they could display the most unfettered masculine competence for all this bodily decadence. Unlike the (literally) upright chaps in uniform who constituted the standard, ideal pose for white English people these men walked, talked and sat with a minimal order and a great deal of impact. Inevitably, we adored them and found in their relaxed postures and physical confidence something utterly seductive. Unfortunately, such admiration was not shared by the staff who saw in these different attitudes to the body a suggestion of disorder and sensuality that was threatening. Not only did our heroes seem comfortable in themselves, they also seemed at one with the object world. I remember being told off at school, endlessly, for sitting on desks and leaning against walls. As far as I was concerned these physical objects were part of my environment, for me to use. I had no real intentions (if many fantasies) about destroying any of my physical surroundings; I just wanted to lean against the wall. Marlon Brando, Humphrey Bogart and James Stewart, I noticed, quite often leaned against walls and sat on desks. [...]

The endless hurdles of middle-class life had been introduced to most of us in childhood. We had all been brought up knowing exactly what we were allowed to do at a particular age, how we had to work hard at school to pass the eleven plus and how we then had to work even harder in order to stay at grammar school and pass our O levels. Then, surprise, no surprise, as soon as we had taken those exams new ones arrived on the scene. If we passed those exams, and passed them well enough, we were then given the licence to go and take more exams. The future stretched before as an endless succession of hurdles. Some of these hurdles were, we realised, public examinations. The other hurdles were the life events that we dimly, and not so dimly, realized were part of the process of becoming fully-fledged members of the middle-class community. Among these hurdles were getting married, buying a house, starting a family and making sure that the children went to good schools. This, we knew, was what the future was all about, and learning to be competent at all these decisions and processes was an important part of our education. If our competence, or our judgment, failed then we could easily find ouselves married to the wrong person or living in the wrong house with too many children, all of them at inadequate schools. In those days nobody had ever dreamt of CSE or GCE examinations in the 'Quality of Life' or 'Health Education' or any of the other subjects which today teach and try to instil 'proper' values in adolescent heads. But even if this formal education in the values of the middle class did not exist, the informal education was there, and centrally so. [. . .]

What the school did not maintain—and if it had then it (and hundreds of other English grammar schools) might have belonged to a completely different tradition—was that its essential business was education for a meritocracy. The school could, and did, rely on the predictability of the English class system to sustain a more or less perfect fit between class and perceived intelligence; when this correspondence broke down it became apparent that class divisions within the school would be maintained. What was striking about the system, therefore, was that parents could protest about the academic judgment of the school on social grounds and have their objection sustained. A friend whose father strongly objected to his daughter being placed in Division Two because 'she would no longer be mixing with A stream girls' was not told to go away and mind his own business but actually had his objection sustained. This example of parental power is the kind of instance that must bring mixed joy to a Thatcherite heart. Here was a man invoking the crudest kind of class snobbery and having that attitude endorsed. In effect the school was saying that it too regarded it as unfortunate that people from different backgrounds had to mix with one another and that as far as possible they would recognize the importance of maintaining social distinctions.

And so my friend remained, struggling, in Division One for Mathematics. But parental class-power had triumphed against the academic judgment of the school. At the same time what had triumphed was male class-power against female lack of power. However powerful our teachers were within the school they were, after all, 'only' women and therefore had none of the 'real' social power and prestige of that group known as 'our fathers'. Between 'our fathers' and the teachers there existed a curious tension. We acquired our social prestige and status (or lack of it) from our fathers and yet our fathers were part of a world against which many of our teachers had battled. If our teachers controlled our day-to-day world then it was our fathers who could, on occasions, control the school and question the autonomy of its arrangements. [. . .]

As girls, even middle-class girls, our chances of getting into university (particularly to read subjects such as medicine or law) were not as good as they were to become ten or twenty years later. Even if our chances were better than the mythical working-class girl in the Robbins Report who had a 1 in

600 chance of going on to higher education, entry was still highly selective and very competitive. Despite the fact that we were used to this (indeed we had just spent seven years being educated into the idea that education necessarily entailed selection and competition) it was nevertheless a daunting prospect to be told that two years' hard work and blood, sweat and tears over A levels could come to nothing. If we failed to make those coveted A level grades of at least three Cs then we would be forced back to the ranks of the training college applicants. There were few polytechnics to offer us alternative places, and we came to realise that conditional offers from universities meant precisely that.

7 HE WHARE TANGATA; HE WHARE KURA?—WHAT'S HAPPENING TO OUR MAORI GIRLS?

NGAHUIA TE AWEKOTUKU

Hoki hoki tonu mai
te wairua o te tau
Ki te awhi rei na ki
tenei kiri e

The shrill excited squeak of a two-year-old's voice lifted in the close night air, bounced off the dark wooden headboard of the great big bed. Bundling a soft feather pillow around her neck, the little girl rolled into the warm warm cushion of her Kuia's side. Her feet were snug beneath her Koro's arm. She was wrapped up in bed with her Kuia and her Koro, and she was happy. They were teaching her a song—one of the songs they did at the concert; one of the songs she loved.

My earliest childhood—before I first caught a school bus—was the time of both my grandparents, my Kuia and my Koro, and living down the *pa*. How desperately I wanted to stay down the *pa*, to be with them all the time! But the two people who adopted me had other ideas, and moved a few miles up the road, to a Maori Affairs home in a new 'pepper potted' suburb. 'Pepper potting' was a government policy of mixed racial housing. Integration. Having Maori and Pakeha live side by side, with goodwill and purpose, as they had so diligently fought side by side in World War II. My mother preferred the *pa*, and her people. Her husband, a well-colonized person from another tribal group, preferred to foster friendships with the Pakehas next door, and across the road. Especially those ones who were English and had a little girl who did elocution and dancing, and got very exciting presents from her relatives in 'the old country' and her daddy who was always in America. I was simply fascinated; she had a stereoscope with views of the ruins of Pompeii and the Changing of the Guard, and she had games with numbers and other bits. And shelves and shelves of books. Books! We never had them. My Kuia and Koro had the Maori Bibles and heaps of the *Weekly News*—but not real books, with thick backs and hard covers. This girl was truly from another world.

Source: Middleton, S. (ed.) (1988) *Women and Education in Aotearoa* (pp. 89–96). Wellington: Bridget Williams Books.

But slowly, I began to explore it. One of my aunties had become a school teacher, and she was very interested in 'tiny tots'. At that stage, I was very much a 'tiny tot', and she was very interested in me. She visited us a lot, and she often looked after me. We played games together, and some months before my fifth birthday, I had stumbled through my first lines of reading, and written my first sentences. Aunty Toria encouraged my mother to give me books; I will always be grateful for that. And I devoured them. I memorized them. I treasured them. Even when I was down the *pa*, my books were my friends. They didn't hit and pinch and laugh at me for my asthma and funny way of talking and *hakihaki* (eczema); I was happiest with books, and the old people, especially my Kuia, who sat weaving in a pool of sunlight, around her a mass of sweetly fragrant green flax. I was seen either as a loner, or a little bit strange. And I was very excited about going to school.

That first day, that first week of school. Rotorua Primary. Cluttered together with lots of other tiny tots. Fear, excitement, panic; we clutched our little chair bags and rattled their contents—chalk, duster, handkerchief. We peered up at the dark, endlessly high, polished walls, where the narrow windows seemed so far away. We sneezed on the smell of chalk dust. I made a friend—actually, she was my cousin. We swapped chair bags straight away. Hers was bright yellow with brown grapes and mine was navy blue with pink daisies. We chattered and made a noise. We got smacked. We learned fast.

By Standard 2, I had hopped a few classes and settled in, when suddenly the world changed. Family matters shifted us to Wellington, where we stayed with another aunt. I had also acquired two newly adopted siblings, who came and went: one was a brother four years older than me; the other a baby girl, a tiny little sister. But during most of the Wellington time, they were not with us. Instead, I had three older male cousins to contend with, and a vastly different, almost foreign, social and cultural environment.

My aunt had married a very wealthy and prominent doctor. Their home was a spacious nineteenth century villa, densely carpeted and richly panelled with dark glowing wood and bevelled glass, gleaming antiques, heavy maroon velvet drapes, and landscapes and horse pictures edged in gilded wood. Huge trees framed their view of the sea, and embraced the house itself. And they even had 'native bush'—an acre of forest trees, just behind the house. And only 12 minutes away from the uncle's Willis Street surgery. The family was devoutly Catholic, and thus I became a somewhat bewildered pupil at the exclusive hilltop convent of Mount Carmel.

It was not easy. Catechism and Christian Doctrine were totally beyond me, and Sister Mary Aden took me into her special care. I was there two terms; I spent what seems, at this point so far along in my life, hours just wandering alone around the school. I examined the vaults below the red brick building, and one day I found some brilliantly coloured banners leaning against a wall. Amazing. I explored the basements, and avoided the classrooms—there were only two. And I became aware that I was different—not just because I was a 'Non-Catholic', but because I was Maori. The only one in the school—my cousins were at boys' schools, and together. I was by myself. And everyone expected me to sing. That was hard, and rather humiliating, despite my early lessons from the old people. After all, I was asthmatic and it was bleak winter in Wellington. However, my clearest memory of that time was the school marching, beneath one of those banners, in the Corpus Christi Festival—with all the trumpeting and pageantry—rich song resonant on the chill grey air. Hundreds of proud, happy people being Catholic. I thought about turning into a Catholic. Seriously.

But again, changes. A transfer for a painful half term in a Palmerston North convent school, St Mary's. Competitive marching teams at play time, and the nuns calling me a nuisance. The only good thing—dawdling to school through the hospital grounds; huge gentle oak trees, softly greening. And daffodils.

My conversion had to wait another year. Back I went to Rotorua Primary; Standard 3 and a Maori teacher who taught us his tribe's version of 'Hey Diddle Diddle Te Pereti me te Whira', and whacked everyone on the back of the legs with a leather strap if we misbehaved, which was often, though I only lined up for one dose. Though I cannot remember why; and had come from a household where a 'damn good hiding' was always threatened and often carried out. Corporal punishment was something I was very used to.

The last three years of primary school crawled by at St Michael's Convent, where I sheltered with the nuns, Sisters of Mercy, with soft Irish accents and gentle pink faces. My home life was in acute crisis; that's all I'll say here. My Koro died; my mother's husband refused to live permanently down the *pa*. My mother refused to leave our Kuia. And my older adopted brother returned to his 'real' (birth) family, while my baby sister stayed, because she was my mother's *mokopuna*.

At this time, I also thought a lot about my 'real' family—but my father had been dead a long time, and my mother had a chronic, crippling illness. Unlike most adopted Maori children, I had no contact with my birth family, though my father's home was Ohinemutu, and my mother would often visit other relatives in the *pa*. I daydreamed a lot about what it would have been like—I wrote long, complicated stories and made up plays.

I trundled about confused, unhappy, but safely concealed behind a veneer of much celebrated 'cleverness', which perhaps in its own way protected me. Once school was done for the day, I would hang about for hours. I did not want to go 'home'—to the suburban house—where I was forced by fear to live, away from my Kuia and my mother, for varying periods. The house, the man in it: both frightened me. So I diligently remained at school, applying myself. I did my best to be brainy and productive, and the nuns loved and rewarded me for it. What treasures they shared! Christian Doctrine revealed not only the deep bewilderment of Eucharist and purgatory and Immaculate Conception; it also planted the seeds of strong political consciousness.

Apart from the lives of the saints—the chaste Agnes and Philomena and Catherine, who chose death before dishonour—we were read the most extraordinary stories. Of Violet Szabo, courageous woman spy and anti-Nazi resistance fighter. Of Douglas Bader, the RAF ace pilot who lost both his legs, but kept his wings and shot down even more enemy planes. Of the Wooden Horse, which enabled prisoners of war to tunnel valiantly to freedom. World War II was not too far behind us, and Battler Britain and Spy Thirteen and Biggles were comic heroes avidly consumed, and brought to life in the playground. Other issues also surfaced in the classroom—the Irish Republican Army and its own heroic struggle; the true meaning of Guy Fawkes Night; and very poignantly indeed, the plight of the Black Babies of South Africa. I clearly remember being told about apartheid; Verwoerd had just attained power, and we attended a special mass for the native people. As well as the politics, and 'the moral of the story', there was the music, the drama, the plainsong, Latin, English and Maori. How often we were told, by visiting 'Inspectors', and church dignitaries, that 'truly we sang like angels'.

Although we were a small convent school, the second in the district and very new, we presented a fascinating ethnic fruit salad. A lot of Maori children. And a few of the others—Italian, Canadian, Portuguese, Cook Island, Yugoslav, Polish, Irish and Dutch, with the balance Pakehas. We were shaped and prodded and readied for secondary school—though there was then no church institution in Rotorua. Academically, the 'clever ones' were cultivated, in the first row of the room. We were groomed on 'Proficiency Test' cards; we sat outside examinations, and we did well. I was awarded the Ngarimu Essay Prize; I was an avid writer, and contributed the serialized version of my second novel to a Bay of Plenty Catholic Schools monthly bulletin. About some kids sailing a raft (not a canoe!) called Te Arawa from Maketu to Motiti Island, in earnest search for adventure. My first extravagant literary effort was about two orphans who inherit a haunted Rhineland castle, complete with Lorelei, and punctuated heavily with lots of 'Achtungs!' and 'Raus! Raus!' and 'Gott in Himmels!' And by this time, I had a set of real books—Arthur Mee's Children's Encyclopaedia, with epics of the glorious Empire on which the sun never set. They satisfied me for a while, but they frustrated me too—because the flowers and trees were foreign, and I never did find a razor shell or a periwinkle on the beach at Maketu.

She scratched, a little to the left, a little to the right. The sunburn was still annoying, flakey and sore. Itchy. She moved again. And suddenly, above the clamouring hymn, a voice shrilled out—'Stop! Stop this instant! You, there! Get out! Get out of this hall! You were doing the twist! Doing the twist at my assembly! Get out! Go, girl, go!' A muffled wavelet of gasps and giggles rolled down the hall. Row after row. She looked up, saw those dark red swan wing glasses flashing fiercely down at her. At her. No one else had moved. 'Do you mean me, Miss Hogan?' She gestured meekly to herself. 'Yes! You! Go to my office. Now!'

Three away from the centre aisle, she lurched across them. And walked the endless walk, under the gape of a thousand eyes, to the head's office. It was the Tuesday of the first week of the first term of her first year at high school.

That year was unspeakably, unprintably ugly. I ran away from home, I got into fist fights with other girls, I wagged school. I sneaked out at night, I imagined I was Elvis Presley and Connie Francis all at once. I chased girls who were running after boys and it looked as if I chased boys too. Which was blatantly untrue and unfair. I passionately, passionately hated that school. Its teachers. Its pupils (except my cousins). And most of all its headmistress.

I was placed in the top third form, privileged to learn Latin and French with the yachting, skiing set. I wanted to study Maori; was told that was impossible, my IQ test results were too high. They were convinced they were doing me a huge favour; they were wrong. I was, after all, from down the *pa*. No different from all those rough Maori widgies in 3 Vocational and 3 Commercial B and 3 Remove—my cousins, my mates. And in the classroom, I had two strange allies—a Canadian immigrant from a family of seventeen kids, and a voluptuous silky-voiced sophisticate whom I persuaded to run away with me (during one of my 'Elvis' episodes).

Three memorable items from that school year. For our class fund-raising stall, I offered to bring Rewena bread. The response: 'Eeek! Ooooh! We don't want stuff like that on our stall!' I raged, 'Look here you Pakehas, I'll bring it and I bet it'll sell before any of your butterfly cakes and coconut ice does!' And of course it did. Second item: hearing the reigning Miss New Zealand, a Maori woman related to many of us, come and address the assembly about poise and pride and all that. Then a few days later, hearing the headmistress request that all Maori girls, Maori girls only, remain in the assembly hall. The Pakehas all filed out, even the dark quarter-caste looking ones. We stayed, and we were told some of us 'had been seen shoplifting. In school uniform. And I know it was a group of Maori girls. I know it.' We knew there was a very active group of Pakeha girls playing that game too. We said nothing. What was the point? Third melting moment: being pushed out in front of the class by the maths teacher, a golfing, cantankerous, vegetarian bigot in tweeds, with the announcement that I was a black abomination, because I hadn't done my homework. Balanced later by the French teacher, a plump bespectacled matron with heart-shaped lips, who counselled in her most soothing voice that I was special because I was a Maori and I was clever and had a responsibility to my race. Hohum. I was expelled.

I survived. Most of the girls I had been following around left school at the end of that year. Got jobs, got pregnant. Boring. I had had enough of being a rebel; I had never stopped writing or thinking, despite all that had been going on. And I desperately wanted to go to a boarding school, to get away. But the problem was simple enough—my family could not afford any fees, did not know about Maori Education Grants, and although I was 'scholarship material' academically, for a Catholic school, I was unacceptable, possibly even corrupt. So that was that. I was bad news.

Luckily for me, the headmaster of the only other high school in the area acknowledged my academic potential (possibly after a chat with the nuns), and offered 'to come halfway to meet me, if I came halfway too'. It was the break I needed. I applied myself; there were other Maori teenagers in the top stream, and we were related. One in fact, was the cousin with whom I'd swapped chair bags in the infants' room.

Those four years at high school whipped me through a series of changes; I tried to bury the Elvis part of my personality in a flurry of affected femininity that never quite fit. Maori culture, the drama club and amateur theatrics, hiking, classical records from the library, and reading Shakespeare aloud to myself were all part of it. Plus writing, copious amounts of writing, in journals long since and tragically lost (that's another story!). And hours in the *whare runanga*, the house Tamatekapua, with the orator/sage Tani Te Kowhai, who told me long, complicated stories. With so many of the other old people of Ngati Whakaue, of Te Arawa Whanui. *E Kui ma, e Koro ma; Kaore Koutou e warewaretia e tenei mokopuna mokai e okioki tonu atu.* Most of my peers thought I was a bit peculiar.

Financially, life was far from easy. I never, ever had a full school uniform—I borrowed when necessary, and improvised with an uncle's reefer jacket, and mother's white blouses. My mother kept down two jobs; her husband was seldom on the scene. I worked too. As a tourist and publicity model (those images are still for sale), as a takeaway bar and coffee shop attendant, as a tourist guide and hostess, as a dishwasher. To keep myself at school, I had to work weekends in my lower and upper sixth years. My mother could not comprehend why I refused to 'get a job in a bank' (high status choice for a Maori girl with School Cert.), or later 'go to training college' (even higher status choice for a Maori girl with UE). By doing this, I could bring money into the house, and also be independent. But these options were not for me—I was determined to go to university, and my determination was seen as rather selfish.

Homework was also a problem, but one shared by just about all the *pa* kids. Our parents got together, some teachers volunteered to supervise, and

Homework was also a problem, but one shared by just about all the *pa* kids. Our parents got together, some teachers volunteered to supervise, and for a brief period we had 'more school after school' at Te Ao Marama, the homework centre. However, supervision and support declined, and soon we were all back at home again, struggling for quietness, privacy and solitude, or just not bothering at all. And I was the only one crazy enough to be thinking about a university degree.

There was only one known model for a Maori woman academic—I followed the achievements of Ngapare Hopa proudly, and with great pleasure. Her success motivated me. She was an anthropologist, as was Te Rangi Hiroa—Sir Peter Buck. Anthropology—what wonders. A way of helping our people, by studying our culture. That was the career for me. I wrote an essay about this ambition, and won another national prize. I was very clear about things when I was fourteen years old!

Not so, two years later. Contact with a family of lawyers convinced me that Law School was the preferable direction—and I believed I had 'the making of a good lawyer'. Until I got there. Totally unprepared for university life, the pace of a big metropolitan city, and the horrors of an elitist hostel, where the only other Maori women were domestic and kitchen staff. How I loved them. Totally unprepared for the snobbery and cliqueyness of the Maori students—each and every one of whom had attended private schools; I was neither in their club, nor their league.

So, with the other Maori girls new to the big city, I inevitably flopped into a life in the fast lane—searching the city's festering underbelly. I discovered Japanese ships and drag queens and nightclubs and hard (and soft) drugs. I experimented, I explored. And I fell—with a sharp push from the faculty fathers—out of Law School.

Eventually after a long series of misadventures, to become an anthropologist, a Doctor of Philosophy. But all that is another story, another chapter, in another book.

He mihi atu tenei kia kotou, e kui ma, e whaca ma
Kua wehe atu ki te po
Kua ngaro atu i te aroaro o Papatuanuku,
Tena ra kotou.

8 FEMINIST PSYCHOLOGY AND THE STUDY OF MEN AND MASCULINITY: ASSUMPTIONS AND PERSPECTIVES

MARGARET WETHERELL AND CHRISTINE GRIFFIN

The role of men and the construction and reproduction of masculinity have been recurrent considerations in contemporary feminism, particularly in Western societies. These issues sharpened into two related concerns during the late 1970s: what political role could men play in relation to feminism; and how were masculinities negotiated and reproduced in patriarchal capitalism? Debates around the 'problem of men' have been central to both everyday feminist practice and to the development of broad political strategies.

While feminism has a long history of engagement with men and masculinity, there have been fewer signs of interest in men as gendered beings within the academic world of psychology and the social sciences. [. . .]

Questioning men within feminist thought and politics has caused this pattern of academic neglect to change. [. . .] Mainstream ('malestream') academic courses, empirical research and theoretical analyses began to take gender relations more seriously through the 1980s, stimulated in part by the critical work on masculinity initiated by socialist men in the 1970s, accompanied also by a growth of encounter-therapy-style projects (particularly in the USA) for men to explore the forms of their masculinity. By the late 1980s, a few men (and a lot more women) were doing various sorts of work around masculinity and gender in academia and as 'practitioners'. [. . .] Since the late 1980s there has been a spectacular explosion of publications around men and masculinity by Western academic men, again principally in the USA but also in Australia and in the UK. [. . .]

This article is based on a series of interviews and written responses from a range of male and female social scientists currently working in the area. Resources and geography inevitably limited our selection, and we do not want to suggest that those we contacted best define this field. We are grateful to these contributors for their time and for their support for this enterprise. [. . .]

The focus on male rather than female academics [. . .] reflects our emphasis on the ways in which men have recently begun to engage with feminism and the study of gender relations. Our selection is certainly not meant to imply that the main impetus for work on masculinity has come from men. Rather,

Source: Abridged from the journal *Feminism and Psychology* (1992), 2, 2, 361–91.

as those we interviewed acknowledged, it was as a result of the academic and 'political' activities of feminists that the gendering of men emerged as an issue in the social sciences and elsewhere.

We try to pull out [...] the models of subjectivity and social processes underlying research, the definitions and theories of gender drawn upon, crucial influences, as well as motives on becoming interested in the topic.

MEN ON MEN: THE PSYCHOLOGISTS

In this section we discuss the work of four British psychologists—John Archer, David Cohen, Paul Pollard and John Rowan. Although they share a disciplinary label in common, these four men represent two very different perspectives within psychological investigations of men and masculinity. John Rowan and David Cohen work outside academic institutions and adopt a mainly humanistic or eclectic perspective. Pollard and Archer are both employed in the Psychology Department of Lancashire Polytechnic and are social psychologists working largely within an experimental framework. Despite these considerable differences, some continuities, which reflect the distinctive history and concerns of psychology, will also become apparent.

John Rowan has been actively working on masculinity since the 1970s and has been involved in *Achilles Heel*, the magazine of the UK men's movement, almost since its inception. Rowan lives in North London and works independently as a psychotherapist. His book *The Horned God* (1987) combines his therapeutic interests with his interest in masculinity, femininity and spirituality. David Cohen is a freelance journalist and film-maker. He is the founder and former editor of *Psychology News* and the author of several biographical studies of eminent psychologists. He published his first work on masculinity in 1990, a book called *Being a Man*, which combines a personal and autobiographical account of his marriage, his experience of his wife coming out as lesbian, and his other sexual relationships, with a review of the psychological literature on masculinity. Both Cohen and Rowan are concerned with the subjective experience of masculinity and draw strongly on their own lives as data.

John Archer and Paul Pollard, in contrast, describe themselves as interested in 'the bad behaviour of other men'. Their work applies conventional social psychological techniques and theories to problems arising from male culture and socialization. Pollard works on sexual violence, particularly acquaintance and 'date rape'; he is interested in researching patterns of 'rape-tolerant attitudes' and attributions of responsibility along with the connections to sex-roles, peer groups and socialization. John Archer was trained as a biologist at Sussex University and remains interested in the biological and sociobiological basis of gender and male violence, he has worked (with Barbara Lloyd) on what used to be called the 'psychology of sex differences'; he is now interested in the social worlds of children and in applying social identity theory to children's gender groups.

Paul Pollard and John Archer both explain their interest in men and masculinity as an outgrowth of earlier intellectual concerns. For Archer, research on the biology of hormones led gradually to an interest in gender.

> **Archer:** I started out as a biologist at the University of Sussex with an interest in sex hormones and behaviour. There were a couple of feminist biologists working there also. In our research group we became interested in the way work on hormones and behaviour was being used by psychologists such as Corinne Hutt and Jeffrey Gray to bolster up their ideas about the biological basis of psychological sex differences. [...] Of course, once you start saying there's something wrong with these biological explanations, your attention becomes drawn to surrounding issues and alternative explanations, and it was at that stage I linked up with Barbara Lloyd.

Paul Pollard described how his PhD research on social judgement and inductive statistics led to an interest in the attribution of responsibility, and from there to the structure of lay explanations of the causes of rape. This shift was mediated by a desire to work on a social problem rather than an abstract issue.

> **Pollard:** I think in a way, unconsciously almost, I began moving through different research areas, stopping whenever I encountered something that I felt was of sociopolitical value to actually spend one's life researching. In terms of my current interests, sexual aggression has always been, as a lay person and as a researcher, one of the things (though not the only thing) I would identify as an important social problem.

Pollard and Archer present familiar academic biographies and motives to account for their current research interests. Not surprisingly, given their very different orientation. John Rowan and David Cohen point instead to personal and political catalysts. Both Cohen and Rowan emphasized the role of significant women in their lives whose turn to feminism encouraged their own self-consciousness about masculinity.

David Cohen noted that his book grew out of his attempts to understand problems in his relationship with his wife. He justifies the use of autobiographical material on the grounds that not only is it more authentic but allows the psychologist to approach topics such as sexuality where it is impossible to gather empirical data in the usual manner. [...]

John Rowan's account of his personal history usefully describes some of the history of segments of the men's movement in the UK:

Rowan: I started vaguely getting into it in 1970 to 71 when I was involved in the 'Camden Movement for People's Power' (which produced a magazine called *Red Camden*), and living with a woman in a revolutionary commune in Holloway. She was interested in feminism and quite concerned about some of the issues. I went on a couple of demonstrations with her and was quite active, got photographed, and so on.

Then I broke up with her, and the group broke up, and I went back to my wife. By this time she had been discovering feminism in the year that I had been away, and was now going to three meetings a week of various groups. She was very keen on feminism and very critical of me. She suggested I should go to a men's group, and introduced me to a friend of hers whose husband was running a group in South London.

And so in 1972 I went to my first men's group and at that time we were discussing should we call ourselves 'Men against Sexism', or 'Men's Liberation', or 'Changing Men'. Already there were these various orientations and labels. [. . .]

So I got involved very early, and I've been involved in five or six different men's groups over the years, consciousness-raising groups, that sort of thing. In 1974 I got involved with the beginnings of what was at first called the 'Radical Therapy Group' and which was later renamed 'Red Therapy.' [. . .]

Feminist ideas began to come into that more and more and it split into a men's group and a women's group, and soon after that disappeared altogether. I think it had really completed all it had to do. Some of the women went and joined the Women's Therapy Centre, and put their energy into that. Some of the men founded *Achilles Heel*. So I think a lot of good came out of it. [. . .]

The differences between David Cohen and John Rowan and John Archer and Paul Pollard become even more marked when we looked at the contrasting ways these researchers theorize gender relations. We focus first on Archer and Pollard.

Do Pollard and Archer think masculine behaviour can be explained in terms of biology? Both men were willing to attribute some role to evolutionary history but disagreed about its importance. John Archer said he had a number of reservations about the sociobiological analysis of social phenomena but was persuaded by biological explanations of some male characteristics such as aggression and violence. [. . .]

Paul Pollard is probably best described as agnostic on this question. He said he found some sociobiological explanations, particularly those concerning male promiscuity and female fidelity, interesting and convincing but that, in terms of sexual aggression, biological male characteristics should be seen, at best, as a distal cause. Pollard argued that there were more important proximal causes for sexual violence and it was simply not parsimonious to drag explanation back to the level of biology.

Pollard and Archer draw strongly on the concepts of sex-roles, social identity, peer groups and socialization to explain different manifestations of gender relations, as John Archer's description of his current research interests indicates:

> **Archer:** I was particularly interested in the social worlds of children because if you look at the dominant social learning and cognitive theories in developmental psychology both trace the same processes in boys and girls. [...]
>
> Well, there is developmental evidence that there are two sorts of male role model. One is the active one of boyhood based on physical toughness and interest in sport, the other develops later and is based on achievement in mostly non-physical spheres. The first one predominates in boyhood up to about 14 or 15, then the other model takes over but presumably not in all cases, predominantly in the middle-class Western world. That's just one of the things that came out of looking at the literature, also the asymmetry about crossing the gender boundaries—how boys from a very early age are prohibited from doing things which are seen as feminine but this doesn't happen as early or as strictly in girls. [...]

Archer has recently been applying social identity theory to children's gender groups. Intergroup relations theory, he suggests, allows us to see these groups as unequal in status and explains how power relations in broader society structure the different sense of identity and roles afforded in each case. For Archer, social identity represents 'a bridge between abstract societal levels of analysis and the actual behaviour of boys' and girls' groups'.

Paul Pollard similarly relies on the concept of socialization to make sense of male violence. He argues that inequality at a social-structural level can in itself give men power over women but inequality is also combined with ideologies of aggressiveness and competitiveness which become socialized into the male child and reinforced in particular masculine subcultures. [...]

> **Pollard:** My point really concerned the presence of inequality and the general acceptance of power and aggression, displayed in the love of wonderful shiny nuclear weapons, for example. I'm not just talking about street corner fights, I'm not even talking about aggression at that level, I'm also talking about more minor forms of sexual harassment, say, which are another way it emerges.
>
> Inequality coupled with the general social reinforcement of aggression means that male—female relations are rife for people executing power.

I don't think it depends upon your socialization at all, you just find
yourself in a situation where as a male you tend to be more often in
powerful relationships with females, and as society condones aggression,
competitiveness, utilization of power over others, it's indirectly supporting you doing that. [. . .]

Pollard [. . .] is interested in individual differences, particularly in 'rape-
tolerant attitudes'. But individual differences are connected, for Pollard, to
cultural differences. In his interview he argued that there are links between
constellations of attitudes to broad political issues and specific attitudes to
sexual aggression, he also argued that men in 'heavily male-oriented cultures'
are more likely to condone sexual aggression and receive 'social reinforcement
not social sanction for their views'.

John Archer is similarly interested in exploring individual differences,
in his case in the context of work on stereotypical and biased perceptions of women and men's actions. An important research aim is
to separate out and investigate the links between attitudes, personality
and the performance of gender-typical or atypical roles in everyday life.
Both Pollard and Archer were sceptical about the value of psychoanalytic
or other psychodynamic explanations of masculinity and individual difference.

Pollard and Archer's views on social change sum up their theoretical orientation. Thus Pollard stresses the importance and difficulty of attitude
change, noting how 'rape-tolerant attitudes' create a social climate in
which women become reluctant to report rape. While Archer, following
the work of Alice Eagly, argues in a similar fashion for the intractability of some psychological aspects of gender and the malleability of
others. [. . .]

Both men found it difficult to specify any general theory of society and
social divisions which influenced their work, and Pollard argued a pragmatic line—if the problem of sexual aggression could be solved it didn't
really matter if a patriarchal or a Marxist analysis of social divisions were
more apposite.

In contrast to Archer and Pollard's emphasis on roles, subcultures, groups
and identities and use of methods such as experiments, surveys and obser-
vational studies, David Cohen and John Rowan emphasized the value and
importance of reporting on direct subjective experience.

Rowan: Humanistic psychology, it seems to me, has always been saying
that the most important thing is your own experience, and not some
abstract theory or great law. [. . .]
    There are moments in my life when I have had this feeling that what
I'm experiencing right now is true and unalloyed and not mixed with
social flim-flam of one kind or another—I'm really seeing this as it is.
Those moments of authenticity, moments of truth, which don't come

that often but which do come sometimes, I really trust. I think there is something in human experience that makes it possible to see things without social veils sometimes. [...]

Cohen similarly describes his book as based on the principle of 'using my own life as evidence' and being 'analytical about my own behaviour in a detached way'. Cohen's approach is eclectic in the sense that his book draws on a range of psychological studies with varying methodologies. [...] This openness makes it difficult to categorize Cohen's approach, but the general flavour can be seen in response to a question about how he theorizes the relationship between gender and power.

> **Cohen:** The first thought that occurred to me when I read feminist books was that men were very powerful but that didn't square with my own experience. I've worked in traditional jobs very little, but the year I did I was as powerless as I've ever been. I had a maniacal boss who was under pressure himself, and I was made to feel ...certainly very bad. Now in the context of the experience to be told that really being a man was about having power I just thought doesn't square with people's experiences.
>
> It seemed to me very strange. There's a whole tradition of left-wing thinking which argues that the workers are downtrodden and exploited, and undoubtedly there are some people who took out their frustrations on their wives and on their children—but I don't think they were powerful people. Many people didn't act in this way. [...]
>
> I accept that women may see men as more powerful than men see themselves. Now that's quite an important point because it doesn't mean men have the power and it doesn't mean that women are wrong—it means there is an interesting set of attitudes to explore.

Later in the interview

> **Wetherell:** But you're saying no simple equation can be made between masculinity and power?
> **Cohen:** None at all, none at all. I think anybody who does is equally making the assumption there is a simple equation between feminity and weakness. [...]

Cohen seems to argue first, that men do not necessarily feel powerful, and that feminists have not paid sufficient attention to men's experiences and vulnerabilities. At another point in his interview he argued that he would like to see more acknowledgement of the vulnerability of 'ordinary men', particularly in heterosexual relations. He is also arguing that power is complex, and such aspects of power as class position and power relations within the workplace should not be ignored. [...]

John Rowan was also concerned to stress, in both his interview and his book, the vulnerability men experience, particularly in relation to feminism, and some of the ways men might 'heal the wound'.

> **Rowan:** As far as men are concerned, feminism is deeply wounding. It hurts men to hear that they're responsible for the world's ills—whatever bad things were done, they have done them. That's hurtful enough, but then to hear that not only have you been doing it for 6000 years or whatever, what you said five minutes ago proves you are still doing it—that's hard to take. There is a wound there. [...]
>
> My angle is to say that unless men actually allow themselves to be wounded, to let that wound go very deep, to shatter their ego, to really experience that shattering, that collapse, and the results from that, they can't heal the wound. Either for themselves or for women or children or for anybody else—you've got to have the wound before you can heal it. Once you have admitted there is something terribly and desperately wrong, and it does affect you, then you can start healing the wound.

Rowan draws on his interest in spirituality, paganism, goddesses and eco-feminism to argue that there are forms of female power which need to be acknowledged.

> **Rowan:** There are three channels of healing which have to be used and explored. One is the conscious channel, where you make obvious changes in your own life. And on the public level—changes in laws, regulations and rules, in illustrations in books, the words you use, pronouns, and all those public things which can be done. All these entail a real understanding of the importance of power in society, and how nothing can change unless those power issues are faced and dealt with.
>
> Second, there is the unconscious level. You have to admit that you have, as a man, lots of prejudices against women which are not constantly owned so they can't be consciously changed. [...] Men have to admit that there is often an unconscious hatred of women, an unconscious loathing or disgust.
>
> The third channel of healing is the spiritual channel. When sociologists talk about power, most of the time they retire baffled, because they have no concept of female power as different from male power. Just because they can't see any examples of female power they have no notion what it might be. It is only by studying mythology that we have any inkling of what female power is all about, and how men have to relate to that if they're going to make the

final radical change. Female power is more fundamental than male power. [...]

Rowan's analysis of gender is based on a mix of psychodynamic influences, some social influences, and spiritual and mythological work concerning channels of power. This position leads Rowan to argue that there are male and female essences which he links to the experience of living in a male or female body. [...]

Rowan is deeply opposed to the concept, therefore of androgyny, and to placing sole emphasis on the social construction of gender. David Cohen, on the other hand, is happy to embrace a social constructionist or sex-roles analysis in this area. Although he thinks there is a biological bedrock to gender, he believes sex-roles are not inherited in the way he thinks intelligence might be. For Cohen, masculinity and femininity should be seen as relational. The extent of social change in the last few decades suggested to him 'that the essence of masculinity lies very much in the expectations that were foisted on men'.

It is important not to underestimate the very real differences which separate David Cohen and John Rowan's analysis of masculinity from Archer and Pollard's social psychological analysis. But we feel that these two strands of work—one solidly based in the academic world and one more precariously based outside academic institutions and tied to the personal and political—sum up two of the main routes male psychologists working on men and masculinity have travelled in recent years both in the UK and elsewhere. [...] To summarize, these concern the reliance, which is evident in both frameworks, in the concept of sex-roles to theorize the social component of gender; the emphasis on 'masculinity' rather than 'masculinities'; that is, the failure to examine the differential operation of gender when combined with other social divisions based on ethnicity, class, age and sexuality; the relative lack of acknowledgement and knowledge of feminist writing and theorizing; the tendency, particularly evident in Cohen, Pollard and Archer's research, to work from 'academic' rather than 'political' definitions of problems; and the emphasis on pragmatic empiricism, reflected in Pollard and Archer's quantitative approach and Cohen and Rowan's prioritizing of the authenticity of experience.

Finally, there was a sense in these interviews of the limits of psychological and social psychological explanation when it comes to explaining the social organization of gender and theorizing male power. [...]

MEN ON MEN: THE SOCIOLOGISTS

As a discipline, sociology has a somewhat longer history of looking at men and masculinity (or rather masculinities) from a critical perspective than psychology. This is primarily due to the more immediate impact of contemporary feminist analyses on sociological research and teaching, and the barriers erected by the dominant theoretical and methodological paradigms in psychology to a feminist perspective. Although there are some important differences between the approaches of those working in sociology and psychology, there are also some obvious shared areas of interest, and feminist ideas have provided the basis for some of the bridges between the sociological and psychological domains.

We contacted a wide range of men who have examined men and masculinity from a sociological perspective. [. . .]

Gary Fine was involved in research on 'pre-adolescent and adolescent male culture' through the 1970s and 1980s. This included studies of Little League baseball, published as *With the Boys: Little League Baseball and Preadolescent Subculture* in 1987. He also looked at fantasy games such as Dungeons and Dragons, published in *Shared Fantasy: Role-playing Games as Social Worlds* in 1983. He is currently Professor and Head of Sociology at the University of Georgia.

Harry Brod has investigated various aspects of men's lives in the USA, including the construction of Jewish masculinity, men and fathering, pornography and the social construction of male sexuality. He has also written about and taught on gender studies and men's studies courses in the USA. Brod is currently Visiting Associate Professor in Women's and Gender Studies and Philosophy at Kenyon College, Ohio. He edited a collection on men and masculinity in 1987, entitled *The Making of Masculinities: The New Men's Studies*.

Michael Kimmel worked in sociology through much of the 1970s and 1980s, looking at the historical construction of masculinity in the USA, particularly men's responses to the emergence of feminism at the turn of the century, and aspects of male sexuality. He is also involved in teaching and writing on gender studies and a course on the Sociology of the Male Experience. Kimmel is currently Professor of Sociology at the State University of New York at Stony Brook. He recently edited a book entitled *Changing Men: New Directions for Research on Men and Masculinity* in 1987, and *Men's Lives* (with Michael Messner) in 1989.

Originally a 'remedial reading teacher in disadvantaged secondary schools working on sexism issues', Gary Dowsett in 1977 became a researcher on issues of class and gender inequality in Australian education and migrant education. Since 1975 he has been 'an active member of gay liberation' (in one of its many forms). Dowsett spent the latter half of the 1980s 'coordinating a series of research projects on gay and bisexual men's responses to HIV/AIDS' in New South Wales. He has also worked on qualitative research into gay sexuality and masculinity which will form part of his PhD at Macquarie University in Sydney. Dowsett is currently Research Fellow in Sociology at Macquarie University, and his work is on the interface between research and campaigning work.

Bob Connell is a colleague of Gary Dowsett's through their work at the

Macquarie University AIDS Research Unit. Connell has been teaching and researching in sociology since the late 1960s. His work on gender and masculinities dates from the late 1970s, with research on schooling in Australia, a life-history study of changes in masculinity, theoretical work on *Gender and Power* (1987) and more recently, research around AIDS prevention with gay men. Connell is currently Professor of Sociology at Macquarie University in Sydney.

Born in the North of Ireland, Mairtin mac an Ghaill worked as a teacher in British schools and colleges until 1990, teaching sociology to 'A' level students. During the late 1980s, he carried out a series of interviews with teachers and students in Birmingham colleges as part of his PhD (1988) on the schooling of Asian and Afro-Caribbean students. This was published as *Young, Gifted and Black* in 1990, focusing on the lives of several groups of students: young Asian and Afro-Caribbean women and men; and their white teachers' perspectives on 'race' and gender. Mac an Ghaill is currently a lecturer in Education at the University of Birmingham, and his most recent research has looked at the construction of sexuality in schools, and the experiences of students who identify as gay or lesbian. [. . .]

Jeff Hearn has been involved in men's groups and various anti-sexist campaigns since 1978. As a sociologist he has researched and written on various aspects of masculinity, including *The Gender of Oppression* (1987); *'Sex' at 'Work'* (1987) (with Wendy Parkin); and *Men in the Public Eye* (1991). He is series editor for a collection of books, 'Critical Studies on Men and Masculinity', published by HarperCollins (formerly Unwin Hyman). He is currently Senior Lecturer in the Department of Applied Social Studies at Bradford University, and has recently started work on a research project linked with another project conducted by Jalna Hanmer in the same department. These projects will look at men and women's experiences of violence and abuse, as abusers and survivors respectively.

Most of these sociologists cited feminist ideas and campaigns or the impact of particular women in their lives as contributing to their involvement in work on men and masculinity. The impact was felt inside and outside of the academy for many of them. [. . .]

For G. Fine, the development of feminist theory in both sociology and social psychology compelled him to look at the gender dimensions of his work. In Fine's main area of research on youth cultures and subcultures, there is a long tradition of studies which have looked only or mainly at young men, but with minimal attention to the gendered elements of their lives. This pattern is found in both the mainstream positivist paradigm and in radical (mainly Marxist) youth subcultural studies. Fine's sense of finding it 'hard to avoid' looking at 'gender differences' needs to be seen in the context of the impact of feminist work on this 'malestream' tradition.

Whilst Fine mentioned gender differences and the impact of social psychological work on sex roles and intergroup relations, Bob Connell described

the main influences on his work rather differently, and he has written critically on the limitations of the 'sex roles' perspective in theories of gender
socialization. In his written contribution, Connell stated that there was no
clear sense of how he became involved in research on masculinity, nor any
one influence:

> **Connell:** It's surprisingly hard to say exactly how I got involved in
> research on masculinity. Even if I wished to be wholly confessional
> (which I don't), the background is tangled. Politics, personal relation-
> ships, sexuality, job demands and fantasy are all intermixed.
> In the mid-1970s I was teaching sociology, researching and writing
> about class, arguing socialist principles, loosely involved in labour politics.
> Women I was involved with in personal or work relationships were
> involved in the women's liberation movement. I listened to what they
> said, read feminist literature, was persuaded its main arguments were
> correct, and that anyone with socialist principles had to support fem-
> inism. [. . .]
> About 1979 I began to write some of this stuff down in the form of
> essays about men in sexual politics, and apply it to labour movement
> issues. A research project on class and education I was involved in became
> increasingly concerned with gender, and gave leads on the formation of
> different kinds of masculinity in schools. In the early 1980s a theoretical
> research project on patriarchy-and-capitalism acquired a focus on 'mascu-
> linity' and led to an extended critique of masculinity-research, especially
> of the 'sex role' literature. [. . .]

For Connell, his research is set in a politicized personal history which is
complex with many intersecting strands. Gender is not the only structuring
element here; sexuality, class and age are also mentioned. The theme of structural relations in patriarchy and capitalism is one which runs through most
(though not all) of the responses from male sociologists.

Jeff Hearn also mentioned in his interview both academic and non-academic
influences on his work, including his relationships with children, women students, and his involvement in specific campaign groups.

> **Hearn:** I first became interested in this area, in the relationship between
> men and feminism, around 1978. In 1978 I became involved in founding,
> with another man, a men's group in the department in which I worked,
> where I still work. [. . .]
> Another thing much on my mind at that time was living with
> young children, a four-year-old and a two-year-old. This was the
> most novel thing in my life, I didn't quite know what to make of
> it. It introduced a whole lot of new experiences—physical exhaustion,
> emotional demands, pleasure and so on. I was also involved in an
> under-fives group, a group mainly of women and a few men,

campaigning around childcare and nurseries, from around 1978 to 1985. [...]

But for quite a few years teaching and experiences outside teaching were kept separate, very separate actually. One of the things that forced me to bring them together was some writing about personal experience—a pamphlet called 'Birth and Afterbirth' published by *Achilles Heel* in 1983. [...]

The pamphlet is very critical of fathers and it's really anti-father actually. The penny dropped that it was pointless keeping those two worlds separate.

Jeff Hearn also mentioned influences from childhood and early family life which shaped his personal, political and intellectual development, though he did not see this as a linear passage based on neat distinctions between 'private' and 'public' spheres. For Hearn, his own recognition that the private or personal could never be separated from the public world of waged work, research and teaching was a formative moment, and he tried to communicate this argument to other men.

Hearn also cited influences from Marxism, ethnomethodology, post-structuralism, gay liberation, feminism and feminist theory. He mentioned radical feminist ideas in particular, but with some ambivalence about the use of such labels.

> **Hearn:** I'd felt for a very long time, that Marxism and ethnomethodology were just two parts of the same account, although neither do justice to gender, they are the two obvious background theories. Following on from that, the label's getting difficult here, I found accounts described as radical feminist personally more, I'm trying not to use the word, challenging. They seemed more accurate actually, that's what I'm trying to say, they seemed more accurate than some other kinds of accounts that haven't been labelled radical feminist. But I know there are problems actually dividing up these things. [...]

On the other side of the Atlantic sociologist Michael Kimmel gave a stark illustration in his written response of the impact of feminism on his view of himself:

> **Kimmel:** I was participating in a graduate seminar in Feminist Theory several years ago when a dispute between a white woman and a black woman froze the casual temper of the group. The white woman claimed that the universal oppression of women by men bound the two of them in a common plight. The black woman disagreed. 'When you wake up and look in the mirror, what do you see?' she asked. 'I see a woman', replied the white woman. 'That's precisely the problem', replied the black woman. 'I see a black woman. For me race is visible every

day, because it is how I am not privileged in this culture. Race is invisible to you, which is why our alliance will always be strained to me.'

I was startled by this exchange. When I, middle-class, white, male, looked in the mirror, I saw a human being, universally generalizable, a generic person—without race, class or gender. What had been so easily concealed had become strikingly visible.

I like to think of this story as a personal and intellectual illustration of the way that feminism has transformed the social and behavioural sciences. Feminism has made it clear that gender is one of the central axes around which social life revolves. [. . .]

Kimmel sees his academic work as a political project, which owes an 'enormous debt' to feminist writers, and which partly arose in opposition to the 'sex-roles' model:

> **Kimmel**: A central theme in my work . . . is to make gender visible to men . . . Making masculinity visible means confronting both accepted academic models of gender relations and political relations between women and men. For me, this has meant challenging the 'sex-role' model that has governed social and behavioural sciences for the last quarter century. [. . .]
>
> As readers can obviously tell, my debt to feminist theorists is enormous. [. . .]

Harry Brod [. . .] is another US social theorist who has taught in the area of 'gender studies', influenced by feminist work and an involvement in sexual politics. Like many social scientists working around issues of sex and gender, Brod's work overlaps into psychology. In his written response, Brod defines his work as follows:

> **Brod**: I construe my work as an attempt to articulate and theorize men's actions and experiences as both causes and effects of patriarchy, as part of the feminist project of articulating and theorizing patriarchy. This has seemed to me important but relatively unexplored territory. By shedding light on men's consciousness of these experiences, I seek to empower women and anti-sexist men by producing knowledge about and hence demystification of masculinities. Part of what motivates the project is my view that understanding *male* experience as particular *gendered* experience is part of overthrowing patriarchy, since male claims to universality of their voices and visions are part of what keeps women's perspectives silenced and suppressed.
>
> I first became seriously interested in these issues when I joined a men's consciousness-raising/support group while a graduate student in San Diego, California in the mid- and late seventies. [. . .] My involvement became more academic following my accepting a teaching job in the

Program for the Study of Women and Men in Society at the University of Southern California.

Like Connell and Kimmel, Brod too is interested in the production, reproduction and negotiation of masculinities. [...] Like many other respondents, Brod sees his work as in a constant process of change:

> **Brod:** [...] More recently, I have been struggling to give up some of my attraction to the tradition of grand theory because of the challenges to such theories by postcolonialist and postmodernist theory. [...]

For Gary Dowsett too, academic work and political activities were intertwined, and research on gender, masculinity and sexuality was an urgent political endeavour, as his written response makes clear:

> **Dowsett:** Over the last four and a half years I have been coordinating a series of research projects on gay and bisexual men's responses to HIV/AIDS ... The bulk of our work concerns monitoring the education programme directed to gay men and advising on educational strategies aimed at sustaining safe sexual behaviour. [...]
>
> Various issues specifically related to work on masculinity have been, not surprisingly, absent from the main research and education agendas in the West for many years, and the main work on male sexuality developed in the last decade by men lies largely (but not entirely) in the marginalized domain of gay studies or in the non-academic work of the largely unemployed, gay intelligentsia. My alarm at the ignorance of medical and proto-medical disciplines, granted the historic right to speak about epidemics, human behaviour and sexuality in their work on HIV/AIDs, virtually demanded that we combine the work I had done on homosexuality, the work Bob Connell had done on sexuality and masculinity and our joint work on education, with the others in the School to produce what is now the programme of research carried out in the Macquarie University AIDS Research Unit.

For Mairtin mac an Ghaill, the influences and the aims of academic work were similarly not confined to texts, abstract theories or empirical studies:

> **Mac an Ghaill:** I went to an all-male boarding school. That was one experience of an all-male environment. I also had contact through the Roman Catholic priest, that was another all-male group. My family in Ireland are in the army, a lot of them are in the army, officer class, of course. There was much talk inside the family of being a man's man. This history was really waiting in some ways for me to reflect on it. It was the idea that men prefer to be with men, prefer their company, that was the start of it, along with the way men acted with other men which was systematically different from the way they acted with women. On the face of it these were all straight men.

But it was partly through working on *Young, Gifted and Black* that I began to theorize masculinity. I suppose from sociology, particularly from feminism, in trying to understand the educational experiences of students, the differences between the male and female, the masculinity thing, emerged again. But not so much in terms of race, I think, as understanding it in terms of class. As with Paul Willis's work, the links for working-class kids between shop-floor culture and notions of work emerged. So there's two levels in my life: looking at masculinity in a more general way and just trying to understand aspects of it, personal meanings of it, and then the teaching and research, looking at it more specifically in terms of educational processes. My own theory and practice merged. As well as always from university onwards, the guy I was initially living with, was in a feminist environment so I was kind of forced into it, I didn't have much choice, it was a very practical thinking, like the division of labour inside the flat and all that kind of thing, the talks and the rows that came from that.

As with Jeff Hearn and Bob Connell, the 'private' and 'public' spheres intersect for mac an Ghaill, with no sense that research is an impersonal, apolitical endeavour.

What marked most of these male sociologists apart from most of the male psychologists we contacted was their understanding of gender as a power relation within structural perspectives which usually made links with parallel and overlapping power relations around 'race', class, sexuality and culture. Once again, this was often understood in terms of their personal histories and subjectivities as well as through abstract theories and empirical research. This was frequently entered through a dissatisfaction with the 'sex-role' model which was prevalent in psychological research. [. . .]

Looking at the research on 'race' and education, mac an Ghaill was initially directed to look at Asian and Afro-Caribbean students as 'problems'. His own research and teaching convinced him that the white teachers (both liberals and explicitly racist traditionalists) and the institutions of education were the source of most problems *for* black students. Research on the experiences of Irish students was defined by him as work around English racism, and by potential supervisors as research on black students, a connection which mac an Ghaill attempted to reverse by constructing white teachers and educational institutions as problematic.

Mac an Ghaill describes himself as anti-sexist and anti-racist, describing himself as able to operate from a position of relative power. Michael Kimmel makes many similar points in his objections to liberal theories of gender inequality, his definition of gender as a power relation which is linked to class, 'race', ethnicity and sexuality:

Kimmel: Gender is a power relation, an historically constituted, socially constructed process that reproduces the power of men over women and the power of some men over other men.

Men's power over women is easily understood, but the power of some men over other men needs a bit of explication. I mean the distribution of power among men by class, race, ethnicity, sexual orientation. Thus I mean the power of upper and middle-class men over working-class men; the power of white, native-born men over non-white and non-native-born; the power of heterosexual men over gay men. But a depoliticized sex role model made these power relations invisible by a sleight of hand. [. . .]

The model didn't need to be more finely tuned; it needed to be jettisoned. Gender wasn't a thing, a *masculinity* as a unitary essence towards which all men strive and some men (conveniently straight, white men) achieve better than others. One studies *masculinities*, the desegregated, multiple constructions of gender, and thus makes central and visible the power dynamics by which hegemonic masculinity is reproduced. This means that the study of gender is linked to the study of class, race and ethnicity and sexuality. Efforts to understand masculinities are, by definition, political; they identify the dynamics that constitute the reproduction of other forms of power relations.

Like many of those who referred to the study of masculinit*ies*, and the notion that masculinity is not a monolithic, unitary entity, Jeff Hearn saw this as something of a double-edged argument. The tension between a sex/gender class analysis and an examination of how particular masculinit*ies* are constructed was linked to debates over structuralist and poststructuralist perspectives.

> **Hearn:** The whole idea of a gender class is, I think, very important as a concept for theoretical and political activity; very few men seem to be interested in looking at that. Feminists have been writing about women as a class for a long time, but very few men want to take that on, that's a real problem. [. . .]
>
> We need to recognize that men are a gender class, in terms of their power over women, but deconstruct at the same time the monolithic implications of that.

Summarizing the main themes emerging from the responses of male sociologists—first, there is the obvious way these men tend to locate their own histories at the intersection between personal and political influences outside academia, and the academic world of research, texts, theory and teaching. Second, feminism(s) appears as a key influence from within and outside of academia. Third, and as a consequence of the above two points, structural theories of power formed the bedrock of their understandings of sex/gender, men and masculinity, a rejection of the 'psychology of sex roles' model. Finally, and in sharper contrast with most of the male psychologists we contacted, these male sociologists made connections between gender and sexuality, 'race' and class, age and culture in their approach to the study of masculinit*ies.*

WOMEN ON MEN: SOME FEMINIST SOCIAL SCIENTISTS

[...] This section examines the work of three women working in the UK—Halla Beloff, Wendy Hollway and Lynne Segal. [...]

Lynne Segal is the author of a recent book on men, *Slow Motion: Changing Masculinities, Changing Men* (1990), and is well known for her socialist feminist politics. Segal works at Middlesex Polytechnic and, although a psychologist, has been influenced by a wide range of social science theorizing. Wendy Holloway works at Bradford University in the Development and Project Planning Centre. In recent years she has been attempting to apply trends in poststructuralist thought, particularly the work of Foucault and Lacan, to understanding discourses framing gender identity and heterosexual rela-tionships. This work is summarized in her book, *Subjectivity and Method in Psychology* (1989). Halla Beloff is a Senior Lecturer in Social Psychology at Edinburgh University. Her research interests include work on male self-presentation and the male gaze using photography and fine art as one arena for studying self-images.

It was clear from all three interviews that for feminist academics one important task is to first justify one's interest in studying men. Why devote time and energy to investigating masculinity? The issues raised here are familiar ones and Phyllis Chesler described in a letter to us how her book, *About Men* (1978), one of the first feminist psychological analyses of mas-culinity, produced a critical response from many feminists concerned at the attention given to men. In defending her own work, Lynne Segal formu-lated both the arguments for and against this focus.

> Segal: Well, of course, the first question is whether feminists should be studying men at all. I know there is a view which some have put forward suggesting that men have had far too much of a platform for too long, and so why should we waste our energy studying men unless immediately you can show this to be in women's interest?
>
> I don't agree with that. Although it's men's voices we've heard, what we haven't heard is men's voices really interrogating themselves—as a sex. So, as I argue very strongly in the book, it is a new thing to regard men and masculinity as a problem. [...] And so I do think that it is a sig-nificant thing to be studying men and masculinity and I do think that in problematizing men and masculinity we are beginning to subvert the taken-for-granted assumption that to be human is to be male and also to be male is in a sense to be all right.

Like Chesler, Segal described receiving a critical and sometimes hostile response to her work. In this next extract from the interview she points to two different routes within feminism and begins to indicate her own political and theoretical convictions: non-separatism, opposition to gender essentialism, and her stress on the heterogeneity of men and masculinity.

> **Segal:** There is one strand of feminism which feels very hostile to me. This strand sees, for instance, men's violence and pornography as the root of men's power and also sees all men as somehow similarly oppressive of women, as a result of biology or through some historically inevitable socialization. This strand definitely sees what I write as dangerous and letting the men off the hook. [...]

Halla Beloff similarly articulated the view that it is time masculinity was problematized in psychology and elsewhere. Indeed, there was a consensus on this point among Hollway, Beloff and Segal.

Wendy Hollway stressed the connections she sees between work on women and femininity on the one hand and men and masculinity on the other. She argued that the two areas are linked because: 'I am convinced that gender difference is a mutual production in social relations, and there's no point in looking at women in isolation. There's a point for descriptive work, but for theoretical work, to answer the question "why" and "how" about gendered identities, it is a waste of time.'

Feminist psychology in Hollway's view, must investigate how men *and* women maintain, reproduce and can change dominant discourses of masculinity (and femininity) and the practices which sustain those discourses. This approach leads her to want to study the whole range of masculinities and not just the abusive extremes of masculinity.

> **Hollway:** If I get time in the future I would like to do some research on the problematic aspects of masculinity, but focusing on the range of men in practice. I think a lot of feminist work, not necessarily the feminist psychology work actually, has been fixated on pornographers, rapists, murderers, child sexual abusers, and so on, quite rightly because those are shocking manifestations of problems of masculinity. But it is a bit difficult to see what the range is and how those extremes actually link to other so-called normal manifestations of masculinity and to men who don't have much problem with the way that masculinity addresses them.

The feminist psychologists we interviewed were not simply wishing to problematize and 'genderize' men, however. Their gaze was not simply questioning, it was also at times sceptical and amused, producing a distinctive feel to their responses compared to those of male academics. As a friend commented when we were writing this piece: 'Masculinity? Neurosis? Why make the distinction?' And this point sums up an important theme in some feminist analyses of masculinity.

Many feminist psychologists have emphasized, not just male vulnerability, but the disturbed, edgy, and almost pathological nature of masculine identity. Male authors, such as David Cohen and John Rowan in psychology, and others in sociology, such as David Jackson (1990) and Victor Seidler (1989), have engaged in critical autobiographical examinations of masculine socialization and male psychology, but the recent feminist exploration feels more in tune with Freud's ironic puzzling over the 'bizarre mysteries' of femininity. For Halla Beloff, male self-presentation, at some points, simply has to be seen as comic.

> **Beloff**: I think at some stage one does come to the psychoanalytic point that the adjustment of men is more precarious than the adjustment of women—going right back to the simplest ideas that you can't dress a boy baby in pink to the idea that men are more fearful of homosexuality than women are.
>
> The self-presentation of men in one sense is always apparently a phallic one—they have to be strong, straight and upright. The feminist psychologist, Janet Sayers, makes this terribly simple point that women who are supposed to be weak have always known that they were strong, and men who are supposed to be strong have always known that they were weak and, well, those two things are very different. We are willing for our true natures to be known, it can only do us good, but the same is not the case for men! [. . .]

Lynne Segal is also curious about the basis for the apparent intractability of gender difference along with the possible psychodynamic roots of male and female development. In her interview she summarized the history of work on masculinity as following a path from optimism to pessimism. Segal argued that early work on men was very much influenced by sex-role theory, as was work on women, which suggested, not only that sex-roles were repressive and oppressive for both women and men, but also implied that change would be relatively straightforward. Segal notes that, more recently, theorists from a variety of persuasions have become more concerned with the fixity of gender which also includes an awareness of the anxiety contained within men's strivings to be masculine.

> **Segal**: The sex-role socialization approach which was popular in the 1970s can't really explain the tenacity and centrality of our attachments to gender, our ambivalence, or our fierce resistance—the complexity and strength with which we hold on to our fight against a deep sense of ourselves as sexed beings—as men and women. Or, the dramas we have around masculinity and femininity. It did seem to me that we do need to look at some of the ideas coming from psychoanalytic thinking, mainly just the introduction of much greater complexity to the psychic, and

the idea of the layerings of activity and passivity which become connected up with ideas of masculinity and femininity. [. . .]
    Psychoanalysis does have something to tell us but there's also going to
be something missing if we attempt to understand masculinity and femininity simply in terms of the familial construction of sexual identity. I
think we have to see that the importance and strength of masculinity,
as a symbol, comes from many sources. [. . .] That's why I say we have
to somehow find ways of connecting the psychic with the complexity
of the social.

Although this point was not directly discussed with Wendy Hollway in
our interview with her, the defensive nature of the male stance in heterosexual relations has also been a crucial theme in her writing (Hollway, 1983;
1989). An important aspect of her analyses of the discourses around heterosexuality is her empirical investigation of the ways in which men articulate,
and fail to articulate, intense feelings of irrationality, vulnerability and desire.
Hollway invokes a Lacanian analysis of the organization of male desire for
the Mother/Other and argues that, typically, men project or displace their
emotions of vulnerability and dependency on to the women with whom
they are involved.
    What rescues this analysis for feminism, however, is Hollway's emphasis
on power. She argues that, although male power is complex, not in any way
unidirectional or unproblematically applied, it is central to understanding the
maintenance of gender difference. Hollway states that male power must be
seen, in part, as a deeply embedded resistance to and negation of the interpreted power of women as mothers and sexual partners. In a fascinating
analysis of men's reactions to feminist women (Hollway, 1983) she argues
that this provides the conditions for men to position women, sometimes
successfully, as 'too powerful'.
    A focus on power also runs through Segal's struggle to connect 'the psychic
with the complexity of the social'. One of the most striking aspects of the
work of both Wendy Hollway and Lynne Segal is the extent to which they
move so readily from psychology to social theory. For both Hollway and
Segal this move allows them to pay more attention to theorizing gender and
power relations. Beloff, in contrast, draws on Goffman's work and is more
interested in microsocial forms of social interaction. [. . .]
    Segal's theoretical position is a complex one and difficult to pin down since
she wishes to draw on both psychodynamic explanations and on social theory
to explain the persistence of gender difference and male power. She also wants
to combine a feminist analysis with a socialist framework which looks at the
class position of the men who have been able to institute changes. Power, she
said in her interview, is not simply about 'bonking someone on the head'. It
is not about these relatively simple acts of assertion, nor is it about phenomenology, or feelings of potency; power is manifested in deeply entrenched

rituals and routines which, she states, continually place men at the centre. There is an interesting overlap here with Beloff's analysis of fine art and photography and Hollway's exploration of discourses on heterosexual relations. And, to sum up, it is possible to see the work of all three feminist social scientists as instantiations of their demand that academic work must investigate the way male power is reproduced through concrete rituals of male self-expression. It is this emphasis, despite differences in topic and theoretical perspective, which unites their work. [...]

CONCLUSION

What, therefore, are some of the main assumptions and perspectives underlying current research on men and masculinity? What are the theoretical and methodological choices? We have tried to indicate through the words of contemporary researchers some of the dominant strands in work by men on men. The approach of the three feminist social scientists considered in the previous section has added some further themes, a more detached view of male vulnerability, and expanded on explanations for the intractability of gender difference.

In summary, the key areas of dispute seem to us to lie around the theorization of male power. The problem of male power provides a useful litmus test for different approaches. How far do phenomenological and sex-role analyses of power take us? The male psychologists we interviewed are clearly convinced that humanistic psychology, on the one hand, and the concept of gender socialization, on the other, provide the key to understanding gender relations. Most male sociologists are equally convinced that sex-role theories have had their day and are inadequate to the task. Whereas John Rowan turns to mythology and work on goddesses for inspiration, male sociologists and the feminist social scientists we interviewed are becoming more and more persuaded of the complexity of the relationship between the psychic and the social.

But, if contemporary sociological analyses of power relations are preferable to psychological analyses, then on what basis and to what extent should social scientists explore the subjectivities and daily experiences of men? How important are men's accounts of their vulnerability? What place should these stories have in a social science of masculinity? There is another set of questions around the commonality of male experience. Are there common sets of social expectations and gender ideologies which cut across other divisions based on social class and ethnicity? Should we talk of 'masculinities' in the plural or 'masculinity' in the singular?

References

Brod, H. (ed.) (1987) *The Making of Masculinities: The New Men's Studies*. Boston: Allen & Unwin.
Chesler, P. (1978) *About Men*. New York: Harcourt Brace Jovanovich.

Cohen, D. (1990) *Being a Man*. London: Routledge.
Connell, R.W. (1987) *Gender and Power*. Cambridge and Oxford: Polity/Blackwell.
Fine, G. (1983) *Shared Fantasy: Role-playing Games as Social Worlds*. Chicago, IL: University of Chicago Press.
— (1987) *With the Boys: Little League Baseball and Preadolescent Subculture*. Chicago, IL: University of Chicago Press.
Jackson, D. (1990) *Unmasking Masculinity: A Critical Autobiography*. London: Unwin Hyman.
Hearn, J. (1987) *The Gender of Oppression: Men, Masculinities and the Critique of Marxism*. Brighton: Harvester Wheatsheaf.
— (1991) *Men in the Public Eye, The Construction and Deconstruction of Public Men and Public Patriarchies*. London: HarperCollins.
Hearn, J. and Parkin, W. (1987) *'Sex' at 'Work': The Power and Paradox of Organisation Sexuality*. Brighton: Harvester Wheatsheaf.
Hollway, W. (1983) Heterosexual sex, power and desire for the other. In S. Cartledge and J. Ryan (eds) *Sex and Love: New Thoughts on Old Contradictions*. London: The Women's Press.
— (1989) *Subjectivity and Method in Psychology: Gender, Meaning and Science*. London: Sage.
Kimmel, M. (ed.) (1987) *Changing Men: New Directions in Research on Men and Masculinity*. London: Sage.
Kimmel, M. and Messner, M.A. (eds) (1989) *Men's Lives*. New York: Macmillan.
Mac an Ghaill, M. (1990) *Young, Gifted and Black*. Milton Keynes: Open University Press.
Rowan, J. (1987) *The Horned God*. London: Routledge.
Segal, L. (1990) *Slow Motion: Changing Masculinities, Changing Men*. London: Virago.
Seidler, V. (1989) *Rediscovering Masculinity: Reason, Language and Sexuality*. London: Routledge.

Part 2 Theorizing Gender and Difference

9 FEMINIST PERSPECTIVES

JUDY LOWN

Feminist theoretical work has always developed in close unison with political activity. This has distinctively influenced the way in which it has used and transformed methods and approaches from a range of academic traditions.

The term 'second wave feminism' was coined in the USA to describe a range of activities which began in the late 1960s, produced by women who saw themselves in some way as feminists. It is often linked to developments taking place in the USA, Europe and Australasia at that time. It is distinguished from the 'first wave'—also characterized by a burgeoning of activity directed at changing the condition of women (Rendall, 1985)—identified as having taken place principally in the USA and parts of Europe during the nineteenth century.

The term 'feminism' came into widespread use only at the beginning of the twentieth century (Cott, 1987). It was first used by early nineteenth-century 'Utopian socialists' in France who aimed to set up communities based on equality, including equality between the sexes (Taylor, 1983). In the UK, there was a widespread concern with what was popularly known as the 'Woman Question'—the issue of the place of women in a society undergoing far-reaching economic transformation entailing the increasing separation of home and workplace. Huge debates took place in many different contexts about the implications of these developments for women. Those who advocated employment in the public sphere for women, accompanied by the right to vote, access to education and a variety of legal and political rights, were labelled as feminists by subsequent generations.

Some recent writers now talk of 'feminisms', rather than the singular 'feminism', in an attempt to capture and convey the variety of different analyses of women's position. The term—whether singular or plural—is also a distinctively Western one. Writers from non-Western traditions have either found other terms more appropriate or have developed a critical approach to the use of the word. Alice Walker, for example, uses the term 'womanist' to describe the distinctive experience of women survivors of a history of colonial exploitation and slavery (Walker, 1985). Other black American writers, like bel hooks and Audre Lorde, emphasize the need for an understanding and a politics based on the interconnectedness of inequalities of race and sex (hooks, 1981, 1984, 1989, 1991; Lorde, 1984a). Such writers have also urged an

Source: U207, *Issues in Women's Studies*. The Open University, (1992), The Course Introduction (updated for this Reader), pp. 53–62.

integration of class issues so that feminism is not restricted to a concern with the lives of white middle-class women.

THE WOMEN'S LIBERATION MOVEMENT

In the late 1960s the term 'feminism' was rarely mentioned even by those beginning to question women's position; more common terms were 'women's liberation' or 'women's rights'.

The year 1968 witnessed, on a global front, the invasion of Czechoslovakia by Soviet troops; widespread student and worker unrest in France; and in the UK, the outbreak of student protest against conditions in higher education, which mainly took the form of criticisms of the curriculum and decision-making processes (Pateman, 1972) and large-scale demonstrations, occupations and strikes in universities and polytechnics. In the USA, radical student organizations were emerging and joining with campaigns linked to struggles against racism and the Vietnam War, as well as the conservative content and structures of university education.

Some observers have tried to connect the emergence of women's liberation with student unrest in the 1960s, and see both as the monopoly of affluent children benefiting from post-war prosperity and the expansion in educational opportunities (Bouchier, 1984). Thus the Butler Education Act in 1944, and the expansion of the universities in the early 1960s, purportedly opened wider opportunities and brought more girls into higher education. Many women became frustrated by the lack of career opportunities to match their educational success and their involvement in student protest was frequently devalued and marginalized by male student activists. In the USA, the first groups to emerge with the prefix of women's liberation are frequently attributed to gatherings of women who were involved in student politics and civil rights activities and were tired of taking a secondary place in the radical movement. When women got together in groups without men they began to share their experiences without tailoring what they said to male presence and without conceding to male organizational structures.

Many such groups were referred to as 'consciousness-raising groups' with their focus on the collective sharing of experiences which had been seen primarily as individually experienced isolated events but were now identified as examples of the general oppression of women. For example, women who might previously have thought of themselves as subordinate in their relationships with men, began to see such experiences in terms of wider patterns of power. This was the beginning of the understanding that the 'personal is political': experiences which seem to belong to the 'private' realm of love, relationships, family life and household arrangements are as much structured by wider power relationships as experiences more commonly associated with the 'public' world of education, employment and political movements. Women's treatment in education and radical activity began to be linked to the ways they were treated individually by men. Meetings in which women met to discuss such issues were generally structured as non-hierarchically as possible. Either there was nobody chairing or, if there was, that role was rotated and leadership was shared, as were skills and tasks. Women developed their own strengths and resources.

In the USA, these developments were accompanied by the identification of 'the problem with no name' (Friedan, 1963). This problem related specifically to the experience of 'housewives'—mainly white middle-class housewives living in the suburbs. The rareness of books like Betty Friedan's led Lee Comer in the UK to write *Wedlocked Women* in 1971: a critique of modern marriage and family life from a woman's point of view. According to Lee Comer, the experience of being in a women's group enabled her to write—a group which she points out was not just composed of young, educated women. These groups were a source of strength to act as well as a means for raising consciousness.

The 'Demands' of the Women's Liberation Movement

The first national Women's Liberation Conference was open to both women and men and was held at Ruskin College in 1970. The second was held in Skegness in 1971. After 1971, conferences were only for women and were held until 1978. They were forums for debate, the co-ordination of campaigns and formulation of policy and what became known as the 'Demands' of the movement. There were initially four Demands: for the right to equal pay, to free nursery care for the under fives, to free contraception and abortion and to equality of opportunity in education. The last arose out of a widespread critique of the post-war notion of equal educational opportunities. An increasing awareness at an experiential level—later strongly substantiated by research—of the gender discrepancies, was added to research showing the social class differentials in education.

Later Demands to be added were the right to financial and legal independence, the right to define one's own sexuality and an end to discrimination against lesbians, and the right to be free of physical violence and abuse from men. Differences around the answers to the question of to whom these demands were addressed were influential both in characterizing some of the different political positions within the Movement and to the growing difficulties of organizing national conferences. The Demands, however, remained an important focus for various campaigns throughout the 1970s.[1]

Socialist/Marxist feminism

One of the political positions to emerge in the Women's Liberation Movement was socialist or Marxist feminism. This position has been more visible in the UK than in the USA, something often attributed to the different political traditions of the two countries. The heritage of wide-spread indigenous slavery created a sharp political focus for the issue of civil rights in the USA, whereas British politics was more dominated by issues of social class. Much early work among 'second wave' British feminists engaged with Marxist arguments linking the position of women with the dominant system of production. Using Marxist tools of analysis, socialist feminists saw the struggle for women's liberation as being an integral part of the struggle against capitalism.

The pamphlet by Sheila Rowbotham, 'Women's Liberation and the New Politics', is an example of this approach (Rowbotham, 1969). In it, she criticizes traditional (mostly male) Marxists for not incorporating an analysis of patriarchal relationships into their understanding of capitalism and argues that male authority over women in both the workplace and the family has specific implications for women as part of the workforce (in terms of relations of production) and as wives and mothers (in terms of relations of reproduction). As subordinates in both spheres, women are doubly exploited as workers and oppressed as the carers of present and future workers. An early formulation of this position, then, focused upon two systems of subordination: capitalism and patriarchy. Capitalism, as an economic system in which the ruling class owns and controls production, exploits workers. Patriarchy, as a form of power in which adult males, through the 'rule of the father', have control over everyone else, including younger men and boys, oppresses women. Subsequent debates among all sorts of feminists have grappled with how these two forms of power can most accurately be conceptualized and with what the consequences of their inter-relationship are for the lived experience of all sorts of women and men. Clearly, the political implications, especially in terms of strategy, have also varied according to the particular conceptualizations that are produced. Perhaps the crux of the socialist feminist position was the contemporary slogan 'No women's liberation without revolution, no revolution without women's liberation'. Sheila Rowbotham expanded on her work in subsequent books (Rowbotham, 1973, 1974, 1989) and similar arguments were developed by other socialist feminists such as Juliet Mitchell (Mitchell, 1971). Mitchell was one of the first feminists to explore what psychoanalysis could tell us about the ways in which primary relationships influence the development of men and women. She tried to link an understanding of the psychic creation of individuals to an analysis of the economic and ideological context in which individuals lived.

Psychoanalytical feminism

From the early 1970s there was interest among some feminists in how psychoanalysis could be used to further an understanding of women's position. These feminists rejected Freudian assumptions of women's deficiency denoted by the lack of a penis and the 'envy' this supposedly evoked. They made use, however, of Freud's central concept of the unconscious to examine both how power relationships between the sexes are formed and the different senses of personal identity accompanying these relationships.

For feminists, the usefulness of the notion of the unconscious lies both in its explanatory value and in the possibilities of personal and social change which it opens up. The existence of an unconscious helps to explain the persistence of particular social relations by showing how these are deeply structured into individual inner psyches as well as in outer social institutions. For example, patriarchy does not only exist 'out there' in the social and political system, but it also exists inside all of us who live in patriarchal societies. Our psychic development will differ according to, among other things, whether we are female or male. One implication is that programmes for change have to take on board those aspects which are unconsciously formed as well as those that are a matter of conscious will.

There are two main strands of feminist psychoanalytical thought emerging from these premises. One derives principally from the work of the French psychoanalyst, Jacques Lacan, and emphasizes that the unconscious, like language, is symbolic. It is the acquisition of language and the accompanying development of the unconscious which is seen as central to an understanding of personal identity. The feminist development of this approach can be seen in the work of Juliet Mitchell in the UK and Julia Kristeva, Hélène Cixous and Luce Irigaray in France. Some of these writers have also been associated with the branch of theory known as postmodernism, an approach which sees human identity as inevitably multi-faceted, fragmented and ever-changing (and consequently, ever-changeable).

The other main strand owes more to British Object Relations Theory in which personal identity and its unconscious components is conceptualized as developing through relationship with others, particularly those who care for us in early life. According to this approach, unmet needs in childhood can result in adulthood in feelings of an inauthentic 'outer' self which we present to the world while concealing, usually unconsciously, a buried 'inner self' that no one sees. Feminist writers to build on this tradition include Nancy Chodorow, and Luise Eichenbaum and Susie Orbach, who have particularly focused upon relationships between mothers and daughters within Western patriarchal societies.

A growing body of psychoanalytical work is also looking at the experience of institutionalized racism (Lipsky, 1987) and the effects of colonialism and cultural difference on psychological development (Espin, 1988).

Similarly, the implications of disabilities are being explored. This work represents another challenge to classic psychoanalytical theory which assumes a universalistic experience of unconscious processes. Other work is questioning the widespread homophobia within psychoanalysis (Ryan, 1983: O'Connor and Ryan, 1993).

Lesbianism

The recognition of the validity of lesbian sexuality (within the Demands of the Women's Liberation Movement) marked another instance of the 'personal' becoming 'political'. For many women who had had lesbian relationships, this area of their lives was predominantly hidden, as a result of the growing stigmatization of same-sex relationships accompanying the emergence of 'sexology' at the turn of the last century (Jeffreys, 1986). For most of the twentieth century, lesbians have occupied a 'twilight' world (Faderman, 1992). Prior to this, 'romantic friendships' between women, which probably included sexual and non-sexual relationships, had been regarded as commonplace (Faderman, 1981). As the Gay Liberation Movement developed at the end of the 1960s, many lesbians joined with gay men in asserting the right to 'come out'—to emerge from an enforced invisibility and enjoy the same social and legal rights as heterosexuals. Many of these women were also involved in women's liberation. A growing consciousness of themselves as women as well as gay, combined with issues distinctive to women in the Gay Liberation Front, led many lesbians to differentiate themselves from men and organize separate activities and meetings. The existence of both the Women's Liberation and Gay Liberation Movements also opened to women, hitherto identifying as heterosexual, possibilities they had not previously known existed.

Gay politics helped stimulate discussions of sexuality in the Women's Liberation Movement. The Sixth Demand was added to the Women's Liberation Demands in 1974. By proclaiming the right for women to define their own sexuality, and calling for the end of discrimination against lesbians, sexuality became a political issue on the women's liberation agenda for the first time. This enabled a recognition that any women can have active sexual feelings. For women already identifying as lesbians this was often the first public recognition of a previously hidden existence. For women exploring their sexuality a new possibility was opened up. There is, of course, no automatic alignment between lesbianism and any particular feminist political position—lesbians can have any, or no, politics.

For other women, the Women's Liberation movement provided a means for making a deliberate choice not to have sexual relationships with men. This has been referred to as 'political lesbianism'. Women who chose this label for themselves or who had it cast upon them were also often associated with what became known as 'separatism'. Whether or not they actually had physical relationships with women, 'separatists' preferred to live their lives as far removed from men as possible since men were seen as the main problem, and heterosexuality, as an institution, as the major stumbling block to women's liberation. An early exposition of lesbian separatism can be found in Jill Johnston's *Lesbian Nation* (Johnston, 1974), and a later analysis of its role in developing a lesbian feminist perspective is contained in Charlotte Bunch's, *Passionate Politics* (Bunch, 1987). This position became more formalized in the UK with the emergence of revolutionary feminism later in the 1970s.

Revolutionary feminism

Revolutionary feminism and radical feminism both identified men as the main enemy. However, they differed in their strategies and tactics. Despite their recognition of the radical nature of the radical feminist critique of the effect of male power on women's lives, many revolutionary feminists argued that radical feminist involvement in the creation of women's culture meant they had opted out of revolutionary politics, politics designed to overthrow male power. Revolutionary feminists therefore adopted strategies aimed at actively challenging the power men hold over women.

This strand of feminism expressed a frustration with what its advocates saw as a watering down of women's liberation politics around the mid 1970s. It argued that women should not only organize and live seperately from men (Leeds Revolutionary Feminist Group, 1981) but should also engage in active struggle against the main forms of men's control over women. These were identified in terms of male violence against women and led to campaigning groups such as Women Against Violence Against Women and to research and action directed towards issues of sexuality and power. The emergence of this strand represented an addition to the two main tendencies of radical feminism and socialist feminism (MacNeill and Rhodes, 1982; Coveney *et al.*, 1984).

Radical feminism

Radical feminists see systematic power relationships as lying at the root of women's oppression. While socialist feminists initially put the emphasis on the class relations of capitalism and argued to incorporate an understanding of sex inequality into such an analysis, radical feminists argued that it was patriarchal relationships which formed the central division upon which all other forms of oppression in society were based. One of the first studies of patriarchy from a radical feminist perspective, was Kate Millett's *Sexual Politics* (Millett, 1970). Millett uses 'sexual politics' to refer to the unequal power relations between the sexes and argues that sexual politics results in women's oppression institutionally and personally. All institutions—the education system, the police, the military, the law, the economic system and the family (and the knowledge which guides such institutions)—are patriarchal. Millett's work served as a major means of theorizing the notion of the 'personal is political'.

Many of the most well-known writers in the radical-feminist tradition are North American (like Kate Millett). Shulamith Firestone wrote *The Dialectic of Sex*, also in 1970. The term 'dialectic' had previously mainly been used by Marxists to depict the way in which history develops by means of contradictions and the reconciliation of contradictions in relation to processes of production. Firestone suggests that it is biological contradictions which form the basis of women's oppression. The main contradiction is that women do not control their own reproductive processes. Women should therefore take that control, if necessary through the use of artificial means of fertility.

Radical feminism also emphasized woman-centredness as a means of combatting male-dominated society. Adrienne Rich, for example, has argued for the need to 're-vision' the past, present and future since women are steeped in patriarchal culture, language and politics (Rich, 1977, 1979). Being woman-centred, or woman-identified, requires putting women's experiences and realities at the centre of women's lives and of a politics aimed at constructing a new vision of history, culture and the human psyche. Writing and poetry have a particular role to play in this process (Rich, 1978, 1979). Mary Daly focused specifically on language, arguing that a radical philosophy involves a voyage of creation aimed at producing a new 'gynomorphic' language (Daly, 1978), one derived from the life force of women embodying spiritual change which can only develop in a separate and self-contained women's culture. Separatism in this context provides a space for women to explore and nourish their own inner processes away from men.

Separatism, as a concept and strategy, has a part to play but is differently interpreted in most forms of feminism. Among socialist feminists it is recognized as an important principle for discussion and organization alongside mixed activity but does not permeate women's lives as much as in radical or revolutionary feminism. Most feminists recognize some need for engagement with or alongside men.

Radical feminism, although emerging initially in the USA, can be seen in women's politics and research in the UK as well. A collection of mainly British writings reflecting this approach is contained in *On the Problem of Men* (Friedman and Sarah, 1983). These papers grew out of conferences held in 1979 and 1980 aimed at explicitly exploring patriarchal institutions and the influences of patriarchy on men and their behaviour. The main premise was that the dismantling of patriarchy requires an understanding of how it affects men and boys, as those who benefit from and frequently resist relinquishing patriarchal power, as well as how it affects women and girls. But since the mid-1980s, the lines between different 'types' of feminism have been far more blurred, particularly with the growing influence of postmodernism, which sees both personal and institutional boundaries as much more permeable than approaches that emphasize structures.

Black feminism

There has been a growing body of black feminist activity and theory during the 'second wave' (earlier 'first wave' activity has also been documented; see, for example, Moraga and Anzaldua, 1981). There is a range of black feminist positions but one of the major arguments of black feminism is aptly summed up in the title of an influential black women's studies collection published in the USA in the early 1980s: *All the Women Are White, All the Men Are Black, But Some of Us Are Brave* (Hull, Scott and Smith, 1982). The title draws attention to the ways in which black women's experiences have been excluded and ignored both by white feminists and within the black community. Many articles highlight the double burden of racism and sexism for black women and the expanding knowledge of the contributions of black women being developed through black women's studies. Any feminism which marginalizes black women is seen as partial and inadequate feminism. White feminists who perceive black women's experience only in terms of victimization are criticized for the racism of such a view. Audre Lorde takes Mary Daly to task, for example, for not acknowledging and including the strengths and wisdom of black women in her analysis (Lorde, 1984b). She points out the false universalism of much white feminist thought and argues that women's liberation can only be achieved by a recognition rather than a denial of differences.

Black feminists also emphasize the need to confront the sexism of black men and stress that only black women are in a position to develop an understanding of gender divisions within black communities (Combahee River Collective, 1981). The crucial point for black feminists is that feminism should include '*all* women: women of colour, working class women, poor women, disabled women, lesbians, old women—as well as white, economically privileged, heterosexual women' (Smith, 1982). bel hooks argues that white feminists need to stop drawing analogies between the experience of women and black people in order to work towards a better integration of an understanding of imperialism and its inter connection with other hierarchies of oppression (hooks, 1981). In her more recent work, bel hooks seeks an integration of postmodernist thought with black feminist perspectives (hooks, 1991). In the UK, the main concern of black feminists has also been an analysis of the contradictions inherent in race, class and gender relations and a challenge to white feminists to take these on board (Amos and Parmar, 1984). A number of women's organizations and campaigns have also been appearing in countries all over the world, addressing themselves to issues of gender, race and class.

Liberal feminism

The tradition of liberal feminism has focused mainly on issues to do with the 'public world' such as employment, education, political and legal rights and strategies aimed primarily at changing legislation. The priority is to secure individual rights for women without discrimination on the grounds of sex.

This tradition can be traced back to 'first wave' feminist struggles to get the vote for women, to expand employment opportunities, to end discrimination against married women through legislation and to extend educational opportunities for girls and women. The roots of liberal feminism go back to at least the eighteenth century when the notions of individual rights, citizenship and democracy were first being widely debated. Although power was being transferred away from the traditional landed aristocracy, it was extended only as far as the men of the newly emerging middle class. Conspicuously absent from inclusion in the ranks of citizenry with equal rights and a share in democratic power were working-class men, black people from the 'colonies' and women of all classes and races. The liberal political tradition has largely been concerned with the gradual extension of democratic rights to every section of the population. A key figure as far as women's rights are concerned was Mary Wollstonecraft who wrote *A Vindication of the Rights of Women* in 1789 (Wollstonecraft, 1982), often regarded as a classic statement of liberal feminism. She argues that women are rational agents whose inferior position results from inadequate education. The main remedy lies through equal educational opportunities (Tomalin, 1977).

For modern liberal feminists, equality in civil rights and education is the main solution to women's situation. The National Organization of Women in the USA, and, in the UK, the Equal Opportunities Commission with its emphasis on reform, particularly in the realm of legislation, continue the tradition. It can also be found in books addressing issues of female education and employment, such as Eileen Byrne's *Women and Education*, written in 1978.

One objective which probably unites socialist feminists, revolutionary feminists, radical feminists and black feminists is that radical change of the complex hierarchies of capitalism, patriarchy and racism is needed in order to liberate women. For liberal feminists the priority is to *reform* the existing institutions, not to replace them. All strands of feminism, however, unite around the kinds of campaigns which derive principally from liberal ideology but also provide a platform for radical strategies and objectives, such as the struggles for equal opportunities policies in employment and education, and issues such as abortion, family allowance and child benefit, childcare provision, domestic violence and rape. Some writers argue that liberal feminism is a radicalizing force in that it does challenge the law (Eisenstein, 1982); others agree that laws can be 'instruments that facilitate the process of change and advance the situation of women' and that campaigns can be extended to other areas of women's oppression such as female sexual slavery (Bunch, 1987).

FRAGMENTING FEMINISM?

In the early 1990s, many of these questions about where power lies and how power relations can be changed have been dramatically influenced by postmodernism. There are varying definitions of postmodernism, mainly depending upon the intellectual discipline from which it emerges and the historical period it is seen to describe (Bordo, 1992). The chief targets of post-modernist criticism are overarching, generalizing theories aimed at producing global explanations of every form of social and political hierarchy and any notion of the individual as a unified, coherent, rational entity. The emphasis on *post*modernism derives from a turn against the dualistic and rational-istic assumptions of Enlightenment thinking in the West seen as heralding the 'modern' era towards the end of the eighteenth century.

The primary dualism characterizing Western 'modernist' theorizing is, for postmodernists, that between 'mind' and 'body'. It is this division, in par-ticular, that is seen as creating an impetus for theoretical work that attempts not only to construct all-embracing explanations but also to presume that all action is motivated by the rational mind. A corollary is that the body belongs to the terrain of the irrational, unordered and untheorizable.

Postmodernism represents a movement away from seeing power as located in one centre. Greatly influenced by writers such as Foucault, power is seen to be a dynamic of non-centralized forces that accrue into dominant his-torical forms through multiple 'processes, of different origin and scattered location' (Foucault, 1979). In different historical conjunctures, different 'dis-courses' come to regulate and normalize the construction of daily life.

In feminist circles, there has been much debate as to the significance of postmodernist claims (Nicholson, 1990). The postmodernist challenge is directed as much towards Marxist/socialist approaches and radical fem-inist approaches (with their conceptualizations of *systems* of capitalism and patriarchy) as towards classical liberalism. If power is not solely vested in one ruling group in society (whether capitalists or men) does this mean that there are greater possibilities for resistance and subversion among a whole variety of social groups? Is it the case that women already have all sorts of means at their disposal for asserting their power and definitions? Are not Madonna and other cultural icons, for example, a new symbol for an unfet-tered freedom to behave as we wish? And isn't it the case that black women, women of colour, lesbians, women with disabilities, among others, have been pointing out for a long time that women are no more of a homogenous group than are men? Surely, each and every one of us is cast within a multiplicity of identities rather than one?

These sorts of questions have highlighted a new preoccupation with issues of epistemology and philosophy as well as politics. Holistic approaches, such as Marxist, liberal and radical feminism, produced different analyses of 'women's position'. More recently, there has been a growing focus on how we even form our means of analysis. How have we come to 'know' what we think we 'know' about women and men? How has the very tradition of what is seen as 'knowledge' influenced our thoughts and actions concerning women and men? Who produces 'knowledge' anyway?

One important argument to emerge around these questions is that of the 'standpoint' theorists. These writers see all knowledge as socially situated. Much of what has been presented as 'objective' knowledge in the past is actually produced from the vantage point of those who can mobilize more power through their control of the dominant discourses. This 'knowledge' is not only partial because it excludes the experience of the socially marginalized, but is distorted by the absence of recognition on the part of those who produced it of their own social location (Haraway, 1991; Harding, 1986). For these writers, it is the questions raised by 'marginal' groups which offer a stronger starting point for knowledge (Harding, 1991). It is not suggested that these perspectives will produce solutions but at least they pose more reliable and far-reaching questions precisely because they come from a marginalized vantage point where power relations are more visible and made more explicit. Moreover, there is a recognition of multiple identities, located within varying bases of power, where, for instance, a Black woman is an 'outsider within' because she is simultaneously 'inside' the category of woman but 'outside' the category of whiteness (Hill Collins, 1991).

In many ways, this approach owes a lot to the whole evolution of 'second wave feminism'. It retains a concern with power, without assuming it as monolithic and all-embracing. It also has links with 'woman-centredness', without, perhaps, the tendency towards idealization of women, or of particular women, which that notion sometimes purveys. It builds on the early attention drawn to the difference between women's and men's bodies and how these can be differently inscribed (Goldstein, 1991) and treated. There are links too, with current psychoanalytical work, whereby not only the body but language as well as relationship are seen to be central to any theoretical exploration. The diversity of experiences among women, highlighted, for example, by critiques of 'second wave feminism' from black women and lesbians, are given central attention. The differences *within*, as well as the differences *between*, are being acknowledged in more and more intellectual disciplines (Moore, 1993).

Alongside these intellectual and theoretical developments, political activity amongst women has been increasingly taking the form of specific campaigns and issues. Many and various groups and organizations now tend to replace the larger, more generalized bodies of the past. Instead of aiming to unite many disparate groups behind one all-embracing cause, the focus is more and more on particular goals which might mobilize many in support but where distinctiveness and difference are openly identified. For example, the campaign in the early 1990s to free Kiranjit Ahluwalia, an

Asian woman who killed her abusive husband, mobilized a cross-section of support from various sections of society but raised particular issues concerning Asian women's lives and was directed towards Kiranjit's release and specific changes in the law. Many issues are recognizably linked to the earlier concerns of 'second wave feminism', such as violence against women, pornography and other cultural representations, equal rights in employment, legislative change, immigration control issues, environmental issues, prejudice against lesbians, housing, single mothers, religious fundamentalism. Perhaps now, however, intersecting identities and interests to do with, for example, racism, sexuality and class have a higher and more explicit profile and the complexity of these issues receives greater attention.

What does this mean for the future of feminist politics? Does a fragmented world mean a fragmented feminism, or even fragmented feminisms? Postmodernism can be in danger of leading up blind alleys where all power is dispersed, all identities are fragmented and all political projects are modernist delusions. Some writers offer salutary reminders that because power is not held by any *one* it does not mean that it is held equally by *all*. People and groups are positioned differently within it. All power relations are unstable, rendering hegemony precarious and resistance continual and unpredictable (Bordo, 1991). In addition, how is postmodernism itself being differently deployed by groups differently located within social and political power relations?

Those of us who have struggled, or are seeking to struggle, to find a voice for our experiences in the 'margins', need to be mindful of those who might wish to use postmodernism as an argument against political critique and collective action, whether these are directed against cultural images or institutional practices. Perhaps we need also to remember that one of the most pervasive ways in which power relations operate is through myth. The discourse of myth can be very effective at portraying those in the margins as 'monsters' who need to be managed and controlled (Warner, 1994).

In the day-to-day existence of many of those living under the shadow of such myths, there is still poverty, homelessness, unemployment, physical danger, legal injustice, stress and hardship. The poorest sections of all societies are still predominantly women and children. Even in a world increasingly defined as 'postmodern', political struggle, based on a recognition rather than denial of difference, might still speak loudest amidst 'the sadly continuing realities of dominance and subordination' (Bordo, 1991).

Note

1. Further details about this can be found in *The Body Politic* (Wandor, 1971) and *Conditions of Illusion* (Allen 1974). Discussions of Activity throughout the 1970s and early 1980s appear in *Sweet Freedom: the Struggle for Women's Liberation* (Coote and Campbell, 1982), *The Feminist Challenge* (Bouchier, 1984), and *Sweeping Statements: Writings from the Women's Liberation Movement, 1981–1983* (Kanter et al., 1984).

References

Allen, S., Sanders, L. and Wallis, J. (eds) (1974) *Conditions of Illusion: Papers From the Women's Movement.* London: Feminist Books.

Amos, V. and Parmar, P. (1984) Challenging imperial feminism. *Feminist Review* 17, 3–21.

Bordo, S. (1992) Review essay: postmodern subjects, postmodern bodies. *Feminist Studies* 18, 1, Spring, 159–75.

—(1991), 'Material Girl': the effacements of postmodern culture. In L. Goldstein (ed.) *The Female Body: Figures, Styles, Speculations.* Michigan: University of Michigan Press.

Bouchier, D. (1984) *The Feminist Challenge:The Movement for Women's Liberation in Britain and the United States.* London and Basingstoke: Macmillan.

Bunch, C. (1987) *Passionate Politics.* New York: St Martin's Press.

Byrne, E. (1978) *Women and Education.* London: Tavistock Publications.

Combahee River Collective (1981) A black feminist statement. In C. Moraga and G. Anzaldua (eds) *This Bridge Called My Back: Writings by Radical Women of Color.* Watertown, MA: Persephone Press.

Comer, L. (1971) *Wedlocked Women.* London: Feminist Books.

Coote, A. and Campbell, B. (1982) *Sweet Freedom: The Struggle for Women's Liberation.* London: Pan Books.

Cott, N. (1987) *The Grounding of Modern Feminism.* New Haven, CT and London: Yale University Press.

Coveney, L., Jackson, M., Jeffreys, S., Kaye, L. and Mahoney, P. (1984) *The Sexuality Papers.* London: Hutchinson.

Daly, M. (1978) *Gyn/Ecology: The Metaethics of Radical Feminism.* Boston, MA: Beacon Press.

Eisenstein, Z. (1982) The Sexual politics of the new right. In N.O. Keohane (ed.) *Feminist Theory.* Brighton: Harvester Press.

Espin, O.M. (1988) Cultural and historical influences on sexuality in Hispanic/Latin women: implications of psychotherapy.

Faderman, L. (1981) *Surpassing the Love of Men.* New York: William Morrow.

— (1992) *Odd Girls and Twilight Lovers: A History of Lesbian Life in Twentieth-Century America.* Harmondsworth: Penguin.

Firestone, S. (1970) *The Dialectic of Sex.* New York: William Morrow.

Foucault, M. (1979) *Discipline and Punish.* New York: Vintage.

Friedan, B. (1963) *The Feminine Mystique.* New York: W.W. Norton.

Friedman, S. and Sarah, E. (eds) (1983) *On the Problem of Men.* London: The Women's Press.

Goldstein, L. (1991) *The Female Body: Figures, Styles, Speculations.* Michigan: University of Michigan Press.

Haraway, D. (1991) *Simians, Cyborgs and Women.* London: Routledge.

Harding, S. (1986) *The Science Question in Feminism.* Ithaca: Cornell University Press.

— (1991) *Whose Science? Whose Knowledge? Thinking From Women's Lives.* Ithaca: Cornell University Press.

Hill Collins, P. (1991) *Black Feminist Thought: Knowledge, Consciousness and the Politics of Empowerment.* London: Routledge.

hooks, b. (1981) *Ain't I a Woman: Black Women and Feminism.* New York: Quadrangle. (Also published in the UK in 1982 by Pluto Press.)

— (1984) *Feminist Theory: From Margin to Centre.* Boston, MA: South End Press.

— (1989) *Talking Back: Thinking Feminist, Thinking Black.* London: Sheba Feminist Publishers.

— (1991) *Yearning: Race, Gender and Cultural Politics.* Boston, MA: South End Press.

Hull, G.T., Scott, P.B. and Smith, B. (eds) (1982) *All the Women are White, All the Men are Black, But Some of Us are Brave.* New York: The Feminist Press.

Jeffreys, S. (1986) *The Spinster and Her Enemies.* London: Pandora Press.

Johnston, J. (1974) *Lesbian Nation.* New York: Simon & Schuster.

Kanter, H., Lefame, S., Shah, S. and Spedding, C. (1984) *Sweeping Statements: Writings from the Women's Liberation Movement, 1981–1983.* London: The Women's Press.

Leeds Revolutionary Feminist Group (1981) *Love Your Enemy? The Debate Between Heterosexual Feminism and Political Lesbianism.* London: Onlywomen Press.

Lipsky, S. (1987) Internalised racism. In *Re-evaluation Counselling.* New York: Rational Island Publishers.

Lorde, A. (1984a) *Sister Outsider: Essays and Speeches.* New York: The Crossing Press.

— (1984b) An open letter to Mary Daly. In A. Lorde *Sister Outsider.* New York: The Crossing Press.

MacNeill, S. and Rhodes, D. (1982) *Women Against Violence Against Women.* London: Onlywomen Press.

Millett, K. (1970) *Sexual Politics.* New York: Doubleday.

Mitchell, J. (1971) *Woman's Estate.* Harmondsworth: Penguin.

Moore, H. (1993) The differences within and the differences between. In Teresa del Valle (ed.) *Gendered Anthropology.* London: Routledge.

Moraga, C. and Anzaldua, G. (eds) (1981) *This Bridge Called My Back: Writings by Radical Women of Color.* Watertown, MA: Persephone Press.

Nicholson, L. (1990) *Feminism/Postmodernism.* London: Routledge.

O'Connor, N. and Ryan, J. (1993) *Wild Desires and Mistaken Identities Lesbianism and Psychoanlysis.* London: Virago.

Pateman, C. (ed.) (1972) *Counter Course: A Handbook for Course Criticism.* Harmondsworth: Penguin.

Rendall, J. (1985) *The Origins of Modern Feminism: Women in Britain, France and the United States, 1780–1860.* London and Basingstoke: Macmillan.

Rich, A. (1977) *Of Woman Born: Motherhood as Experience and Institution.* London: Virago.

— (1978) *The Dream of a Common Language: Poems 1974–1977.* New York: W.W. Norton.

— (1979) *Of Lies, Secrets and Silence.* New York: W.W. Norton.

Rowbotham, S. (1969) *Women's liberation and the new politics.* Pamphlet.

— (1973) *Woman's Consciousness, Man's World.* Harmondsworth: Penguin.

— (1974) *Hidden from History: Three Hundred Years of Women's Oppression and the Fight Against It.* London: Pluto Press.

— (1989) *The Past is Before Us: Feminism in Action Since the 1960s.* Harmondsworth: Penguin.

Ryan, J. (1983) Women loving women. In S. Cartledge and J. Ryan (eds) *Sex and Love.* London: The Women's Press.

Smith, B. (1982) Racism and women's studies. In G.T. Hull, P.B. Scott and B. Smith (eds) *All the Women are White, All the Men are Black, But Some of Us are Brave.* New York: The Feminist Press.

Taylor, B. (1983) *Eve and the New Jerusalem: Socialism and Feminism in the Nineteenth Century.* London: Virago.

Tomalin, C. (1977) *The Life and Death of Mary Wollstonecraft.* Harmondsworth: Penguin.

Walker, A. (1985) *In Search of Our Mothers' Gardens.* London: The Women's Press.

Wandor, M. (ed.) (1971) *The Body Politic.* London: Stage 1.

Warner, M. (1994) *Managing Monsters.* New York: Vintage.

Wollstonecraft, M. (1982) *A Vindication of the Rights of Women.* M.B. Kramnick (ed.). Harmondsworth: Penguin.

10 FEMINIST THEORIES OF THE STATE: TO BE OR NOT TO BE?

JANE KENWAY

One purpose in this article is to map the broad terrain of feminist theories of the state, and to identify recent developments. A second is to identify some of the challenges which postmodern and post-structuralist theorizing poses for feminist state theory, and to assess its potential contribution.

ESTABLISHED THEORIES OF THE STATE: SOCIAL FEMINISM

[...] The radical stance suggests that existing theories of the state are totally distorted by the world view of men and that this problem cannot be solved simply by writing women into such theories. [...]

It is argued that because feminist theories of the state usually draw on liberalism or Marxism, 'feminism has no theory of the state' (Mackinnon, 1989, p. 158) and 'has not confronted, on its own terms, the relations between the state and society within a theory of social determination specific to sex' (p. 159). [...]

Radical feminism's basic premise is that the most fundamental and long-lasting division in society is that which exists between the sexes. In this view the biological differences between the sexes have been converted by men into sets of social relationships which oppress women. Women's reproductive capacities have been transposed into oppressive family forms. Biological differences in physical strength and associated ideologies of masculinity and aggression have enabled men to control women through the threat of violence. The term patriarchy is used (not uncontroversially) to describe the institutional arrangement through which men as a sex-class exert power over women. State politics and legal and administrative arrangements are seen overwhelmingly to reflect men's interests. The particular focus of radical feminism's critique of the state has been on its complicity in sustaining the patriarchal family; its judicial and other arrangements concerning matters of rape, domestic violence, prostitution, abortion, pornography and reproductive technology; and its involvement in militarism and warfare.

Source: Abridged from Muetzelfeldt, M. (ed.) (1992) *Society, State and Politics in Australia* (pp. 108–44). Annandale: Pluto Press.

Catherine MacKinnon's (1989) focus is on the 'consciousness and legiti-
macy conferring power of law' (p. xiii) which 'sees and treats women the
way men see and treat women' (p. 126). She centres most of her critique
on the liberal state which 'constitutes the social order in the interests
of men as a gender—through its legitimatizing norms, forms, relations
to society and substantive policies' (p. 162). [...] MacKinnon proposes
a 'feminist jurisprudence' which moves beyond the mainstream—malestream point of view and which recognizes, at the outset, that inequality
between men and women arises from relationships of power, from dominance and subordination.

Given that the state is so inextricably linked to patriarchy, radical feminists
have not usually, in theory at least, looked to the state to help bring about
gender justice, preferring separate and different modes of political analysis
and practice. None the less, radical feminism, in practice, has had an impact
on state activities. It has been a dominant, although not exclusive, force
behind the establishment of rape crisis centres, women's refuges, the modi-
fication of laws on sexual violence and the creation of sexual harassment
legislation. [...]

In contrast, the liberal and socialist feminist projects involve both a critique
of male-stream political theory and a reconstruction of the theoretical field in
order that it may adequately address gender-related matters and inform feminist politics.

Liberal feminism and the state

Liberalism, with its opposition to the 'divinely ordained' power of mon-
archs, its enthusiasm for equality between free individual citizens and its
emphasis on equal rights, has provided the two waves of the feminist
movement with a battery of politically useful concepts. In the late nineteenth and early twentieth centuries, it led women to claim their rights
as citizens to vote, to hold property in their own names and to participate
in the labour force without legal barrier. Beyond the 1960s, the second
wave of liberal feminism has involved further calls for sexual equality in
the form of equal rights and equal opportunities in the public sphere.
More specifically, liberal feminism has had four central themes to its policy
initiatives. Firstly, it has sought to bring into effect anti-discrimination legislation. (For a discussion of the implications of this legislation in Australia,
see Mumford, 1989, ch. 11.) A second policy initiative has centred on
attempts to place women in positions of power and influence in elec-
toral politics, the administrative and judicial apparatus of the state, and
various other public authorities. Aligned to this strategy is a third approach,
which seeks a more balanced distribution of the sexes across the paid
labour force but most particularly in male-dominated areas where the
power, prestige and rewards are highest. Finally, because liberal

feminists attribute the inequalities between males and females to the sex stereotyping associated with various dimensions of the public and private sphere, it has sought to prompt agencies of the state to discourage sex stereotyping.

It is clear from this set of policy initiatives that liberal feminists have a strong belief in the power of the state to protect women and better their lot. [...] Despite its current dominance by men and by ideologies which benefit them, the state is regarded, ultimately, as sufficiently neutral to accommodate women and women's interests once women are able to achieve balanced representation and to exert sufficient pressure.

Even though liberalism and feminism may share elements of common history, feminist social and political theorists find in liberal theory a number of features which contribute to women's subordination to men. Carole Pateman (1989) demonstrates how liberal theories regarding the social contract 'presuppose the sexual contract and that civil freedom presupposes patriarchal right' (p. x). Others focus on the distinction between public and private realms and 'the sleight of hand through which one becomes male and the other female.' (Phillips, 1987, p. 13). Many feminists argue, in defining the family as a private terrain which should be free from government interference, liberalism fails to recognize the connections between the so-called public and private spheres, and that much which we might conventionally think of as personal is, in fact, political.

There are a range of other ways in which the liberal distinction between public and private has been considered by feminists. In liberal theory the public sphere may, in one sense, be equated with government and the private with the family and the two are deemed completely separate. [...]

Two strands are identified in early liberal theory; one emanating from John Locke endorses the notion of women's inferiority in both spheres, and another (emanating from J. S. Mill) announces their absolute equality to men while denying the existence of a domestic division of labour which contributes to women's inequality in both spheres. The tensions between these views are part of the politics of the modern state and also raise certain dilemmas for feminism.

There is a constant strain amongst liberal feminists concerning the extent to which their demands upon the state should emphasize girls' and women's equality with or difference from men. [...] MacKinnon (1989) acknowledges that the sameness/difference doctrine does attempt to address the important but paradoxical problem of gaining access for women to men's benefits while simultaneously valuing women's ways of being. However, she notes that the doctrine also acts to conceal.

Concealed is the substantive way in which man has become the measure
of all things. [. . .] Approaching sex discrimination as if sex questions
were difference questions and equality questions were sameness questions, merely provides two ways for the law to hold women to a male
standard and to call that sex equality (MacKinnon, 1989, pp. 220–41).

[. . .] The modern liberal democratic welfare state does, in fact, blur the
distinction between public and private realms. In some cases it makes policies
which impinge on the family, in others (e.g. until recently, marital rape) it
neglects to, but in both cases it 'behaves' in ways largely detrimental to
women even if ambiguously so. As Carole Pateman (1987) and others point
out, liberalism makes a second distinction between private and public by
splitting the public sector into a further separation between the public and
the private; the former referring again to government and the latter to
civil society. However, while the family can indeed claim to be part of civil
society, most liberal theorists have tended to ignore it, preferring to concern
themselves with the economy, markets, and the appropriate balance between
the freedom of private enterprise and the degree of government regulation
of the political and social rights of individual citizens. Under liberalism the
ethic guiding civil society is atomistic individualism. [. . .]
    It is clear that feminism has drawn from liberalism in a selective way,
while at the same time recognizing the contribution that the theory and
practice of liberalism has made to women's generally subordinate social
position. This ambivalence is indicative of a general ambivalence within
feminism towards the role of the state. On the one hand, it is regarded
as a central agency in contributing to male/female power relations; on
the other it is the site, par excellence, for much feminist political agi-
tation. [. . .]

Socialist feminism and the state

While Marxism offers a critique of liberalism, socialist feminism is censorious
of liberalism, Marxism and liberal feminism. Socialist feminists argue that in
concentrating so closely on legal rights, political equality before the law, equal
opportunity, affirmative action and so forth, liberal feminist analysis tends
to diminish the significance of the various sources of power in civil society,
particularly those rooted in the economy. The formal, legal equality guar-
anteed by liberalism is seen to mask and indeed legitimate those social and
cultural inequalities associated with differences in economic power. [. . .]
Socialist feminists argue that liberalism's focus on the individual not only
makes the theoretical accommodation of women as a sex-class difficult, but
that it also virtually prohibits an analysis of the class differences amongst
women. [. . .]
    Socialist feminists draw selectively from Marxist theories of the state. They

argue that the categories of Marxism are either sex-blind or underdeveloped in their potential for the analysis of the role that the state plays in men's domination of women and women's position within particular modes of production. Despite this, they believe that Marxism has considerable analytical power, particularly with regard to the relationship between the state and the economy, and so its insights are useful providing it can be sufficiently 'revised'. They further contend that while radical feminist analyses of patriarchy may have their problems, they nevertheless have opened up a range of areas for inquiry which Marxism has neglected. These include, in particular, the social role of the family and domestic labour, the economic subordination of women in the home and in the paid labour force and, more broadly, the relationship between patriarchy, capitalism and the state. In examining such matters, socialist feminists have tended to allude to the role of the state only indirectly. [...]

It is possible to recognize three tendencies and within each a variety of different lines of argument. One tendency is to highlight the role that the state plays in serving the interests of capital through its complicity in sustaining women's subordination and segmentation in the paid work force and the home (Wilson, 1977). Within this line of thinking, some writers argue that women have been discouraged from full and equal participation in the paid labour force by interrelated state policies on the family, welfare and taxation. Others argue that in participating in the determination and regulation of conditions of work through, for example, restrictive legislation, definitions of skill and discriminatory wage structures, the state has reinforced the sexual division of labour. [...]

A second tendency is to characterize the state as a dual system of oppression, operating a partnership between the semi-autonomous structures of capital and patriarchy (Hartman, 1981). Because of their servicing role in the family and the domestic ideology associated with it, women's labour-force participation is seen to be restricted while men's is enhanced. Reinforcing this, it is argued, is the behaviour of male-dominated trade unions which historically have sought to protect men's position in the workforce by supporting sexist definitions of skill, not supporting equal pay and instead, supporting the family wage. Collectively such practices are seen to underscore men's domination over women in both the private and public sphere.

None of the writers who develop the above analyses deny the complexity and changing nature of the processes involved. [...]

In recent years the socialist feminist perspective began to widen to include analyses of such other state activities as budgetary and monetary policies: taxation and its allowances and benefits; the provision of goods and services such as housing, health, communication, transportation and education; and macroeconomic theories and policies. But still lacking are developed analyses of the effects of these policies on women from different class groups, and any theoretical framework that explains the contradictory and consistent ways in which the state relates to women across the various policy fields. Most socialist feminist accounts of the state have difficulty in accounting both for the impact on the state of class and feminist struggles which have demanded that the state improve the condition of women's lives. Nor do they accommodate the fact that the state is a major employer of women and that it has, in some instances, acted progressively on women's behalf. [...]

From what I have said so far, it is clear that radical, liberal and socialist feminist theories of the state all have limitations, not the least being their inability to critically reflect on the possibilities and limitations of the state's capacities to effect positive change for all women and girls.

Recent departures

Recent departures have called for a more empirically based, historically dynamic and holistic feminist theory of the state which takes into account changing social and political conditions, and the work of Showstack Sassoon (1987), Franzway, Court and Connell (1989) and Watson (1990) are important here. Overall these contributions suggest that there is a clear and urgent need both for a more complete engagement between feminist state theory and actual political practice, and for more empirical research—in particular, that which explores the difficult and tense processes of reform and change i.e. 'the problems of working in and around the state' (Franzway, Court and Connell, 1989, p. 164). Marian Sawer's (1990) very comprehensive study of 'women and public policy in Australia' offers a valuable starting point to this theoretical project.

The discussion so far also suggests that no state theory is at all adequate unless it recognizes that the state:

- interacts with the intermeshing patterns of power associated with gender, class and race in ways which cannot be reduced to functionalist or conspiratorial accounts but which must be understood as in a complex condition of tension,
- participates in producing the shifting patterns of power which make up the social formation, but in ways which take into account its own diverse and contradictory sets of interests as a structure of power,
- is, therefore, neither unitary nor rational in the ways in which it negotiates and institutionalizes these competing sets of interests,
- is able to assist the political projects of social movements (such as feminism) but under conditions of considerable constraint,
- is best analysed in historical context.

TO BE OR NOT TO BE?

[...] Some writers claim that in the late twentieth century we live in social and cultural conditions which differ markedly from those of the early twentieth and late nineteenth centuries. New and particular forms of cultural

practice in fields as diverse as architecture and film, town planning and literature are included in such discussions, as are new information technology
and the social and cultural changes it has brought. These changes and differences, such writers argue, are so fundamental that the new cultural forms and
indeed the current condition must be named in order that they may be distinguished from earlier periods. They also make the case that certain social
theories have developed in concert with these changed conditions and that
further theories must be developed which are able to explain these shifts
and their implications. The current condition is thus described as one of
'postmodernity' and the many different theoretical perspectives which have
arisen in association have been labelled collectively as 'postmodernist'. Such
theories question many of the fundamental assumptions of the modernist
social theories which arose in connection with the period which has come
to be called 'modernity'. Post-structuralism is one of the theories which has
been included under the rubric 'postmodernism', and it is post-structuralism
which I will focus on here. The two terms are often and confusingly used
interchangeably, and indeed in some senses they are interchangeable.

Postmodernism, the state and feminism

The relationship between feminism and postmodernism is both ambiguous
and contentious, for the following reasons (see Nicholson, 1990: Intro;
Morris, 1988: Intro). The rise of such social movements as feminism has
been one defining feature of the condition of postmodernity. Further,
feminist theories have helped to create the conditions of possibility for
postmodernist theories. None the less, feminist theories can still be loosely
classified according to whether they draw from the theoretical tenets of modernism or postmodernism. While it is clear that postmodernist theory in
its various forms has provoked considerable interest amongst feminists, the
politics which arise from such theory are by no means clear. [. . .]

One strand of postmodernism is fascinated by new technologies of information and communication, i.e. the communications revolution. This revolution, it is argued, is what characterizes the condition of postmodernity. This
strand is concerned with the implications of the communications revolution
for our 'culture, economy and social form' (Hinkson, 1990). More particularly, it is concerned with its implications for the production, analysis and
transfer of knowledge and information, and the nature and culture of paid
work. It is also concerned with the cultural dominance of the commodity
and the invasiveness of its images; the reconstitution of time and space relationships as a consequence of new technologies; and the implications of all
the above for social interaction and human subjectivity. [. . .] A second strand
concerns itself with the growth of science and scientific rationality, and the
increasing pervasiveness of their influence over many aspects of our life form.
The pertinent questions to ask are: 'What are the implications for the state
of the postmodern condition?' and 'What are the implications for women

and feminist politics of both?'

One of the implications is the way in which these new technologies interact with economic matters to help facilitate the internationalization of capital and labour and the growth of international enterprises, the operations of which challenge the capacities of nation states to control their own economies and cultural and natural environments. Another is the way in which the state attempts to steer but is also steered by the cultural and economic logic of the communications revolution. The new technologies of communication are demonstrating an increasing potential to bypass state boundaries. Information culture cuts across the processes of the state. For example, some analysts suggest that the media played a significant role in the politics of recent changes in Eastern Europe. Anna Yeatman summarizes this point well when she says:

> As the new global society develops with its plethora of communication networks and its relative lack of clearly identifiable institutional centres of policy determination, the boundaries of the policies of the state will become highly permeable. Jurisdictionally specific policies will become driven increasingly by non-jurisdictionally bounded global discourses. (Yeatman, 1990, p. 169)

[...] As states struggle to transform their national economies within international economies, and as they direct their resources accordingly, we see a shedding of welfare responsibilities. It also becomes evident that information and communication technologies and scientific discourses are deployed to legitimate such adjustments and to reassert control over populations which are increasingly dispersed across international information cultures. Policy-making becomes increasingly caught up in the marketing and policing of images, and the difference between the image and 'the real' becomes difficult to determine as the state variously uses and abuses media outlets and is used and abused by them. [...]

Clearly the strands of postmodernism just outlined have brought into question feminist (and other) theories of the state which define it as a centre of power *par excellence*, and much more work needs to be done to develop these ideas. Another interrelated strand of postmodernism makes feminist (and other) notions of the state even more problematic. I refer here to post-structuralism. Predictably, post-structuralist theories stand in opposition to structuralism which is regarded as a characteristic feature of modernist theoretical practice.

Post-structuralism, feminism and state theory

Post-structuralism arises from somewhat overlapping approaches to psychoanalytic, linguistic, literary and social theorizing. It is a term applied to a very loosely connected set of ideas about meaning, the way in which meaning is made, the way it circulates amongst us, the impact it has on human subjects, and finally the connections between meaning and power. The emphasis is on discursive and textual practices. Predictably, the unifying premise of all post-structuralist theories, whether they apply to language, institutions, 'human nature' or power, is that they are anti or *post*-structure. They resist any tendency to totalize what they regard as complex and multifaceted. Post-structuralism is concerned with the local and contextual, and regards theories which incorporate grand narratives and essentialist notions of causation as reductionist and unable to deal with complexity. It is thus opposed to 'large scale historical narratives and social and theoretical analyses of pervasive relations of dominance of subordination (Fraser and Nicholson, 1990, p. 20). Indeed, it is opposed to any notion of history as linear and evolutionary (Nicholson, 1990, p. 3). It recognizes fragmentation, dispersal and discontinuity, and celebrates plurality. It attends to 'difference' and 'otherness', to the worlds and voices of the most silent and repressed. [. . .]

For post-structuralists, meaning is not fixed in language or in consistent power relations of dominance and subordination. It shifts according to a range of linguistic, institutional and cultural contextual factors. It is influenced by and influences shifting patterns of power. Such a view of meaning makes problematic the notion of truth and the truth claims of science, and, in part, leads post-structuralists to reject the legacy of the Enlightenment and the foundational role of philosophy as the provider of 'transcendental reason'. [. . .] Further, it is hostile towards humanism's presuppositions about human nature, and instead argues that subjectivity is multiple and contradictory and constituted by discourse. This view of human subjects means that post-structuralism is suspicious of any discourse which promises enlightenment and freedom.

Given these general tenets of post-structuralism, it is predictable that when feminists draw on this mode of theorizing to think about government institutions and processes, they are unlikely to seek to contribute to theories of the state. Indeed, to do so would be regarded as something of an anathema. From a post-structuralist point of view, such theories would be regarded as structuralist or, more broadly, modernist on the following grounds.

They draw on the logic of binary oppositions and on the principles of humanism and the Enlightenment legacy; they construct meta-narratives, predicated on unified subjects; they construct unified groups of oppressor, oppressed and revolutionary agents; and they see power as centrally located and dispersed downwards. The picture is of course more complicated than this brief résumé of the post-structuralist critique allows, and to sustain the proposition that feminist theories of the state tend to be modernist, one would need to look more closely at each particular theory at various stages of development. A more interesting question that we can ask is: 'Why would post-structuralist feminists be likely to regard the above features of feminist theories of the state as a problem, and what do they offer as an alternative?'

To answer this question it is necessary to outline the theoretical apparatus of Michel Foucault, who is a dominant figure in the way in which post-structuralists discuss the institutions and processes of government.

Foucault, discourse, knowledge and power   Foucault 'warns against the seductions of totalizing theory, which appears to resolve all differences and contra-dictions through unified and cohesive explanation' (Diamond and Quinby, 1988, p. xii). Equally, too, Foucault warns against a search for origins and closure, and exhorts us to recognize plurality and, in particular, the struggle over both meaning and the construction of subjectivity. Such views suggest an understanding of the state which is in stark contrast with those discussed earlier. Indeed, in some senses they call into question any theory of the state which too readily lapses into generalization. In the section to follow, I will introduce a number of concepts which form part of Foucault's theoretical framework and which help to explain his 'view' of the state. I will begin with the concept 'discourse' and show how he relates discourse to the politics of meaning and subjectivity, to power and so to government institutions. The point to keep in mind here is that Foucault is preoccupied with the relationship between forms of power and knowledge, and I will mention something about the ways in which he believes power and knowledge become part of the operations of the state. I will conclude this section by briefly noting the sorts of politics which arise from a foucaultian perspective.

Foucault uses the term 'discourse' to designate the conjunction of power and knowledge (Foucault, 1976). [. . .] In his early work, Foucault seeks to make clear the structures, rules and procedures which determine the different forms of our knowledge, those aspects of knowledge so fundamental that they remain 'unvoiced and unthought' (Young, 1981, p. 10). He calls this an 'archeology of knowledge', a study of the rules which determine what can and cannot be said within a particular discourse at a particular time; rules which include such procedures as prohibition, exclusion and the opposition between true and false. In discussing how different disciplines are constituted, he shows how knowledge can fix meaning, representation and reason; how the very organization of the discourse can be an exercise of power, controlling and restraining what can be said as well as the right to speak. For Foucault, discourses are 'practices that systematically form the objects of which they speak . . . Discourses are not about objects; they do not identify objects, they constitute them and in the practice of doing so conceal their own inter-vention' (Foucault, 1977a, p. 49). It is through discourse, then, that the social production of meaning takes place and through which subjectivity is pro-duced and power relations are maintained.

Suggested in this is a propostion which Foucault develops in his later studies of 'genealogies', that is the study of the historical emergence of discourses and their relationship to the state or, to be more specific, its institutions. The proposition is that knowledge and power are inseparable, that forms of power are imbued within knowledge, and that forms of knowledge are permeated by power relations. In order to suggest that power and knowledge are two sides of a single process he coins the term 'power/knowledge', and says:

> Power produces knowledge. Power and knowledge directly imply one another. There is no power relation without the correlative constitution of a field of knowledge, nor any knowledge that does not presuppose and constitute at the same time, power relations. (Foucault, 1987, p. 93)

Knowledge, he argues, is not a reflection of power relations but is immanent in them.

Knowledge is not regarded by Foucault as neutral or pure or, in itself, true or false. In considering knowledge or 'rationality' historically and politically, Foucault points to the 'politics of truth telling', the manner in which social and self government proceeds through the production and institutionalization of 'regimes of truth' (in Gordon, 1989, pp. 108–33). Through genealogical analysis, Foucault suspends questions of truth and falsity and examines the institutional field over and through which a discourse gains and assigns power and control. He considers 'regimes of truth' as they have effects through apparatuses of power (Benton, 1984, p. 177). He is concerned to examine 'how forms of rationality inscribe themselves in practices or systems of practices and what role they play within them' (Foucault, 1981, p. 8) suppressing a plurality of alternative discourses and reducing their credibility. Regimes of truth may also be accompanied by or be the same thing as regimes of morality or moral technologies. These proselytize a particular morality, claim its higher status, and at the same time exercise a relationship of power (Minson, 1980).

[...] According to Foucault, analysis should begin with the 'micro-physics' of power (power/knowledge configurations), with localized mechanisms, histories and trajectories, techniques and procedures. From here, he says, analysis should ascend to reveal how these have been colonized or appropriated by various forms of macro domination. Connections to a dominant state apparatus or a ruling group cannot be generalized; they must be reached through analysis (Smart, 1983, pp. 83–4).

With regard to discussions of the state, then, the important point to be made about Foucault is that his conception of politics and the location and exercise of power is very different from those whose perceptions are inspired by forms of Marxism or liberalism or, indeed, radical feminism. Foucault's conception of power is complex and multi-layered. [...] As the following rather difficult quotation indicates, power is a relation within and between discourses. It is:

> the multiplicity of force relations immanent in the sphere in which they operate and which constitute their own organization; as the process which, through ceaseless struggles and confrontations, transforms, strengthens or

reverses them; as the support which these force relations find in one another, thus forming a chain or a system, or on the contrary, the disjunctions and contradictions which isolate them from one another; and lastly, as the strategies in which they take effect, whose general design or institutional crystallization is embodied in the state apparatus, in the formulation of the law, in the various social hegemonies. (Foucault, 1981, p. 92)

From this point of view, the state may be conceptualized as an apparatus of social control which achieves its regulatory effects over everyday life through dispersed, multiple and often contradictory and competing discourses. It is a composite of micro powers. So, rather than focusing on the state *per se* and the interests which steer it, when Foucault discusses power his focus is on the local, everyday and intimate; indeed, it is on the body itself—the prime site for discursive regulation. Power, he says 'seeps into the very grain of individuals, reaches right into their bodies, permeates their gestures, their posture, what they say, how they learn to live and work with other people' (quoted in Martin, 1988, p. 6).

What, then, is Foucault's notion of human nature? This is exemplified in his theory of the subject. For him, the subject is neither unitary, rational nor possessed of free will. It is, rather, an effect of discourse. It is, particularly, an effect of the institutionalization of regimes of truth. As suggested earlier, subjectivity is produced by discourse and representation and does not exist prior to either. Identity becomes the shifting consequence 'of the complicated and often paradoxical ways in which pleasures, knowledges and power are produced and disciplined in language and institutionalized across multiple social fields' (quoted in Martin, 1988, p. 9). As there is no place outside of discourse, freedom or emancipation from the power relations immanent in discourse are unthinkable. None the less, the conditions which make resistance possible are, he claims, inherent in all discourses and discursive relations. Such a view suggests that people are formed, at least in part, through the discourses which comprise the state's various institutions. Let us now explore this point a little.

Foucault links technologies of power with the emergence of the human sciences, the 'disciplines', arguing that they take people as both their object and their subject. They not only study practice, they bring it into effect. For Foucault, the power/knowledge couplet, which arises through the use to which government institutions put the human sciences, exists beneath the judicial and political structures which make up the state. The 'judicio political', according to Foucault, formally guarantees an egalitarian system of rights. The 'disciplines', however, run counter to such law, constructing inegalitarian technologies of power and regimes of truth. How does this happen?

Foucault discusses the individualizing and totalizing forms of power employed by institutions and governments via systems of power/knowledge relations. These individualizing techniques may be seen in Foucault's discussion of the three modes of the objectification of the subject (in Rabinow, 1984). He talks, for instance, of 'dividing practices'. This refers to those procedures which distribute, contain, manipulate and control people through the ways in which they classify and categorize them. Such methods divide people from each other and within themselves, giving them an identity which is both social and personal. In *Madness and Civilization* (1967), *The Birth of the Clinic* (1975) and *Discipline and Punish* (1977b), Foucault shows how 'dividing practices' interconnect with the growth of the social sciences, how they relate historically to humanitarian rhetoric of reform and progress, how they become increasingly efficient and widely applied, and how they were usually applied to dominated groups.

The totalization procedures identified by Foucault arose as governments came to accept responsibility for the economy, for order and for the lives of people through all aspects of society. This resulted in centralized administrative apparatuses and a 'will to knowledge' about people's everyday lives and the state's resources. Through an ever expanding archive containing intricate statistical details of individuals, the state developed an administrative grid which provided a means of both surveillance and regulation of everyday life. The human sciences assisted in this process through the provision of methods, plans, programmes, data and knowledge. The objectification of the human body via the combination of knowledge and power resulted in what Foucault calls 'disciplinary technologies'. The aim of such 'technologies', was to develop a 'docile body which may be subjected, used, transformed and improved' (in Rabinow, 1984).

The rationality accompanying these disciplinary technologies is primarily directed towards efficiency and productivity through a system of 'normalization' (in Gordon, 1989, pp. 104–8). This normative rationality has, Foucault claims, become an integral part of such state apparatuses as medicine, law and education. Matters of values, justice, right and wrong have been superseded by concern with the 'norm' and deviation from it. Normalizing technologies function to identify deviations. Other, accompanying, technologies provide corrective and disciplinary mechanisms. Such technologies include a vast apparatus for testing and documentation. Methods provided by the social sciences facilitate diagnostic and prognostic assessments and hierarchization, that is, normative judgements to be made about the individual. The 'objective' knowledges produced as a result of such inquisitions become part of the 'web of control' of the state bureaucracy. Thus, a characteristic feature of modern power structures is its capacity to both totalize and individualize the 'subject'. [...]

Given Foucault's rejection of 'Enlightenment', his tendency towards relativism, and his sceptical view of emancipation, what are the implications of his theories for the political practice of those who would challenge relationships of dominance and subordination which are institutionalized by the state's various bodies and process? This has been a matter of considerable speculation, and answers abound. My reading is that Foucault talks of a new politics of truth, saying:

> The problem is not changing people's consciousness—or what's in their heads—but the political, economic, institutional regime of the production of truth; to detach the power of truth from the forms of hegemony, social, economic and cultural within which it operates. (in Rabinow, 1984, pp. 74–5)

For Foucault, oppositional politics should take the form of critique, beginning with a suspicion of universal truths. He suggests 'maybe the target nowadays is not to discover what we are but to refuse what we are (in Rabinow, 1984, p. 22) and argues that:

> the real political task in a society such as ours is to criticize the workings of institutions which appear to be both neutral and independent; to criticize them in such a matter that the political violence which has always exercised itself obscurely through them, will be unmasked, so that one can fight them. (in Rabinow, 1984, p. 6)

In standing 'offside' in relation to certain knowledges, Foucault shows the value of refusing to think and act in accordance with the 'rules' of knowledge. As Biddy Martin (1988, p. 10) says: 'What is crucial is the capacity to shift the terms of the struggle, the ability to see our position within existing structures but to respond from somewhere else'. [...]

Foucault and feminism   Feminists who use Foucault's 'game openings' do not do so unreflectively and none fail to notice that gender does not particularly figure in his discussions of power/knowledge, rationality and sexuality. Sandra Lee Bartkey (1988, p. 63) notes that Foucault's 'docile bodies' are remarkably gender neutral, asserting that he is 'blind to those disciplines that produce a modality of embodiment that is peculiarly feminine'. As Bartkey also demonstrates, Foucault's focus on institutions ignores those disciplinary practices which are unbounded and which have particular implications for women. Her superb documentation of the disciplinary regime of femininity, and the forces and experts which produce the female body as a spectacle, shows how this regime is 'everywhere and it is nowhere; the disciplinarian is everyone and yet no-one in particular (Bartkey, 1988, p. 74). Feminists note further that despite Foucault's expressed interest in 'the insurrection of subjugated knowledges' and marginalized voices he pays little attention to feminist knowledge. None the less, Foucault has proved useful for feminists. [...]

Drawing from a foucaultian perspective, Judith Allen makes the case that feminism does not need a theory of the state. She says:

The state is a category of abstraction that is too aggregative, too unitary and too unspecific to be of much use in addressing the disaggregated, diverse and specific (or local) sites that must be of most pressing concern to feminists. 'The state' is too blunt an instrument to be of much assistance (beyond generalizations) in explanations, analyses or the design of workable strategies. (Allen, 1990, p. 22)

In contrast, Allen opts for historical and locational specificity in analysis, and suggests that feminist theory would be better informed by analyses of such discursive regimes as policing, legal culture, medical culture, bureaucratic culture and masculinity. Her implication is that feminist politics would be more effective if it recognized and targeted diverse and localized sites of struggle.

However, a foucaultian view of the workings of government institutions does not necessarily preclude a recognition of the existence of the macro structures of the state or macro forms of domination. As Biddy Martin (1988, p. 6), quoting Foucault, says: 'The state is not the origin but an overall strategy and effect, a composite result made up of a multiplicity of centers and mechanisms. What I am suggesting here is that discourse theory in general—and in particular such concepts as discourse, power/knowledge, technologies of power, dividing practices, regimes of truth, the politics of truth telling and so forth—may assist current feminist theories of the state to grapple with the fine grain of state politics. Such a view of the state challenges those theories which draw on the grand narratives of capitalism and patriarchy in a totalizing and simplistic manner, to identify the detail, complexity and subtlety of the workings of the state.

[...] Rosemary Pringle and Sophia Watson (1990), in the concluding chapter of *Playing the State* (Watson, 1990), draw on Foucault's conception of power, choosing to retain 'the state' as a concept, recognising it as a complex network of discursive practices. Further, Anna Yeatman (1990) suggests that a discourse-theoretical view of the state also has strategic implications for democratic practice. She argues that we must participate in the struggle over meaning, i.e. 'enter the politics of discourse', in order firstly to refuse 'the monological, mono-vocal and mono-centric constructions that non and anti-democratic individual groups and parties currently practice' (Yeatman, 1990, p. 151), and secondly to develop alternative meanings which help to produce a new reality by naming it.

In my view, developing a feminist foucaultian perspective on government institutions and their relationship to civil society need not mean abandoning our attempts to theorize and influence the state. What it does mean, however, is some careful work exploring the relationships between discourses. It means assessing the ways that micro powers intersect, articulate and rearticulate in order to bring about the effects of broad structural dominance. It also necessitates work which explores, empirically, how feminists have and might continue to participate in the politics of discourse. The overall lesson here is that feminist state theories must attend much more closely to post-structuralism in order for them to better understand the ways in which meaning is produced, distributed, negotiated and transformed in relation to the shifting articulations of power which comprise the state.

Using post-structuralism for feminist state theory: the difficulties and dilemmas
[...] There are, however, some important incompatibilities between the two bodies of literature which must be named and addressed.

One dilemma concerns the category 'woman' and the identity politics which arise from it. Post-structuralism has made the category women problematic. [...] Feminists recognize that women are usually positioned on the negative side of most dualities: man/woman, reason/emotion, culture/nature, public/private and so forth. For some feminists, the way around this problem is to celebrate what women have been socially constructed to become, and so to name women's side of the duality as positive. However, for those feminist post-structuralists who draw their inspiration from Derrida, this simply confirms the binary at the same time as escape from its problems is sought. For them, feminist politics must be about abandoning gender dualities altogether, and this also means abandoning the gendered dualities which often inform feminist critique, theory and political action: oppressor/oppressed; public/private and so on.

A discourse-theoretical perspective on subjectivity comes to the problem somewhat differently. According to Valerie Walkerdine (1981), females 'are not unitary subjects uniquely positioned, but produced as a nexus of subjectivities in relations of power which are constantly shifting'. This belief that women are constituted by discourse permits the recognition of differences amongst women of class, race, ethnicity, sexuality and so forth. It suggests that a woman is, in fact, many women, shifting her identity according to the range of discourses which make up her world and the moment. [...] She can also, of course, not be positioned or identified as a woman at all. Broadly, post-structuralism regards the categories 'woman' and indeed 'women' as fictions of discourse, and the task of feminism is seen to be the dismantling of the fiction.

Such views are a helpful corrective to the problems of binary logic and essentialism which are evident in some feminist theories of the state. However, they also place in jeopardy the notion of identity politics, and contrast particularly strongly with liberal and radical feminist approaches. If identity is so fractured, how can politics be based upon the notion of women? How can this emphasis on plurality recognize the extent to which discourse and subjectivity are located within broad and recognizable patterns of dominance and subordination which arise from intersecting structures of gender, class and race, and their institutionalization via the state? Indeed, Nancy Fraser and Linda Nicholson (1990, p. 20) accuse post-structuralism and postmodernism of political naivete, saying they 'prelude an arguably essential genre of political theory ... (namely) the identification and critique of macrostructures of inequality and injustices which cut across the boundaries separating relatively discrete practices and institutions'.

If theories cannot be built, and if political campaigns cannot be mounted, on the concept of woman or women and on such notions as inequality, subordination and oppression, then how can feminists play a role in the politics of the state? As Biddy Martin [1988, pp. 13–18] observes, post-structuralism runs the risk of conceptualizing notions of oppression, sexual difference and identity out of existence. Linda Alcoff sums up these points well when she asks:

> If gender is simply a social construct, the need and even the possibility of a feminist politics becomes immediately problematic. What can we demand in the name of women if 'women' do not exist and demands in their name simply reinforce the myth that they do? How can we speak out against sexism as detrimental to the interests of women if the category is a fiction? (Alcoff, 1988)

[...] This set of dilemmas alerts me to another. Post-structuralist feminism has most frequently been concerned with critique. Its politics are about deconstruction: 'refusing what we are'; exposing the politics of 'truth'. There are valuable lessons for other feminisms to learn here. Among other things, deconstructive methodologies encourage feminists to reflect on feminist thinking itself. If discourse is productive of subjectivity then this suggests that feminists must be wary of producing discourses which reduce woman to less than they are and might be or which prescribe for women what they should be. Such dangers are evident in radical and liberal feminist theories. Certainly, according to the edicts of post-structuralism, feminism must adopt a sustained deconstruction of itself: it must undo its own meanings and categories in the never-ending story of its development. But the difficulty that post-structuralism faces in making this point is that its construction of subjectivity denies intentionality, that is, it will not recognize the subject's ability to reflect on discourse and to challenge its determination. No longer positioned by patriarchal truths, are women again to be denied agency and to be equally helplessly positioned by new feminist truths? Indeed, if truth has no guarantees then how can feminism justify its existence given that its historical understanding has been that women live out their lives in various conditions of subordination? If all truths are relative, then why seek to build feminist theory? In such a scenario does a feminist theory of the state, or anything else for that matter, have any place at all? (Harstock, 1990.) Is there no longer any possibility of political and theoretical coherence for feminism? Do feminism's truths simply service feminism's truth tellers and the status of feminist knowledge itself? Clearly then, there are a number of problems for feminists in abandoning the Enlightenment belief that science and reason will lead to the discovery of knowledge and truth.

Of course, when it comes to the politics of the state, deconstruction is not enough. As Linda Alcoff (1988: 270) observes: 'Following Foucault and Derrida, an effective feminism could only be a wholly negative feminism, deconstructing everything and refusing to construct anything.' According to Alcoff, 'negative struggle' cannot be the only form of struggle. She says 'you cannot mobilize a movement that is only and always against; you must have a positive alternative, a vision of a better future that can motivate people to sacrifice their time and energy toward its realization (Alcoff, 1988, pp. 270–1).

Clearly those feminist politics which are directed at the state must involve critique and vision, but they must also offer suggestions for strategy and organization. Interestingly, radical and liberal feminism are strong on all four necessities, while socialist feminism, like post-structuralist feminism, stops short at critique.

At this stage it is not at all clear how post-structuralist feminism can deal with these epistemological and very much political dilemmas. This problem is one which is currently engaging much feminist energy and the outcomes of such engagements have very evident implications for feminist theories of the state and, by implication, strategies to assist women's action in and on the state. Linda Nicholson's (1990) edited collection *Feminism/Postmodernism* brings together many writers who, although coming from a range of different feminist positions, engage critically and positively with the relationship between feminism and postmodernism in its post-structuralist and other manifestations. [. . .]

Nancy Fraser and Linda Nicholson (1990, p. 20) argue that the arrival of postmodernism on the scene need not 'demand the elimination of all big theory, much less theory *per se*, to avoid totalization and essentialism. They make the case for theorizing which situates its concepts within explicitly cultural and historical contexts and frameworks.

CONCLUSION

Post-structuralist and, more broadly, postmodernist feminism have provided feminist theories of the state, and feminist theory more generally, with some inescapable challenges. And the practical necessity for feminism to act in and on the state has set postmodernism and post-structuralism a demanding political and theoretical task. The extent to which feminists are able to work through and beyond the tensions between modernist and postmodernist feminisms towards feminist theories of the state which accommodate and transcend the best of both worlds will determine whether, in the future, feminist state theory is 'to be or not to be'.

Acknowledgement

I wish to thank Lindsay Fitzclarence and Bill Green for their helpful comments on earlier drafts of this article.

References

Alcoff, L. (1988) Cultural feminism versus post-structuralism. In E. Minnich, J. O'Barr and R. Rosenfield (eds) *Reconstructing the Academy: Women's Education and Women's Studies* (pp. 257–89). Chicago: University of Chicago Press.

Allen, J. (1990) Does feminism need a theory of the state? In S. Watson (ed.) *Playing the State: Australian Feminist Interventions* (pp. 21–37). Sydney: Allen & Unwin.

Bartkey, S. Lee (1988) Foucault, femininity and the modernisation of patriarchal power. In I. Diamond and L. Quinby (eds) *Feminism and Foucault: Reflections on Resistance* (pp. 61–86). Boston, MA: Northeastern University Press.

Benton, T. (1984) *The Rise and Fall of Structural Marxism: Althusser and His Influence.* London: Macmillan.

Diamond, I. and Quinby, L. (eds) (1988) *Feminism and Foucault: Reflections on Resistance.* Boston, MA: Northeastern University Press.

Foucault, M. (1967) *Madness and Civilization.* New York: Pantheon.

— (1975) *The Birth of the Clinic.* New York: Vintage Books, Random House.

— (1976) Politics: the study of discourse. *Ideology & Consciousness* 3, 7–26.

— (1977a) *The Archeology of Knowledge.* London: Tavistock.

— (1977b) *Discipline and Punish: The Birth of the Prison.* London: Penguin.

— (1981) *The History of Sexuality, Volume One: An Introduction.* Harmondsworth: Pelican.

Franzway, S., Court, D. and Connell, R.W. (1989) *Staking a Claim: Feminism, Bureaucracy and the State.* Sydney: Allen & Unwin.

Fraser, N. and Nicholson, L. (1990) Social criticism without philosophy. In L.J. Nicholson (ed.) *Feminism/Postmodernism* (pp. 19–35). New York: Routledge.

Gordon. C. (ed.) (1989) *Michael Foucault, Power/Knowledge: Selected Interviews and other Writings 1972–1977.* Brighton: Harvester Press.

Harstock, N. (1990) Foucault on power: a theory for women? In L.J. Nicholson (ed.) *Feminism/Postmodernism* (pp. 157–76). New York: Routledge.

Hartman, H. (1981) The unhappy marriage of Marxism and feminism: towards a more progressive union. In L. Sargent (ed.) *Women and Revolution* (pp. 1–41). Boston, MA: South End Press.

Hinkson, J. (1990) Post modernism and structural change. *Public Culture* 2, 2, Spring, 82–101.

MacKinnon, C. (1989) *Toward a Feminist Theory of the State.* Cambridge, MA: Harvard University Press.

Martin, B. (1988) Feminism, criticism and Foucault. In I. Diamond and L. Quinby (eds) *Feminism and Foucault: Reflections on Resistance* (pp. 3–19). Boston, MA: Northeastern University Press.

Minson, J. (1980) Strategies for socialists: Foucault's conception of power. *Economy and Society* 19, 1, 1–43.

Morris, M. (1988) *The Pirate's Fiancée: Feminism and Reading, Postmodernism.* London: Virso.

Mumford, K. (1989) *Women Working: Economics and Reality.* Sydney: Allen & Unwin.

Nicholson, L.J. (ed.) (1990) *Feminism/Postmodernism.* New York: Routledge.

Pateman, C. (1987) Feminist critiques of the public/private dichotomy. In A. Phillips (ed.) *Feminism and Equality* (pp. 103–27). Oxford: Basil Blackwell.

— (1989) *The Sexual Contract.* Cambridge: Polity Press.

Phillips, A. (ed.) (1987) *Feminism and Equality.* Oxford: Basil Blackwell.

Pringle, R. and Watson, S. (1990) Fathers, brothers, mates: the fraternal state in Australia. In S. Watson (ed.) *Playing the State: Australian Feminist Interventions* (pp. 179–229). Sydney: Allen & Unwin.

Rabinow, P. (ed.) (1984) *The Foucault Reader.* New York: Pantheon Books.
Sawyer, M. (1990) *Sisters in Suits: Women and Public Policy in Australia.* Sydney: Allen & Unwin.
Showstack Sassoon, A. (ed.) (1987) *Women and the State: The Shifting Boundaries of Public and Private.* London: Hutchinson.
Smart, B. (1983) *Foucault, Marxism and Critique.* London: Routledge & Kegan Paul.
Walderkine, V. (1981) Sex, power and pedagogy. *Screen Education* 38, 14–24.
Weedon, C. (1987) *Feminist Practice and Post-structuralist Theory.* Oxford: Paul Blackwell.
Wilson, E. (1977) *Women and the Welfare State.* London: Tavistock.
Yeatman, A. (1990) *Bureaucrats, Technocrats, Femocrats.* Sydney: Allen & Unwin.
Young, R. (ed.) (1981) *Untying the Text: A Post Structuralist Reader.* London: Routledge & Kegan Paul.

11 POSTMODERNISM AND GENDER RELATIONS IN FEMINIST THEORY

JANE FLAX

As the thought of the world, (philosophy) appears only when actuality is already there cut and dried after its process of formation has been completed . . . When philosophy paints its grey in grey, then has a shape of life grown old. By philosophy's grey in grey it cannot be rejuvenated but only understood. The owl of Minerva spreads its wings only with the falling of the dusk. (G.W.F. Hegel, preface to *Philosophy of Right*)

It seems increasingly probable that Western culture is in the middle of a fundamental transformation: A 'shape of life' is growing old. In retrospect, this transformation may be as radical (but as gradual) as the shift from a medieval to a modern society. Accordingly, this moment in the history of the West is pervaded by a profound yet little comprehended change, uncertainty, and ambivalence. This transitional state makes certain forms of thought possible and necessary, and it excludes others. It generates problems that some philosophies seem to acknowledge and confront better than others.

I think there are currently three kinds of thinking that best present (and represent) our own time apprehended in thought: psychoanalysis, feminist theory, and postmodern philosophy. These ways of thinking reflect and are partially constituted by Enlightenment beliefs still prevalent in Western (especially American) culture. At the same time, they offer ideas and insights that are only possible because of the breakdown of Enlightenment beliefs under the cumulative pressure of historical events such as the invention of the atomic bomb, the Holocaust, and the war in Vietnam.[1][. . .]

My focus here will be mainly on one of these modes of thinking: feminist theory. I will consider what it could be, and I will reflect upon the goals, logics and problematics of feminist theorizing as it has been practised since the mid 1980s in the West. I will also place such theorizing within the social and philosophical contexts of which it is both a part and a critique. [. . .]

A fundamental goal of feminist theory is (and ought to be) to analyze

Source: Nicholson, L. (ed.) (1990) *Feminism/Postmodernism* (pp. 36 – 62). London: Routledge.

gender relations: how gender relations are constituted and experienced and how we think or, equally important, do not think about them.[2] The study of gender relations includes, but is not limited to, what are often considered the distinctively feminist issues: the situation of women and the analysis of male domination. Feminist theory includes an (at least implicit) prescriptive element as well. By studying gender we hope to gain a critical distance on existing gender arrangements. This critical distance can help clear a space in which reevaluating and altering our existing gender arrangements may become more possible.

Feminist theory by itself cannot clear such a space. Without feminist political actions, theories remain inadequate and ineffectual. [. . .]

METATHEORY

Feminist theory seems to me to belong within two, more inclusive, categories with which it has special affinity: the analysis of social relations and postmodern philosophy.[3] Gender relations enter into and are constituent elements in every aspect of human experience. In turn, the experience of gender relations for any person and the structure of gender as a social category are shaped by the interactions of gender relations and other social relations such as class and race. Gender relations thus have no fixed essence; they vary both within and over time.

As a type of postmodern philosophy, feminist theory reveals and contributes to the growing uncertainty within Western intellectual circles about the appropriate grounding and methods for explaining and interpreting human experience. Contemporary feminists join other postmodern philosophers in raising important metatheoretical questions about the possible nature and status of theorizing itself. [. . .]

Postmodern philosophers seek to throw into radical doubt beliefs still prevalent in (especially American) culture but derived from the Enlightenment, such as the following:

(1) The existence of a stable, coherent self. Distinctive properties of this Enlightenment self include a form of reason capable of privileged insight into its own processes and into the 'laws of nature'.

(2) Reason and its 'science'—philosophy—can provide an objective, reliable, and universal foundation for knowledge.

(3) The knowledge acquired from the right use of reason will be 'true'—for example, such knowledge will represent something real and unchanging (universal) about our minds and the structure of the natural world.

(4) Reason itself has transcendental and universal qualities. It exists independently of the self's contingent existence (e.g. bodily, historical, and social experiences do not affect reason's structure or its capacity to produce atemporal knowledge).

(5) There are complex connections between reason, autonomy, and freedom.

All claims to truth and rightful authority are to be submitted to the tribunal of reason. Freedom consists of obedience to laws that conform to the necessary results of the right use of reason. [...] In obeying such laws, I am obeying my own best transhistorical part (reason) and hence am exercising my own autonomy and ratifying my existence as a free being. [...]

(6) By grounding claims to authority in reason, the conflicts between truth, knowledge, and power can be overcome. Truth can serve power without distortion; in turn, by utilizing knowledge in the service of power, both freedom and progress will be assured. Knowledge can be both neutral (e.g. grounded in universal reason, not particular 'interests') and also socially beneficial.

(7) Science, as the exemplar of the right use of reason, is also the paradigm for all true knowledge. Science is neutral in its methods and contents but socially beneficial in its results. [...]

(8) Language is in some sense transparent. Just as the right use of reason can result in knowledge that represents the real, so too, language is merely the medium in and through which such representation occurs. There is a correspondence between word and thing (as between a correct truth claim and the real). Objects are not linguistically (or socially) constructed; they are merely made present to consciousness by naming and the right use of language.

[...] Despite an understandable attraction to the (apparently) logical, orderly world of the Enlightenment, feminist theory more properly belongs in the terrain of postmodern philosophy. Feminist notions of the self, knowledge, and truth are too contradictory to those of the Enlightenment to be contained within its categories. The way(s) to feminist future(s) cannot lie in reviving or appropriating Enlightenment concepts of the person or knowledge.[4]

Feminist theorists enter into and echo postmodernist discourses as we have begun to deconstruct notions of reason, knowledge, or the self and to reveal the effects of the gender arrangements that lay beneath their neutral and universalizing facades. (See Jardine, 1985; Haraway, 1983; Ferguson, 1984; Irigaray, 1985). [...]

In fact, feminists, like other postmodernists, have begun to suspect that all transcendental claims reflect and reify the experience of a few persons — mostly white, Western males. These transhistoric claims seem plausible to us in part because they reflect important aspects of the experience of those who dominate our social world.

A FEMINIST PROBLEMATIC

[...]To understand the goals of feminist theory we must consider its central subject—gender.

Here, however, we immediately plunge into a complicated and controversial morass. For among feminist theorists there is by no means consensus on such (apparently) elementary questions as: What is gender? How is it related to anatomical sexual differences? How are gender relations constituted and sustained (in one person's lifetime and, more generally, as a social experience over time)? How do gender relations relate to other sorts of social relations such as class or race? Do gender relations have a history (or many)? What causes gender relations to change over time? What are the relationships between gender relations, sexuality, and a sense of individual identity? What are the relationships between heterosexuality, homosexuality, and gender relations? Are there only two genders? What are the relationships between forms of male dominance and gender relations? Could/would gender relations wither away in egalitarian societies? Is there anything distinctively male or female in modes of thought and social relations? If there is, are these distinctions innate or socially constituted? Are gendered distinctions socially useful or necessary? If so, what are the consequences for the feminist goal of attaining gender justice? (Stacey, 1983; Chodorow, 1985).

Confronted with such a bewildering set of questions, it is easy to overlook the fact that a fundamental transformation in social theory has occurred. The single most important advance in feminist theory is that the existence of gender relations has been problematized. Gender can no longer be treated as a simple, natural fact. [...]

Contemporary feminist movements are in part rooted in transformations in social experience that challenge widely shared categories of social meaning and explanation. In the United States, such transformations include changes in the structure of the economy, the family, the place of the United States in the world system, the declining authority of previously powerful social institutions, and the emergence of political groups that have increasingly more divergent ideas and demands concerning justice, equality, social legislation, and the proper role of the state. In such a decentered and unstable universe it seems plausible to question one of the most natural facets of human existence—gender relations. On the other hand, such instability also makes old modes of social relations more attractive. [...]

THINKING IN RELATIONS

'Gender relations' is a category meant to capture a complex set of social processes. Gender, both as an analytic category and a social process, is relational. That is, gender relations are complex and unstable processes (or temporary totalities in the language of dialectics) constituted by and through interrelated parts. These parts are interdependent, that is, each part can have no meaning or existence without the others.

Gender relations are differentiated and (so far) asymmetric divisions and attributions of human traits and capacities. Through gender relations two types of persons are created: man and woman. Man and woman are posited as exclusionary categories. One can be only one gender, never the other or both. The actual content of being a man or woman and the rigidity of the categories themselves are highly variable across cultures and time. Nevertheless, gender relations so far as we have been able to understand them have been (more or less) relations of domination. That is, gender relations have been (more) defined and (imperfectly) controlled by one of their inter-related aspects—the man.

These relations of domination and the existence of gender relations themselves have been concealed in a variety of ways, including defining women as a 'question' or the 'sex' or the 'other'.[5] and men as the universal (or at least without gender). In a wide variety of cultures and discourses, men tend to be seen as free from or as not determined by gender relations. Thus, for example, academics do not explicitly study the psychology of men or men's history. Male academics do not worry about how being men may distort their intellectual work, while women who study gender relations are considered suspect (of triviality, if not bias). [. . .]

To the extent that feminist discourse defines its problematic as 'woman', it, too, ironically privileges the man as unproblematic or exempted from determination by gender relations. From the perspective of social relations, men and women are both prisoners of gender, although in highly differentiated but interrelated ways. That men appear to be and (in many cases) are the wardens, or at least the trustees within a social whole, should not blind us to the extent to which they, too, are governed by the rules of gender. [. . .]

THEORIZING AND DECONSTRUCTION

The study of gender relations entails at least two levels of analysis: of gender as a thought construct or category that helps us to make sense out of particular social worlds and histories, and of gender as a social relation that enters into and partially constitutes all other social relations and activities. As a practical social relation, gender can be understood only by close examination of the meanings of 'male' and 'female' and the consequences being assigned to one or the other gender within concrete social practices.

Obviously, such meanings and practices will vary by culture, age, class, race, and time. We cannot presume *a priori* that in any particular culture there will be a single determinant or cause of gender relations, much less that we can tell beforehand what this cause (or these causes) might be. Feminist theorists have offered a variety of interesting casual explanations including the sex/gender system, the organization of production of sexual division of labour, child-rearing practices, and processes of signification or language. These all provide useful hypotheses for the concrete study of gender relations in particular societies, but each explanatory scheme also seems to me to be deeply flawed, inadequate, and overly deterministic.

For example, Gayle Rubin (1975) locates the origin of gender systems in the 'transformation of raw biological sex into gender'. However, Rubin's distinction between sex and gender rests in turn upon a series of oppositions that I find very problematic, including the opposition of 'raw biological sexuality' and the social. This opposition reflects the idea predominant in the work of Freud, Lacan, and others that a person is driven by impulses and needs that are invariant and invariably asocial. This split between culture and natural sexuality may in fact be rooted in and reflect gender arrangements. [. . .]

Socialist feminists locate the fundamental cause of gender arrangements in the organization of production or the sexual division of labour. However, this explanatory system also incorporates the historical and philosophical flaws of Marxist analysis. Marxists (including socialist feminists) uncritically apply the categories Marx derived from his description of a particular form of the production of commodities to all areas of human life at all historical periods. Socialist feminists replicate this privileging of production and the division of labour with the concomitant assumptions concerning the centrality of labour itself. Labour is still seen as the essence of history and being human. Such conceptions distort life in capitalist society and surely are not appropriate to all other cultures.[6]

An example of the problems that follow from this uncritical appropriation of Marxist concepts can be found in the attempts by socialist feminists to widen the concept of production to include most forms of human activity. These arguments avoid an essential question: Why widen the concept of production instead of dislodging it or any other singularly central concept from such authoritative power?

This question becomes more urgent when it appears that, despite the best efforts of socialist feminists, the Marxist concepts of labour and production invariably exclude or distort many kinds of activity, including those traditionally performed by women. Pregnancy and child rearing or relations between family members more generally cannot be comprehended merely as 'property relations in action' (Kuhn, 1978, p. 53). Sexuality cannot be understood as an exchange of physical energy, with a surplus (potentially) flowing to an exploiter (Ferguson, 1984). Such concepts also ignore or obscure the existence and activities of other persons as well—children—for whom at least a part of their formative experiences has nothing to do with production.

However, the structure of child-rearing practices also cannot serve as the root of gender relations. Among the many problems with this approach is that it cannot explain why women have the primary responsibility for child rearing; it can explain only some of the consequences of this fact. In other words, the child-rearing practices taken as causal already presuppose the very social relations we are trying to understand: a gender-based division of human activities and hence the existence of socially constructed sets of gender arrangements and the (peculiar and in need of explanation) salience of gender itself.

The emphasis that (especially) French feminists place on the centrality of language (e.g. chains of signification, signs, and symbols) to the construction of gender also seems problematic.[7] A problem with thinking about (or only in terms of) texts, signs, or signification is that they tend to take on a life of their own or become the world, as the claim that nothing exists outside of a text; everything is a comment upon or a displacement of another text, as if the model human activity is literary criticism (or writing).

Such an approach obscures the projection of its own activity onto the world and denies the existence of the variety of concrete social practices that enter into and are reflected in the constitution of language itself (e.g. ways of life constitute language and texts as much as language constitutes ways of life). This lack of attention to concrete social relations (including the distribution of power) results, as in Lacan's work, in the obscuring of relations of domination. Such relations (including gender arrangements) then tend to acquire an aura of inevitability and become equated with language or culture (the 'law of the father') as such. [...]

All of these social practices posited as explanations for gender arrangements may be more or less important, interrelated, or themselves partially constituted in and through gender relations depending upon context. As in any form of social analysis, the study of gender relations will necessarily reflect the social practices it attempts to understand. There cannot, nor should we expect there to be, a feminist equivalent to (a falsely universalizing) Marxism; indeed, the epistemologies of feminism undercut all such claims, including feminist ones.[8]

[...] We cannot simultaneously claim (1) that the mind, the self, and knowledge are socially constituted and that what we can know depends upon our social practices and contexts and (2) that feminist theory can uncover the truth of the whole once and for all. Such an absolute truth (e.g. the explanation for all gender arrangements at all times is X) would require the existence of an Archimedes point outside of the whole and beyond our embeddedness in it from which we could see (and represent) the whole. What we see and report would also have to be untransformed by the activities of perception and of reporting our vision in language. The object seen (social whole or gender arrangement) would have to be apprehended by an empty (ahistoric) mind and perfectly transcribed by/into a transparent language. The possibility of each of these conditions existing has been rendered extremely doubtful by the deconstructions of postmodern philosophers.

[...] Any episteme requires the suppression of discourses that threaten to differ with or undermine the authority of the dominant one. Hence, within feminist theory a search for a defining theme of the whole or a feminist viewpoint may require the suppression of the important and discomforting voices of persons with experiences unlike our own. The suppression of these voices seems to be a necessary condition for the (apparent) authority, coherence, and universality of our own.

Thus, the very search for a root or cause of gender relations (or more narrowly, male domination) may partially reflect a mode of thinking that is itself grounded in particular forms of gender (and/or other) relations in which domination is present. [...] Criteria of theory construction such as parsimony or simplicity may be attained only by the suppression or denial of the experiences of the other(s).

THE NATURAL BARRIER

Thus, in order for gender relations to be useful as a category of social analysis we must be as socially and self-critical as possible about the meanings usually attributed to those relations and the ways we think about them. Otherwise, we run the risk of replicating the very social relations we are attempting to understand. We have to be able to investigate both the social and philosophical barriers to our comprehension of gender relations.

One important barrier to our comprehension of gender relations has been the difficulty of understanding the relationship between *gender* and *sex*. In this context, *sex* means the anatomical differences between male and female. Historically (at least since Aristotle), these anatomical differences have been assigned to the class of natural facts or biology. In turn, biology has been equated with the pre- or nonsocial. Gender relations then become conceptualized as if they are constituted by two opposite terms or distinct types of being—man and woman. Since man and woman seem to be opposites or fundamentally distinct types of being, gender cannot be relational. If gender is as natural and as intrinsically a part of us as the genitals we are born with, it follows that it would be foolish (or even harmful) to attempt either to change gender arrangements or not to take them into account as a delimitation on human activities.

Even though a major focus of feminist theory has been to denaturalize gender, feminists as well as nonfeminists seem to have trouble thinking through the meanings we assign to and the uses we make of the concept 'natural'.[9] What, after all, is the natural in the context of the human world? There are many aspects of our embodiedness or biology that we might see as given limits to human action which Western medicine and science do not hesitate to challenge. For example, few Westerners would refuse to be vaccinated against diseases that our bodies are naturally susceptible to, although in some cultures such actions would be seen as violating the natural order. The tendency of Western science is to disenchant the natural world (Weber, 1972; Horkheimer and Adorno, 1972). More and more the natural ceases to exist as the opposite of the cultural or social. Nature becomes the object and product of human action; it loses its independent existence. Ironically, the more such disenchantment proceeds, the more humans seem to need something that remains outside our powers of transformation. Until recently, one such exempt area seemed to be anatomical differences between males and females.[10] Thus, in order to save nature (from ourselves) many people in the contemporary West equate sex/biology/nature/gender and oppose these to the cultural/social/human. Concepts of gender then become complex metaphors for ambivalences about human action in, on, and as part of the natural world.

But the use of gender as a metaphor for such ambivalences blocks further investigation of them. [...] What remains masked in these modes of thought is the possibility that our concepts of biology and nature are rooted in social relations; they do not merely reflect the given structure of reality itself.

Thus, in order to understand gender as a social relation, feminist theorists need to deconstruct further the meanings we attach to biology/sex/gender/nature. This process of deconstruction is far from complete and certainly is not easy. Initally, some feminists thought we could merely separate the terms *sex* and *gender*. As we became more sensitive to the social histories of concepts, it became clear that such an (apparent) disjunction, while politically necessary, rested upon problematic and culture-specific oppositions, for example, the one between nature and culture or body and mind. As some feminists began to rethink these oppositions, new questions emerged: Does anatomy (body) have no relation to mind? What difference does it make in the constitution of my social experiences that I have a specifically female body?

Despite the increasing complexity of our questions, most feminists would still insist that gender relations are not (or are not only) equivalent to or a consequence of anatomy. Everyone will agree that there are anatomical differences between men and women. These anatomical differences seem to be primarily located in or are the consequence of the differentiated contributions men and women make to a common biological necessity—the physical reproduction of our species.

However, the mere existence of such anatomical differentiation is a descriptive fact, one of many observations we might make about the physical characteristics of humans. [...]

It is also the case that physically male and female humans resemble each other in many more ways than we differ. Our similarities are even more striking if we compare humans to, say, toads or trees. So why ought the anatomical differences between male and female humans assume such significance in our sense of our selves as persons? Why ought such complex human social meanings and structures be based on or justified by a relatively narrow range of anatomical differences?

One possible answer to these questions is that the anatomical differences between males and females are connected to and are partially a consequence of one of the most important functions of the species—its physical reproduction. Thus, we might argue, because reproduction is such an important aspect of our species life, characteristics associated with it will be much more salient to us than, say, hair colour or height.

Another possible answer to these questions might be that in order for humans physically to reproduce the species, we have to have sexual intercourse. Our anatomical differences make possible (and necessary for physical reproduction) a certain fitting together of distinctively male and female organs. For some humans this 'fitting together' is also highly desirable and pleasurable. Hence, our anatomical differences seem to be inextricably connected to (and in some sense even causative of) sexuality. [. . .]

A problem with all these apparently obvious associations is that they may assume precisely what requires explanation—that is, gender relations. We live in a world in which gender is a constituting social relation and in which gender is also a relation of domination. Therefore, both men's and women's understanding of anatomy, biology, embodiedness, sexuality, and reproduction is partially rooted in, reflects, and must justify (or challenge) pre-existing gender relations. In turn, the existence of gender relations helps us to order and understand the facts of human existence. In other words, gender can become a metaphor for biology just as biology can become a metaphor for gender.

PRISONERS OF GENDER

The apparent connections between gender relations and such important aspects of human existence as birth, reproduction, and sexuality make possible both a conflating of the natural and the social and an overly radical distinction between the two. In modern Western culture and sometimes even in feminist theories, the words *natural* and *social* become conflated in our understanding of 'woman'. In nonfeminist and some feminist writings about women, a radical disjunction is frequently made between the natural and the social. Women often stand for/symbolize the body, 'difference', the concrete. These qualities are also said by some feminist as well as nonfeminist writers to suffuse/define the activities most associated with women: nurturing, mothering, taking care of and being in relation with others, preserving (compare Ruddick, 1984a; 1984b). Women's minds are also often seen as reflecting the qualities of our stereotypically female activities and bodies. Even feminists sometimes say women reason and write differently and have different interests and motives than men.[11] Men are said to have more interest in utilizing the power of abstract reason (mind), to want mastery over nature (including bodies), and to be aggressive and militaristic.

The re-emergence of such claims even among some feminists needs further analysis. Is this the beginning of a genuine transvaluation of values or a retreat into traditional gendered ways of understanding the world? In our attempts to correct arbitrary (and gendered) distinctions, feminists often end up reproducing them. Feminist discourse is full of contradictory and irreconcilable conceptions of the nature of our social relations, of men and women and the worth and character of stereotypically masculine and feminine activities. The positing of these conceptions such that only one perspective can be correct (or properly feminist) reveals, among other things, the embeddedness of feminist theory in the very social processes we are trying to critique and our need for more systematic and self-conscious theoretical practice.

As feminist theorizing is presently practised, we seem to lose sight of the possibility that each of our conceptions of a practice (e.g. mothering) may capture an aspect of a very complex and contradictory set of social relations. Confronted with complex and changing relations, we try to reduce these to simple, unified, and undifferentiated wholes. We search for closure, or the right answer, or the motor of the history of male domination. The complexity of our questions and the variety of the approaches to them are taken by some feminists as well as nonfeminists as signs of weakness or failure to meet the strictures of pre-existing theories rather than as symptoms of the permeability and pervasiveness of gender relations and the need for new sorts of theorizing. [...]

Within feminist discourse, women sometimes seem to become the sole bearers of both embodiedness and difference. Thus, we see arguments for the necessity to preserve a gender-based division of labour as our last protection from a state power that is depersonalizing and atomizing (see, e.g. Bethke Elshtaine, 1981; 1982). In such arguments the family is posited as an intimate, affective realm of natural relations—of kinship ties, primarily between mothers, children, and female kin—and it is discussed in opposition to the impersonal realms of the state and work (the worlds of men). Alternatively, feminists sometimes simply deny that there are any significant differences between women and men and that insofar as such differences exist, women should become more like men (or engage in men's activities). Or, the family is understood only as the site of gender struggle and the reproduction of person—a miniature political economy with its own division of labour, source of surplus (women's labour), and product (children and workers).[12] The complex fantasies and conflicting wishes and experiences women associate with family and home often remains unexpressed and unacknowledged. Lacking such self-analysis, feminists find it difficult to recognize some of the sources of our differences or to accept that we do not necessarily share the same past or share needs in the present.[13]

Female sexuality is sometimes reduced to an expression of male dominance, as when Catherine MacKinnon (1982, p. 531) claims 'gender socialization is the process through which women come to identify themselves as sexual beings, as beings that exist for men'. Among many other problems, such a definition leaves unexplained how women could ever feel lust for other women and the wide variety of other sensual experiences women claim to have—for example, in masturbation, breast feeding, or playing with children. Alternatively, the essence of female sexuality is said to be rooted in the quasi-biological primal bonds between mother and daughter.[14]

For some theorists, our fantasy and internal worlds have expression only in symbols, not in actual social relations. For example, Iris Young (1984) claims that gender differentiation as a category refers only to 'ideas, symbols, and forms of consciousness'.[15] In this view, fantasy, our inner worlds, and sexuality may structure intimate relations between women and men at home, but they are rarely seen as also entering into and shaping the structure of work and the state. Thus, feminist theory recreates its own version of the public/ private split. Alternatively, as in some radical feminist accounts, innate male drives, especially aggression and the need to dominate others are posited as the motor that drives the substance and teleology of history (as in Firestone, 1970; Mackinnon, 1982).

Feminist theorists have delineated many of the ways in which women's consciousness is shaped by mothering, but we often still see fathering as somehow extrinsic to men's and children's consciousness (see Chodorow and Contratto, 1983). The importance of modes of child rearing to women's status and to women's and men's sense of self is emphasized in feminist theory; yet we still write social theory in which everyone is presumed to be an adult. For example, in two collections of feminist theory focusing on mothering and the family (Trebilcot, 1984; Thorne and Yalom, 1983),there is almost no discussion of children as human beings or mothering as a relation between persons. The modal 'person' in feminist theory still appears to be a self-sufficient individual adult.

These difficulties in thinking have social as well as philosophical roots, including the existence of relations of domination and the psychological consequences of our current modes of child rearing. In order to sustain domination, the interrelation and interdependence of one group with another must be denied. Connections can be traced only so far before they begin to be politically dangerous. For example, few white feminists have explored how our understandings of gender relations and theory are partially constituted in and through the experiences of living in a culture in which asymmetric race relations are a central organizing principle of society.[16]

Furthermore, just as our current gender arrangements create men who have difficulties in acknowledging relations between people and experiences, they produce women who have difficulties in acknowledging differences within relations. In either gender, these social relations produce a disposition to treat experience as all of one sort or another and to be intolerant of differences, ambiguity and conflict.

The enterprise of feminist theory is fraught with temptations and pitfalls. In so far as women have been part of all societies, our thinking cannot be free from culture-bound modes of self-understanding. We as well as men internalize the dominant gender's conceptions of masculinity and femininity. Unless we see gender as a social relation rather than as an opposition of inherently different beings, we will not be able to identify the varieties and limitations of different women's (or men's) powers and oppressions within particular societies. Feminist theorists are faced with a fourfold task. We need to (1) articulate feminist viewpoints of/within the social worlds in which we live; (2) think about how we are affected by these worlds; (3) consider the ways in which how we think about them may be implicated in existing power/knowledge relationships; and (4) imagine ways in which these worlds ought to and can be transformed.

Since within contemporary Western societies gender relations have been ones of domination, feminist theories should have a compensatory as well as a critical aspect. That is, we need to recover and explore the aspects of social relations that have been suppressed, unarticulated, or denied within dominant (male) viewpoints. We need to recover and write the histories of women and our activities into the accounts and stories that cultures tell about themselves. Yet, we also need to think about how so-called women's activities are partially constituted by and through their location within the web of social relations that make up any society. That is, we need to know how these activities are affected but also how they effect, enable, or compensate for the consequences of men's activities, as well as their implication in class or race relations.

There should also be a transvaluation of values—a rethinking of our ideas about what is humanly excellent, worthy of praise, or moral. In such a transvaluation, we need to be careful not to assert merely the superiority of the opposite. [. . .] Our upbringing as women in this culture often encourages us to deny the many subtle forms of aggression that intimate relations with others can evoke and entail. For example, much of the discussion of mothering and the distinctively female tends to avoid discussing women's anger and aggression—how we internalize them and express them, for example, in relation to children or our own internal selves.[17] [. . .]

Since we live in a society in which men have more power than women, it makes sense to assume that what is considered to be more worthy of praise may be those qualities associated with men. As feminists, we have the right to suspect that even praise of the female may be (at least in part) motivated by a wish to keep women in a restricted (and restrictive) place. Indeed, we need to search into all aspects of a society (the feminist critique included) for the expressions and consequences of relations of domination. We should insist that all such relations are social, that is, they are not the result of the differentiated possession of natural and unequal properties among types of persons.

However, in insisting upon the existence and power of such relations of domination, we should avoid seeing women/ourselves as totally innocent, passive beings. Such a view prevents us from seeing the areas of life in which women have had an effect, in which we are less determined by the will of the other(s), and in which some of us have and do exert power over others (e.g. the differential privileges of race, class, sexual preference, age, or location in the world system).

Any feminist standpoint will necessarily be partial. Thinking about women may illuminate some aspects of a society that have been previously suppressed within the dominant view. But none of us can speak for 'woman' because no such person exists except within a specific set of (already gendered) relations—to 'man' and to many concrete and different women.

Indeed, the notion of a feminist standpoint that is truer than previous (male) ones seems to rest upon many problematic and unexamined assumptions. These include an optimistic belief that people act rationally in their own interests and that reality has a structure that perfect reason (once perfected) can discover. Both of these assumptions in turn depend upon an uncritical appropriation of the Enlightenment ideas discussed earlier. Furthermore, the notion of such a standpoint also assumes that the oppressed are not in fundamental ways damaged by their social experience. On the contrary, this position assumes that the oppressed have a privileged (and not just different) relation and ability to comprehend a reality that is out there waiting for our representation. [. . .]

I believe, on the contrary, that there is no force or reality outside our social relations and activity (e.g. history, reason, progress, science, some transcendental essence) that will rescue us from partiality and differences. Our lives and alliances belong with those who seek to further decentre the world—although we should reserve the right to be suspicious of their motives and visions as well.[18] Feminist theories, like other forms of postmodernism, should encourage us to tolerate and interpret ambivalence, ambiguity, and multiplicity as well as to expose the roots of our needs for imposing order and structure no matter how arbitrary and oppressive these needs may be.

If we do our work well, reality will appear even more unstable, complex, and disorderly than it does now. In this sense, perhaps Freud (1961, pp. 50–1) was right when he declared that women are the enemies of civilization.

Notes

1. For a more extended discussion of these claims, see Flax (1980)
2. Representative examples of feminist theories include Barbara Smith (1983); Cherrie Moraga and Gloria Anzaldua (1981); Annette Kuhn and Ann Marie Wolpe (1978); Joyce Trebilcot (1984); Sandra Harding and Merill B. Hintikka (1983).
3. Sources for and practitioners of postmodernism include Friedrich Nietzsche (1966; 1969); Jacques Derrida (1967); Michel Foucault (1977); Jacques Lacan (1968; 1973); Richard Rorty (1979); Paul Feyerabend (1975); Ludwig Wittgenstein (1970; 1972); Julia Kristeva (1981); Jean-François Lyotard (1984).
4. In 'The instability of the analytical categories of feminist theory' Sandra Harding (1986) discusses the ambivalent attraction of feminist theorizing to both sorts of discourse. She insists that feminist theorists should live with the ambivalence and

retain both discourses for political and philosophical reasons. However, I think her argument rests in part on a too uncritical appropriation of a key Enlightenment equation of knowing, naming, and emancipation.

5. For example, the Marxist treatments of the 'woman question' from Engels onwards, or existentialist, or Lacanian treatment of woman as the 'other' to man.

6. Marx may replicate rather than deconstruct the capitalist mentality in his emphasis on the centrality of production. Compare Albert O. Hirschman (1977) for a very interesting discussion of the historical emergence and construction of a specifically *capitalist* mentality.

7. The theories of French feminists vary, of course. I am focusing on a predominant and influential approach within the variations. For further discussion of French feminism, see the essays in *Signs*, Vol. 7, No. 1. Autumn 1981, and *Feminist Studies*. Vol. 7. No. 2. Summer 1981.

8. Catherine MacKinnon (1982) seems to miss this basic point when she makes claims such as: 'The defining theme of the whole is the male pursuit of control over women's sexuality—men not as individuals nor as biological beings, but as a gender group characterized by maleness as socially constructed, of which this pursuit is definitive' (p. 532). On the problem of the Archimedes point, see Myra Jehlen (1981).

9. But see the work of Evelyn Fox Keller on the gendered character of our views of the natural world, especially her essays 'Gender and science', in Harding and Hintikka (1983) and 'Cognitive repression in physics'. (1979).

10. I say 'until recently' because of developments in medicine such as sex change operations and new methods of conception and fertilization of embryos.

11. On women's 'difference' see the essays in Eisenstein and Jardine (1980) and Marks and Courtivron (1981); also Carol Gilligan (1982).

12. This seems to be the basic approach characteristic of socialist-feminist discussions of the family. See, for example, the essays by Ann Ferguson (1984) and Annette Kuhn (1978).

13. See, for example, Barbara Smith's discussion of the meanings of *home* to her in the introduction to *Home Girls* (Smith, 1983). Smith's definition contrasts strongly with the confinement and exploitation some middle-class white women associate with *home*. See, for example, Michele Barrett and Mary McIntosh (1983), and Heidi I. Hartmann (1981).

14. This seems to be Adrienne Rich's argument in 'Cumpulsory heterosexuality and lesbian existence (1980).

15. Iris Young (1984, p. 140). In this essay, Young replicates the split Juliet Mitchell posits in *Psychoanalysis and Feminism* (1974) between kinship/gender/superstructure and class/production/base.

16. But see the dialogues between Gloria I. Joseph and Jill Lewis (1981), and Marie L. Lugones and Elizabeth V. Spelman (1986), and Phyllis Marynick Palmer (1983). Women of colour have been insisting on this point for a long time. Compare the essays in Barbara Smith (1983), and Cherrie Moraga and Gloria Anzaldua (1981). See also Audre Lorde (1984).

17. Compare the descriptions of mothering in Joyce Trebilcot (1984), especially the essays by Whitbeck and Ruddick.

18. I discuss the gender biases and inadequacies of postmodern philosophy in *Thinking Fragments* (1990). See also Naomi Schor (1987).

References

Barrett M. and McIntosh, M. (1983) *The Anti-Social Family*. London: Verso.
Bethke Elshtain, J. (1981) *Public Man, Private Woman*. Princeton, NJ: Princeton University Press.
— (ed.) (1982) *The Family in Political Thought*. Amherst, MA: University of Massachusetts Press.
Chodorow, N. (1980) Gender, relation, and difference in psychoanalytic perspective. In H. Eisenstein and A. Jardine (eds) *The Future of Difference*. New Brunswick, NJ: Rutgers University Press.
Chodorow, N. and Contratto, S. (1983) The fantasy of the perfect mother. In B. Thorne and M. Yalom (eds) *Rethinking the Family*. New York: Longman.
Derrida, J. (1967) *L'écriture et la différence*. Paris: Editions du Seuil.
Eisenstein, H. and Jardine, A. (1980) *The Future of Difference*. New Brunswick, NJ: Rutgers University Press.
Ferguson, A. (1984) Conceiving motherhood and sexuality: a feminist materialist approach. In J. Trebilcot (ed.) *Mothering: Essays in Feminist Theory* (pp. 156–8). Totowa, NJ: Rowman & Allanheld.
Ferguson, K.E. (1984) *The Feminist Case Against Bureaucracy*. Philadelphia: Temple University Press.
Feyerabend, P. (1975) *Against Method*. New York: Schocken.
Firestone, S. (1970) *The Dialectic of Sex*. New York: Bantam Books.
Flax, J. (1990) *Thinking Fragments: Psychoanalysis, Feminism, and Postmodernism in the Contemporary West*. Berkeley, CA: University of California Press.
Foucault, M. (1977) *Language, Counter-Memory, Practice*. Ithaca, NY: Cornell University Press.
Fox Keller, E. (1979) Cognitive repression in physics. *American Journal of Physics* 47, 718–21.
— (1983) Gender and science. In S. Harding and M.B. Hintikka (eds) *Discovering Reality: Feminist Perspectives on Epistemology, Metaphysics, Methodology, and Philosophy of Science*. Boston, MA: D. Reidel Publishing.
Freud, S. (1961) *Civilization and its Discontents*. New York: W.W. Norton.
Gilligan, C. (1982) *In a Different Voice*. Cambridge, MA: Harvard University Press.
Haraway, D. (1983) A manifesto for cyborgs: science, technology, and socialist feminism in the 1980s. *Soicalist Review*, 80, 65–107.
Harding, S. (1986) The instability of the analytical categories of feminist theory. *Signs: Journal of Women in Culture and Society* 11, 4, Summer, 645–66.
Harding, S. and Hintikka, M.B. (eds) (1983) *Discovering Reality: Feminist Perspectives on Epistemology, Metaphysics, Methodology, and Philosophy of Science*. Boston, MA: D. Reidel Publishing.
Hartmann, H.I. (1981) The family as the locus of gender, class, and political struggle: the example of housework. *Signs: Journal of Women in Culture and Society* 6, 3, 366–94.
Hirschman, A.O. (1977) *The Passions and the Interests*. Princeton, NJ: Princeton University Press.
Horkheimer, M. and Adorno, T.W. (1972) *Dialectic of Enlightenment*. New York: Herder & Herder.
Iragaray, Luce (1985) *Speculum of the Other Woman*. Ithaca, NY: Cornell University Press.
Jardine, A.A. (1985) *Gynesis: Configurations of Woman and Modernity*. Ithaca, NY: Cornell University Press.

Jehlen, M. (1981) Archimedes and the paradox of feminist criticism. *Signs: Journal of Women in Culture and Society* 6, 4, 575–601.

Joseph, G.I. and Lewis, J. (1981) *Common Differences: Conflicts in Black and White Feminist Perspectives.* New York: Doubleday.

Kristeva, J. (1981) Women's time. *Signs: Journal of Women in Culture and Society* 7, 11, Autumn, 13–35.

Kuhn, A. (1978) Structure of patriarchy and capital in the family. In A. Kuhn and A.M. Wolpe (eds) *Feminism and Materialism.* Boston, MA: Routledge & Kegan Paul.

Kuhn, A. and Wolpe A.M. (eds) (1978) *Feminism and Materialism.* Boston, MA: Routledge & Kegan Paul.

Lacan, J. (1968) *Speech and Language in Psychoanalysis.* Baltimore: John Hopkins University Press.

— (1973) *The Four Fundamental Concepts of Psychoanalysis.* New York: W.W. Norton.

Lorde, A. (1984) *Sister Outsider.* Trumansburg, NY: Crossing Press.

Lugones, M.L. and Spelman, E.V. (1986) Have we got a theory for you. In M. Pearsall (ed.) *Women and Values.* Belmont, CA: Wadsworth.

Lyotard, J.-F. (1984) *The Postmodern Condition.* Minneapolis: University of Minnesota Press.

MacKinnon C. (1982) Feminism, Marxism, method, and the state: an agenda for theory. *Signs: Journal of Women in Culture and Society* 7, 3, 515–44.

Marks, E. and de Courtivron, I. (eds) (1981) *New French Feminisms.* New York: Schocken Books.

Marynick Palmer, P. (1983) White women/black women: the dualism of female identity and experience in the United States. *Feminist Studies* 9, 11, 151–70.

Mitchell, J. (1974) *Psychoanalysis and Feminism.* New York: Pantheon Books.

Moraga, C. and Anzaldua, G. (1981) *This Bridge Called My Back.* Watertown, MA: Persephone Press.

Nietzsche, F. (1966) *Beyond Good and Evil.* New York: Vintage.

— (1969) *On the Genealogy of Morals.* New York: Vintage.

Rich, A. (1980) Compulsory heterosexuality and lesbian existence. *Signs: Journal of Women in Culture and Society* 5, 4, 631–60.

Rorty, R. (1979) *Philosophy and the Mirror of Nature.* Princeton, NJ: Princeton University Press.

Rubin, G. (1975) The traffic in women: notes on the 'political economy' of sex. In Rayna Rapp Reiter (ed.) *Toward an Anthropology of Women.* New York: Monthly Review Press.

Ruddick, S. (1984a) Maternal thinking. In J. Trebilcot (ed.) *Mothering: Essays in Feminist Theory.* Totowa, NJ: Rowman & Allanheld.

— (1984b) Preservation love and military destruction: some reflections on mothering and peace. In J. Trebilcot (ed.) *Mothering: Essays in Feminist Theory.* Totowa, NJ: Rowman & Allanheld.

Schor, N. (1987) Dreaming dissymmetry: Barthes, Foucault, and sexual difference. In A. Jardine and P. Smith (eds) *Men in Feminism.* New York: Methuen.

Smith, B. (ed.) (1983) *Home Girls: A Black Feminist Anthology.* New York: Kitchen Table, Women of Color Press.

Stacey, J. (1983) The new conservative feminism. *Feminist Studies* 9, 3, 559–83.

Thorne, B. and Yalom, M. (eds.) (1983) *Rethinking the Family.* New York: Longman.

Trebilcot, J. (ed.) (1984) *Mothering: Essays in Feminist Theory.* Totowa, NJ: Rowman & Allanheld.

Weber, M. (1958) Science as a vocation. In H.H. Gerth and C. Wright Mills (eds)

From Max Weber. New York: Oxford University Press.
Wittgenstein, L. (1970) *Philosophical Investigations.* New York: Macmillan.
— (1972) *On Certainty.* New York: Harper & Row.
Young, I. (1984) Is male gender identity the cause of male domination? In J.
    Trebilcot (ed.) *Mothering: Essays in Feminist Theory.* Totowa, NJ: Rowman &
    Allanheld.

12 FEMINISM AND THE CHALLENGE OF RACISM: DEVIANCE OR DIFFERENCE?

RAZIA AZIZ

In the long and uneven history of women's liberation in the West, its project has been frequently and seriously challenged by imperialism and racism. This is because—in combination with class—imperialism and racism have repeatedly posed the question of differences between women in the starkest terms. Slavery, conquest and colonialism created dominant and subject peoples within global structures of material exploitation and political subordination. They also involved the representation of the dominated peoples discursively—in language—as an inferior Other (as against the 'superior' white peoples of Europe and North America).[1] These processes—political, discursive and economic—provided the breeding ground for various racisms.

What has this to do with women's liberation? It indicates that women on different sides of these global processes have significantly different interests: most crucially, women oppressed and exploited by racism and/or by imperialism, have some interests in common with our menfolk, and in opposition to those of white Western men *and* women. In reality this maps out a vast area of complex solidarities, contradictions and struggles which women, seen globally, inhabit.

Thus both terms in the phrase 'women's liberation' have come under question and we are led to ask *which women?* or *what is a 'woman'?*; and *whose liberation?* or *liberation from what?* [. . .]

The political context within which the British racism-and-feminism 'debate' has taken place continues to be one in which racism and imperialist domination figure strongly. In this context black women's critiques frequently have a particular vibrancy derived from an insistence on placing the question of history centre stage. This is more a political than an academic point. History is not given, it has to be made. In making a history that takes black women as its *subjects* and agents, not its *victims*, black women have challenged feminism with a project of the kind that is arguably dear to all feminists. Yet

Source: Abridged and adapted from Crowley, H. and Himmelweit, S. (1992) *Knowing Women: Feminism and Knowledge* (pp. 291–305). Cambridge: Polity Press.

it is exacting in the demand that white women acknowledge and take responsibility for their own agency, witting or otherwise, as *oppressors* of black women *and* men. [...]

'RACE', RACISM AND BLACK STRUGGLE

Any racism relies on two assertions: the first is the 'self-evident truth' that different races exist in the world (determined in some way by biology); the second is that these races exist in a hierarchy of superiority and inferiority. In ths article, I write of 'race', not race. I seek in doing this to problematize the concept, and ask you to consider what use it would serve if racism (or race-ism) did not exist. Put another way, what cause is furthered by the assertion that there exist in the world discrete and identifiably different 'races' (quite aside from whether it is factually correct)? As food for thought, I would like to give the word a health warning: 'If its meaning is treated as self-evident, this word may impede critical thought'!

The meaning of *black* varies *between* contexts; it is also contested *within* a context. I use it mostly to refer to people of African and Asian descent living in Britain.[2] Black people do not comprise a hermetically sealed or homogeneous category: skin colour, history and culture all play a part in their definition. Black-ness is a product of self-conscious political practice: its meaning has been given by, and has in turn affected the struggles of people in Britain who have identified themselves (and have been identified) as black. (The fact that many black people do not identify as black has continued to be a weakness in black strategy, and one to which I will return towards the end of this article.)

The term 'black' was appropriated in a movement involving those social groups who were the main targets of post-World War Two racism. Black *culture*, in this sense, is not the same as ethnicity: it acknowledges that migration and racism have not left so-called traditional cultures untouched; and that a *racialized* First World context demands more than a conservative defence of, for example, 'Muslim', 'Sikh' or 'African-Caribbean' cultures. Black political identification implies a complex understanding of the need for common strategies and visions.

At this point it is worth considering ethnicity—a concept as widely used as it is strongly criticized. In spite of their commonalities, different communities clearly differ in language, religion and other social practices. Ethnicity could be a way of theorizing this. But the language of ethnicity has some very odd qualities. At home it is used euphamistically to transform the problem of racism into the less thorny one of cultural difference and prejudice. The acquisition of 'ethnic minority' status by some white communities is critical in this because it is used to obscure further the reality of racism. Abroad the language of ethnicity soothes our incredulity over murderous civil wars by offering us 'ethnic cleansing' where words like racism, nationalism, facism and genocide would leave us uneasy. Unsurprisingly white British, non-Jewish, non-Irish people appear to have no ethnicity at all. This is because the language of ethnicity is a product of racism, not a serious device for helping us contextualize cultural difference in a historically and politically informed way.

Culture is frequently important to people's sense of self, but both culture and ethnicity must be carefully defined to be analytically useful *and* politically appropriate. Cultural prejudice and misunderstanding form part of racism but alone cannot explain its violence, its preoccupation with genetically determined characteristics or its economic dimension. The ethnicity issue continues to confound black politics partly because it is backed by the funding strategies of central and local government *and* positively regarded by (often the most conservative) elements of the said 'ethnic minorities'.[3] This can divert attention from racism, and from the really interesting question of how black people can negotiate the actual differences between us which find cultural expression.

Black refusal of shades of colour, ethnic or biologically racial bases for resistance has not always been easy to sustain,[4] but it has tended to undermine commonly held conceptions of 'race' and therefore—I would argue—racism itself. *It emphasizes that 'race' is a social category, not a natural one,* and that people acquire 'race' through their entry into historically specific and racist social relations, just as they acquire black political identity through historically specific practices. The creative appropriation of experiences of imperialism, colonialism and slavery, encourages common struggles across ethnic and class divisions. It does not mean that black identity is the same as Third World identity, but that identification with Third World struggles forms an important part of black politics.

Furthermore, while black people are not 'a class', our common struggles respond to an important extent to local and global economic processes. The various labour migrations which brought black peoples to British shores were products of an imperialist international economic and political order. Migration, exploitation and class mobility are all prominent features of black histories. Compare these migrations (including the forced migration of Africans as slaves) with the nature of the intimately related migrations of white peoples to North and South America, Africa, Asia and Australasia, and the global dimension of black/white difference becomes still clearer. *Anti-black racism is one of the great political facts of our time, in large part because of its relationship to immense wealth creation and appropriation on a global scale.*

In Britain, black resistance has emerged strongly in confrontations with the state and its representatives: over immigration controls that have explicitly institutionalized racism since the early 1960s, and which continue to divide black families; over police brutality towards black youth on the one hand, and their failure to take racist crimes seriously on the other; over the racism of the courts, schools, social services and the state as an employer; and in the inner-city riots, in combination with white people who suffered similar economic disadvantage, against the system as a whole. These struggles strongly inform black women's critiques of feminism.

However, black resistance is not just about state power and material goals. Identity and culture are integral to a struggle that responds to the complexity of racism, but goes far beyond the agenda it sets. In his book, *There Ain't No Black in the Union Jack*, Gilroy (1987) demonstrates the importance of culture both to the resilience of racism and to the process of resisting it. He alerts us to the prevalent cultural representations of black people as either 'problem' or 'victim'—both of them categories of deviance. This means that the representation (including self-presentation) in speech, writing, music and forms of political action of black people *outside these categories*—that is, as the subjects of history and agents of historical change, as people who struggle, resist and live incredibly varied and complex lives—is in itself a weapon against racism (as it is against women's subordination).

Though subversive forms of representation in isolation cannot defeat racism, the *culture* of resistance is inseparable from the *goals* of liberation. An appropriation of history can establish black people as subjects of history, contemporary and past. To the extent that language, culture and discourse constitute reality, this process is pivotal. (The *denial* of history is, by contrast, a centrepiece of racism—as demonstrated, for instance, by the curious synonymity of 'black' and 'immigrant' which invisibilize the fact of a black presence in Britain over centuries. What needs to be placed at the heart of discourse about 'race' is a history which allows black people the complexity, passion, intelligence and contradictions of thought, action and word that white people are implicitly credited with when black people are seen as victims or problems. It is a history that 'sees' *difference* precisely because it insists on a fundamental human *commonality*, namely the capacity for agency.

The elements of such a history are present in the understanding of blackness as *not defined by common oppression so much as a common context of struggle and resistance* (Mohanty, 1988, p. 67). That context, as I have tried to show, is infused with a historically specific blend of economic exploitation, cultural oppression and social subordination in which the state is prominent. It needs, furthermore, to be seen in an international perspective.

Racism requires a perspective of deviance. It speaks (implicitly or explicitly) from the position of the dominant white group. A racist perspective is composed of two elements: first, the failure to own the *particularity* of white-ness; second, the failure to acknowledge that, in a racist context, a 'white' voice stands in a relationship of authority to a 'black' voice. To 'see' deviance instead of difference means to take the experience of the dominant group as the implicit or explicit *universal* standard or norm. [. . .]

THE PROBLEM OF DIFFERENCE

[...] Black women bring to feminism lived realities of a racism that has marginalized and victimized us in the wider world. [...] The bid for a feminism that 'sees' the agency and the struggle and the celebration in black women's lives is explicit in the writing of black feminists. This involves giving black women centre stage, and refusing consignment to the role of exotic sideshow.

In attempting to shift the ground of feminist discourse, the adversary has at times appeared to be *white feminists* but is in fact, I would venture, White feminism—by which I expressly do *not* mean any feminism espoused by white feminists. I refer, rather, to any feminism which comes from a white perspective, *and* universalizes it.

It is not that White feminism is a clearly defined, coherent and internally consistent body of thought based on conscious racist intentions. It is, rather, a way of seeing. It subsists through a failure of white feminists to consider both the wider social and political context of power in which feminist utterances and actions take place, and the ability of feminism to influence that context.

Much of black women's critique has highlighted the suppression within feminism of black/white *difference*. This can happen in one of two ways: the first is the denial of difference which is implicit in the assumption that all women have certain interests (rather than others) in common. On closer inspection supposedly universal interests turn out to be those of a particular group of women. For instance, the pro-abortion feminist stance of the 1970s did not take into account the fact that many black women's reproductive struggles were around the right to retain and realize their fertility. For black women abortions, sterilizations and Depo Provera[5] were all-too-easily available, and were often administered without adequate consultation and/or under the shadow of economic repression.[6] These are not experiences restricted to black women, but it was the intervention of black women which exposed the in fact narrow base of what seemed to some to be a universal demand, and transformed the campaign—which has subsequently focused on choice and reproductive rights.

The second way in which black/white difference has been suppressed in feminism is through its representation as black deviance. The issue is that black women have been marginalized in feminist discourses, so that when they are depicted, it is as the exception. This problematizes the ways in which black women differ from White feminism's standard of Woman, rather than the general applicability of this standard.

To address this problem requires the prior recognition that black women's historical position as peripheral to the grand workings of power in society has precluded us hiding behind a mask of generality: too often the exception, the special case, the puzzling, more-oppressed or exotic anomaly (even within feminism), we have been largely denied the voice of authority by which white women appear to speak on behalf of the female sex as a whole. Black women's particularity is transparent because of racism; any failure of white women to recognize *their* own particularity continues that racism.

THE INSEPARABILITY OF BLACK AND WHITE EXPERIENCE

In keeping with the politics of black resistance, an appropriation of imperialist history has been integral to black women's political practice. In this way forged an identity deeply imbued with temporal and spatial solidarities: solidarity with political and ancestral predecessors on the one hand, and with Third World liberation movements on the other. It is not my view that black women have a monopoly on internationalism, *or* that black women—in the First World—have an automatic identity of interests with Third World women. Nevertheless, black women, especially black working class women, have frequently been left 'holding' the argument for the simultaneous consideration of class, 'race', imperialism and gender. This is not because no one else can see it, but because no one else lives it in such an acute way.

White women are as much part of social relations as black women are. Therefore, they must be as knowledgeable about the interactions of these structures of domination, albeit from a very different position. Racism, however, relies on a perspective of deviance which obscures white particularity. This masks the fact that white-ness is every bit as implicated as black-ness in the workings of racism. Thus, whether or not they are aware of it, *racism affects white women constantly.*

In articulating black women's experiences of the British state, the labour market, their families and their sexualities, black feminist writers have emphasized black/white difference (sometimes at the expense of other issues—see the next section). However, it is important to note that ours are not stories parallel to those of white women, but intricately intertwined with them. Black women cannot—even if we wanted to—speak of our struggles outside of the context of racism and resistance (if only because our colour is never 'invisible'); white feminists, on the other hand, can speak—and many do—as if that context did not exist.

The point is not, I would argue, that white women experience the state (to take one example) as patriarchal, whereas black women experience the state as racist *and* patriarchal: if the state is racist, it is race-ist in relation to everyone; it is merely more difficult for white people to see this, because part of the racism of the state is their privilege.

THE ISSUE OF MEN

Another important contribution of black women has been to raise awareness about how racism undermines black *masculinity*, treating it as pathological in relation to white masculinity (another form of Other-ness). The myth of black men as rapists of white women, for example, justifies violence against these men and is an indication that not all men are equal—or equally favoured—in patriarchy. The failure to recognize these issues independently is only one example of the poor track record of British feminism where racism is concerned.[7] As Ramazanoglu pointed out: 'Racism divides feminists not because our attitudes, statistics or concepts need correcting (although, of course, they do), but because *black women have real political interests in common with black men'* (1986, p. 85 emphasis added). To which may be added: and because racism really does reside in relationships between white women on the one hand and black women and men on the other. These two claims demand much more from feminism than an adding on of the special concerns of black women. Racism is only one of many reasons why the oppression and exploitation of men matters to feminism (class is another). The thrust of black women's arguments is that the feminist project itself had to be re-evaluated.

What are the implications for feminism of these critiques? A key piece of the re-evaluation demanded by black women is that feminism should abandon the notion that all women automatically have common interests (and that men and women have opposing interests). The underlying logic is that common interests between women only emerge as a consequence of common appropriation of historical experiences of oppression, subordination and exploitation through the essentially political practices of solidarity, alliance and resistance.

In other words, feminism has been challenged to place itself in history, and to locate itself in relation to other forms of resistance such as black and Third World liberation and class struggles. As a consequence, it needs to work for its coherence as a political force, rather than assuming a ready-made, but false, coherence by placing itself outside history, and shirking the responsibilities attendant on its power as a social movement.

Many of the issues raised by black women—about who sets the political agenda, about marginalization in language and practice, in short about Other-ness—are familiar to white feminists from their own history of resistance. What has not been so easy to come to terms with is the need to acknowledge the uncomfortable dual position of oppressor and oppressed. In this way the 'debate' however acrimonious, provided feminism with a fresh opportunity to address its most troublesome weaknesses and to move on from them. [. . .]

BEYOND THE DEBATE

Black women are an immensely varied social group spanning different histories, classes, sexualities, languages and religions. What I have attempted to
do is distil the recasting of the politics of history which *some* black women
have brought to feminism. The works I have drawn upon do not constitute an
internally consistent body of scholarship, much less unerringly espouse what
I have termed a perspective of difference. In fact, I shall argue below that
the strategy of highlighting black/white difference has involved certain tactics
that undermine the move towards such a perspective. I am not suggesting
that the strategy is entirely misguided (I have adopted it myself up till this
point!). But it is also important to place it under scrutiny. In doing so, I
make a point which is conceptually simple, but politically complex: namely
that the energetic assertion of black/white (or any other) difference tends to
create fixed and oppositional categories which can result in another version
of the suppression of difference. Differences *within* categories—here black and
white—are underplayed in order to establish it *between* them. Consequently,
each category takes on a deceptive air of internal coherence, and similarities
between women in the different categories are thus suppressed.[8] [. . .]

The problem of class

There has been some acknowledgement by black women that white working-
class women have also been marginalized in the feminist movement. [. . .]

However in the attempt to deliver a jolt to White feminist complacency, certain issues of political significance are negated with the effect of
homogenizing white women on the one hand and black women on the other.
The significance of such omissions is that they de-emphasize the oppression
of *white* women by other white women, leaving black women *apparently* the
sole aspirants to that dubious accolade.

A different problem arises when we consider the *self-preservation* of black
women. Here class has been used selectively in a way that seems to deny the
diversity of black women. The most common manifestation of this is the
majoritarian approach: since *most* black people are working class, it is okay
to behave as if they *all* are. I am not attacking analyses of the exploitation
of black people and the role of capitalism in producing it, only noting a tendency to *class*-ify black people—a social group that displays class diversity *and*
mobility.

This tendency inadvertently supports the unexamined position demonstrated in the following quotes:

> All black people are subordinated by racial oppression, women are sub-
> ordinated by sexual domination, and *black women are subordinated by*
> *both as well as class.* (Foster-Carter, 1987, p. 46 emphasis added)

> . . .black women are subjected to the *simultaneous* oppression of
> patriarchy, class and 'race' . . . (Carby, 1982, p. 213)

The effect of this is to represent black women as *homogeneously oppressed in almost every politically significant way.* In bringing this argument, I could (as a black middle-class woman) be accused of special pleading: which is precisely my point: unless black identity *is* class identity, black middle-class people cannot be considered a 'special', or deviant, case. [. . .]

The problem of culture and identity

The tendency to homogenize the oppression of black people comes from an understandable desire to find common ground and to resist the power of racism to divide black people from one another. However, it remains the case that perhaps more than half the people who may be labelled 'black' do not identify as such: I refer, of course, to a large proportion of people of South Asian descent living in Britain.

In spite of the criticisms of the 'ethnicity' approach which I offered earlier, there is a real political and experiential issue to be answered which is not just about divisive strategies of *racism* but about actual historical differences in the nature of colonialism, imperialism, racism and representation—and in how these are appropriated.

The growth of anti-Muslim racism and the Islamization of Muslim communities in Britain during and since the Rushdie Affair is only one particularly acute example of why cultural *identity* matters. This example is of interest to all black women because of the profound consequences for Muslim *women* (many of whom identify with Islam) of the move towards fundamentalism (which is, of course, not confined to Muslim communities). The strategy of underplaying inter-black difference has never been equal to this challenge of *subjectivity*: at a time like this, it can appear at best politically naive, and at worst irresponsible.

Any line of argument chosen to emphasize black/white difference will tend to deny the complexity of both black and white experience. This may be unavoidable, but unless it is explicitly acknowledged a racial essentialism can emerge through the back door of fixed and oppositional identities. If alliances are seriously sought, the strategy of stressing one difference is limited. The dilemma is clear, even if its solution is not: in order for difference to be taken seriously it has to be established in debate and action; but it is important to take a broad view of the political consequences of this process, otherwise there is a risk of again detaching difference from history.

The issue of identity is one which best crystallizes this dilemma. Rooted as it is in complex layers of struggles and contexts, identity is not neat and coherent, but fluid and fragmented. Yet attempts to assert it seem to undermine potential solidarities between specific groups of women. [. . .]

Locating a feminism of difference

Recent years have seen the demise of grand (or modernist) theories; namely
those which claim to establish *a fundamental determinant* of history (such
as class or patriarchy). This demise is very closely related to the inability
of such theories to respond to the complexities of difference and power.
Socialist-feminists have attempted to juggle the grand structures of 'race',
class and gender without giving one of them overall primacy. This strategy
has not, however, been totally successful. It has become increasingly apparent
that the attempt to combine (and so 'democratize') grand theories of 'race',
class and gender may be unworkable. The endeavour tends to produce and
multiply unwieldy and static categories without much analytical power (such
as 'the white, middle-class male') as the list of oppressions became as long as
the range of political struggles was multitudinous.

This 'democratization' of oppressions can be seen in retrospect as an attempt
to push grand theory to its limits. It was accompanied by the growth of
a phenomenon often labelled 'identity politics'. Oppressions tended to be
increasingly regarded as 'relative', with attached identities that tended to be
elevated above criticism. This can lead to an inward-looking identity politics
where oppressions are added and subtracted. The capacity to analyze the
interrelations between identities and social relations, and to establish political
priorities, is thereby seriously weakened.

Identity politics ceases to be progressive when it sees the assertion of
identity *as an end in itself.* Jenny Bourne (1983) urges us to ask what
identity *does* in relation to the politics of resistance? Does identity politics
promote or does it divert resistance by providing a sanctuary for people who
do not want to acknowledge that they are oppressors? Bourne laments the
analytical and political loss of privilege of the *material* (particularly the economic) as a determining factor separate from and somehow more real than
language, culture and representation. Yet this dethroning need not take the
ahistorical route Bourne criticizes. The view that language is constitutive of
reality can, instead, open the field for historically aware analyses of the relationship between, for example, 'race', class and culture.

A focus on representation as a social *act* allows us to understand the ways
in which the historical, the biological and the material are given a reality
and meaning through language. It offers us a more complex conception of
power as exercised in all manner of social interactions. Crucially, it allows
us to see competing discourses—for instance those of dominant racism, of
ethnicity and of black resistance—as *intrinsic* to the exercise of power in
society.

This paradigmatic shift is rightly labelled *postmodernist* as it is a response
to—and an attempt to move beyond—the weaknesses of grand theory. At its
heart is an entirely different treatment of *subjectivity*—or the way in which
people live and understand their selves and identities.

Postmodernism is *deconstructive*: it sees subjectivity as a *product* of power rather than its author; and agency as power's way of acting through the individual. Power, in this understanding, is exercised in historically specific discourses (or ideologies) and practices: in contrast to the modernist conception, it is not unitary and zero-sum, but diffuse, constantly changing and plural. Postmodernism is therefore antithetical to essentialism of any kind—racial, sexual or human.[9] It proposes that the selves we think are fixed and unitary are actually unstable, fragmented and contradictory. It can thus potentially help us look at changes and tensions (such as that of oppressor/oppressed) in who we understand ourselves as being.

Such a perspective can save identity from 'mummifying' by challenging us self-consciously to deconstruct our identities. This act of deconstruction is *political*, as it exposes the intricate operations of power that constitute subjectivity. Thus the particular deconstruction of the identity 'woman' that black women have achieved can be seen as exposing the link between racism at large and its subjective articulation. Nor is black identity somehow privileged (as I have tried to show): the cost of a 'home' in any identity is the exercise of a power to include the chosen and exclude the Other.

I may appear at this point to be espousing contradictory positions—am I *for* or *against* the assertion of identity?—in response to which I simply restate the question: 'What is identity for?'

In providing us with self-presentations of black women as subjects of history, black women have established their identity as an influential political fact. An anti-humanist insistence on always *de*-constructing subjectivity ignores political context and the importance of identity in resistance. The assertion of identity is a process people can relate to because it reclaims agency and makes them feel powerful. The importance of this cannot be underestimated. Furthermore, any focus on language and subjectivity which divorces them from material forces (such as the current crisis and restructuring of capitalism) also divorces theory from some of the things that affect people most severely.

Postmodernism does not immunize us from the responsibility to locate ourselves relative to the political movements of our time as a discourse, it is part of—and is implicated in—the very power relations in society that we analyze and aim to change. If a feminism of difference is to compete with reactionary forces for the spaces caused by political schisms, it needs to incorporate *both* the deconstruction of subjectivity *and* the political necessity of asserting identity. Additionally, its recognition of the fact that language and culture constitute reality needs to coexist with a recognition of the unmitigated realities of violence, economic exploitation and poverty. For a feminism of difference, these questions need to be answered in relation to the imperatives of each historical moment. This requires a degree of self-consciousness and responsibility of thought, utterance and action from our oppressed and oppressor selves alike which is nowhere near prevalent as yet.

But the potential for alliance between and among black and white women depends upon it.

Notes

1. See the excellent essay 'Orientalism' by E.W. Said (1979), in which he critically investigates the process by which this has occurred.
2. The strongest competing definition of 'black' (and the most prevalent) confines it to people of the African diaspora only.
3. This means that different black communities are effectively pitched in competition with each other for scarce resources, so the 'ethnic minority' approach, dressed up as an attempt to encourage racial harmony, in fact divides and separates black communities.
4. Black people of all kinds experience allegiances based on one or more of these characteristics, which some would argue is partly because of what racism has done to us—a view with which I concur.
5. A long-acting, injectible contraceptive banned in the United States because of disturbing side-effects.
6. Angela Davis (1981), in *Women, Race and Class,* informs us that the US-backed sterilization campaign in Puerto Rico in the 1970s claimed the fertility of 35% of all women of reproductive age.
7. See Amos and Parmar (1984) for other examples.
8. See Phoenix (1988) for a good, short study which challenges this tendency.
9. In other words it is anti-*humanist*, rejecting the idea of an essential human-ness shared by all human individuals.

References

Amos, and Parmar (1984) Challenging imperial feminism. *Feminist Review* 17, 3–20.
Bourne, J. (1983) Towards an anti-racist feminism. *Race and Class* xxv, 1.
Carby, H.V. (1982) White woman listen! Black feminism and the boundaries of sisterhood. In Centre for Contemporary Cultural Studies (eds) *The Empire Strikes Back: Race and Racism in 1970s Britain.* London: Hutchinson.
Davis, A. (1981) *Women, Race and Class.* London: The Women's Press.
Foster-Carter, V. (1987) Ethnicity: the fourth burden of Black Women—political action. *Critical Social Policy* 20, 46–56.
Gilroy, P. (1987) *There Ain't No Black in the Union Jack.* London: Hutchinson.
Mohanty, C.T. (1988) Under Western eyes: feminist scholarship and colonial discourses, *Feminist Review* 30, 61–88.
Phoenix (1988) Narrow definitions of culture: the case of early motherhood. In S. Westwood and P. Bachu (eds) *Enterprising Women: Ethnicity, Economy and Gender Relations.* London: Routledge.
Ramazanoglu, C. (1986) Ethnocentrism and socialist-feminist theory: a response to Barrett and McIntosh. *Feminist Review* 22, 83–6.
Said, E.W. (1979) *Orientalism.* New York: Vintage.

13 CONTESTED DISCOURSES ON MEN AND MASCULINITIES

JEFF HEARN AND DAVID H.J. MORGAN

Much sociology and sociological theory has been implicitly about men, without explicitly saying so. A number of sociological fields, for example, criminology and the study of juvenile deliquency, have a long tradition of the study of men and masculinity. Furthermore, in the 1950s a number of significant sociological texts were published on men, in several cases written by women, prior to the growth of second wave feminism. Just as feminist scholarship has demonstrated that 'woman', 'women', and 'femininity' are socially and historically constructed, and thus problematic, so too has it demonstrated the problematic nature of 'man', 'men', and 'masculinity' (for example, Delphy, 1977; Chesler, 1978; Friedman and Sarah, 1981). Then there has been, often in association with gay liberation, the growth of gay scholarship and studies on homosexuality and gay men. Much of this has comprized detailed socio-historical research into the social contruction of the 'male homosexual' (for example, Weeks, 1977). While gay research undoubtedly has major implications for the deconstruction of men (Carrigan et al., 1985), it has not always addressed 'men' and 'masculinity' as its explicit topic. Some of his work has been criticized for its neglect of feminist critiques, especially around sexuality and power (Stanley, 1984).

From the late 1960s, there developed alongside the Women's Liberation Movement (WML) and the Gay Liberation Movement (GLM), in a number of western countries, a small but identifiable series of groups and networks of 'men against sexism'. In some cases, and particularly in the United States, these have sometimes been seen as a 'movement' of their own. These networks have generated a variable and irregular literature, in the form of news-sheets, journals and autobiographical and political writings. A relatively early example of a book from this social context is *Unbecoming Men* (Bradley et al., 1971), recording the personal experiences of five men in a consciousness-raising group. Meanwhile, more academic studies of men and masculinity were developing from a mixture of largely sex-role culturalist sociology, social psychology, and some 'men's movement' writing. The obvious landmark text for this strand is Pleck and Sawyer's (1974) edited collection, *Men and Masculinity.* By the late 1970s this kind of sociological and psychological work together with literary and historical studies on men were being

Source: Hearn, J. and Morgan, D.H.J. (eds) (1990) *Men, Masculinities and Social Theory* (pp. 4–17). London: Unwin Hyman.

referred to in the United States at least, as 'men's studies'. In the United Kingdom, the landmark text was Tolson's (1977) *The Limits of Masculinity*, which developed an economic class analysis of postwar masculinities. By now there were courses on men in universities and similar institutions, networks of scholars in North America and Europe, the *Men's Studies Review* based in the United States, numerous special issues of journals, a number of recently produced textbooks and readers, and at least five bibliographical studies on men and masculinity (Grady, Brann and Pleck, 1979: Massachusetts Institute of Technology Humanities Library, 1979; August, 1985; Ford and Hearn, 1988; Treadwell and Davis, n.d). Some indication of the internationalism of these concerns can be gauged from the high level of interest at symposia on these questions at two recent major conferences: 'Men's response to the feminist challenge' at the Third International Interdisciplinary Congress on Women, Trinity College, Dublin, July 1987 (Hearn, 1987b); and 'Men in gender studies' at the Joint Congress of the German, Austrian and Swiss Sociological Associations, University of Zurich, October 1988 *(Männer in der Geschlecterforschung*, 1988).

This limited institutionalization of these recent studies on men and masculinities has generated further controversy, not least because of the danger of this being used against the interests of women, now or in the future. These controversies operate at various levels and in various arenas. There are worrying issues around the gender/sexual politics of the allocation of scarce resources for teaching and research, and legitimate fears that 'men's studies' will become yet another variation on a well-established patriarchal theme. Then there are the uses and impacts of different social science traditions on the study of men, particularly differences between positivism and critical theory, culturalism and structuralism, and increasingly modernism and postmodernism (Hearn, 1989a; b). To some extent these kinds of differences have become mapped on to differences between North American and European approaches to the study of men. In this sense the study of men reproduces tensions between North American and European traditions found in other branches of social science. One of the many implications of feminist critiques is a deep questioning of the possibility of being simultaneously a man, a positivist, and a critic of men. Such debates have been reproduced in uncertainties around the very naming of this area of study. As noted, the term 'men's studies' is favoured by some, and has been used particularly in the United States; others favour 'male dominance studies', 'the critical study of men', and so on. (We outline our own position on some of these questions in the next section.)

THE CRITIQUE OF MEN

First, we see it necessary for men to support the development of feminist scholarship in general and women's studies in particular. This is not just an abstract principle but something which involves concrete actions, including the recommendation of and use of feminist texts in teaching and research, and the vigorous institutional support for and defence of women's studies programmes, whether they be whole degrees or parts of other courses.

Second, we consider the proper focus for men interested in and concerned about gender, and gender politics is men, ourselves. This particularly applies in the development of research and publication. There are a number of necessary caveats to this, including the need for men students to write required course essays about women; the obvious need to read feminist writings and scholarship and the need to study men in terms of the impact of men's power upon women; and the need in that research and writing which is collaborative with women to devise an appropriate division of labour, separation of information, and sharing of information.

Third, there is no parity between women's studies and the critique of men. While we see women's studies as being by women, of women, and for women, the critique of men is by both women and men. While women may wish to study men critically, there is no equivalent leeway for men to study women, although we noted above that this may be appropriate under certain conditions.

Fourth, men's critique of men, ourselves, is to be developed in the light of feminism. This critique needs to be anti-sexist, anti-patriarchal, pro-feminist, and gay-affirmative. It means not just a positive academic relationship with feminism but also a positive political relationship with feminism, including men's support for feminist initiatives and political projects.

Fifth, the underlying task of the critique of men is to change men, oursleves, and other men. This involves men in both individual and collective change. It is premissed on the assumption that we learn to understand the world by trying to change it and not by trying to detach ourselves from it. Again, this necessitates concrete actions, notably self-criticism and the critical attempt to change other men, to encourage others to turn their attention to feminist scholarship, to review their reading lists, and so on.

Lastly, we see it as crucial to attend also to the longer-term implications of men studying men. In particular, there is the possibility that 'good intentions' are not enough. Thus men must also vigorously support equal opportunities and similar policies at every level. We must refrain from applying for teaching and research jobs on women's studies. We also believe that men should generally refrain from applying for research grants from funds earmarked for 'equal opportunities', 'gender studies', and 'women's studies'. Instead, men might usefully apply for funds on men and gender, perhaps in collaboration with women, from supposedly non-gendered research funds. We also believe that there is a need to monitor carefully any moves towards the institutional development of studies on gender. We say this with some caution, aware that some feminists support the term 'gender studies' as an umbrella term.

[...] We see these suggestions as first steps in clarifying men's activity in sociology in relation to feminism and women's studies. In particular, we urge men to come out publicly and institutionally in support of the continuing development of feminist scholarship, teaching, and research, and of women's studies.

The critical study of men and masculinities is clearly not just a question of institutional development; it is also very much a series of developments in relation to theory and theorizing. This is to be seen in a wide range of ways and through a variety of sometimes contradictory themes. [...] One of the most important themes which certainly informs many of the recent writings about men is the relative invisibility of men, as an explicit focus in research and sociological theory. For example, this is noted by Duroche (1990), where he notes the relative absence of analysis of the male body. This argument is, of course, somewhat paradoxical. Feminists have justly argued that the central theoretical concerns and the general orientations to research have been dominated by the concerns of men. Research has often been about men, conducted by men and for men; where research has been carried out on women, it has often been by men and has reflected men's versions of the world. The term 'malestream' has been developed to describe the numerical and ideological domination of men and their concerns within sociology (O'Brien, 1981). Feminism has, clearly, challenged this male dominance although the impact has been somewhat uneven.

Moreover, if there has been an invisibility of men in sociological and other research this may not be entirely accidental. As Kimmel (1990) notes, the invisibilities of men may serve men's interests, keeping their activites apart from critical scrutiny, by other men as well as by women. Many men's fraternal institutions have indeed been dedicated, directly or indirectly, to the preservation of men's secrets. Hence, when we write about the invisibility of men within sociology we are writing about an invisibility constructed through and within a wider framework of male dominance. Studies which are routinely about men, in that men constitute the acknowledged or unacknowledged subjects, are not necessarily about men in a more complex, more problematized, sociological sense. They tend to be resource rather than topic. Studies of social mobility, for example, may be about men for methodological reasons or administrative convenience but they are rarely, if ever, about men in the sense that researchers believe that such studies might make any contribution to the sociology of gender or the critical understanding of men and masculinities.

Such an adjustment of focus, seeing texts which routinely use men as subjects as also telling us something about men and masculinities, can itself be a critical exercise since it problematizes what is routinely taken for granted (Morgan, 1981; 1990; 1992). However, we should not overstate this question of invisibility. For the most part, as has been argued, we are talking about the invisibility of men within 'malestream' sociology. Feminist research and theory, while it has been by women and for women, has never been just *about* women. A consideration of such issues as pornography, sexual harassment and violence against wives, or such concepts as patriarchy, sexism and reproduction, should serve as reminders that men have always been under critical consideration within feminist scholarship. It is likely that the recent articulated development of studies of masculinities has made some significantly new contributions, to certain aspects of fatherhood and to men's bodies and sexualities, for example, but the theoretical (as well as the political) inheritance from feminist writings should always be remembered (Stanley, 1990).

Theory is an area where for the most part questions of gender and masculinity have been even less visible than in some other sections of sociology. The links between theory and gender may be understood in at least two ways. In the first place, we may focus on the process of theorizing gender—in this case with specific reference to men and masculinities—and on the ways in which existing theoretical approaches may contribute to, or possibly inhibit, our understandings of the substantive gender issues. [...] So the focus may be upon the problems of theorizing men and masculinities. But we may see the relationship in the opposite direction, that is, from gender to theory. In this case, questions may be asked as to the extent to which and the ways in which various discussions and debates around gender issues might contribute to the reformulation of sociological theory and provide a critique of the practice of theorizing itself. [...]

Feminist theorizing has confirmed the socially constructed and gendered nature of social theory itself in its various forms, as epistemology, ontology, methodology, sociology of science, science, and so on (for example, Harding and Hintakka, 1983; Harding, 1986; 1987). Such problematizations of social theory have often drawn together major structural questions of power, and very immediate issues of practice, of how sociology and the social sciences more generally should be done. They have also necessarily prompted a growing interest in the relationship of social theory, men, and masculinities. The questions raised range from the impact of men's power upon the historical development of social theory, to the connections between masculinities and dominant conceptions of rationality, to ethical and political problems in researching by men and on men. Thus the relationship of social theory, men, and masculinity has implications not only for social theory in a generalized way but also for the full range of malestream sociological activities and traditions.

The need to theorize gender, in particular to theorize men and masculinity, arises largely because of the dangers of reification, essentialism, and reductionism that arise when using such categories as 'women' and 'men', 'femininity' and 'masculinity'. In some cases, for example, there may be a danger of importing taken-for-granted understandings of masculinity—men as competitive, striving, future-oriented and aggressive—into our analyses or re-analyses of existing texts. Preliminary moves in the business of theorizing of men and masculinity have been to argue for the socially constructed nature of these antics and for a pluralizing of the terminology such that we talk of 'masculinities' rather than of 'masculinity'. These moves are not, without their own difficulties and dangers, although they would seem to be necessary preliminary moves in this theoretical undertaking.

This is not the place to provide a complete stocktaking of the sociology of gender and of masculinity. It is worth noting, however, that the actual use of the term 'gender' is still relatively recent within sociology and that the sociology of gender (as opposed, say, to the narrower study of sex roles) is not a well established area. Given this, it is impressive how much progress has been made. Feminist research and the analysis of gender/sexual stratification have already made substantial contributions to a sociology of gender, although it would not be wise to consider these as equivalents. Some recent work in the analysis of men and masculinities (for example, by Hearn, 1987a; Connell, 1987) has placed considerable emphasis upon theoretical considerations. Clearly, however, much more remains to be done, perhaps especially in the analysis of micro-gender processes and the ways in which these might be related to wider structural processes. [...]

Two particular examples of the need to theorize gender in general and masculinity in particular may be provided in the linked areas of the sociology of the body and the sociology of sexuality. [...] The study of the body has, like the sociology of men, made considerable strides in recent years, perhaps more on the theoretical front than on the empirical front (Foucault, 1980; Turner, 1984). Clearly, such studies have been influenced by feminist research and other studies on gender although it remains the case that many such studies, particularly of men and masculinities, remain somewhat disembodied. It is as if the conventional mapping of the nature/culture distinction on to women/men (Ortner, 1974) has been carried over into the study of men and masculinities. Yet many of the central concerns of men and masculinities are directly to do with bodies—war and sport are two obvious examples. We need to elaborate theoretical links between constructions of the body and bodily processes in society (including denials or marginalizations of bodily processes) and constructions of gender and gender identities. How far, for example, are popular accounts of 'body language' a reflection of and a reification of men's interests and concerns? We need to direct the study of gender and masculinities away from the ideological and the cultural, narrowly conceived, and towards the bodily without falling into biological reductionism. We can see some moves in this direction in, for example, Duroche's (1990) linking of issues to do with perceptions of sound and smell to themes of

class and gender, historically located, and in Brod's (1990) discussion of pornography as it affects men or is supposed to affect men. Connell has provided
some interesting clues as to possible developments in the sociology of the
body as applied to men (Connell, 1983; 1987).

The sociology of sexuality is certainly closely connected with the sociology
of the body (although it is not the same thing) and it is also a central concern
of the recent developments in the study of men and masculinities. However,
some of the theoretical links between and distinctions between gender and
sexuality have not always been fully explored. Sexualities are clearly implicated in the constructions of gender and indeed vice versa. Notions of
hegemonic masculinity (Carrigan, Connell and Lee, 1985) are bound up with
hegemonic sexualities. The use of terms of stigmatized sexualities ('poof' or
'wanker') in encounters between young men may illustrate the interplays
between the two. The links and interconnections are clear enough; indeed so
much so that there may be a danger of importing relatively fixed notions of
sexualities just as there may be dangers of constructing relatively fixed notions
of masculinities. Perhaps we need more theoretical discussion not only of
gender salience, the range and kinds of situations and encounters in which
gender may be of greater or lesser significance, but also of 'sexual salience'.
Socially prescribed 'rights' to sexuality, for example, are not uniformly distributed and may be denied or severely restricted to certain groups or
categories such as the young, the old, the disabled, or the mentally ill. If
we are to provide links between gender and sexuality, it should be to an
understanding of sexuality that has been informed by perspectives, such as
those of Foucault, which seek to problematize the very deployment of the
term 'sexuality' itself.

A major theme, therefore, in the processes of theorizing gender is that of
deconstruction, of breaking down artificial unities of genders and sexualities.
As has been said, one influential line of argument has been not simply to
write of 'masculinities' in the plural but to attempt to examine relationships between masculinities within a given society, including relationships
of dominance and subordination. Generally speaking, the concept of 'hegemonic masculinities' addresses itself to these issues, pointing to the dominance within society of certain forms and practices of masculinity which
are historically conditioned and open to change and challenge. Thus today
such a model might be white, heterosexist, middle-class, Anglophone, and
so on. This implies that men too, within a society that may be characterized as 'patriarchal', may experience subordinations, stigmatizations or
marginalizations as a consequence of their sexuality, ethnic identity, class
position, religion, or marital status. The interplay between hegemonic and
subordinate masculinities is a complex one, but should serve to underline the
fact that experience of masculinity and of being a man are not uniform and
that we should develop ways of theorizing these differences. For example,
Westwood (1990) has examined the complex interplays between masculinity,

ethnicity, and class in the context of a society structured by racism as well as by patriarchy. Similarly, issues of gay men and sexualities (especially in the context of concerns about AIDS) have been addressed by Edwards (1994). Linked to this overall emphasis on deconstruction there is a common desire to overcome a variety of dichotomies. These have been widespread within sociology and have their own significance in the development of the discipline. However, they can also be seen as misleading and reificatory. Here we would include distinctions between nature and nurture, nature and culture, and between biology and culture; these are all distinctions which inform another central distinction between 'sex' and 'gender'. While this distinction has clearly been important in getting the sociology of gender off the ground, it has also presented further difficulties, particularly in so far as it leaves the biological 'sex' element of the distinction and its links to gender relatively undertheorized. An important point of departure is to see these distinctions as being themselves historically situated.

Of course the major dichotomy that pervades discussions of gender is that between women and men. Whilst the distinction is important in terms of gender/sexual politics and the analysis of power relations within society as well as being an important aspect of the ways in which most people order their everyday lives and understandings, it is not an unproblematic distinction. For example, a structural analysis of patriarchy, based upon distinctions between men and women, may not immediately translate into everyday practices. Indeed, unexamined and continued use of the everyday categories 'women' and 'men' (as, for example, in the routine analysis of quantitative data 'by sex') may have the effect of reproducing the power structures that gave rise to these distinctions. A theoretical analysis of gender must provide for the critical examination of the everyday deployment of the term 'men', 'women', 'femininity', and 'masculinity', and the occasions of their deployment.

As well as the discussions, already mentioned, dealing with issues of class, sexuality, and ethnicity, there are other ways in which we can look critically at the distinction between 'men' and 'women'. Thomas's (1990) discussion of 'gender salience', for example, sees variation in the degree to which men (and women) see their gender as something which is central and clearly defined in their everyday lives and understandings. From a different perspective, Richards (1990) shows how the Freudian tradition may be seen as generating three variations on the father/son relationship rather than a single model and that these might be deployed to examine variations in masculinities.

It should be stressed that such attempts to overcome or to criticize the everyday taken-for-granted assumption about men and women should not be allowed to take away the critical edge that developed through the analysis of patriarchy and sexual politics. [...] Both an understanding of diversity and a recognition of the whole are required in order to elaborate a critical analysis of masculinites. Perhaps this may best be achieved if we allow the critical examination of the distinctions between women and men to feed back into

a critical examination of other dichotomies which are part of the deep ideological structure that maintains gender inequalities—especially those between
biology and culture, and between sex and gender.

This may also apply to other dichotomics as well, for example that between
the public and the private, one very much implicated in systems of patriarchy
and one which has its own cultural histories (Hearn, 1992). Another distinction is that between agency and structure. While it can be argued that a
major sociological project is to find ways of providing for the interplay
between such distinctions, it may also be argued that the very setting up
of the problem in these terms is problematic. It may be problematic in that
it may perpetrate distinctions which have their own history and which may
have their particular impact on the present social and gender order. The topic
of pornography, for example, raises all kinds of theoretical difficulties. Does
the distinction between agency (men as producers and users of pornography)
and structure (pornography as a form of gendered speech, pornography as
a multi-million enterprise exploiting women) help or hinder the analysis of
this topic, one which is clearly so crucial in the understanding of the construction of genders and sexualities in contemporary society, and one which
is at the heart of gender/sexual political debate. A critical examination of
the distinction between agency and structure may be necessary in order to
develop further the critical analysis of masculinities and of the diversities
of men's responses, including the ways in which some men are themselves
beginning to provide (for) a critique of the gender order of which they themselves are a part.

[. . .] In the process of theorizing men and masculinities, we find a variety of
overlapping and contrasting traditions being drawn upon: feminisms, Marxism,
phenomenology, symbolic interactionism, ethnomethodology, structuralisms,
psychoanalysis, social psychology, and so on. However, such studies do not simply
draw upon existing theoretical traditions; they also make contributions to these
traditions. One aspect of this is the critical analysis of theorizing and the process
of theorizing themselves.

One central aspect of this is an understanding of theory as itself being an
experientially located activity, and not simply as something which goes on
inside people's (mostly men's) heads. When we argue that feminism is a point
of departure for the critical examination of men and masculinities we do not
simply refer to a set of ideas or theories but to the experiences of women
as they confront patriarchal structures and sexist practices. Similarly, and yet
simultaneously *not* similarly, we are concerned with the experiences of men
as we/they live and work in a world which includes the theories and practices
of feminisms. Here we are restating the obvious point that theories do not
simply exist within a closed world of theorizing (although the structure of
academic life may sometimes make it seem like that) but exist in response to
individual and collective experiences, human needs, and historical changes; in
the broadest sense, theories have a material base or material bases. However,

experience itself is not just something which is direct or unmediated; it is itself shaped by and given meaning by theories, latent or manifest, lay or professional, acknowledged or unacknowledged. We wish to examine this circuit, this interplay between theory and experience as it applies to particular issues of men and masculinities.

Here, one or two general points may be made. First, as has already been stressed, the main influences have been the impact of feminisms and a growing sense of perceived 'crisis' on the part of men, partly although rarely straightforwardly in response to, or as a consequence of, the development of feminism. Of course, the idea of 'crisis' is the complex outcome of a historically situated set of influences and circumstances. It is almost certainly not evenly distributed throughout society and it would seem that many men, at all social levels, find little that is problematic about their gender or about the gender order in general (Brittan, 1989). However, it would be wrong to say that this sense of crisis, or at least unease, is simply confined to intellectuals or sociologists. At least some theoretical traditions argue for a deep-rooted male insecurity and these may be given particular content and meaning by particular historically situated experiences. Richards (1990) provides some illustrations of how this process might be seen and understood.

While there are clearly some experiential roots in the recent developments in studies of men and masculinities, it should be stressed that the relationships between experience and theory are not the same for men as for women. Thomas (1990) notes that even where men are developing a consciousness of their gender identity and a desire to challenge gender ideologies, the basis of these desires often appears to be more in terms of abstract principles or general political programmes than direct experience. This lack of equivalence between women and men in these respects should always be stressed and may indeed be generalized. Superordinates, whether in terms of gender, class or race, are not routinely called upon to theorize their own situations in either a sociological or mundane sense, except perhaps in order to provide legitimations of their superordinate position (see Goode, 1982). In the normal course of events, men, elites, or ruling classes generally have no more need to theorize their situations than fish need to theorize about water; yet even saying that does not quite ring true, for there are also numerous contradictions, disjunctures, ambivalences, uncertainties, and just temporary wonderings in the ordinary lives of men which need to be acknowledged too.

Women, therefore, have every right to be sceptical about and critical of many aspects of the recent ways of studies of men and masculinities. How much of this will have the unintended consequences of providing yet another set of legitimations or justifications on the part of men remains to be seen, although we should always be aware of such possibilities. Yet, as Segal (1989) has argued, it would be unfortunate if all these developments in the critical study of men and masculinities, together with all the attempts on the part of men to confront and to change their own practices, were to be rejected. Hence, many writers show how the study of gender might contribute to the study of theory by providing a particular, and central, example of the relationships between experience and theorizing. It is to be hoped that the critical studies of men and masculinities will not simply draw upon existing theoretical traditions but will also provide for a general critique of the process of sociological theorizing. [...] This kind of scepticism about existing theoretical traditions and the practice of theorizing, whether it arises out of the experiences of actual men and women in relation to the feminist challenge or from some other source, will undoubtedly be needed if the critical interplay between gender and theory is to continue and to develop.

One final point may be worth mentioning. The growth of critical studies on men and masculinities is not to be confused with the alleged development of the 'new man'. This 'new man' is supposed to demonstrate a wider range of domestic involvements, a wider range of emotional responses and a greater willingness to criticize his own practices. Most of these recent texts are sceptical of this formulation and point instead to the relative lack of change on the part of men in many areas. [...] Certainly critical, theoretical discussion of men and masculinities must address itself to the forces making for relative lack of change as well as the forces making for change. However there are some reasons for optimism as are illustrated in Cockburn's (1990) references to some of the more positive aspects of equal opportunities legislation or Richard's (1990) consideration of some potentially positive features of Freudian theory. There are positive signs which show the possibilities for the beginnings of debates between women and men around issues of gender inequalities and exploitation. It is unlikely that these debates will be easy and they will not achieve any ready or artificial synthesis. Nevertheless, the fact that these debates are taking place at all is a reason for some guarded optimism.

Note

1. Achilles Heel is a men's publishing collective which produced the journal of the same name from 1977 to 1983, and again in 1987, as well as a number of pamphlets. While the political position of the collective developed over this time, it was broadly concerned with the relationship between men's sexual politics and socialism (see Achilles Heel Collective, 1978; Morrison, 1980). I was a member from 1977 to 1983. The journal was relaunched in 1990.

References

Achilles Heel. *By Way of an Introduction*, vol. 1, pp. 3–7.
Bradley, M., Danchik, L., Fager, M. and Wodetzki, T. (1971) *Unbecoming Men*. New York: Times Change Press.
Brod., H. (1990) Pornography and the alienation of male sexuality. In J. Hearn and D.H.J. Morgan (eds) (1990) *Men, Masculinities and Social Theory*. London: Unwin Hyman.
Brittan, A. (1989) *Masculinity and Power*. Oxford: Basil Blackwell.

Carrigan, T., Connell, R.W. and Lee, J. (1987) Toward a new sociology of masculinity. *Theory and Society* 14, 5, 551–604. Reprinted in H. Brad (ed.) *The Making
   of Masculinities: The New Men's Studies* (pp. 63–100). Boston: Allen & Unwin.
   Extracts in M. Kaufman (ed.) *Beyond Patriarchy. Essays by Men of Power, Pleasure
   and Change* (pp. 139–92), Toronto: Oxford University Press.
Cockburn, C.K. (1990) Men's power in organizations: 'Equal Opportunities' inter-
   views. In J. Hearn and D.H.J. Morgan (eds) (1990) *Men, Masculinities and Social
   Theory.* London: Unwin Hyman.
Connell, R.W. (1983) *Which Way Is Up?* London: Allen & Unwin.
— (1987) *Gender and Power.* Cambridge: Polity, and Stanford, CA: Stanford Uni-
   versity Press.
Duroche, L.L. (1990) Male perceptions as social contract. In J. Hearn and D.H.J.
   Morgan (eds) (1990) *Men, Masculinities and Social Theory.* London: Unwin
   Hyman.
Edwards, T. (1994) *Erotics and Politics: Gay Male Sexuality, Masculinity and Feminism.*
   London: Routledge.
Ford, D. and Hearn, J. (1988) *Studying Men and Masculinity. A Sourcebook of Lit-
   erature and Materials.* Bradford: Department of Applied Social Studies, University
   of Bradford (Revised 1989).
Foucault, M. (1980) *The History of Sexuality,* vol. 1. New York: Vintage.
Goode, J. (1982) Why men resist. In B. Thorne and M. Yalom (eds) *Rethinking the
   Family: Some Feminist Questions* (pp. 131–50). White Plains, NY: Longman.
Grady, K.E., Brannon, R. and Pleck, J.H. (1979) *The Male Sex Role: A Selected and
   Annotated Bibliography.* Mass: Massachusetts Institute of Technology Humanities
   Library.
Harding, S. (1986) *The Science Question in Feminism.* Ithaca, NY: Cornell University
   Press, and Milton Keynes: Open University Press.
— (1987) *Feminism and Methodology: Social Science Issues.* Bloomington, IN: Indiana
   University Press, and Milton Keynes: Open University Press (1988).
Harding, S. and Hintakka, M. (eds) (1983) *Discovering Reality: Feminist Perspectives
   on Epistemology, Metaphysics, Methodology and Philosophy of Science.* Dordecht:
   Reidel.
Hearn, J. (1987a) *The Gender of Oppression. Men, Masculinity and the Critique of
   Marxism.* Brighton: Wheatsheaf, and New York: St Martin's Press.
— (1987b) Theorising men and masculinity, specific problems and diverse approaches.
   Introductory paper to Symposium 'Men's responses to the feminist challenge:
   relationships of theory and practice', Third International Interdisciplinary Con-
   gress on Women, Women's Worlds, Visions and Revisions, Trinity College,
   Dublin, July.
— (1989a) Reviewing men and masculinities or mostly boys' own papers. *Theory,
   Culture and Society* 6, 3, 665 – 89.
— (1989b) Some Sociological Issues in Researching Men and Masculinities. Hallsworth
   Research Fellowship Working Paper No. 2. Manchester, Department of Social
   Policy and Social Work, University of Manchester.
— (1992) *Men in the Public Eye. The Construction and Deconstruction of Public Men and
   Public Patriarchies.* London: Routledge.
Joint Congress of the German, Austrian and Swiss Sociological Associations,
   University of Zurich, October, 1988.
Morgan, D.H.J. (1981) Men, masculinity and the process of sociological enquiry.
   In H. Roberts (ed) *Doing Feminist Research* (pp. 93–113). London: Routledge &
   Kegan Paul.
— (1990) *Discovering Men.* London and Winchester, MA: Unwin Hyman.
— (1992) *Discovering Men.* London: Routledge.

Morrison, P. (1980) *Our Common Ground, Anti-Sexist Men's Newsletter,* 10.
O'Brien, M. (1981) *The Politics of Reproduction.* London: Routledge & Kegan Paul.
Ortner, S. (1974) Is female to male as nature is to culture? In M. Rosaldo and L. Lamphere (eds) *Women, Culture and Society* (pp. 67–88). Stanford, CA: Stanford University Press.
Pleck, J.H. and Sawyer, J. (1974) *Men and Masculinity.* Englewood Cliffs, NJ: Prentice-Hall.
Richards, B. (1990) Masculinity, identification and political structure. In J. Hearn and D.H.J. Morgan (eds) (1990) *Men, Masculinities and Social Theory.* London: Unwin Hyman.
Segal, L. (1989) Slow change or no change: feminism, socialism and the problem of men. *Feminist Review* 31, 5–21.
Stanley, L. (1990) The impact of feminism in sociology: the last twenty years. In C. Kramarae and D. Spender (eds) *The Knowledge Explosion.* New York: Pergamon.
Thomas, A.M. (1990) The significance of gender politics in men's accounts of their gender identity. In J. Hearn and D.H.J. Morgan (eds) (1990) *Men, Masculinities and Social Theory.* London: Unwin Hyman.
Tolson, A. (1977) *The Limits of Masculinity.* London, Tavistock.
Treadwell, P. and Davis, T (n.d.) *Men's Studies Bibliography on Disc.* IBM-MS/DOS. Atlanta, GA. 409, Oakvale Road, Atlanta GA 30307.
Turner, B.S. (1984) *The Body and Society. Explorations in Social Theory.* Oxford: Basil Blackwell.
Westwood, S. (1990) Racism, black masculinity and the politics of space. In J. Hearn and D.H.J. Morgan (eds) (1990) *Men, Masculinities and Social Theory.* London: Unwin Hyman.

14 TRUE CONFESSIONS: A DISCOURSE ON IMAGES OF BLACK MALE SEXUALITY

KOBENA MERCER AND ISAAC JULIEN

I went through a lot when I was a boy. They called me sissy, punk, freak and faggot. If I ever went out to friends' houses on my own, the guys would try to catch me, about eight or twenty of them together. They would run me. I never knew I could run so fast, but I was scared. They would jump on me, y'know, 'cos they didn't like my action ... Sometimes white men would pick me up in their car and take me to the woods and try to get me to suck them. A whole lot of black people have had to do that. It happened to me and my friend, Hester. I ran off into the woods. My friend, he did it ... I was scared.

(Little Richard Penniman. White, 1984, p. 24)

In recent years questions of pleasure and desire have been in the foreground of debates around photography and the politics of representation. In many ways this reflects the political priority given to the issue of pornography in debates led by the women's movement and the gay movement. From our point of view one of the most notable features of this political activity around sexual representation is the marked absence of race from the agenda of concerns—it is as if white people had 'colonized' this agenda in contemporary cultural politics for themselves alone. While some feminists have begun to take on issues of race and racism in the women's movement, white gay men retain a deafening silence on race. Maybe this is not surprising, given the relative apathy and depoliticized culture of the mainstream gay 'scene'.

On the other hand there is a bitter irony in this absence of political awareness of race in the gay male community, especially when we consider recent trends in gay sub-cultural 'style'. After the clone look in which gay men adopted very 'straight' signifiers of masculinity—moustache, short cropped hair, work-clothes—in order to challenge stereotypes of limp-wristed 'poofs', there developed a stylistic flirtation with S&M imagery, leather gear, quasi-military uniforms and skinhead styles. Politically, these elements project highly ambivalent meanings and messages but it seemed that the racist and fascist connotations of these new 'macho' styles escaped gay consciousness as those who embraced the 'threatening' symbolism of the tough-guy look were really only interested in the eroticization of masculinity.[1]

Source: Chapman, R. and Rutherford, J. (eds) (1988) *Male Order: Unwrapping Masculinity* (pp. 131 – 41). London: Lawrence and Wishart.

If the *frisson* of eroticism conveyed by these styles depends on their connotations of masculine power then this concerns the kind of power traditionally
associated with *white* masculinity. It is therefore ironic that gay men have
ignored this ethnic dimension when we also recall that the origins of the
modern gay liberation movement were closely intertwined with the black
liberation movements of the 60s. The documentary film *Before Stonewall*[2]
shows how the American gay community learned new tactics of protest
through their participation in the civil rights struggles for equality, dignity
and autonomy, led by figures like Dr Martin Luther King Jr. As Audre Lorde
points out in the film, the black struggle became the prototype for all the
new social movements of the time—from women's and gay liberation, to the
peace, anti-war and ecology movements as well. But although gays derived
inspiration from the symbols of black liberation—Black Pride being translated into Gay Pride, for example—they failed to return the symbolic debt,
as it were, as there was a lack of reciprocity and mutual exchange between
racial and sexual politics in the 70s. The marginalization of issues of race in
the white gay movement in Britain has already been highlighted by the Gay
Black Group (1982) which questions the ethnocentric assumptions behind the
exhortation to 'come out', regardless of the fact that as black gays and lesbians
our families provide a necessary source of support against racism. However
such concerns with cultural differences have been passed by as the horizon
of gay men's political consciousness has been dominated by the concern
with sexuality in an individualistic sense. Here other aspects of ethnocentrism have surfaced most clearly in debates around the cultural politics of
pornography.

During the 1970s feminist initiatives radically politicized the issue of sexual
representation. The women's movement made it clear that pornography was
condemned for objectifying and exploiting women's bodies for the pleasure
and profit of men. This cultural critique, closely linked to the radical feminist argument that 'porn is the theory, rape is the practice', has had
important effects in society as it found an inadvertent alliance with the
views on obscenity held by the New Right. Mary Whitehouse and others
also helped to politicize sexual representation, arguing that certain types of
imagery were responsible for causing actual violence or abuse.

These developments have also highlighted conflicts of interest between
women and gay men. Gays have often defended porn with libertarian arguments which hold the desire of the individual to do what 'he' wants as
paramount. Such sexual libertarianism is itself based on certain ethnic privileges as it is their whiteness that enables some gay men to act out this
'freedom of choice', which itself highlights the consumer-oriented character
of the metropolitan gay subculture. In this context what interests us are the
contradictory experiences that the porno-photo-text implicates us in, as pornography is one of the few spaces in which erotic images of other black men
are made available.

Our starting point is *ambivalence* as *we want to look, but don't always find the images we want to see.* As black men we are implicated in the same land-scape of stereotypes which is dominated and organized around the needs, demands and desires of white males. Blacks 'fit' into this terrain by being confined to a narrow repertoire of 'types'—the supersexual stud and the sexual 'savage' on the one hand or the delicate, fragile and exotic 'oriental' on the other. These are the lenses through which black men become visible in the urban gay subculture. The repetition of these stereotypes in gay pornography betrays the circulation of 'colonial fantasy', that is a rigid set of racial roles and identities which rehearse scenarios of desire in a way which traces the cultural legacies of slavery, empire and imperialism. Ths circuit for the structuring of fantasy in sexual representation is still in existence. The 'Spartacus' guidebook for gay tourists comments that boys can be bought for a packet of cigarettes in the Phillipines.

Against this backdrop, Robert Mapplethorpe's glossy images of *Black Males* are doubly interesting as the stereotypical conventions of racial representation in pornography are appropriated and abstracted into the discourse of 'art photography'.

Mapplethorpe first made his name in the world of 'art photography' by taking portraits of patrons and protagonists in the post-Warholian subculture of celebrity. In turn he has become something of a 'star' himself as the dis-courses of journalists, critics, gallery curators and collectors have woven a 'mystique' around his persona—the artist as author of 'prints of darkness'.

As he has extended his repertoire the fundamental conservation of Mapplethorpe's aesthetic has become all too apparent: a reworking of the old modernist tactic of 'shock the bourgeoisie' (and make them pay) given a new 'aura' by his characteristic trademark, the pursuit of perfection in photo-graphic technique. The vaguely transgressive quality of his subject matter — S&M rituals, lady body builders, black men—is given a heightened allure by his self-evident mastery of the technological apparatus. However, once we consider the author of these images not as the origin of their meanings but as a 'projection, in terms more or less always psychological, of our way of handling texts' (Foucault, 1977, p. 127) then what is interesting about the images of black men is the way they facilitate the public projection of certain erotic fantasies about the black male body. Whatever his personal motivation or artistic pretentions, Mapplethorpe's camera opens an eye on to the fetishistic structure of stereotypical representations of black men which circulate across a range of surfaces, from pornography to sport, newspapers and advertising, cinema and television.

In pictures such as *Man in a Polyester Suit*, the dialectics of white fear and fascination underpinning colonial fantasy are reinscribed by the exaggerated centrality of the black man's 'monstrous' phallus. The black subject is objec-tified into Otherness as the size of the penis signifies a threat to the secure identity of the white male ego and the position of power which whiteness entails in colonial discourse. Yet, the threatening phobic object is 'contained', after all this is only a photograph on a two-dimensional plane; thus the white male viewer is returned to his safe place of identification and mastery but at the same time has been able to indulge in that commonplace white fixation with black male sexuality as something 'dangerous', something Other.[3] As Fanon argued in *Black Skin, White Mask* the myths about the violent, aggressive and 'animalistic' nature of black sexuality were fabricated and fictioned by the all-powerful white master to allay his fears and anxieties as well as providing a means to justify the brutalization of the colonized and any vestiges of guilt. Mapplethorpe's carefully constructed images are interesting, then, because, by reiterating the terms of colonial fantasy, the pictures service the expectation of white desire; but what do they say to our needs and wants?

Here we return to that feeling of ambivalence because while we can recognize the oppressive dimension of the fantasies staged in such sexual representation, we are fascinated, we still want to look, even if we cannot find the images we want to see. What is at issue is that the same signs can be read to produce different meanings. Although images of black men in gay porn generally reproduce the syntax of commonsense racism, the inscribed, intended or preferred meanings of those images are not fixed. They can at times be prised apart into alternative readings when different experiences are brought to bear on their interpretation. Colonial fantasy attempts to 'fix' the position of the black subject into a space that mirrors the object of white desires, but black readers may appropriate pleasures by reading against the grain, over-turning signs of 'otherness' into signifiers of identity. In seeing images of other black gay men there is an affirmation of our sexual identity.

This touches on some of the qualitative differences between gay and straight pornography: because 'homosexuality' is not the norm, when images of other men, coded as gay, are received from the public sphere there is something of a validation of gay identity. For isolated gays porn can be an important means of saying 'other gays exist'. Moreover, pornographic conventions sometimes slip, encouraging alternative readings. One major photographic code is to show single models in solo frames, enabling the imaginary construction of a one-to-one fantasy; but sometimes, when models pose in couples or groups, other connotations—friendships, solidarities, collective identity—can come to the surface. The ambivalent mixture of feelings in our response to porn is of a piece with the contradictions black gays live through on the 'scene'. While very few actually conform to the stereotypes, in the social networks of the gay subcultures and the circumscribed spaces of its erotic encounters, some black gay men appear to accept and even play up to the assumptions and expectations which govern the circulation of stereotypes. Some of the myths about black sexuality are maintained not by the unwanted imposition of force from 'above', but by the very people who are in a sense 'dominated' by them. Moreover, this subtle dialectic between representation and social interaction is at work in the broader heterosexual context as well—to explore this dimension, and its implications for cultural politics, we pursue Michel Foucault's (1980) idea that sexuality constitutes a privileged 'regime of truth' in our societies (see also Gordon, 1980). From this perspective we may uncover issues around the construction of black masculinities in and through different forms of representation.

Social definitions of what it is to be a man, about what constitutes 'manliness', are not 'natural' but are historically constructed and this construction is culturally variable. To understand how and why these constructions are 'naturalized' and accepted as the norm we cannot rely on notions of ideology as false consciousness. Patriarchal culture constantly redefines and adjusts the balance of male power and privilege and the prevailing system of gender roles by negotiating psychological and personal identity through a variety of material, economic, social and political structures such as class, the division of labour and the work/home nexus at the point of consumption. Race and ethnicity mediates this at all levels, so it's not as if we could strip away the 'negative images' of black masculinity created by Western patriarchy and discover some 'natural' black male identity which is good, pure and wholesome. The point is that black male gender identities have been culturally constructed through complex dialectics of power.

The hegemonic repertoire of images of black masculinity, from docile 'Uncle Tom', the shuffling minstrel entertainer, the threatening native to 'Superspade' figures like *Shaft*, has been forged in and through the histories of slavery, colonialism and imperialism. A central strand in this history is the way black men have incorporated a code of 'macho' behaviour in order to recuperate some degree of power over the condition of powerlessness and dependency in relation to the white male slave-master. The contradiction that this dialectic gives rise to continues in contemporary Britain once we consider images of black males in political debates around 'law and order'. The prevailing stereotype projects an image of black male youth as a 'mugger' or 'rioter'; either way he constitutes a violent and dangerous threat to white society, he becomes the objectified form of inarticulate fears at the back of the minds of 'ordinary British people' made visible in the headlines of the popular tabloid press. But this regime of representation is reproduced and maintained in hegemony because black men have had to resort to 'toughness' as a defensive response to the prior aggression and violence that characterizes the way black communities are policed (by white male police officers). This cycle between reality and representation makes the ideological fictions of racism empirically 'true'—or rather, there is a struggle over the definition, understanding and construction of meanings around black masculinity within the dominant regime of truth.

This paradoxical situation is played out in other areas of popular culture such as sport. Classical racism involved a logic of dehumanization in which African peoples were defined as having bodies but not minds; in this way the super-exploitation of the black body as a muscle-machine could be justified. Vestiges of this are active today in schools for instance, where teachers may encourage black kids to take up sport because they're seen as academic under-achievers. But on the other hand there are concrete advantages to be gained from appearing to play up to such general expectations. Without black ath-letes it is doubtful whether Britain would win any medals at the Olympics — sport is a circumscribed zone where blacks are allowed to excel. And we have also seen how black people have entered sport not just for their own individual gain; by using their public status, they have articulated a political stance — recall those newsreel images of the Black Power salute at the 1968 Olympic Games.

Although black men have been able to exploit the contradictions of the dominant ideological regimes of truth, the political limitations of remaining within its given structure of representation became acutely apparent in the context of the black liberation movements of the 1960s. Slogans such as 'Black is Beautiful', and new idioms of cultural and political expression like the Afro hairstyle (Mercer, 1988), signified the rejection of second-class citizenship and 'negative self-image'. The movement sought to clear the ground for the cul-tural reconstruction of the black subject—but because of the *masculinist form* this took, it was done at expense of black women, gays and les-bians. Figures such as Eldridge Cleaver promoted a heterosexist version of black militancy which not only authorized sexism—Stokely Carmichael said the only position of black women in the movement was 'prone' — but a hidden agenda of homophobia, something which came out in Cleaver's (1970) remorseless attack on James Baldwin. Revolutionary nationalism implied a very macho-oriented notion of black struggle and this pertains to Britain also as the term 'black youth' really means black *male* youth (their sisters were invisible in debates on race and crime in the 70s) and this has been taken, rather romantically, by some black male activists and intellectuals to embody the 'heroic' essence of black people's resistance.

This emphasis on politics as 'frontline confrontation' not only ignores the more subtle and enduring forms of cultural resistance which have been forged in diaspora formations, it also depoliticizes 'internal' conflicts and antagonisms —especially around gender and sexuality—within the black communities. It was precisely because this one-dimensional masculinist rhetoric colludes and compromizes black struggle within existing regimes of representation, that black women organized autonomously as feminists in the 1970s. The issues raised by black feminists—and it has only been with their interventions and leadership that questions of pleasure, desire and sexual politics have entered the agenda of black political discourse—all point us towards the 'unfinished business' of the 60s. And as Cheryl Clarke (1983) demonstrates in her essay 'The Failure to Transform', the issue of homophobia in the black commu-nities cannot be avoided any longer. Contrary to the misinformed idea that homosexuality is a 'white man's disease', something into which we've been corrupted, she shows that lesbians and gay men have always been an integral part of black society—active in politics, the church and cultural activities like music, literature and art—even though our existence is publicly denied and disavowed by self-appointed 'community leaders'.

Although the organizational forms of black sexual politics are only recently emerging, questions of sexuality, pleasure and desire have always been on the black political agenda in so far as our aspirations—for freedom—have always found cultural forms of expression. Above all, it is in the arena of music that black people have endorsed and re-articulated the radical slogan that 'the personal is political'. While the music of the Afro-Christian church—hymns, spirituals, gospel—sang of the intense desire and yearning to transcend the misery of oppression, the blues or the Devil's music of the street sought wordly transcendence in the here and now through the sensual pleasures of the flesh. And as Paul Gilroy has argued[4] it is this emotional realism and the candid expressive voicing of sexual desire that also accounts for the immense popularity of black musics among whites in modern Western societies. It is in the medium of music—always associated with dance and the erotic potentialities of the dance floor—that black men and women have articulated sexual politics. Male–female antagonisms are openly acknowledged in soul; sex is celebrated in the blues, but it is also problematized; some of Billie Holiday's songs offer succinct critiques of black men's manipulative attitudes, but they also address the ambivalent 'messiness' of longing for their intimate embrace.

While machismo was big box-office in the 'blaxploitation' movie genre of *Shaft* and *Superfly* in the early 70s, black male musicians like Sly Stone, Stevie Wonder and Marvin Gaye undercut the braggadoccio to make critiques of conventional models of black masculinity. In this period, classic Motown like 'I'll be There' by the Four Tops or 'Papa Was a Rolling Stone' by the Temptations spoke of a whole range of concerns with reliability and responsibility in personal relationships, critiquing some of the vagaries in certain models of black family life and fatherhood. Today, artists and stars like Luther Vandross and the much maligned Michael Jackson disclose the 'soft side' of black masculinity (and this is the side we like!). We feel it is important to tap into and recognize these resources in popular culture because they reveal that masculinity can be constructed in a diversity of ways. If we attune our ears we may also acknowledge that black male artists in music have been involved in a 'struggle' around the political meanings of masculinity—in contrast to the 'emotional illiteracy' which is regarded as one of the most malignant consequences of patriarchal role models, the sexual discourses of black popular music enables and invites men to find a means of making sense of their feelings. It will be crucial for the left to realize that far from being 'mindless entertainment', music is the key site in everyday life where men and women reflect on their gendered and sexual identities and make adjustments to the images they have of themselves.

Once we can reclaim the camp and crazy 'carnivalesque' qualities of Little Richard—the original Queen of Rock and Roll himself—we can appreciate the way in which some black men have been in the popular vanguard when it comes to sexual politics. Little Richard's outrageousness was a model for many who have deployed the subversive potential of irony and parody like George Clinton's Parliament and Funkadelic, Cameo and perhaps even Prince, as they 'play' with stereotypical codes and conventions to 'theatricalize' and send-up the whole masquerade of masculinity itself. By destabilizing signs of race, gender and sexuality these artists draw critical attention to the cultural *constructedness*, the artifice, of the sexual roles and identities we inhabit. In this way they remind us that our pleasures are political and that our politics can be pleasurable.

Notes

1. For an examination of how these issues erupted around S&M dress styles at the London Lesbian and Gay Centre, see Ardhill and O'Sullivan (1986).
2. *Before Stonewall: The Making of a Gay and Lesbian Community*, directed by Greta Schiller; distributed. by The Other Cinema, Wardour Street, London.
3. The concept of 'colonial fantasy' is developed by Bhabba (1983). See also Bhabba's introduction, 'Remembering Fanon' in the reprint of *Black Skin, White Masks* (Fanon, 1986).
4. In 'Diaspora, Utopia and the critique of capitalism', Ch. 5 of *There Ain't No Black in the Union Jack* (Gilroy, 1987).

References

Ardhill, S. and O'Sullivan, S. (1986) Upsetting the applecart: difference, desire and lesbian sadomasochism. *Feminist Review*, 23.
Bhabba, Homi (1983). The Other question—the stereotype and colonial discourse. *Screen*, 24, 4.
— (1986) Remembering Fanon. In *Black Skin, White Masks* (reprint). Pluto.
Clarke, C. (1983) The failure to transform: homophobia in the black community. In B. Smith (ed.) *Home Girls: A Black Feminist Anthology*. New York: Kitchen Table/Women of Color Press.
Cleaver, E. (1970) *Soul on Ice: Notes on a Native Son*. London: Panther.
Fanon, F. (1986) *Black Skin/White Masks*. London: Pluto. (First published in French (1952) and in English (1968) Grafton Books; (1970) London: Paladin).
Foucault, M. (1977) What is an author? In *Language, Counter-Memory and Practice*. Oxford: Basil Blackwell.
Gay Black Group (1982) *Gay News*, 251, October.
Gilroy, P. (1987) *There Ain't No Black in the Union Jack*. London: Hutchinson.
Gordon, C. (ed.) (1990) *Power/Knowledge: Selected Interviews and Other Writings 1972–1977*. Brighton: Harvester.
Mercer, K. (1988) Black hair/style politics. *New Formations*, 3.
White, C. (1984) *The Life and Times of Little Richard*. London: Pan.

15 THE CENTRALITY OF RELATIONSHIP IN PSYCHOLOGICAL DEVELOPMENT: A PUZZLE, SOME EVIDENCE, AND A THEORY

CAROL GILLIGAN

There are certain risks—including, here, the risk of becoming unable to risk—that we cannot close off without a loss of human value, suspended as we are between beast and god, with a kind of beauty available to neither. (Martha Nussbaum, 19)

A PUZZLE

In the late nineteenth century, psychiatrists treating young women observed that girls 'are more liable to suffer' in adolescence, and that girls who suffer are among the most psychologically vital. Henry Maudsley makes this observation in England in the 1870s. Shortly thereafter, Josef Breuer records a similar impression in Vienna:

> Adolescents who are later to become hysterical are for the most part lively, gifted, and full of intellectual interests before they fall ill. Their energy of will is often remarkable. They include girls who get out of bed at night so as secretly to carry out some study that their parents have forbidden for fear of their overworking.

Countering the generally held impression that hysteria is a sign of mental degeneracy, Breuer concludes, 'The capacity for forming sound judgements is certainly not more abundant in [these girls] than in other people, but it is rare to find in them simple, dull intellectual inertia or stupidity.'

Freud expands this characterization. Describing his patient, Fraulein Elisabeth von R., he says that she shows:

> the characteristics one meets with so frequently in hysterical people: her giftedness, her ambition, her moral sensibility, her excessive demand for love which, to begin with, found satisfaction in her family, and the independence of her nature which went beyond the feminine ideal and found expression in a considerable amount of obstinancy, pugnacity, and reserve.

Like other hysterical young women, Elisabeth suffered from a physical and psychological paralysis: the pains in her legs made it difficult for her to take even a single step forward, her nature was frozen, she found it painful to stand alone.

Source: This article has been specially commissioned for this Reader.

This picture persists across the twentieth century. Karen Horney attributes girls' psychological troubles in adolescence to a revival of Oedipal conflicts and rivalries, leading to tensions around sexuality and problems in relationships with mothers. Melanie Klein locates the source of the difficulties further back in the relational struggles of infancy. Helene Deutsch focuses on femininity and advises young women to develop an 'as if' personality—to wear their femininity like a cloak. Clara Thompson vividly describes the loss of vitality, and Jean Baker Miller ties the constriction in girls' sense of self to a narrowing of relationship.

Michelle Fine's research on adolescents who drop out of school provides a corollary to these clinical observations. Adolescent girls who dropped out of a large, urban high school, at the time of their leaving, were among the least depressed and the brightest of the girls. The association of risk in adolescence with girls' psychological vitality thus extends not only through time but also across class and cultural differences.

Research on adolescent development finds consistent evidence of sex differences. Adolescent girls are more liable than boys to suffer from depression, eating disorders ranging from anorexia to obesity, dissociative processes, suicidal gestures, poor body-image, low sense of self-worth, and lack of resilience or the ability to recover psychologically from trauma or stress. Boys are more psychologically at risk in childhood, more prone to depressive episodes, learning disorders, bed wetting, out of control behaviour; boys who are in trouble at adolescence usually have a history of trouble reaching back into early childhood. Among girls, there is a sudden loss of resiliency or psychological immunity at adolescence. One longitudinal study finds that girls show a sharp drop in resilience around the age of eleven; there was no corresponding finding for boys. This pattern holds across culture, but with significant variation: white girls in the US show a drop in their sense of self-worth around the age of 11; hispanic girls show a sharper drop that occurs later, around 14; black girls maintain their sense of self-worth but are more likely to become involved in open conflict with teachers which leads to trouble at school.

Epidemiological studies of the relationship between life stress and psychological illness find that when families are under stress (from marital discord, economic depression, or the outbreak of war), the children who are most likely to suffer psychologically are boys in childhood and girls in adolescence. Seligman notes the sharp reversal that occurs in the incidence of depression around puberty and concludes that whatever happens to cause the flip-flop, leading girls suddenly to become afflicted at a rate twice as high as boys, it does not have its roots in early childhood. Something, he says, must happen around puberty.

This collection of clinical observations, research findings, and epidemiological data points to an impasse in girls' development, where psychological strengths or vitality are either lost or associated with psychological and

social/economic risk. The puzzle is that consistent evidence of a developmental asymmetry between time of heightened risk in women's and men's
development, despite its clear implications for prevention and treatment, has
until recently remained for the most part unexplored and unexplained theo-
retically. Freud's (1933) observation that 'the riddle of femininity remains
unsolved', has continued to be true for the next half-century. Although girls'
psychological problems at adolescence are frequently explained as a function
of their nature (hormones or puberty) or their culture (femininity or socialization), there has been a striking inattention to the evidence of girls' psychological strength before puberty and the indication of a sudden reversal.

SOME EVIDENCE

Studies of women's psychological development, particularly studies of adolescent girls, have been a phenomenon of the 1980s. Prior to that time,
the psychology of human development was, 'the psychology of the male
youngster writ large'. Key concepts such as self, identity, relationship, sexuality, morality, creativity, achievement and even development itself were
drawn for the most part from a man's perspective or reflected the viewpoint of a male child. Elizabeth Mayer's case study of a young girl
who sees boys' bodies as closed and worries about them having 'no holes'
by its very reversal draws attention to this bias. Whether because of anatomy
or culture, women's openness to relationship has been interpreted as detrimental to the development of a sense of self, sexuality, and the capacity to
love, as well as the ability to think clearly and take decisive action. Consequently, psychologists have encouraged women in a variety of ways and for
a variety of reasons to become more separate and closed.

The studies of women's and girls' psychology which began in the 1980s can
be divided into at least two types. One sought to assess women and girls,
using standard psychological concepts and measures, asking in effect how they
were doing with respect to sense of self, sense of self-worth, sexuality, relationships, work, achievement, creativity, morality or mental health. Another
approach began with the recognition that the categories of psychology were
not for the most part grounded in women's experience and that psychological
research typically imposed a condition of non-relation which perpetuated this
problem. Therefore, the aim of the research was to learn from women and
girls and on that basis to reconceptualize psychology. This approach has led to
the development of a new 'relational psychology', because listening to women
revealed the extent to which psychology itself was out of relation with the
human world (with women, people who are not of European descent, gay
men, lesbians—with everyone who does not fit) and also because women drew
attention to the centrality of relationship in human development.

The imperial 'I' of the Cartesian legacy is so deeply embedded in psychological theory and methods that it is for the most part unobserved within the

field. Malcolm Bowie, reading Lacan in the light of his studies of Proust and Freud, suggests the roots and the costs of the aspiration to autonomy and control:

> From within its early 'insufficiency'—its dependence on others and its lack of motor co-ordination—the human infant anticipates the ego that will in due course offer it autonomy and control. But this ego, once in place, proves to be too strong and too thickly armoured for the individual's own good, and threatens to bring a reverse temporal mechanism into play: against the forward thrust of anticipation a retrospective movement may be established that leads back to the very fragmentation and 'insufficiency' from which the infant had formerly recoiled. Going forward in time to an 'alienating destination' brings one to the start of a painful and disintegrating journey back.

The terms of this analysis—autonomy versus disintegration—convey the anxieties surrounding women: the tendency to equate relationship with loss of autonomy, pain, insufficiency, and disintegration.

Against this backdrop of interpretation, relational psychology has recast the most basic psychological constructs: the sense of self and the experience of relationship. The starting premise is connection rather than separation. Thus the sense of self grows in relationship rather than in separation, and relationship itself is an active process of making and maintaining connection rather than a passive state. Recent research with infants and mothers provides strong empirical support for this theoretical shift by revealing the relational nature of the human infant and documenting an active process of relationship which is evident even before birth.

This change in theory both implies and comes from a change in method. The research on infancy which has proved so revolutionary studied infants with their mothers, taking seriously Winnicott's observation that the human infant is a member of a couple. Making connection the focus of research rather than imposing a condition of non-relation (such as the aptly named 'strange situation' in attachment research), psychologists observed that infants show the capacity both to be and not to be in relationship—to tune in with others, creating relational patterns which Trevarthen compares with jazz improvizations, and also to close themselves and be alone. Tronick has shown that trust in relationships is built not from good connection or attachment *per se* but rather on the ability of the couple to repair the inevitable disconnections or breaks in their relationship.

These findings, then, have direct bearings on the method or structuring of psychological research. Research conducted in a condition of non-relation will observe a closed and cut off person, whereas research conducted in a condition of relationship will encourage vulnerability and elicit relational processes. Tronick's work would suggest that trust in the research setting would hinge on the potential for identifying and repairing relational breaks.

Research psychologists, and to a lesser extent clinicians, traditionally have imposed a condition of non-relationship on their psychological work and then observed psychological processes under these conditions as if they were objective or true. Researchers have used instruments and probes to get at the psyche and skirted relationship through deception; clinicians have relied on various forms of withholding in order to create the conditions for observing the psyche through transference. In contrast, a relational approach, while concerned with truth and cognizant of transference, relies on voice and relationship for gaining access to another person's psyche. As the temperature and humidity of a chemistry laboratory will affect chemical reactions, so the relational atmosphere of research and psychotherapy affects psychological processes.

A series of studies that began in 1981 explored girls' development using a voice-centred relational method, which itself was articulated more fully and clarified in the course of this work. Girls drew our attention constantly to our relationships with them. Over and over again, in a myriad subtle ways, we tried to establish that we had come not to judge them—to see how well they were doing—but to learn from them and with them about girls and women. After much testing, the girls took us into a world which seemed previously unobserved — a girls' world which we, as women, found at once familiar and surprising.

My strongest impression in the first few years of this project was of being let in and then being shut out, shown a glimpse of something that was then covered. I became more adept at picking up cues and asking questions (Do you really feel that way? Is that true? Do you believe that?). Listening to girls, I discovered that they were often speaking without listening to themselves. So that questions created an opening for them to listen and a resonance encouraging them to say what they 'really' thought or felt. It was then that girls revealed an underworld of psychological experience and knowledge and spoke of what they were doing in their relationships, how they really felt about things, what they really thought. It was as if my questions restored the ground or credibility of their voice, or their experience.

Pressed to write a paper about this research, I titled it, 'The willing suspension of disbelief: conflicts of female adolescence', and then wondered about the word 'willing'. Girls were living in what seemed to be, in terms of their own understanding, a fictional world that was taken as real. To live in the world, it seemed necessary, then, for girls not to know what they know, or to act as if they did not see, hear, feel, listen, put together, figure out, make sense of what was going on around them.

In 1986, my colleagues and I moved our project back in developmental time. Lyn Mikel Brown and I initiated a five-year research with close to a hundred girls who at the time we began yearly interviewing were six, nine, eleven, fourteen and sixteen. Subsequently, in 1989, Annie Rogers and I started a three-year more intensive developmental and prevention project. With Normi

Noel, we formed Theatre, Writing and Outing Clubs with two groups of girls who were, respectively, nine and ten, and eleven, when we began.

It took us a while to listen to the strong and open voices of young girls, without hearing their openness as rude, hurtful, unfeeling or selfish—labels which girls in time learn to apply to themselves. By 13, girls regularly call honesty in relationships (speaking your mind, opening your heart) 'stupid'. Young girls are fearlessly open in relationship, saying what is on their mind and hearts. They also can close and simply say nothing.

When Diane at eight is asked about a time when she was not being listened to, she said that at dinner, when she tries to speak, her brother and sister interrupt her, 'stealing' her mother's attention. Diane's response was to bring a whistle to dinner; when she was interrupted, she blew the whistle. This succinct illustration exemplifies girls' ready naming and response to relational breaks or violations. Diane's strategy was effective. Mother, brother and sister stopped speaking and turned to Diane, who said, 'in a nice voice, "That's much nicer."' Eight-year-old Karen walked out of her class on the third day when her teacher did not call on her to do a hard problem. She knew that people seeing her standing in the hall would think that she was in trouble, but she also knew that this was not why she was in the hall: 'I just couldn't take it,' she explained. Asked if her teacher knew why she left, she said 'She didn't listen, but I told her, so I guess she knows.' This fine distinction between the teacher knowing (taking in what Karen said) and the teacher listening (bringing herself into relation with Karen) illustrates how closely girls can observe relationship, but also how readily they are misunderstood. Because listening is often taken to mean agreement, rather than responding to feelings and thoughts.

Jessie, at eight, reveals a more complex picture of relationship. Asked about not being listened to, she speaks of a time when she went over to play with her friend. The friend had another friend over and they did not play with Jessie. Asked what she did, she said that she went up to her friend and whispered in her ear that this wasn't any fun for her, that if they didn't play with her, she would just go home. 'What happened?' her interviewer asks. Jessie says, 'She said, "Just go home".' The friend had not listened to Jessie's feelings. Lauren spoke of a time when her friend responded casually when Lauren told her that her dog had been killed. She realized that her friend wasn't listening to what she was saying. Otherwise, she could not be her friend.

Non-relation was not imagined as a possibility in close relationships by many of these girls, or rather the possibility of relation was constantly imagined. Jessie went home and dreamed up a plan for teaching her friend how it feels to be excluded, so that her friend could be with her in her feelings, could know how Jessie felt. Lauren waited until she had her friend's full attention before she repeated her sad news.

Girls pay close attention to their parents and teachers, know when they are listening and when they are distracted. They also keep close track of what they say and do, recording conversations in their memory and repeating them to their friends. This allows girls to anticipate relational turns and to become caught by anticipation in repetitive patterns.

By remaining open to the human world and taking in the relational sur- round (who is speaking to whom, who is feeling what, when, why, and so forth), girls began to pick up relational dynamics: how things go at home, in school, with friends, with best friends, with mothers, with fathers, and so on. They learn how feelings move between people, how anger lies over sadness and vulnerability, how people mask their feelings by raising their voices, how people cover their faces with smiles or blank looks. Girls' dramatic skits and stories reveal a keen ear and eye for what is real and what is fake, what is true and what is false in relationships.

In this way, girls become very canny about human psychology. They pick up and register in the course of daily living: women's depression, women's and men's sadness and anger, closeness and distance, moments of love, hate, fear, violence, the manifestations of poverty in a world of wealth ('The centre- piece on our family dinner table is a pile of unpaid bills.'), the vulnerability of unemployed or disabled fathers, the disappearance of women in patriarchal marriages ('She's called Mrs Jim Hanson, as if she wasn't there.'), the dif- ference between being physically and psycholocially present ('Every night he says the same thing, "It's a great dinner", no matter what.'), the pleasure of love and closeness in families ('My mother is my best friend.').

Girls watch around psychological corners, listening under the surface, picking up the edges in people's voices, the shifts in expression. If their ability to read relational signals has not been jammed by confusing and traumatic experiences which force not knowing or dissociation, girls can be very canny in knowing who is and is not worthy of trust. Girls brought their relational knowledge into our research project, and we found that to stay in connection with the girls, we had to be clear about our relationship with them.

At eleven, the girls in our project had strong voices. Relational violations ('stealing my mother's attention', 'stealing our teacher') aroused strong feelings and were often severely punished by scapegoating, exclusion, and the like; inclusion and exclusion were constant problems. In groups, girls validated one another's perceptions, which provided a powerful counterforce to adults. In the face of what they experienced as adult non-relation, girls often formed a wall against adult entry, in the same way that they could close out one another, by becoming impassive or by attack. They also could be exceptionally warm, close, empathic, and straightforwardly present with one another and with adults, offering comments, responding to others, saying what they feel and know, knowing by reaching into their 'deep, deep heart'.

Knowing with your heart, feeling in your body, having a gut feeling, are phrases which describe the sense I was left with from this work with girls, because I could not readily explain how they know what they know. We gathered strong evidence indicating that girls know a human world which is said to be unknowable. And then, in the course of our studies, we began to witness girls not-knowing.

As girls approached adolescence, they described a relational crisis. If they continued to speak their minds and show their hearts, they were in danger of losing their relationships—no one would want to be with them. But if they did not speak their minds and say what they were feeling, no one would know what was happening to them and they would be all alone. The talk about separation as key to development in adolescence simply rides over this problem. Girl after girl described a paradoxical situation: that in order to make and maintain relationships, it was necessary to keep large parts of herself out of relationship. By staying out of relationship, girls also protected vulnerable parts of themselves from attack and denigration.

Girls, however, resisted these moves out of relationship. They resisted dissociative processes—not knowing what they knew, not feeling what they felt, not being where they were, not staying in their bodies and in their relationships. In our interviews with girls at the edge of adolescence, the phrase 'I don't know' became repetitive, increasing often year by year. Girls were marking their own not knowing, because when their phrase, 'I don't know', was questioned or pressed slightly, it often turned out that in fact they knew.

The relational nature of this crisis in girls' lives was further indicated by another phrase that became repetitive—the tag phrase 'you know', which girls regularly interspersed in their narratives. It seemed a way of taking relational soundings, assessing what it was possible to say to the woman with whom they were sitting without suddenly feeling all alone, weird, stupid, bad, or crazy.

In talking about giving up relationship for the sake of 'relationships', girls most often spoke about their friends. Jessie, at 11, like many girls at this age, is afraid to tell her friends that she is mad at them, because she fears they will get madder at her and she will just end up making a mess.

Jessie: A lot of times (my friends) get really mad and it terrifies you because you feel like they are going to tell somebody and they are going to get almost the whole class on her side, and it would be one against, I don't know, ten.
Interviewer: In those situations, how do you feel?
Jessie: I don't feel very good. I feel like I'm making this whole fight, that it is really turning out to be a mess.

Girls become wary in their relationships, and often seek safety and solace with their mothers, sometimes with fathers, sometimes with a sister or best friends. As the girls in our studies reached adolescence, they began increasingly to look at their 'looks', and to listen to themselves carefully, monitoring whether they sounded too loud, too sexual, too angry, too aggressive, too inquisitive, too boisterous, too sad. To hide feelings which were dangerous to reveal or potentially offensive, girls separated their voices from their bodies. At 12, Ritu located anger in her stomach and sadness in her heart. But with adolescent sexuality, revealing embodied feelings can become dangerous for girls. It is, however, also dangerous for girls to cut themselves off from what they are feeling in their body. If girls separate their voices from their bodies, they lose their ready capacity to speak their minds and their hearts.

The dissociative processes or internal splits which girls make within themselves as they reach adolescence have commonly been taken as signs of development—separation, the creation of a separate identity or self, subjectivity, autonomy, self-containment, independence. From girls, we picked up strong signs of distress. Dissociation, evidence of exhaustion and depression, the onset of anorexia, bulimia, obesity, suicide attempts (which peak at age 13), and a readiness to back down or back off in the face of strong conviction and feelings (their own or those of others), to simply not mind or not care.

Malka, at 11, speaks about closeness which she equates with knowing and being known. Talking about a long-standing friendship with a boy in her neighbourhood, she says,

> Like, you know, most people, you stand up and say goodbye at the door. And with him, we can be playing a game or whatever, and we just say, 'Bye!' Because we're so intimate ... We're so, I guess it's sort of close. We've known each other for so long and so, we really *know* each other.

We speak about whether people can know when someone really knows them. Malka describes different ways of knowing—the kind you can tell by a test, what you can learn from reading books, and what you 'can just tell', Speaking of how you know when someone knows you, she says:

> You can't tell by a test. Sometimes you know. And even then, they might not know certain things about you. There was a book, there was a quote from it, it was, um, 'Her heart was a secret garden and the walls were very high.' I think everybody has a little bit like that, that they tell *nobody, no matter what.* And so, nobody knows everything about you. There are some things that *you* don't know about you [Sigh]. But sometimes there's just someone who knows you very well, and you *know* that, and you can't find out by any sort of test ... I've noticed recently that I can just tell how people feel about certain things, you know, why they don't want to talk about it.

In adolescence, many girls speak of sudden and shocking betrayal: a best friend who proves untrustworthy, a teacher who acts out of relation, a mother who seems suddenly to stand on the other side of a chasm. Jamaica Kincaid and Maxine Hong Kingston both record the sense of shock in novels about coming of age, and their bi-cultural situation (Caribbean-English; Chinese-American) may sharpen their perception of something more muted in other girls' lives: an earth-rending disconnection or dissociation which leaves the girl with a 'duck voice' or in 'the long rain' of hysteria and craziness.

The relational paradox which forces dissociative processes in girls at adolescence has been observed retrospectively in women's psychotherapy by Jean Baker Miller and her colleagues. Miller formulates this paradox as central for understanding the etiology of psychological problems and also the therapeutic process. In our studies of adolescence, we found that the quick of the dissociation, the stem around which the splitting occurs, is the seemingly impending loss of relationship: one girl goes off in search of relationship, while another girl stays in relationships.

Anne Frank, with the eye of a writer, describes this split within herself. She has the reputation, 'little bundle of contradictions' and she finds that it fits. But 'like so many words, it can mean two things: contradiction from without and contradiction from within'. The external contradiction comes from speaking her mind and not giving in: '[It] is the ordinary not giving in easily, always knowing best, getting in the last word, *enfin*, all the unpleasant qualities for which I am renowned.' This resistant, 'know-it-all' voice which Anne calls 'unpleasant' sounds like the willful side of the hysterics whom Breuer and Freud describe. (Freud reports that Fraulein Elisabeth's father called her 'cheeky' and 'cock-sure'.) In contrast to Anne Frank, the hysterics have lost their voices and become paralyzed.

Anne plumbs her own psychology and finds evidence of an internal contradiction or split personality: 'Nobody knows about it, that's my own secret. I have, as it were, a split personality.' She then describes the two sides. One is sexual, light-hearted, insouciant, giddy—she calls this her bad side and says that it leads others to find her 'insufferable'. The other Anne is pure, deep, good and quiet, but she is underwater or frozen; she never appears in public.

A voice speaks from somewhere outside this division; her subjects are voice, honesty, hurt, vulnerability and the seeming impossibility of relationship:

> I never utter my real feelings ... If I'm to be quite honest, then I must admit that it does hurt me ... If I'm watched to that extent [by my family] I start by getting snappy, then unhappy, and finally I twist my heart round again so that the bad is on the outside and the good is on the inside and keep on trying to find a way of becoming what I would so like to be and what I could be if—there weren't any other people living in the world.

It is easy to move from these diary entries to the various descriptions of what happens to girls at adolescence: the loss of voice, the constriction or division of self, episodes of depression, signs of hysteria, and the giftedness, intelligence, demand for love, and persistence which characterize girls at risk in adolescence. Anne hears her strong voice and character called 'unpleasant', her open sexuality and high spirits lead others to find her 'insufferable'. When she hears on the radio that people are interested in diaries kept during the occupation and decides to revise her diary for future publication, she heeds these voices and deletes the offending passages. Her ear is perfect, because in fact after the war the diary was further censored, after 19 publishers had turned it down. With a Catholic priest who offered to help him, Otto Frank deleted further passages where Anne voiced her sexuality, her resistance, and her open rejection of her mother as a model, given the patriarchal structure of her family.

Dissociative processes are psychologically necessary for girls at adolescence because they have to straddle incommensurate realities and because the split between good and bad women is enforced. Girls experience intense feelings of helplessness, powerlessness and betrayal if they lose the sense that they can say what they mean and be heard. When a girl or her actions are named in ways that directly contradict her experience of herself or what she thinks she is doing, she may feel and be powerless to contest the interpretation, except by jeopardizing herself and her reputation. In effect, she loses her voice or finds herself in frank contradiction with people who have greater power than she does.

Girls' healthy resistance to losing their voice or giving up on relationship thus becomes a political resistance or struggle, given the tension between women's voices and relationships and the perpetuation of patriarchal societies and cultures. Girls' fight for relationship and their ability to repair relational breaks would explain their psychological strengths throughout childhood, their immunity, their vitality, their psychological health. The strongest finding on psychological resilience or a person's ability to withstand stress, is that a confiding relationship affords the best protection against psychological illness. Girls' struggle to maintain their voices in their relationships is so important for this reason. Because once girls stop saying what they are feeling and thinking and often stop knowing it as well, confiding relationship becomes impossible.

A THEORY

> But human excellence grows like a vine tree,
> fed by the green dew, raised up
> among wise men and just,
> to the liquid sky . . .
> We have all kinds of needs for those we love,
> most of all in hardships,
> but joy, too, strains
> to track down eyes that it can trust.
>   Pindar (translated by Nussbaum)

CLOV: They said to me, That's love, yes yes,
not a doubt, now you see how ... How easy it
is. They said to me, That's friendship,
yes, no question, you've found it. They
said to me, Here's the place, stop, raise
your head and look at all that beauty.
That order! They said to me, Come now,
you're not a brute beast, think upon these
things, and you'll see how all becomes
clear. And simple! They said to me, what
skilled attention they get, all these
dying of their wounds.

I say to myself—sometimes, ...
(Samuel Beckett, *Endgame*)

This soil is bad for certain kinds of flowers. (Toni Morrison, *The Bluest Eye*)

If psychological development occurs in relationship, then the human psyche, like a vine tree, becomes vulnerable to the elements it grows in: the human weather, the earth, the quality of the society and culture. If the human psyche or voice is not disembodied, if it has a rich resource of language, if a person can speak and be heard and understood, then she or he/she is likely to flourish. But this soil, as Morrison observes, 'is bad for certain kinds of flowers'.

Morrison is talking about race and racism, but I will talk about gender and patriarchy. Psychological development occurs in society and culture, and patriarchy which requires the disconnection from women on the part of women and men affects women's and men's development differently, from a psychological standpoint. The new and brilliant research on infants and mothers firmly establishes the relational foundation of human development. From the beginning of life, most people have the capacity to make and maintain connection with others. Presumably, this capacity would develop in the course of human life.

Connection or relationship, however, entails vulnerability—the opening of oneself to others. And vulnerability means the ability to be wounded. The zen of development is that relationship, which is the condition for development, also carries with it the potential for being psychologically wounded.

My theory is simply that a relational crisis—a moment when vulnerability becomes unbearably heightened—occurs at different times in the lives of boys and girls living in patriarchy or civilization. For boys, the initiation into patriarchy or the disconnection of self and voice from women, occurs typically in early childhood. Boys who resist this initiation are commonly called 'Mamma's boys' or 'wimps'. For girls, the initiation into patriarchy or the disconnection of voice from women involves an active and ongoing dissociation and occurs typically at adolescence. The consequences of this asymmetry are potentially radical.

To put this in more familiar psychological terms. When Freud described the Oedipus complex as a turning point in boys' early childhood, he described a heightened intersection between psychological health and civilization. The young boys' sexual desires were in tension, on a fantasy level, with his bodily integrity and his masculine identification. Freud saw the Oedipus Complex as a turning point in development because it aligned desire or sexuality with civilization, because it signified the replacement of relationship with identification, because it led to the internalization of cultural prohibitions, because it solidified gender identity. But seeing the relationship between psychological health and civilization as strained and always tenuous, Freud saw the tension between desire and culture as necessitating a 'compromise formation', which leaves a psychological wound or scar. This then provided the seedbed for neurosis.

To reframe this conception in relational terms, boys tend in early childhood to experience a relational crisis. Paradoxically, they must take large parts of themselves out of relationship if they want to enter the world of boys and men and have 'relationships'. This crisis forces the inherently paradoxical split between 'self' and 'relationships'. Suzanne Langer named this split as one of the 'deadlocked paradoxes' of Western culture. Boys resist the internal and external pressures to separate themselves from their relationships, and this healthy resistance to losing voice and connection involves them in what is essentially a quixotic political struggle, which they must lose if patriarchy is to continue.

Boys, then, must find some compromise between their human desire for relationship and the need to make relationships in a world of boys and men where disconnections and dissociations are taken for granted: the ability to be hurt without feeling hurt, the ability to experience loss or hurt without feeling sadness, the ability to separate oneself from relationships—to disconnect oneself psychologically from women. Some boys, often with the help of mothers or fathers, find ways to stay in relationship and also to have relationships. Some outwardly resist and show 'separation anxiety'. Many young boys develop symptoms: speech problems, learning disorders, hyperactivity, depression, and a variety of behaviour problems, or a general loss of vitality manifest in an absence of feelings, a psychological numbness.

The relational crisis in boys' early childhood and girls' adolescence heightens vulnerability because psychological vitality stimulates resistance and resistance leads to trouble: either the external contradiction of open, political resistance, or the internal contradiction of dissociation. These times of relational crisis are thus times of opportunity for resistance but also times of great psychological risk.

The asymmetry between girls' and boys' development with respect to time of heightened psychological risk also creates an opportunity, because of the developmental differences. It is one thing to be four or five years old and have to give up relationship in order to have 'relationships', and it is another to be 11, or 12, or 13. It is also one thing to claim masculinity within a patriarchal society and culture, and another to claim femininity or to perform both or neither. The implicit parallelism in discussions of gender identity or development are profoundly misleading because they imply that psychological development is culturally insensitive or neutral.

When girls enact dissociations at adolescence, they initially name what they are doing and why. Ritu explains that she was angry at her friends, but if she spoke her anger to them they would only get madder at her. So, she explains, 'I just went up to them and said (voice rising) "So hi, what's up?"' Girls understand the importance of relationships: 'You have to have relationships,' Iris explains, but all she can see, psychologically, is a landscape of separation. 'If I were to say what I was feeling and thinking, no one would want to be with me. My voice would be too loud'; Iris is not an outcast or one of the 'leftovers'—she is president of her class, the chosen speaker for their graduation, a top student who has been admitted to a highly competitive college, a young women who describes her family as encouraging and supportive.

Girls' ability to articulate a relational crisis which for boys tends to be inchoate, laced with early loss and terror, means that girls in the course of their development bring to the surface a psychological problem which has been unspoken or taken for granted—a relational problem built into the structure of patriarchy. Boys resist separating from women in early childhood; the costs of both separating and not separating for them are high. For girls, separating from women means creating an inner split within themselves—separating themselves not only from their mothers and other women, but also from themselves.

Girls at adolescence are in school as well as in families; they have friends as well as parents and siblings; they have far more experience of relationships than boys in early childhood and they have the advantages of years of emotional and cognitive development. Girls' resistance is consequently more robust. But the symptoms of dissociation are remarkably similar: like boys in early childhood, girls at adolescence experience a loss of voice or problems in speaking, learning problems, depression, hysteria, and mind–body splits which can lead to numbness but also to eating disorders. Young women who cut themselves may be showing on the surface of their body, the wounds which they have suffered psychologically—as a kind of initiation rite, but also a way of digging deeper, getting to the root, the heart of the problem.

The implication of the theory which I have presented is that women's psychological development raises a question which goes to the heart of patriarchy: is this compromise which has been taken for granted between voice and relationship, psychological health and civilization, necessary—is it psychologically too costly and costly to society and the world as well? The move out of relationship and the dissociations set the scene for violence and violation. Girls' resistance draws attention to the cost for boys of a much earlier disconnection. Civilization, rooted psychologically in the experiences of powerful men, is built around psychological losses and splits. The importance of girls' resistance to making these splits lies in the fact that if listened to it challenges us to think of alternatives.

Psychological development, like human excellence, flourishes in close relationships. The human psyche is like a plant, open to the elements, rooted in the soil. We have come now, at the end of the age of modernism—the end of the ego's era—after a century of unparalleled violence, at a time when violence has become appalling, to appreciate again the fragility of humans. We understand better the closeness and vulnerability which create the conditions for psychological growth, and also the costs of their violation.

Part 3 Marginalized Identities

16 DOES SHE BOIL EGGS? TOWARDS A FEMINIST MODEL OF DISABILITY

MARGARET LLOYD

'Even if we can't lift an egg [it is assumed that] we can boil an egg.' This statement, from the Disabled Women's Conference in Manchester (Manchester Disabled Women's Conference, *Conference Report*, 1990), neatly encapsulates the simultaneous discrimination which disabled women experience, as people with physical or intellectual impairments, and as women. The past decade has seen a growing and stimulating literature exploring the experience, nature and definition of disability within sociological, political and economic discourse, but the emergence of particular strands out of somewhat monolithic earlier formulations of disability culture is more recent. One such strand, in British and American literature, is the perspective of disabled women. Through the writings of disabled women themselves and qualitative research with disabled women (e.g. Deegan and Brooks, 1985; Hannaford, 1985; Lonsdale, 1990; Morris, 1989), the experience of everyday living for women with disabilities is being richly documented. These studies are largely framed within the social structural analysis of disability, which takes as its starting point a critique of individual and pathologizing constructions. These can increasingly be seen as representing mainstream thinking within the disability movement (e.g. Brisenden, 1986; Oliver *et al.*, 1988). Moving along the avenues of thought defined by disabled men in exploring the social and economic discrimination experienced by disabled people (e.g. Finkelstein, 1980; Oliver, 1986) the literature of and about disabled women pauses to identify to what extent and in what ways disabled women may in fact be further disadvantaged (see, for example, Lonsdale's [1990] discussion of employment benefits). The essential boundaries for the discussion remain unquestioned and the issue which emerges instead is the dilemma of identity for an individual experiencing multiple disadvantage and oppression:

I'm a disabled woman now. Two strikes. (Hanna and Rogovsky, 1991)

I'm a woman, Asian and disabled. Which do I identify with most strongly? (quoted in Saxton and Howe, 1988)

For some, the dilemma is resolved by creating a hierarchy of inequalities with disability assuming the greatest significance:

Disability is the primary problem in our lives. Once we identify ourselves

Source: Abridged from Lloyd, Margaret (1992) *Disability, Handicap & Society*, 7, 3.

as powerful disabled individuals, we can go back into our secondary
communities, whether it is to be the black community, or Chicano community, the women's community, or some combination of these. (quoted
in Saxton and Howe, 1988)

For these women, whose primary identification is with their disability, it is
important to consider the role of the women's movement.

Has the women's movement taken our concerns on board? Quite simply,
no. (Manchester Disabled Women's Conference, 1990)

The charge can justifiably be levelled at non-disabled feminists that their
'blindness' in relation to disability issues has contributed to disabled women
finding the disability movement more hospitable than the women's movement
(Hannaford, 1985). It should not be assumed, however, that the disability
movement automatically embraces the issues for disabled women, nor that disabled women should accept an analytical framework which may not adequately
reflect their own experience:

Has the disabled people's movement taken our concerns on board? Again,
no. (Manchester Disabled Women's Conference, 1990)

It is the purpose of this article to examine the appropriateness and usefulness for disabled women of models which are in the forefront of current
disability thinking, but which have been largely constructed by disabled men
(particularly in terms of the British experience). A possible reframing of this
paradigm from a feminist perspective will then be explored.

THE SOCIAL MODEL OF DISABILITY

In the process of bringing to bear critical perspectives from disabled people
themselves on the 'accepted wisdom' about disability, a new paradigm has
emerged which is increasingly known as the Social Model of Disability (e.g.
Oliver, 1983). Briefly stated, exponents of the social model argue that it is
not the physical or mental impairment of the individual which disables, but
the handicapping effects of a society geared to 'ablebodiedness' as the norm.
The disablement is therefore socially created and the experience of disability is
another form of social oppression. Exponents of the social model have arrived
at this position via a sharp critique of individual models, which largely see disability as some form of personal tragedy which the individual must learn to
accept, and to 'cope' with life lived in its shadow.

Two particular axes are emphasized in the formulation of the arguments
leading to the social model: first, socio-economic discrimination which has
significant financial implications; and second, the medicalization of disability
and its relationship with health care. I would not wish to question basic tenets
which have been established elsewhere—for example, that disabled people

are unfairly discriminated against in gaining and sustaining employment (Graham, Jordan and Lamb, 1990); the relationship between disability and poverty (Martin and White, 1988); the control in defining and pathologizing disability exerted by the medical profession (e.g. Morgan, Calnan and Manning, 1985)—but it is important to consider the way in which the discussion has been framed and the extent to which this reflects the real significance of impairment for disabled *women*.

Socio-economic discrimination

A careful scrutiny of disabled people's aspirations and experiences in the key areas of education and employment reveals subtle and interesting variations for disabled women. In many instances, the disadvantage and discrimination experienced by disabled people generally is simply exacerbated for disabled women. For example, higher proportions of women with disabilities are in unskilled work than both men with disabilities and non-disabled women (Lonsdale, 1990). However, other evidence shows a reduction of the differential between disabled and non-disabled women, where marked differences continue to exist between disabled and non-disabled men. For example, the Office of Population Censuses and Surveys 1988 survey revealed 28% of disabled women and 60% of non-disabled women in employment as compared to 33% of disabled men and 78% of non-disabled men.

Home working is an expanding field of employment which offers flexibility in hours worked and when, and might appear to offer a reasonable answer to the employment problems of disabled people. Lonsdale's (1990) study showed that the growing numbers of disabled women who find themselves resorting to home working do so because they are excluded from suitable paid employment outside, and the isolation, low esteem and exploitative low pay which attend such work in fact compound their experience of disadvantage. It is not only *disabled* women who are engaged in home working in disproportionately high numbers, however. Non-disabled women who are mothers of young children and/or married also frequently resort to such means because of the obstacles they face in obtaining and sustaining more satisfactory forms of employment. There is accumulated evidence of the concentration of women in low-paid employment or unemployment (Graham, 1984; Lonsdale, 1992). The disadvantage, discrimination and inappropriateness of employment structures which disabled people encounter in their struggle for valued employment (Oliver, 1990), are *faced by women anyway* as an inevitable consequence of their gender. Any analysis which frames the problem simply in terms of disability must be seen as inadequate in the case of disabled women. We are led towards what Hanna and Rogovsky (1991) identify as the female/disabled 'plus factor', where the disadvantages attending these two characteristics compound each other.

Tracing the employment disadvantages back in search of causes raises questions about the education received, [. . .] and the degree to which it equipped the individual for a range of employment. Whilst the central issue must remain the question of whether disabled children should receive a segregated education in special schools or be integrated within mainstream schooling [...] the related subsidiary question of the type of education received is also of crucial importance. The common complaint amongst disabled people that undue attention is given to training in living skills at the expense of academic qualifications, has the *added* dimension for disabled women that societal expectations of their fulfilling a domestic role makes this a *central criterion* in determining the success or failure of their education. The women in Morris's (1989) study illustrate the effect of this assumption:

> [My GP's] advice was: 'So long as you can cheerfully wave your husband and children off in the morning and welcome them home with a real smile, the problems during the day are immaterial'. (p. 52)

> No one knew what to do with a tetraplegic 14-year-old, so no one suggested that I return to school or try to find work ... In the main, I am satisfied with my achievements. I manage 90 per cent of the housework which I feel compensates my parents to some extent for the help they give me. (p. 110)

It is important to recognize that both these women are satisfied that they are succeeding along the lines expected of them. Similar criteria for 'success' do not appear to be shared by disabled men. The thrust of their arguments are directed towards the barriers they experience in fulfilling valued economic and professional roles (see, for example, Oliver, 1990). Thus, the experiences of these disabled women are circumvented as much by the oppression of their gender as by the discrimination they encounter because of their disability, and both disabled men and disabled women experience the negative, but different, effects of gender stereotyping (feminine women are good home-makers; real men are independent and successful providers). The continuing experience for many girls and young women of relatively low expectations and a lack of interest in the family in their educational achievement (Smithers and Zientek, 1991), a dominance of male role models in school management and the more academically-oriented subjects areas (Smithers and Robinson, 1988), and the proportionately low numbers of girls pursuing sciences, mathematics and computer technology (Kelly, 1981; Parry, 1990), suggests that disabled *and* non-disabled women suffer from the same basic prejudicial assumptions. If we simply look at the lack of useful skills and appropriate qualifications which disabled women have and see the problem as lying in their disability, we are seeing only part of the problem.

Disability and health care

Turning to the second axis, it is apparent that rejection of the 'medical model' of disability is fundamental to the Social Model. This rejection is usually couched in passionate terms, as writers recall experiences of insensitive and patronizing treatment from doctors. [. . .] The significant argument holds: the narrow definition of disability as clinical condition results in all-pervasiveness of doctors' power over disabled people's lives, of which the power to make decisions about fitness for work and entitlement to welfare benefits are but examples. This does not *necessarily* mean, however, that the medical aspects of their lives are unimportant for disabled people. The wholesale minimizing of medicine which is sometimes heard alongside dismissal of the medical model of disability may be, rather, an understandable consequence of the emotional impact of devaluing attitudes and behaviours encountered in medical staff.

There are a number of complex, interrelated factors here, particularly when analysed in the context of gender. It can be argued that the devaluing and stigmatizing factors operating in the relationship between disability and medical treatment are present in a wider context, particularly for women. First, the élitism and power of the medical profession and the often negative effects of this on doctor–patient relationships (e.g. Morgan, Calnan and Manning, 1985; Albrecht and Higgins, 1979). Secondly, the hierarchies operating in medicine and health care are male dominated and male-oriented (e.g. Webb, 1986). Third, female health care workers, both the proportionately small numbers of women doctors and the almost exclusively female lower status occupations are variously drawn into reinforcing these attitudinal biases. Navarro (1979) points to the fact that female doctors are closer and more supportive to male doctors than to lower-status female colleagues; Eisner and Wright (1986) show how difficult it is for female GPs to counter their professional socialization when seeking to integrate feminist values in their dealings with patients; Orr (1986) comments that the role of the health visitor epitomizes female stereotypes of the nurturant, passive, submissive handmaiden or helpmate. Fourth, it is women, as patients, who have experienced most markedly the individualizing and pathologizing of their problems and stigmatizing treatment from doctors and other health care workers (e.g. Graham, 1984; Hannaford, 1985; Webb, 1986).

Clearly, inappropriate uses of power and control, insensitive and patronizing behaviours, and stereotypical attitudes are not confined to *disabled* people's encounters with the health care system. They *are* particularly experienced by women, both as patients and as workers. We must ask whether the automatic linking of the rejection of the medical model with the minimizing of medical aspects is the most helpful construction of the relationship between disability and ongoing health care for disabled women. Undoubtedly, disabled women complain of the same bad experiences with doctors as do disabled men (Lonsdale, 1990), but the same devaluing denial of rights and exclusion from information and choices, to which disabled people are subjected, is the common experience of women anyway. The clearest articulation of this can be found in the struggle for maternity and gynaecological services which adequately meet the wishes and serve the needs of women as defined by themselves. That disabled women are more regularly and intensively subjected to intimate procedures, insensitively handled, than are their non-disabled sisters is not disputed. It may be, however, that the way forward is to acknowledge the centrality of good health care in their lives and direct attention towards the redefining of need and the reshaping of services. The existence of well-women and family planning clinics and the growing consciousness amongst midwives of the need to wrest control from male obstetricians and return it to female providers and recipients of the service, testify to the success of this approach for women generally. It should be possible for disabled women to build into such initiatives their particular perspective.

To summarize the argument thus far: In both areas to which the social model of disability gives particular attention to the experience of disability as socio-economic discrimination and the medicalization of disability, for a disabled woman, the negative effects are not only a consequence of the way in which she is perceived as a disabled person, they are *also a consequence of the way in which she is perceived as a woman*. This model 'stops short' and may even fail to identify the significant issues for disabled women.

EXPERIENCING DOUBLE DISCRIMINATION

The agenda for disabled women

If we take the views of disabled women as our starting point rather than an additional consideration, however, we find a somewhat different emphasis. The women are as concerned as the men to affirm that it is society which disables and oppresses, but the discussion is not confined to the modes of economic and social discrimination identified by disabled men. Disabled women are concerned to explore questions of sexuality and sexual identity; to challenge stereotypical images and oppressive mores relating to child-bearing, rearing and motherhood; to integrate physical and social aspects of self-presentation with critical analysis of the dependent, non-assertive disabled woman which society 'requires'. To judge by the attention given to such issues (Morris, 1989; Lonsdale, 1990; Hanna and Rogovsky, 1991) they are central, not adjunctive to these women's implicit 'social model'.

> You feel yourself insecure as a woman, as well you're insecure as a mother. (quoted in Lonsdale, 1990, p. 67)

> They think I won't ever get married, or what boy would ever look at me. (quoted in Lonsdale, 1990, p. 71)

> It's very difficult to be sexy from a wheelchair. (quoted in Morris, 1989, p. 68)

Many women complain that their challenging of the 'helpless child' role to any degree is interpreted, particularly by welfare professionals, as evidence of their inability to accept their disability.

Issues of such fundamental and pervasive impact cannot be separated from any other sphere of (political) action. To campaign against government indifference towards disabled people's employment, for example, is insufficient unless consistently coupled with challenges to prevailing attitudes about what roles and functions are 'appropriate' for disabled women. Small comfort can be gained, then, from the scant attention paid by disabled men to the perspective and particular concerns of disabled women. What *is* evident, however, is that these are *women's issues*, albeit in sharp relief and peculiarly discriminating for disabled women:

> The nature of a women's dependency on her spouse is complex and lies in the roles and duties which women are expected to perform.... They are simultaneously expected to be sexual playthings, responsive and caring companions and good mothers. ... Physical disability represents a threat to these expectations and this role. (Lonsdale, 1990, p. 83)

Indeed, for some disabled women [...] their political consciousness concerning their disability is developed *only* through their understanding of the experience as a woman:

> I have a strong sense of my accident having liberated me ... Society had rejected me, but that also meant it didn't have any power over me either. I didn't have to achieve the role of wife and mother any more. (quoted in Morris, 1989, p. 98)

Lest it be assumed at this point that the true home for disabled women is located within the women's movement, it is necessary to restate the reality: non-disabled feminists have consistently failed to recognize disability issues. To turn from a context in which disabled women may be invisible *as women* (that is, the disability movement) to one in which their *disability* is ignored or subsumed (that is, the women's movement) is no answer. In returning to Hanna and Rogovsky's (1991) 'female/disabled plus factor' it is instructive to consider the progress of black feminism.

Simultaneity and the example of black feminism

In her helpful summary of feminist critiques of the welfare state, Williams (1989) discusses the ways in which the experiences of black women are mediated *simultaneously* through race, gender and class. She goes on to argue that, historically, the male-oriented Black Power movement and white-oriented women's movement have both failed to recognize this simultaneity. Hence, they have neither adequately recognized nor appropriately represented the cause of black women. In developing their alternative praxis and autonomous organization, black women have not only identified where they share the discrimination experienced by all women, and may in fact be doubly disadvantaged, but have gone on to turn certain issues 'inside out'. Thus, for example, whereas motherhood confers some degree of status on even the most marginalized white young women, for black women it may be a further stigmatizing experience as they become caught up in a web of notions around black sexuality and promiscuity and the pathologized black family.

The arguments of black feminism offer some interesting comparative insights for disabled women. Like black women, they experience ambiguous and sometimes frightening messages about their sexuality. Their physical impairment may deem them 'failures' in relation to the dominant sexual ideal, yet the construction of them as helpless and vulnerable raises another spectre—there is growing (though as yet anecdotal) evidence of physical and sexual abuse of disabled women (Hannaford, 1985). Like children, they must be protected from danger and exploitation, yet there is an assumption that they would never wish for, or be desired in an adult relationship. Their sexuality is constructed in disablist rather than sexist terms, much as black women have argued that their sexuality is constructed in racist terms.

Another illustration of the way in which disabled women become caught up in the 'simultaneity' to which Williams refers in relation to black women is to be with women and 'caring'. Not only is the link between women and caring at the heart of feminist debate, it is integral to the way in which disabled women are viewed in relation to the valued roles of 'wife' and 'mother'. For many disabled women, pregnancy is actively discouraged by both medical practitioners and family, not least because such women are not deemed capable of fulfilling the maternal caring role. In many cases, there is an automatic assumption that they will be sterilized (see Morris, 1989; Lonsdale, 1990). Arguments around functional limitation merge into value-laden stereotypes of the mother figure. This becomes even clearer when the wifely role is being considered, particularly where the male partner is not disabled:

There is a big difference between a disabled husband and a disabled wife. A disabled husband needs a wife to nurture him, but a disabled wife is not seen by society of capable of nurturing a husband who is not disabled. (quoted in Hanna and Rogovsky, 1991, p. 56)

One woman in Lonsdale's study described the shame expressed by her future in-laws that their son had chosen to marry a disabled woman, and their concern that she would ruin his life. Another commented: 'The world does not accept what they have done lightly, but imputes to them motives of sexual inadequacy, kinkiness or saintliness' (quoted in Morris, 1989, p. 99). There is in fact considerable evidence that disabled women are less likely to marry and more likely to be divorced or separated than either disabled men or non-disabled women (Lonsdale, 1990). In sum, disabled women experience the effects of two forms of discrimination simultaneously: they are subject to (and often aspire to) prevailing stereotypes of wife and mother, but as for black women, assuming these roles may not confer valued social status but is often viewed negatively.

There is a further twist for disabled women in the issue of caring. Feminist attacks on so-called 'community' care, which in fact relies exploitatively on the 'labour of love' of informal carers and low-paid formal carers (see Finch and Groves, 1983), must be welcomed by disabled women in its challenge of an assumed female role which some disabled women are unable to fulfil, at least in stereotypical guise. But as Oliver (1990) has pointed out, the force of the feminist argument has been provided through the construction of the disabled person as a burden. Thus the issue can only properly be represented for disabled women through a simultaneous expression of both their female and their disabled identities (see Davis, 1984).[1]

TOWARDS AN ALTERNATIVE PRAXIS

Williams (1989) argues that the failure of both the Black Power movement and feminism to recognize and reflect this simultaneity of experience for black women led to the emergence of black feminism as an autonomous organization. In this analysis of the interrelationships between health, disability and black minorities, Atkin (1991) suggests that problems arise when cultures are asserted to be monolithic. He continues:

> The debate must be informed by an account of disability and health in terms of black people's perceptions, without these perceptions being perceived as deviant or pathological. Black minorities' perceptions, however, do not occur in a void but are interpreted and framed by the wider society. Fundamental to the analysis, therefore, are the political, social, and economic position of black minorities and the context of racism. (Atkin, 1991, pp. 44–5)

Taken together, these arguments would seem to offer an alternative way forward for disabled women which breaks out of monolithic formulations of disability culture, yet does not minimize their disabled identity in the cause of feminism. Speaking of black feminism, Williams (1989) states:

> It is in this attempt ... to grapple much more exhaustively with the notion of difference between women, not just in its subjective sense of culture or experience or struggle, but in its objective sense of how such difference is structured through the interweaving of patriarchy, imperialism and capitalism, and how it is variously reinforced by the state and other institutional structures and by ideologies, that black feminism makes a major methodological contribution. (Williams, 1989, p. 80)

Thus, built on to the assertion of radical feminism that the personal *is* political and hence of *central* concern, black feminism reconstitutes that centre through its integrative rather than incremental treatment of different forms of oppression (Figure 16.1).

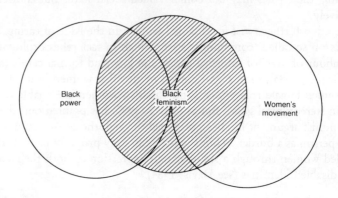

FIGURE 16.1 Black feminism as central

It has been argued here that the 'simultaneity' experienced by disabled women is being denied in two ways. First, they are rendered virtually invisible by the women's movement. Second, they are rendered peripheral by the disability movement. Oliver (1990) acknowledges, for example, that the experience of disability is structured by the ideology of masculinity, but he does not follow this argument through in his analysis of social movements. The combined impact for disabled women is thus a fragmentation and marginalization of their experience. If disabled women are to experience their subjective concerns as an integrative part of the objective structural analysis which the social model of disability provides, then these concerns must be central to that analysis. Further, if they are to be empowered by strength of feminism, then feminist analysis must recognize and embrace disability issues (Figure 16.2).

Disabled men and non-disabled women (such as the writer) can, and indeed must, recognize the issues and work towards an adequate framework. They can never, however, move that framework from the realm of theory to that of genuine praxis. It is for disabled women themselves to claim the 'centrality' towards which this paper has pointed. [. . .] Hannaford (1985), a feminist before her disability, saw radical feminism as the vehicle for expressing the concerns of disabled women without those concerns becoming dangerously individualized. Davis (1984) argues that disabled women must first critique and claim that feminist theory. Fine and Asch (1985), citing evidence of the conservative attitudes shown by both the women's and the disability movements towards disabled women, argue that the way forward must lie in increasing the range and number of roles available to disabled women. Several writers (e.g. Saxton, 1985) examine the usefulness of self-help support and therapeutic groups, of which there are growing numbers in Britain today (Rae, 1991).

That these initiatives are sporadic and disabled women often divided in their response, is itself a function of the fragmentation and marginalization discussed earlier. Nowhere is this more painfully realized than amongst disabled women themselves (e.g. Manchester Disabled Women's Conference, 1990). It is suggested here that disabled women have been struggling to locate themselves within organizations whose theoretical and ideological base is for them inadequate or partial, and they will not fully achieve solidarity or identity or coherence of action until this problem is addressed.

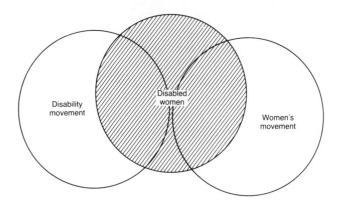

FIGURE 16.2 Disabled women's experience as integrative

CONCLUSION

The reconceptualisation of disability from a pitiful and problematic experience for the individual to a socially created experience of stigma and discrimination has emerged out of the convergence of two strands: the growing realization amongst sociologists that disability research must re-analyse micro level concepts such as individual stigma, deviance and the 'sick role' in the context of macro political, economic and structural concepts (see, for example, Bynder and New, 1979) with the increasing self-confidence and collectivization of disabled people themselves. This paper has suggested that the time is ripe for a further and significant conceptual development which more adequately recognizes the experience of disabled women and locates it within the broader context of women's social experience, thereby instigating new directions in the empowering of women who have to often been under-educated, isolated, marginalized and remain unpoliticized. To describe some disabled women thus does not mean that such women do not recognize and express their problems and concerns, but that the lack of any socio-political analysis which fully embraces their situation leads to alienation from existing political movements, be they the women's movement, the disability movement or party politics. Such alienation (and hence isolation) inevitably reinforces the tendency for those women to personalize and individualize their problems and to refer to prevailing stereotypes as the only means of understanding their situation.

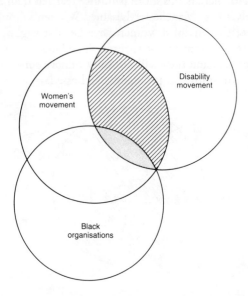

FIGURE 16.3 Model for understanding multiple discrimination. (▨) White disabled women; (▩) black disabled women

Other disabled women have long been active in the disability movement and for them a different problem is raised. Recognizing, as they increasingly do, that the disability movement is primarily male-oriented, they see absorption into such a movement as a considerable threat to their agenda as women. The alternative of separate organization is no more comforting. For an already marginalized minority, the cold winds of separatism may pose an even greater threat. The model suggested here (Figure 16.2) making links for disabled women with the experience of black women, proposes an integrated approach, whereby disabled women's concerns are *central* to both disability and feminst agendas. Such an approach can be extended. This paper has considered the issue of double discrimination, but the problems of stigma, disadvantage, oppression, identity and 'voicelessness' are compounded for people experiencing multiple discrimination. For black disabled women, for example, achieving centrality within feminist, black and disability agendas may be the way out of the trap of fragmentation, marginalization or absorption (Figure 16.3).

This is not an easy process and it is another form of oppression for an already marginalized minority to struggle with it alone. Whilst only disabled women can speak *as* and *for* disabled women, others (particularly those with overlapping concerns such as non-disabled women and disabled men), are equally responsible in the task of working towards change. [. . .] In order that 'disabled people' should cease to mean, effectively, 'disabled men', non-disabled feminists must lend their strength to the naming of women's experience within any analysis of disability. For 'women' to cease to mean, effectively, 'non-disabled women', disabled men must lend their strength to the naming of disability within feminism. A crucial lesson to be drawn from the progress of black feminism, however, is that separate articulation of disabled women's concerns is not enough. The model must be reconstituted.

Dedication

This article is dedicated to the memory of Kathy Avieson, disabled woman, colleague and fellow traveller in this exploration.

Acknowledgements

The author would like to thank Howard Parker, Paul Wilding and Suzy Braye for their comments on a draft of this article.

Note

1. Since this paper was written Jenny Morris has published *Pride against Prejudice* (Women's Press, 1991). The reader is referred to Morris's section on feminist research and community care.

References

Albrecht, G. and Higgins, P. (eds) (1979) *Health, Illness and Medicine.* Chicago, IL: Rand McNally.

Atkin, K. (1991) Health, illness, disability and black minorities: a speculative critique of present day discourse. *Disability, Handicap & Society* 6, 1, 37–47.

Brisenden, S. (1986) Independent living and the medical model of disability. *Disability, Handicap & Society* 1, 2, 173–78.

Bynder, H. and New, P. (1979) Time for a change: from micro- to macro-sociological concepts in disability research. In G. Albrecht and P. Higgins (eds) *Health, Illness and Medicine.* Chicago, IL: Rand McNally.

Davis, B.H. (1984) Women, disability and feminism: notes towards a new theory. *Frontiers* 8, 1, 1–5.

Deegan, M. and Brooks, N. (eds) (1985) *Women and Disability.* New Brunswick, NJ: Transaction Books.

Eisner, M. and Wright, M. (1986) A feminist approach to general practice. In C. Webb (ed.) *Feminist Practice in Women's Health Care.* London: Wiley.

Finch, J. and Groves, D. (1983) *A Labour of Love: Women, Work and Caring.* London: Routledge & Kegan Paul.

Fine, M and Asch, A. (1985) Sexism without the pedestal. In M. Deegan and N. Brooks (eds) *Women and Disability.* New Brunswick, NJ: Transaction Books.

Finkelstein, V. (1980) *Attitudes and Disabled People: Issues for Discussion.* New York: World Rehabilitation Fund.

Graham, H. (1984) *Women, Health and the Family.* Hemel Hempstead: Harvester Wheatsheaf.

Graham, P., Jordan, A. and Lamb, B. (1990) *An Equal Chance? A Study of Discrimination against Disabled People in the Labour Market.* London: Spastics Society.

Hanna, W.J. and Rogovsky, B. (1991) Women with disabilities: two handicaps plus. *Disability, Handicap & Society,* 6, 1, 49–63.

Hannaford, S. (1985) *Living Outside Inside: A Disabled Woman's Experience.* Berkeley, CA: Canterbury Press.

Kelly, A. (ed) (1981) *The Missing Half.* Manchester: Manchester University Press.

Lonsdale, S. (1990) *Women and Disability: The Experience of Physical Disability Among Women.* Basingstoke: Macmillan.

— (1992) Patterns of paid work. In C. Glendinning and J. Millar (eds) *Women and Poverty in Britain: The 1990s.* 2nd edn. Hemel Hempstead: Harvester Wheatsheaf.

Manchester Disabled Women's Conference (1990) *Conference Report.* Manchester: Disability Forum.

Martin, J. and White, A. (1988) *The Financial Circumstances of Disabled Adults Living in Private Households, Office of Population Censuses and Surveys: Surveys of Disability in Great Britain.* London: HMSO.

Morgan, M., Calnan, M. and Manning, N. (1985) *Sociological Approaches to Health and Medicine.* Beckenham: Croom Helm.

Morris, J. (ed) (1989) *Able Lives: Women's Experience of Paralysis* London: Women's Press.

Navarro, V. (1979) Women in health care. In G. Albrecht and P. Higgins (eds) *Health, Illness and Medicine.* Chicago, IL: Rand McNally.

Oliver, M. (1983) *Social Work with Disabled People.* Basingstoke: Macmillan.

— (1986) Social policy and disability: some theoretical issues. *Disability, Handicap & Society* 1, 1, 5–17.

— (1990) *The Politics of Disablemen.* Basingstoke: Macmillan.

— Oliver, M., Zarb, G., Silver, J., Moore, M. and Salisbury, V. (1988) *Walking into Darkness: The Experience of Spinal Injury.* Basingstoke: Macmillan.

Orr, J. (1986) Feminism and health visiting. In C. Webb (ed.) *Feminist Practice in Women's Health Care.* London: Wiley.

Parry, G. (ed) (1990) *Engineering Futures: New Audiences and Arrangements for Engineering Higher Education.* London: Engineering Council.

Rae, A. (1991) *On the Box, Coalition.* Greater Manchester Coalition of Disabled People.

Saxton, M. (1985) A peer counselling training program for disabled women: a tool for social and individual change. In M. Deegan and N. Brooks (eds) *Women and Disability.* New Brunswick, NJ: Transaction Books.

Saxton, M. and Howe, F. (eds) (1988) *With Wings: An Anthology of Literature by Women with Disabilities.* London: Virago Press.

Smithers, A. and Robinson, P. (1988) *The Shortage of Mathematics and Physics Teachers.* Department of Education, University of Manchester.

Smithers, A. and Zientek, P. (1991) *Gender, Primary Schools and the National Curriculum.* London: NASUWT/Engineering Council.

Webb, C. (ed) (1986) *Feminist Practice in Women's Health Care.* London: Wiley.

Williams, F. (1989) *Social Policy: A Critical Introduction.* Cambridge: Polity Press.

17 THE HISTORICAL ROOTS OF THE MODERN LESBIAN IDENTITY

MARTHA VICINUS

[...]
Lesbian history is in its initial stages, inhibited both by the suspect nature of the subject and the small number of individuals willing and able to pursue half-forgotten, half-destroyed, or half-neglected sources. Nevertheless, since the late 1970s there has been an encouraging efflorescence of work, breaking from the old psychological paradigms and insisting upon the necessity of a historical understanding of women's same-sex sexual behavior. These studies have concentrated on issues of concern to contemporary lesbians, especially the origins of an individual and group identity.

This attention to identity politics, past and present, has had two obvious pitfalls. As the editors of *Signs* pointed out in the introduction to their 1984 special issue on lesbians:

> Such focus on identity may in fact limit inquiry to those cultures in which lesbian identity and survival *as lesbians* are crucial matters of concern; it may hinder cross-cultural analysis, for example, because it provides inadequate vocabulary for discussion of relationships among Third World women. ... Discussion of lesbianism in these terms has relevance only where identity and sexuality are intertwined and where personal identity is itself a cultural value. (Freedman, 1984)

Such pioneering collections as *This Bridge Called My Back: Writings by Radical Women of Color* (Moraga and Anzalduá, 1981); *Nice Jewish Girls: A Lesbian Anthology* (Beck, 1982), and *Home Girls: A Black Feminist Anthology* (Smith, 1984), have problematized the contemporary relationship between a lesbian identity and a racial identity in the United States. But possible role conflicts, personal opportunities, or individual self-definition in the past remain largely unknown. Moreover, the homosexual possibilities for women in the Third World, past or present, are still little understood by Western writers.

Lesbian desire is everywhere, even as it may be nowhere. Put bluntly, we lack any general agreement about what constitutes a lesbian. Jackie Stacey (1987) has suggested one alternative to any rigid definition of the lesbian identity. In an unpublished article questioning feminist psychoanalysis, she

Source: Abridged from *Feminist Studies* 18, 3, Fall 1992 (by permission of the publisher, Feminist Studies, Inc., c/o Women's Studies Program, University of Maryland, College Park, MD 20742, USA.).

recommends instead that 'it might be possible to consider questions of lesbian identity and desire within the models of fragmented subjectivity'.

> The diversity of our experience of lesbianism is enormous. . . . We cannot assume any coherent or unified collective identity when we recognize the diversity of definitions and experiences of lesbians. . . . Lesbian experiences are not only fragmented within 'lesbian cultures,' but also within cultures dominated by heterosexuality, in which lesbians are ascribed the contradictory positions of the invisible presence. (Stacey, 1987)

'Diversity' is a salutary reminder that not all questions can be answered, but it hardly resolves the problems facing a historian. If we are to make sense of our history, we must look for connections embedded in differences and contradictions.

Virtually every historian of sexuality has argued that the present-day sexual identity of both homosexuals and heterosexuals is socially constructed and historically specific. Yet same-sex erotic attraction appears to be transhistorical and transcultural and to appear repeatedly in a limited range of behaviours. As Eve Kosofsky Sedgwick (1990, p. 85) has pointed out, most of us hold contradictory notions in regard to sexual preference without attempting to resolve them. We recognise a distinct group of homosexual peoples or individuals and also understand that sexual behavior is unpredictable, various, and strongly affected by both same-sex and opposite-sex desires and influences.

The history of lesbianism also demonstrates a continual jostling of two competing perspectives on the origins of homosexual feeling. Is it a product of social conditions or of one's innate propensity? Onlookers have usually chosen the former, and medical experts have chosen the latter, although by the twentieth century the two models are often postulated simultaneously. Lesbians themselves seem to use both explanations, but those privileging butch-femme relations lean toward a model of innate predisposition, and those preferring romantic friendships favor a conditioned, sexual continuum. [. . .]

The question of when and under what circumstances the modern lesbian identity arose is, perhaps, impossible to answer. If we turn to a larger historical context within which such an identity might have grown, all the usual criteria used by historians to explain social change do not seem sufficient. A lesbian identity did not result from economic independence or from an ideology of individualism or from the formation of women's communities, although all these elements were important for enhancing women's personal choices. In 1981 Ann Ferguson argued that financial independence was a necessary precondition for the formation of a lesbian identity, but this does not seem to be the case. We have examples from the eighteenth and nineteenth centuries of women who were economically dependent upon their families and yet were successfully involved with women. The sexually active upper-class Anne Lister (1791–1840) was often frustrated that she had to live with her wealthy uncle and aunt in provincial Yorkshire but she arranged her social life to take advantage of every sexual opportunity. Over the course of eight years she managed numerous meetings with her married lover and had several affairs (Whitbread, 1988).[1]

The onset of the industrial revolution appears to have had little impact upon the formation of a lesbian culture, although it led to more occupational opportunities for women of all social classes. The development of a mercantile economy in seventeenth and eighteenth-century northern Europe may have encouraged some women to think of themselves as individuals apart from their families. Both religion and politics united to emphasize the importance of the individual's soul; those women who found strength through their religious beliefs to seek nontraditional roles may also have felt—and acted upon —nonconforming sexual desires.

The formation of self-conscious women's communities can be seen as a necessary precondition for a lesbian identity. But here again we find a tradition going back into the Middle Ages that yielded feminine and proto-feminist independence and bonding but hardly anything one could recognize as a lesbian identity. During the eighteenth and nineteenth centuries women organized salons, artistic coteries, religious organizations, and educational institutions. Although these were rarely self-consciously lesbian such groups clearly provided opportunities for the development of intense friendships.[2]

[. . .]

THE SEVENTEENTH AND EIGHTEENTH CENTURIES: THEATRICS OR NATURE?

By the late seventeenth and eighteenth centuries, when the traditional hierarchies of social order, private and public, were giving way, in Europe and among Europeans in the Americas, to ideas of individualism and egalitarianism, lesbian desire appears to have been defined in four dominant ways, closely linked to the social class of the women concerned. This correlation between class, public appearance, and sexual behaviour suggests an effort to categorize women's deviancy in a satisfactory manner that did not threaten the dominant heterosexual and social paradigms of the age. Biological explanations seem to have been confined to educated, often medical, men, but the general public preferred a 'social constructionist' approach that emphasized the individual's circumstances.

The most common figure of female deviance was the transvestite. Early modern Europeans took cross-dressed women in their stride, even as they excoriated the effeminate man.[3] Virtually all the examples of 'passing women' that have survived (and many women must have died with their true identity unknown) are of working-class and peasant women who sought more job opportunities, better pay, and greater freedom.[4] Contemporaries accepted such economic necessity but often reinterpreted it in more romantic, hetero-sexual terms. Eighteenth-century broadside ballads praised the 'female war-rior' who went into battle in order to find her beloved. Most versions raised the possibility of sexual transgression but resolved matters in the final verse with a happy marriage or other appropriate female destiny.

The precursor to the modern 'butch' cannot be traced back to those women who passed as 'female soldiers'. Such women retained their biological identity as women and simply donned the outward clothing of men. They managed to be courageous fighters, gentle helpers, and loyal wives simultaneously—and to be universally admired. In her examination of the records of modern 'military maids,' Julie Wheelwright documents how many women depended upon the collusion of fellow soldiers to safeguard their secret.[5] When faced with a heterosexual proposition, the 'soldier' either deserted or capitulated to a common-law marriage.

The female soldier's closest relative was the immensely popular cross-dressed actress of the eighteenth-century stage. Wandering actresses, or even less reputable vagrants, made up most of this group. Most of these women were notoriously heterosexual; only the infamous Londoner Char-lotte Charke wore breeches in public. She delighted in playing with the possibilities of sexual transgression; her 1755 memoir robustly declared on the title page, 'Her Adventures in Mens Cloaths, going by the Name of Mr. *Brown*, and being belov'd by a Lady of great Fortune, who intended to marry her.' However, she cast her autobiography in terms of a theatrical comedy, so as to mitigate the dangerous implications of her actions. Neither theatrical nor military dress implied a permanent identity but, rather, a tem-porary, if bold, seizing of opportunity.

More troubling, because more difficult to place, were those women who either appeared 'mannish' or continued to cross-dress after the wars were over. Rudolph Dekker and Lottie van de Pol have argued that in Holland women who dressed as men did so because they could conceive of love for another woman only in terms of the existing heterosexual paradigm. If this was so, the highly risky marriages that so many cross-dressed women undertook make sense, for they were 'the logical consequence of, on the one hand, the absence of a social role for lesbians and the existence of, on the other hand, a tradition of women in men's clothing' (Dekker and van de Pol, 1988, pp. 54–5, p.71). Although this suggestion is attractive, we lack sufficient personal information to generalize with confidence about the many and complicated psychosocial reasons why a woman might have cross-dressed in the past. [...]

Far more common was the 'free woman' who seemed to choose a flagrantly varied sexuality. Her appearance and behaviour could signal an erotic interest in women, but at other times—as prostitute, courtesan, or mistress—she chose men. The subject of gossip or pornography, she was invariably portrayed as consuming both women and men. I would label this third category of publicly identified lesbian desire as the occasional lover of women. This woman was frequently attacked as a danger to the normal political hierarchies because of her undue influence upon male leaders. The evidence for her activities can be best described as 'porn and politics,' pamphlets, gossip, and similarly suspect sources describing flagrant sexual freedom. The connection between sexual deviance and political deviance is hardly unique to women; indeed, the libertine libertarian John Wilkes (1727–97) was the subject of an intense pamphlet war linking him with excessive freedoms of all sorts.[6]

The most famous example of this kind of political linkage is Marie Antoinette, who was repeatedly accused of political intrigue and bisexual debauchery (Bonnet, 1981, pp.137–65; see also Faderman, 1981, pp.42–3). Although her female lovers were of her own social class, she was accused of taking on male lovers from the lower classes. Much of the evidence against her was generated by those determined of destroy an effeminate aristocracy and to replace it with a purified masculine democracy. In several cases Marie Antoinette was woven into preexisting pornographic plots with little consideration for historical facts. But we should not dismiss this material, for such culturally influential male fantasies, derived from both pornography and high art, had a lasting impact upon the public (and, occasionally, the private) image of the lesbian.

The fourth and increasingly common form that lesbian desire took is the romantic friendship. Nancy Cott (1977, p. 186) has documented the ways in which the definition of 'friend' changed in the eighteenth century to refer specifically to an elective, nonfamilial relationship of particular importance. Maaike Meijer (1983) in her description of the friendship of two famous late eighteenth-century Dutch blue-stockings, Betje Wolff and Aagje Deken, points to the importance of a shared interest in learning, often in the face of family and public opposition, as a crucial element in romantic friendships.[7] A sense of being different, of wanting more than other young women, symbolized by a love of learning, characterizes many of the romantic friendships described by Faderman (1981) in *Surpassing the Love of Men*. Yet even here, women's friendships were tightly controlled by external definitions of respectability. All bourgeois families feared any emotions that would overturn the conventional hierarchies in the private and public spheres. The discipline of study was supposed to teach women friends to be rational, to control their love for each other. In actuality, it probably led to a desire for greater independence—and consequently, an increased labelling of such friendships as deviant.[8]

These four forms of lesbian sexual desire were united less by the behavior or attitudes of the women than by the ways in which men interpreted women's same-sex desire. On the one hand, we have amusement, curiosity, and romanticization; on the other, we have horror, punishment, and expulsion. In either response, however, women's same-sex behaviour remained marginal to male sexual and societal discourses.[9] The vocabulary used to define these visibly aberrant women, drawn from the classical world, emphasized either an unnatural act or a congenital defect. The Greek word 'tribade' appears only in the sixteenth and early seventeenth centuries in France and England, as a description of a woman who rubbed her genitals against another woman's. Well before the pioneering sexologists of the late nineteenth century, medical theorists assigned an essentialist identity to same-sex behavior, arguing that it must be rooted in the individual's physiology. The most common medical term was 'hermaphrodite'. 'Sapphic,' the word used most frequently in memoirs, does not even merit a sexual definition in the *Oxford English Dictionary*.[10]

Only when a woman seemed to contravene directly masculine priorities and privileges was she punished. But even in these cases, sexual deviancy had to be compounded by a trespassing upon the male preserves of religion or politics in order to draw the full wrath of masculine authority. Lesbian sexuality remained a muted discourse. The usual punishment for a woman who married another woman was a public whipping and banishment. One notable exception, however, was the early eighteenth-century case of the respectable innkeeper, 'James How'. Mary East and her friend had opened a public house in the 1730s in a village north of London, and by dint of hard work and honesty they prospered. But East, known everywhere as 'James How', had been forced to pay a blackmailer for years. Finally, after the death of her partner, she took her case to the magistrates; they did not arrest her for fraud but imprisoned the blackmailer. All surviving accounts of How treat her sympathetically. The most acceptable model for understanding her 35-year 'marriage' was the female-warrior ballad, and reports were circulated that she and her 'wife' must have decided to join together after they had been jilted by men. Marjorie Garber (1991, pp. 69–70) has labelled this 'normalization' of the transvestite as a 'progress narrative,' which recuperates an individual into a bourgeois tale of economic struggle and social success.[11] [. . .]

This casual and seeming indifference to women's relationships needs to be contrasted with those occasions when women clearly threatened the dominance of men or of the traditional family. The actress Charlotte Charke, in spite of her notoriety, was never a public threat because she remained a liminal figure of farce, but the multifarious sins of the German Catharina Margaretha Linck led to her trial for sodomy and her execution in 1721. She had joined an egalitarian, woman-led religion and later had converted to Roman Catholicism and then Lutheranism. Dressing as a man, she served in a Prussian volunteer corps, worked as a weaver, and married a woman with whom she had sex, using a homemade dildo. After hearing complaints from her daughter, Linck's mother-in-law and a neighbour 'attacked her, took her sword, ripped open her pants, examined her, and discovered that she was indeed not a man but a woman' (Erickson, 1981, p. 33).[12] In her defence, Linck insisted she had been deluded by Satan and that it was no sin for a maiden to wear men's clothes. Both reasons depend upon circumstances;

Linck did not argue that she was biologically different or that she had been born 'that way.'

Women who avoided a direct confrontation with male prerogatives, whether sexual or political, fared best. The most famous example of romantic friendship in the eighteenth century was the upper-class 'Ladies of Llangollen,' who ran away from threats of marriage and the convent to live with each other in remote north Wales. Eleanor Butler (1739–1829) and Sarah Ponsonby (1755–1831) succeeded because they each had a small income and made a determined effort to reproduce a happy marriage in rural retirement. (James How and his 'wife' had followed the working-class equivalent of this pattern in their moral probity, modesty, and hard work.) In their riding habit and short, powdered hair they looked like a pair of old men when seated (they still wore skirts), and their eccentricities were brushed aside by a wide circle of admirers. Yet even they were subject to gossip. In 1790 a journalist described Lady Eleanor as 'tall and masculine and appearing in all respects a young man, if we except the petticoats she retains'. (Butler's and Ponsonby's lives are recounted in Maver, 1971, p. 74.) She was actually short, dumpy and fifty-one at the time. During their long lives they faced down snide comments by appearing intellectual, desexualized, and otherworldly.

Samuel Johnson's friend, the well-known gossip Mrs Piozzi, made a distinction that was typical of the age, in respecting the intellectual Ladies of Llangollen and loathing the sexual antics of the aristocracy. In 1789 she noted, 'The Queen of France is at the Head of a Set of Monsters call'd by each other *Sapphists* who boast her example and deserve to be thrown with the *He* Demons that haunt each other likewise, into Mount Vesuvius. *That* Vice increases hourly in Extent—while expected *Parricides* frightened us no longer. . . .' (Balderston, 1951: 1, p.740).[13] The dislike of such behaviour seems to have stemmed from the growing political hatred of the dissolute aristocracy as much as a distaste of their frolics. Nevertheless, the fear of active female sexuality in places of power was a potent threat, as Marie-Jo Bonnet (1981, p.165) reminds us. She argues that the Revolutionary crowd's decapitation and mutilation of Mme. Lamballe's genitals was an effort to destroy lesbian friendships and not just the friend of the imprisoned queen. (See also Castle, 1992.)

THE NINETEENTH AND TWENTIETH CENTURIES: NATURAL AFFECTION OR *FEMME DAMNÉE?*

By the early years of the nineteenth century we can see two changes in same-sex relations. First, male commentary on occasional lesbian love-making, whether hearsay, journalism, or literature, became much more common. Public gossip shifted from Marie Antoinette's bedroom politics to the overtly sexual, unconventional women in artistic circles. Now women who were not necessarily prostitutes or well-connected could—at the price of respectability—choose to live a sexually free life. In addition, a few middle-class working women began to wear masculine (or simply practical) clothing. The active, mannish woman from the middle classes can be found throughout Europe and America by the 1820s. Most insisted upon their sexual respectability but also asserted their right to enter such predominantly male arenas as medicine, literature, art, and travel. While professional single women emphasized their emotional ties, the bohemians flaunted their sexuality. George Sand (1804–76) is the most important representative of the latter type, and Rosa Bonheur (1822–99) of the former; not coincidentally both were economically independent artists.

Sometime in the early nineteenth century the cross-dressed masculine woman (the mannish lesbian) appeared, whose primary emotional, and probably also her sexual, commitment, was to women. [. . .] In effect, these women combined the outward appearance of the cross-dressed woman and the inner, emotional life of a romantic friendship. The mannish lesbian, a forerunner of the twentieth-century 'butch' is the result of this double inheritance. It is one which denied the theatricality of gender and instead inscribes it upon the body as a permanent identity. As I will discuss below, this figure became the identified deviant 'invert' in the later-nineteenth and early-twentieth-century work of such sexologists as Richard von Krafft-Ebing, Havelock Ellis and Sigmund Freud. At the same time, both romantic friendships and passing women, continued well into the twentieth century. In 1929, for example, in the midst of Radclyffe Hall's *The Well of Loneliness* obscenity trial, a Colonel Barker was arrested after passing as a World War I hero for over a decade; she had been 'married' for three years before deserting her wife.[14] Romantic friendships flourished among women activists in the national Woman's Party in the 1940s and 1950s, according to Leila Rupp (1989).

None of these familiar types includes what we would now call the 'femme' of the butch–femme couple.[15] Like the younger woman in a Sapphic romance, she was presumed to be only an occasional lover of women—someone who could, like Mary in *The Well of Loneliness* (1928), be lured away from her aberration by a handsome man. Teresa de Lauretis concludes: 'Even today, in most representational contexts Mary would be either passing lesbian or passing straight, her (homo)sexuality being in the last instance what can not be seen. Unless . . . she enter the frame of vision *as* or *with* a lesbian in male body drag' (de Lauretis, 1988). The impossibility of defining her by appearance or behaviour baffled the sexologists. Havelock Ellis, by defining the sexual invert as someone who possessed the characteristics of the opposite sex, was unable to categorize the feminine invert. As Esther Newton has pointed out, he argued tentatively, 'they are always womanly. One may perhaps say that they are the pick of the women whom the average man would pass by. . . . So far as they may be said to constitute a class they seem to possess a genuine, though not precisely sexual, preference for women over men' (quoted in Newton, 1989, p. 288). Perhaps Ellis sensed that the 'femme' was not a passive victim but an active agent in defining her own sexual preference. Certainly by the late 1950s, scandal sheets had identified her as the consummate actress who deceived unsuspecting husbands—in effect, she had overtaken the butch as the threatening female who undermined masculinity.[16] An instability of gender identity adheres to the feminine invert in spite of every effort to categorize her.

The publication of excerpts of Anne Lister's diaries for the years 1817–24 has given us new insight into the life of a self-consciously mannish lesbian.[17] Her entries reveal that many educated women had covert sexual relations with other women, often as a pleasurable interlude before or during marriage, sometimes as part of a long-term commitment. Lister, 25 when her published diary begins, spends little time analyzing why she preferred a masculine demeanor, even at the expense of public effrontery. But she was deeply distressed when her more conventional (and married) lover was uneasy about being seen with her at a small seaside resort because she looked 'unnatural'. Lister defended her carefully contrived appearance, recording in her diary that 'her conduct & feelings [were] surely natural to me in as much as they are not taught, not fictious, but instinctive' (Whitbread, 1988, p. 28).[18] Lister was a forerunner of those women who sought to change their appearance to accord with their souls; she assumed that her behaviour was innate and instinctual, even though she had gradually and self-consciously adopted more masculine accoutrements. Her lover on the other hand, denied that she might be pursuing an adulterous affair with 'Freddy' Lister; economic circumstances had driven her into marriage and emotional circumstances led her into Lister's arms. Both were choices made under social constraints, but in no way were they part of her intrinsic identity.[19] Within a self-consciously sexual couple, two conflicting justifications for their behavior coexisted uneasily.

George Sand dressed as a male student in order to sit in the cheap seats at the theatre, and into her forties she wore informal male dress at home. She was also for a brief period madly in love with the actress Marie Dorval; each of the men in Sand's life was convinced that she was having an affair specifically to torment them.[20] Given her reputation as a sexually free woman, rumours swirled around Sand, inviting different interpretations of her identity then and now. Sand fits male fantasies of the devouring lesbian, of the woman who is all body. When this remarkable woman cross-dressed, it represented not her soul but her all-too-dominating body (de Courtiran, 1979). The bisexual Sand symbolized the strong woman who devoured weak men and found her pleasure in the arms of other women. The 1830s in France spawned novels about monsters, of whom lesbians were among the most titillating. This male-generated image of sexual deviance proved to be especially powerful and one that would return repeatedly in twentieth-century portrayals of the lesbian *femme damnée*. (See also Moses, 1993; Faderman, 1981, pp. 274–99; Kraakman, 1987.)

[. . .]

Lillian Faderman (1981, pp. 190–230) has defined the nineteenth-century as the heyday of romantic friendships, when women could love each other without fear of social stigma (see also Faderman, 1978). In New England the longevity and the erotic undertones of relations between women appear to have been publicly accepted, for 'Boston marriages' were commonplace in literary circles; we have numerous other well-documented examples in every northern European country where women were making inroads into the professions. Most of these highly respectable couples had one partner who was more active and public, while the other was more retiring. The nineteenth-century English educational reformers, Constance Maynard and Louisa Lumsden, for example, spoke of each other as wife and husband, respectively; as headmistress of a girls' school, Lumsden expected her 'wife' to support her decisions and to comfort her when difficulties arose (Vicinus, 1982). Lumsden was repeatedly described by her friends as assertive, even 'leonine', although photographs reveal her to our eyes as an upper-class lady much like her peers in physical appearance.

The mannish Bonheur worked hard to keep the image of respectable independence which characterized romantic friendships. Nevertheless, her square craggy features and men's clothes placed her in a suspect category. When French taste turned against her realistic paintings, she hinted to friends that the criticism was as much a personal attack on her life with Nathalie Micas as it was her artistry (Ashton and Browne Hare, 1981, p. 162). However proud she may have been of her androgynous appearance, Bonheur was also self-conscious enough to insist that her lifelong relations with Micas and Anna Klumpke were pure. Both Lister and George Sand, one moneyed the other an aristocrat, were willing to risk public slander, but Bonheur needed public acceptance to succeed as a painter.

I think that we may have exaggerated the acceptability of romantic friendships. A fear of excess—whether of learning or of emotion—may well have been a cover for opposition to the erotic preference implied by a close friendship. The vituperation launched against Marie Antoinette and her best-known lovers had political roots, but it is only an extreme form of similar warnings found in etiquette books, medical tracts, and fiction, describing the dangers of over-heated friendships. The Queen could endanger the state; less lofty women could endanger the state of marriage. The notorious example of the feminist Emily Faithful (1835–95) provided ample opportunity to editorialize against romantic friendships. In 1864 Admiral Henry Codrington petitioned for divorce on the grounds of his wife's adultery; in addition, Faithful was accused of alienating his wife's affections. Helen Codrington in turn, accused him of attempted rape upon Faithful one night when the two women were sleeping together (the known facts are briefly outlined in Banks, 1985). Faithfull herself first signed an affidavit claiming that this incident had taken place, but in court she refused to confirm it. The scandal permanently damaged her standing with other feminists, and she never regained the position of leadership she had held as the founder of the Victoria Press and *The Victoria Magazine*.

During the first half of the nineteenth century we can see the accelerating efforts of the medical and legal professions to define, codify, and control all forms of sexuality and thereby to replace the church as the arbiters of sin and morality. Women's deviant sexual behaviors, whether heterosexual prostitution or homosexuality, continued to be male-defined transgressions dominated by male language, theories, and traditions. Such narrow terms as 'hermaphrodite' were replaced with a plethora of competing words, such as 'urning', 'lesbian', 'third sex', and 'invert'. Writing in the 1830s, Alexandre Jean-Baptiste Parent-Duchâtelet, the pioneering French medical hygienist, linked the lives of prostitutes with those of cross-dressed lesbians. Both represented possibilities and fears for men, for each embodied an active, independent, uncontrollable sexuality.[21] Underneath their veneer of scientific language, the medical and legal tracts betray many of the same interests and biases as pornography and literature.

It has become a truism that the sexologists, such as Richard von Krafft-Ebing and Havelock Ellis, did not so much define a lesbian identity as describe and categorize what they saw about them. [. . .]

Several feminist historians in Britain, following the lead of Lillian Faderman, have argued that the sexologists created a climate of opinion that stigmatized single women and their relationships and favoured heterosexuality (see Coveney et al., 1984; Jeffreys, 1985). Others have argued that the sexologists stimulated the formation of lesbian identity (Ruehl, 1982) or that their influence has been greatly exaggerated. All these scholars have, to date, looked almost exclusively at the medical debates rather than placing these debates in a wider historical context. A host of competing sociobiological ideologies and disciplines grew at the end of the nineteenth century, including social Darwinism, eugenics, criminology, and anthropology; women's sexual relations could hardly remain unaffected by them.

Have we too readily categorized these early sexologists and their embarrassingly crude classifications of sexual behaviour? Rather than labelling the sexologists' descriptions benighted misogyny, we might learn more from them about both contemporary lesbian mores and masculine attitudes. Esther Newton (1989, p. 291) has suggested that Havelock Ellis's biological determinism at the very least made available a sexual discourse to middle-class women, who 'had no developed female sexual discourse; there were only male discourses—pornographic, literary, medical—*about* female sexuality'. I would add that these three male discourses had long affected the traditional categories of transvestite, romantic friend, occasional lover, and androgynous woman; all four types had already been defined as suspect before they were taken up by Krafft-Ebing and Ellis. In effect, women's sexual behaviour has never been isolated from or independent of the dominant male discourses of the age. [. . .]

By the end of the nineteenth century, wealthy and/or intrepid women had consciously migrated not only to Paris but also to Berlin, Amsterdam, New York, San Francisco, Chicago, and other cities, where they hoped to find other homosexuals.[22] They were specifically attracted to cities with bohemian subcultures, which promised to give women space to explore their sexuality, their bodies. An extraordinary number of homosexual clubs and bars—surviving photographs indicate a passion for elegant butch—femme attire—flourished in Berlin, Munich, Hamburg, and other German cities, attesting to the cultural richness of Weimar Germany; none survived the Nazi takeover of 1933.

Some of the excitement and fragility of Germany's lively gay night life was also characteristic of Harlem of the 1920s. As Lillian Faderman (1991, pp. 62–92) has argued, it was a decade when bisexuality was fashionable, and the sexually freer world of Harlem attracted both white and black women. (See also Garber, 1984; 1988.) [. . .]

But for literary English and American lesbians, Paris symbolized sexual freedom.[23] It was already known for its lesbian subculture thanks not only to Sand's reputation but also to the poetry and fiction of such notable male writers as Balzac, Gautier, Baudelaire, Louÿs, Zola, Maupassant, and Daudet. [. . .]

The bohemian world of George Sand did not need to be re-created because these women were living their own version of it.[24]

The most striking aspect of the lesbian coteries of the 1910s and 1920s was their self-conscious effort to create a new sexual language for themselves that included not only words but also gestures, costume, and behaviour.[25] These women combined the essentialist biological explanation of lesbianism with a carefully constructed self-presentation. The parties, plays and masquerades of the wealthy American Natalie Barney (1876–1970) are the best known 'creations'.

[. . .]

An insistence upon the flesh, the very body of the lesbian, distinguished this generation. But if Barney celebrated the tactile delights of a woman's body, for Radclyffe Hall the lesbian body could be a curse because society refused to acknowledge its inherent validity. Without public, and especially family, acceptance, self-hatred was inevitable for her heroine Stephen in *The Well of Loneliness*: 'She hated her body with its muscular shoulders, its small compact breasts, and its slender flanks of an athlete. All her life she must drag this body of hers like a monstrous fetter imposed on her spirit. This strangely ardent yet sterile body' (Hall: 1968, p. 217). Moreover, contemporaries had the example of Reneé Vivien (1877–1909) to remind them of the psychic dangers of lesbian love. Vivien embodied the doomed lesbian by changing her name, her religion, and her body, finally drinking and starving herself to death by the age of 31.

The privileged Barney declared that a woman's body was her greatest pleasure, but Hall contended that a woman's body was her unavoidable destiny, sterile and fertile. Both positions have an altogether too familiar ring, for both had long been encoded in male discourse. This generation of extraordinary women could not escape a familiar paradox that feminists still confront: by privileging the body, positively or negatively, women necessarily became participants in an already defined language and debate. Woman as body had been a male trope for too long to be overcome by a spirited or tragic rejection (see Suleiman, 1986).

Newton has argued that Radclyffe Hall chose to portray Stephen as a congenital invert, based upon Havelock Ellis's theories, because it was her only alternative to the asexuality of romantic friendships. Actually, by the late 1920s Hall had numerous other alternatives, including Barney's hedonistic lesbianism, Vivien's self-created tragedy, Colette's theatrical affair with the marquise, and the many less colourful monogamous couples in Paris's literary world. For Hall, these women were either too secretive or too ostentatious and therefore too close to heterosexual fantasies about the life of the deviant.[26] Hall's militant demand for recognition made Ellis's congenital invert the most natural choice. This model, with its emphasis upon an innate, and therefore unchangeable, defect, also carried the status of scientific veracity. Ironically, as soon as a woman's body—specifically Stephen's 'monstrous' body—became the focus of discussion, the book was legally banned in England. [. . .]

The demand for respect, for acceptance of one's innate difference, assumed a kind of sexual parity with men which has never been widely accepted. Hall's radical message was lost, but her portrait of Stephen remained. The complex heritage of the first generation of self-identified lesbians, experimental and flamboyant, collapsed into the public figure of the deprived and depraved *femme damnée*. The open-ended confidence and playfulness of the 1910s and 1920s did not survive the court case against *The Well of Loneliness*. The political and economically turbulent 1930s narrowed women's sexual options. The lesbian community in Paris continued but shorn of its former glamour. Those who could find work often had to support relatives. The women's movement itself seemed increasingly irrelevant in the face of such competing ideologies as communism and fascism. Unfortunately, generalizations are difficult to make, for we know little about the isolated lesbian of the 1930s. Characteristic of the decade, class divisions appear to have increased, so that the middle-class lesbian disappeared into discreet house parties, the aristocratic lesbian popped up at favourite expatriate spas, and the working-class lesbian could be found among the unemployed hitchhikers described by Box-Dar Bertha.[27] Our only evidence of her public role is fleeting references in popular psychology books—like Krafft-Ebing's — labelling her as dangerously independent.

The doomed lesbian was a remarkably durable image. By the 1950s everyone knew what a lesbian was; she had been assigned a clearly defined role. Defiance and loneliness marked her life, according to the pulp romances.

The *femme damnée* was not simply a product of a fevered literary imagination; if her sexual preference became public knowledge during the witchhunts of the McCarthy period she became literally outlawed. After acceptance during the labour-hungry years of World War II, lesbians and gays faced expulsion from military and government jobs (see Bérubé, 1990). Nevertheless, Elizabeth Wilson in England found the *femme damnée* an attractive alternative to bourgeois marriage in the 1950s; she was disappointed when progressive friends told her she was sick, not damned (Wilson, 1986, p. 175).

In the 1950s both the general public and lesbians themselves privileged the predictable figure of the mannish lesbians. Romantic excess, forbidden desires and social marginality were all represented by her cross-dressing. But, as I have demonstrated, she was also the product of a tangled history which embodied the outlawry of passing, the idealism of romantic friendship, and the theatricality of aristocratic play. What adhered to her identity most powerfully during these years, however, was a sense of being born different, of having a body that reflects a specific sexual identity. The femme who could pass had disappeared. Although the American Joan Nestle (1987) has argued forcefully for her importance, Wilson (1986, p. 141) experienced being a woman's woman as 'the lowest of the low' in the liberal heterosexual world she inhabited.

But the old playfulness of an earlier generation never completely died. Now it had returned not to re-create the past but rather to celebrate the identification of homosexuality with defined, and inescapable, roles or to imagine a utopian world of transformed women. Like the women of the early twentieth century, many lesbians of our time have set themselves the task of creating a lesbian language, of defining lesbian desire, and of imagining a lesbian society. Monique Wittig, in *Les Guérillères* (1969), *Le Corps lesbien* (1973), and *Brouillon pour un dictionnaire des amantes* (1975), has presented the most sustained alternative world. Her wholesale rewriting of history, in which all mention of man is eliminated, makes it possible to imagine a woman's body outside male discourse. Even here, however, our history is incomplete. In their heroic comedy *Brouillon pour un dictionnaire des amantes*, Wittig and her coauthor, Sande Zeig, leave a blank page for the reader to fill in under Sappho. Dyke, butch, amazon, witch, and such 'obsolete' words as woman and wife are included. But androgyne, femme, invert, and friendship are missing.[28] Rosa Bonheur, who so disliked rigid sex roles, is strangely absent from this world. And what about the occasional lover of women? Historians are more confined to their evidence than writers of fiction and cannot create utopias, but they can and do create myths. When we rewrite, indeed, recreate, our lost past, do we too readily drop those parts of our past that seem unattractive or confusing to us? Can (and should) utopian language and ideas help us recuperate a history full of contradictions?

Notes

This is a (1992) revised and updated version of a paper originally presented at the 'Homosexuality, Which Homosexuality?' conference (Amsterdam, December 1987)

1. Lillian Faderman's (1981) *Surpassing the Love of Men: Romantic Friendship between Women from the Renaissance to the Present* contains the best account of the pleasure and limitations of romantic friendship without financial means.

2. I am indebted to Laurence Senelick for drawing my attention to Pidansat de Mairobert's pre-revolutionary quasi-pornographic romance. *Histoire d'une jeune fille* (Paris: Bibliothéque des Curieux, n.d. (1789)), in which a fictional 'Secte des Anandrynes' meet for lesbian frolics under the leadership of a statuesque woman described as possessing 'something of the masculine in her appearance' ('quelque chose d'hommasse dans toute sa personne'). 23.

3. Randolph Trumbach (1987) has documented the shift from the rake's bisexual freedom to the effeminate sodomite in 'Gender and the homosexual role in modern Western culture: the eighteenth and nineteenth centuries compared'.

4. The one obvious exception to this generalization is James Barry (1795?–1865), a well-known British army surgeon, whom contemporaries assumed was hermaphrodite on account of her small stature, lack of beard, and high voice. See Rae (1958).

5. See especially the case of the American Civil War volunteer Frank Thompson (Emma Edmonds) in Wheelwright (1989, pp. 62–6).

6. See Richard Sennett's (1978, pp. 99–106) discussion of the ways in which John Wilkes's body—and sexual freedom— came to represent political freedom.

7. These ideals also characterized the friendship of Ruth and Eva in *Dear Girls: The Diaries and Letters of Two Working Women, 1897–1917* (Thompson, 1987), a century later.

8. These issues are touched on, but not completely developed in Martha Vicinus (1989).

9. Joanne Glasgow argues that 'misogyny, thus, accounts in significant ways for the official neglect of lesbianism' in the Roman Catholic church. See Glasgow (1990, p. 249).

10. The *Oxford English Dictionary*, not always the most reliable source on sexual matters, records the first use of tribade in 1601: tribady in 1811–19 in reference to the famous Miss Woods and Miss Pirie vs. Lady Cumming Gordon trial of 1811. Hermaphrodite receives the most complete coverage, with the first reference to its use as 1398. Sapphic is defined simply as 'of or pertaining to Sappho, the famous poetess of Lesbos,' or 'a metre used by Sappho or named after her.' Sapphism is not mentioned.

11. Garber's discussion is in regard to the jazz musician Billy Tipton, whose sexual identity was revealed at 'his' death in 1989.

12. See also Theo van der Meer 'Tribades on trial: female same-sex offenders in late-eighteenth-century Amsterdam'. These women, drawn from a similar class as Linck's, were seen as public nuisances and prostitutes as well as tribades.

13. Trumbach (1991) documents Mrs Piozzi's growing awareness of English 'sapphists' and the reference to them in slang as early as 1782 as 'tommies'.

14. The fullest account of 'Colonel' Barker can be found in Wheelwright (1989, pp. 1–11; p. 159.) Wheelwright points out that Barker married only after her father-in-law caught the two women living together. In court 'his' wife, Elfrida Haward, denied all knowledge of her husband's true sex. Characteristically, the judge was most concerned with Barker's deception of the Church of England. See also Baker (1985, p. 254).

15. But see Colette's (1966, pp. 114–29) attempt to define her in an evocative re-creation of Sarah Ponsonby in *The Pure and the Impure*.

16. See, for example, 'The shocking facts about those lesbians'. *Hush-Hush* 5 (September 1959), unpaginated; 'Do lesbian wives swap husbands?' *On the Q.T.* 5 (July 1961), pp. 28–29; pp. 56–57; p. 60; Tague (1965, pp. 20–21; p. 58). I am indebted to Laurence Senelick and the Lesbian Herstory Archives, New York City, for these references.

17. See also the more elusive life described in Betty T. Bennett's (1991) biography, *Mary Diana Dods: A Gentleman and a Scholar*. One of two illegitimate daughters of the fifteenth earl of Morton, Dods earned a precarious living as a writer using several different male pseudonyms. In 1827 Mary Shelley helped Dods escape from England to the Continent as Walter Sholto Douglas, 'husband' of the pregnant Isabel Robinson. Although they gained entry to the highest literary circles in Paris, the Douglases were totally dependent upon funds from their families. Dods appears to have died in penury in 1829, freeing her 'wife' to make a highly respectable marriage to an Anglican minister resident in Florence, Italy.

18. For examples of attacks on Lister by men, see Whitbread, 1988, pp. 48–49; p. 106; p. 110; pp. 113–15.

19. We have, of course, only Lister's interpretation of her behaviour, but see Whitbread (1988, p. 104): 'I felt she was another man's wife. I shuddered at the thought & at the conviction that no soffistry (*sic*) could gloss over the criminality of our connection. It seemed not that the like had occurred to her'. The use of a masculine (or androgynous) nickname for the more mannish partner can be found repeatedly in these relations.

20. As Ruth Jordan (1976, p. 68) describes it: 'George was credited with at least three simultaneous affairs (with men): one with Sandeau, unwanted but still officiating, another with Latouche, who had retired to the country, and yet another with Gustave Planche, the unkempt, uncombed, unwashed brilliant critic of the *Revue des Deux Mondes*. Marie Dorval was the latest, most sensational addition to a cohort of unproven lovers'. Biographers of Sand fall into two camps, those who sensationalize her life and those who normalize it; the latter, of course, are most reluctant to identify her relationship with Dorval as sexual.

21. A.J.B. Parent-Duchâtelet claimed that 'lesbians have fallen to the last degree of vice to which a human creature can attain, and, for that very reason, they require a most particular surveillance on the part of those charged with the surveillance of prostitutes. . . .' (*La Prostitution dans la ville de Paris* (1836). 1, p. 170), quoted in Stambolian and Marks (1979, p. 148).

22. Gayle Rubin has coined the phrase 'sexual migrations' to describe 'the movement of people to cities undertaken to explore specialized sexualities not available in the traditional family arrangements, and often smaller towns, where they grew up'. Quoted by Rapp (1980, p. 106, n. 4) In her autobiography Gidlow (1898–1986) makes clear that until the 1970s her homosexual community was comprised primarily of men and a few close women friends (Gidlow, 1986).

23. Benstock (1986, p. 49) quotes Elyse Blankley in characterizing Paris as 'a double edged sword, offering both free sexual expression and oppressive sexual stereotyping. It might cultivate lesbianism like an exotic vine, but it would never nourish it. In front of (Renée) Vivien—and indeed every lesbian yawned the immense, unbridgeable chasm separating men's perceptions of lesbian women and lesbian women's perceptions of themselves. See Blankley (1984).

24. We have very little evidence of a working-class lesbian subculture at this time. Elsa Gidlow's (1986) memoirs (pp. 68–71) seem to indicate a similar pattern of seeking out a bohemian artistic culture. During World War I, while working as a secretary and living at home, she started a literary group in Montreal which attracted a young gay man who introduced her to the Decadent writers of the late nineteenth century, avant-garde music, and modern art.

25. In her essay 'The new woman as androgyne', Smith-Rosenberg (1985) discusses the revolutionary nature of this project—and its failure, which she attributes to the writers' unsuccessful effort to transform the male discourse on female sexuality (pp. 265–6, 285–96).
26. This point is also made by Gillian Whitlock (1987). See also Benstock's (1986, p. 59) comment about this generation of lesbian writers as a whole: 'Without historical models, (their) writing was forced to take upon itself the double burden of creating a model of lesbian behaviour while recording the personal experience of that behaviour'.
27. See Bullough and Bullough (1973)(1977) Sanders on Dorothy Thompson (Thompson was the lover of Christa Winsloe, playwright and author of the play and novel upon which *Madchen in Uniform* was based): Box-Car Bertha, *Sister of the Road: An Autobiography*, as told to Reitman (1975). See also Faderman (1991, pp. 93–117); and Gidlow (1986, pp. 250–81).
28. I am using the English translation (Wittig and Zeig, 1980).

References

Ashton, D. and Browne Hare, d. (1981) *Rosa Bonheur: A Life and a Legend*. New York: Viking.

Baker, M. (1985) *Our Three Selves: The Life of Radclyffe Hall*. London: Hamish Hamilton.

Balderston, K. (ed.) (1951) *Thraliana: The Diary of Hester Lynch Thrale (Later Mrs Piozzi)* (2nd edn.) Oxford: Clarendon Press.

Banks, O. (1985) *The Biographical Dictionary of British Feminists, 1800–1930*. New York: New York University Press.

Beck, E. Torton (1982) *Nice Jewish Girls: A Lesbian Anthology*. Waterton, Mass: Persephone Press.

Bennett, B.T. (1991) *Mary Diana Dods: A Gentleman and a Scholar*. New York: William Morrow.

Benstock, S. (1986) *Women of the Left Bank, Paris,1900–1940*. Austin, TX: University of Texas Press.

Bérubé, A. (1990) *Coming Out under Fire: A History of Gay Men and Women in World War II*. New York: Free Press.

Blankley, E. (1981) Return to Mytilène: Renée Vivien and the City of Women. In S. Merrill Squier (ed.) *Women Writers and the City.* (pp. 45–67). Knoxville: University of Tennessee Press.

Bonnet, M. -J. (1981) *Un Choix sans équivoque*. Paris: Denoël.

Bullough, V. and Bullough, B. (1977) Lesbianism in the 1920s and 1930s: a newfound study. *Signs* 2, 895–904.

Castle, T. (1991) Marie Antoinette obsession. *Representations* 38, Spring, 1–38.

Colette (1966) *The Pure and the Impure* (trans. Herma Briffault). New York: Farrar, Straus & Giroux.

Cott, N. (1977) *The Bonds of Womanhood. 'Woman's Sphere' in New England, 1780–1835*. New Haven: Yale University Press.

Coveney, L. *et al.* (1984) *The Sexuality Papers: Male Sexuality and the Sexual Control of Women*. London: Hutchinson.

Dekker, R. and van de Pol, L. (1988) *The Tradition of Female Transvestism in Early Modern Europe*. London: Macmillan.

de Courtivon, I. (1979) Weak men and fatal women: the Sand image. In G. Stambolian and E. Marks (eds) *Homosexualities and French Literature* (pp. 224–16). Ithaca: Cornell University Press.

de Lauretis, T. (1988) Sexual indifference and lesbian representation. *Theatre Journal* 40, May, 177.

Ericksson, B. (trans) (1981) A lesbian execution in Germany, 1721: the trial records. In S.J. Licata and R.P. Petersen (eds) *Historical Perspectives on Homosexuality*. New York: Haworth Press.

Faderman, L. (1978) The morbidification of love between women by nineteenth-century sexologists. *Journal of Homosexuality* 4, Fall, 73–90.

— (1981) *Surpassing the Love of Men: Romantic Friendship between Women from the Renaissance to the Present*. New York: William Morrow.

— (1991) *Odd Girls and Twilight Lovers: A History of Lesbian Life in Twentieth-Century America*. New York: Columbia University Press.

Ferguson, A. (1981) Patriarchy, sexual identity and the sexual revolution. *Signs* 7, Autumn, 158–72.

Freedman, E.B. *et al.* (1984) Editorial—The lesbian issue. *Signs* 9, Summer.

Garber, M. (1987) A spectacle in colour: the lesbian and gay subculture of jazz age Harlem. In M.B. Duberman, M. Vicinus and G. Chauncey, Jr (eds) *Hidden from History: Reclaiming the Gay and Lesbian Past* (pp. 318–31). New York: New American Library.

— (1988) Gladys Bentley: the bulldagger who sang the blues. *Out/Look* Spring, 52–61.

— (1991) *Vested Interests: Cross-dressing and Cultural Anxiety*. New York: Routledge.

Gidlow, E. (1986) *Elsa: I Come with My Songs*. San Francisco: Booklegger Press.

Glasgow, J. (1990) What's a nice lesbian like you doing in the Church of Torquemada? Radclyffe Hall and other Catholic converts. In K. Jay and J. Glasgow (eds) *Lesbian Texts and Contexts: Radical Revisions*. New York: New York University Press.

Hall, R. (1968) *The Well of Loneliness*. London: Corgi Books. (First published 1928.)

Hunt, L. (1991) The many bodies of Marie Antoinette: political pornography and the problem of the feminine in French Revolution. In L. Hunt (ed.) *Eroticism and the Body Politic* (pp. 108–30). Baltimore: Johns Hopkins University Press.

Jeffreys, S. (1985) *The Spinster and Her Enemies: Feminism and Sexuality, 1880–1930*. London: Pandora.

Jordan, R. (1976) *George Sand: A Biography*. London: Constable.

Kosofsky Sedgwick, E. (1990) *Epistemology of the Closet*. Berkeley, CA: University of California Press.

Kraakman, D. (1987) Sexual ambivalence of women artists in early nineteenth-century France. Unpublished paper delivered at the 'Homosexuality, Which Homosexuality?' conference, Amsterdam, December.

Maver, E. (1971) *The Ladies of Llangollen*. London: Michael Joseph.

Meijer, M. (1983) Pious and learned female bosomfriends in Holland in the eighteenth century. Unpublished paper delivered at the 'Among Men, Among Women' conference, June, Amsterdam.

Moraga, C. and Anzaldúa, G. (1981) *This Bridge Called My Back. Writings by Radical Women of Color*. Watertown, MA: Persephone Press.

Moses, C. Goldberg (1993) Difference in historical perspective: Sain-Simonian feminism. In C.G. Moses and L.W. Rabine *The Word and the Act: French Feminism in the Age of Romanticism*. Bloomington: Indiana University Press.

Nestle, J. (1987) Butch—femme relationships: sexual courage in the 1950s. In J. Nestle *A Restricted Country* (pp. 100–9). Ithaca: Firebrand Books.

Newton, E. (1989) The mythic mannish lesbian: Radclyffe Hall and the new woman. In M.B. Duberman, M. Vicinus and G. Chauncey, Jr (eds) *Hidden from History: Reclaiming the Gay and Lesbian Past*. New York: New American Library.

Rae, I. (1958) *The Strange Story of Dr James Barry*. London: Longmans.

Rapp, R. (1980) An introduction to Elsa Gidlow: memoirs. *Feminist Studies* 6, Spring.

Reitman. L. (1975) *Sisters of the Road: An Autobiography*. New York: Harper & Row. (First published 1937.)

Ruehl, S. (1982) Inverts and experts: Radclyffe Hall and the lesbian identity. In R. Brunt and C. Rowan (eds) *Feminism, Culture, and Politics* (pp. 15–36). London: Lawrence & Wishart.

Rupp, L. (1989) Imagine my surprise: women's relationships in mid-twentieth-century America. In M.B. Duberman, M. Vicinus and G. Chauncey, Jr (eds) *Hidden from History: Reclaiming the Gay and Lesbian Past* (pp. 395–410). New York: New American Library.

Sanders, M.K. (1973) *Dorothy Thompson: A Legend in Her Time*. Boston: Houghton Mifflin.

Sennett, R. (1978) *The Fall of the Public Man: On the Social Psychology of Capitalism*. New York: Vintage.

Smith, B. (1984) *Home Girls: A Black Feminist Anthology*. New York: Kitchen Table, Women of Color Press.

Smith-Rosenberg, C. (1985) The new woman as androgyne: social disorder and gender crisis, 1870–1936. In C. Smith-Rosenberg *Disorderly Conduct: Visions of Gender in Victorian America*. New York: Alfred Knopf.

Stacey, J. (1987) The invisible difference: lesbianism and sexual difference theory. Unpublished paper delivered at the 'Homosexuality, Which Homosexuality?' conference, Amsterdam, December.

Stambolian, G. and Marks, E. (eds) (1979) *Homosexualities and French Literature*. Ithaca: Cornell University Press.

Suleiman, S.R. (ed.) (1986) *The Female Body in Western Culture: Contemporary Perspectives*. Cambridge, MA: Harvard University Press.

Tague, S. (1965) How many US wives are secret lesbians? *Uncensored* 14, February.

Thompson, T. (ed.) *Dear Girls: The Diaries and Letters of Two Working Women, 1897–1917*. London: Women's Press.

Trumbach, R. (1987) Gender and the homosexual role in modern Western culture: the eighteenth and nineteenth centuries compared. In D. Alman (ed) *Homosexuality, Which Homosexuality?* (pp. 149–70). Amsterdam: An Dekker.

— (1991) London's Sapphists: From three sexes to four genders in the making of modern culture. In J. Epstein and K. Straub (eds) *Body Guards: The Cultural Politics of Gender Ambiguity* (pp. 112–41). New York: Routledge.

van der Meer, T. (1991) Tribades on trial: female same-sex offenders in late-eighteenth-century Amsterdam. *Journal of the History of Sexuality* 1, January, 424–45.

Vicinus, M. (1982) 'One life to stand beside me': emotional conflicts in first-generation college women in England. *Feminist Studies* 8, Fall, 610–11.

— (1989) Distance and desire: English boarding school friendships. In M.B. Duberman, M. Vicinus and G. Chauncey, Jr (eds) *Hidden from History: Reclaiming the Gay and Lesbian Past* (pp. 212–29). New York: New American Library.

Wheelwright, J. (1989) *Amazons and Military Maids*. London, Pandora.

Whitbread, H. (ed.) (1988) *I Know My Own Heart: The Diaries of Anne Lister*. London: Virago.

Whitlock, G. (1987) 'Everything is out of place': Radclyffe Hall and the lesbian literary tradition. *Feminist Studies* 13, Fall, 576.

Wilson, E. (1986) *Hidden Agendas: Theory, Politics and Experience in the Women's Movement*. London: Tavistock.

Wittig, M. and Zeig, S. (1980) *Lesbian Peoples: Materials for a Dictionary*. London: Virago.

18 (IN)VISIBILITY: 'RACE', SEXUALITY AND MASCULINITY IN THE SCHOOL CONTEXT

MÁIRTÍN MAC AN GHAÍLL

We are only beginning to understand the complex articulation between schooling, masculine cultural formations and sexual/racial identities. Feminist theory has enabled us to move beyond the ahistorical gender/sexual essentialism and determinsm of sex-role theory, acknowledging that young people are not such '*tablae rasae*, to be injected or even constructed with the ideology of the day' (Rowbotham, 1989, p.18). As Carrigan, Connell and Lee (1985, pp. 88–9) argue:

> The history of homosexuality obliges us to think of masculinity not as a single object with its own history but as being constantly constructed within the history of an evolving social structure of power relations. It obliges us to see the construction as a social struggle going on in a complex ideological and political field in which there is a continuing process of mobilization, marginalization, contestation, resistance and subordination.

Modern schooling systems are significant cultural sites that actively produce and reproduce a range of differentiated, hierarchically ordered masculinities and femininities that are made available for students to inhabit. It is within historically specific school gender regimes that we may locate the development of black and white lesbian and gay sexualities (Mac an Ghaill, 1993).

A main argument here is that the major problem in the schooling of black gay students is not their sexuality but the phenomena of homophobia, heterosexism and racism which pervasively circumscribe their social world. Furthermore, these phenomena are mediated and reproduced both through existing formal and hidden curriculum, pedagogical and evaluative systems that set out to regulate subordinated young people and through gender/sexual specific mechanisms, such as the processes of gender/sexual representations, which in turn are 'race', class and age specific. An idealist analysis of the curriculum that reduces the heterosexist structuring of schooling to aberrant teacher prejudice is insufficient to explain the complex social interaction of white male and female teachers with black male students in racialized, male

Source: Abridged from Epstein, D. (ed.) (1994) *Challenging Lesbian and Gay Inequalities in Education* (pp. 189–225). Buckingham: Open University Press.

dominated institutions. For example, the students' teachers claimed that they found it difficult to discuss lesbian and gay issues within the school context. However, at a deeper level specific age relations operate in English schools that serve to marginalize and alienate many young people. White teachers' difficulty in communicating with black gay students is not simply an issue about sexuality and racism. It is also premised on the low epistemological status ascribed to all students.

THE CASE STUDY

The Asian and Afro-Caribbean young gay men involved in this qualitative study were aged between 16 and 19 years. They were all attending local post-16 education institutions situated in the Midlands. I taught a number of them, who were following A-level courses. Within their schools and colleges they were not 'out' as gay. My own students informed me that they were open to me about their sexuality because of my anti-homophobic stance. In the staffroom, classroom and more informal school arenas I presented a pro-gay perspective. They introduced me to their friends, who in turn introduced me to their friends. We operated as an informal support group. [. . .]

Our being together provided the conditions for us to start a conversation about the politics of oppression with particular reference to contemporary state schooling. This produced an unexpected and unintended effect. By the early 1990s in post-primary schools there tends to be less evidence among minorities of the 'black unity' of the mid 1980s, with its emphasis on the shared experience of anti-black racism. The black gay students here in exploring the politics of complex difference involving the articulation of homophobia, heterosexism and racism, are a sector of the younger generation among whom 'syncretic black identities are being formed . . .' (Mama, 1992, p. 80), focusing on racial, gender and sexual communalities as well as on the specificities of personal histories, memories, desires and expectations.

Methodology

Space does not allow for a detailed discussion of the study's methodology, particularly with reference to questions concerning the politics and ethics of researching oppressed groups (see Mac an Ghaill, 1989a). Much of the material reported here was collected from observation, informal discussions and recorded semi-structured interviews with the students and their teachers at their schools and colleges. The material is taken from life and school histories that involved discussion of family/kinship network, peer groupings, work experience, political views/activities and school/college experiences. This methodological approach helped to locate schooling within the larger socio-political processes (see Connell, 1989; Morgan, 1992). Sharing our life histories helped to challenge the power asymmetries between the students and myself. My main influences include feminist methodology and praxis-based pedagogy (see Freire, 1985; Bryan, Dadzie and Scafe, 1985, and hooks, 1991). In adopting a student-centred methodological approach that prioritizes their epistemological accounts of schooling, I have attempted to operate within a framework that served to empower the students who were actively involved in the construction of the research stance (Griffin, 1987, p. 21; Bhavnani, 1991).

ADMINISTRATIVE SYSTEMS OF TEACHER RACIAL AND GENDER/SEXUAL TYPIFICATIONS

As Westwood (1990, pp. 56–7) points out within the context of the need to de-essentialize black masculinity:

> The essentialism of the constructions that surround the black man and black masculinity have given plenty of scope for racist accounts through stereotyping and the construction of black men as 'the other'. [...] The fixity of these stereotypes places 'races', genders, motivations and behaviours in such a way that they become naturalized and a substitute for the complex realities that they seek to describe.

For the young men in this study these processes of naturalization and objectification were most immediately experienced through the highly contradictory dominant systems of teacher racial and gender/sexual discourses which are 'embedded in social relationships of structured domination and subordination' (Bhavnani, 1991, p. 181). These administrative systems operate as processes of teacher signification, that form the basis for the creation of ethnically structured student hierarchies. In turn, they serve to establish regulatory criteria by which to develop allocative and exclusionary processes within specific institutional sites, in relation to the Afro-Caribbean and Asian groups (Miles, 1989).

In earlier work (Mac an Ghaill, 1989b) I set out to reconceptualize black students' experience of schooling within a framework that moved beyond mono-causal explanations and examined the multifaceted dimensions of racially structured English schooling. The Afro-Caribbean and Asian young men in this study, all of whom are academically successful, recall schooling biographies that have significant convergences and differences. What emerges is how racialized social and discursive configurations with their own local histories are grounded in specific material cultures at classroom and playground levels. For the students, the white teachers' racial and gender/sexual typifications did not take a unitary form but rather were differentially structured and experienced, mediated by the specificity of different school cultures and individual and collective student responses. In particular, the racial and gender composition of each school was a significant variable in the construction of teacher typifications. So, for example, in working-class schools where there was a majority Asian student population with a mainly white minority, the dominant representations of Asian youths tended to be negative, with caricatures of them as 'sly' and 'not real men'. However, in working-class schools which included significant numbers of Afro-Caribbeans, the students felt that the Asians were caricatured in a more positive way in relation to the Afro-Caribbeans, who were perceived as of 'low ability', 'aggressive' and 'anti-authority'. In contrast, in middle-class grammar schools with predominantly white student populations, such attributes as 'hard-working' and 'ambitious' were assigned to Asian students (Rattansi, 1992).

A major limitation of much 'race-relations' theoretical and empirical work in education has been the failure to incorporate psychodynamic explanations (Henriques, 1984; Cohen, 1987; Nava, 1992). As students point out, their schooling cannot be reductively conceptualized in terms of a simple binary social system, composed of a juxtaposed white straight superiority and a black gay inferiority. The relations between white teachers and black students also involve a psychic structure, including such elements as: desire, attraction, repression, transference and projection in relation to a racialized 'sexual other'. (Pajaczknowska and Young, 1992) [...] In the following accounts the young men discuss the range of split responses from white males to themselves, that were manifested in terms of the interplay between racial and sexual fear and desire and the accompanying contradictory elements of repulsion, fascination and misrecognition (Klein, 1960; Rutherford, 1990).

Andrew: It's like with the straights, all the bits they don't like about themselves or they're afraid of, they push on to us.

Rajinder: Thinking about it, it's very complex. Straight men don't really have a problem with gays, they have a problem with themselves. Straight men seem to fear and love women but fear and hate gay men. Then whites, especially white men, have that fear and hatred for Asians and Afro-Caribbeans. So, black gay men are a real threat to white straight men. Like James Baldwin says, they act out their fears on us, on our bodies ... But then there's other complications. Like at our school, you could see some of the white teachers, the men, they really admired the Caribbeans and not just in sport and music, where it was really homoerotic, though of course they could never admit it to themselves. I think for a lot of teachers there, who felt trapped in their jobs, the macho black kids represented freedom from the system. There were anti-school macho whites and Asians but the teachers with their stereotypes fantasized about the Caribbean kids, who they saw as anti-authority, more physical and athletic, everything they couldn't be but greatly admired.

Stephen: Like you say black kids know that most white teachers would never live in our areas even though they make their living here. English middle-class people have always lived off immigrants; the blacks and the Irish around here. The teachers' kids go to their white grammar and private schools on the backs of the mis-education that their parents impose on us every day ... But at

night the teachers creep out of their white ghettoes to live it
up among the 'black folk'. Emotionally they're really screwed
up. And somehow although they don't want us as neighbours,
they are obsessed with our food, music, dance, with our sex.
You see they fantasize that these poor black folk they're not
repressed like the whiteys and in a different way their kids are
doing the same ... another generation of patronization from the
white boys and girls!

SUBORDINATED BLACK MASCULINITIES: SUBCULTURAL RESPONSES AND SELF REPRESENTATIONS

There is a danger in examining black gay students' schooling experiences of
unintentionally adopting a passive concept of subject positioning, with the
student portrayed as unproblematically accepting an over-determined racial
and gender/sexual role allocation (Walkerdine, 1990). In fact, as the students
here make clear, they are active curriculum and masculine makers. Male
ethnographic research on white and black working-class males has finely
illustrated how subordinated youth, drawing on resources from their own
communities and wider youth cultural forms, have actively constructed a
range of masculinities. This has taken place within the interrelated nexus
of teacher authoritarianism, their own survivalist peer-group cultures, the
negotiation of their sexual coming-of-age and the anticipation of their future
location in low-skilled local labour markets. In the 1990s for many black
and white working-class young people, their post-school anticipation is for
the status of a condition of dependency as surplus labour in late-industrial
capitalism (Cohen, 1987).

Cockburn (1987, p. 44) has pointed out that 'The social construction of
gender is riddled with resistance and the resistance is complex. While some
boys refuse the macho mode of masculinity and pay the price of being
scorned a "wimp" or a "poofter", others resist the class domination by
means of masculine codes'. For black male students this resistance is also
developed in relation to racially administered schooling systems. Here, the
students reflected on the specific dynamics and interplay between state
schooling and the construction of black ethnic masculinities. They were
aware of how class-based differentiated curricula helped to shape differentiated
masculinities, with sectors of black and white working-class students developing compensatory hyper-masculine forms in response to their experience
of academic failure. They were also aware of how black students defensively
responded to racialized and gendered discourses that constructed juxtaposed
images of 'weak' Asian and 'tough' Afro-Caribbean males. They acknowledged the colonial legacy and present day validity of Mercer and Julien's
argument that:

Whereas prevailing definitions of masculinity imply power, control and authority, these attributes have been historically denied to black men since slavery. The centrally dominant role of the white male slave-master in eighteenth and nineteenth-century plantation society debarred black males from the patriarchal privileges ascribed to the male masculine role. .... Shaped by this history, black masculinity is a highly contradictory formation as it is a subordinated masculinity. (Mercer and Julien, 1988, p. 112).

What emerges are the specific dynamics for young black men of their psychosexual development within state school systems and a wider culture that systematically devalues and marginalizes black masculinities, while elevating and celebrating dominant forms of white straight masculinity. In the following extracts the students make clear the contextual contingency in which racial and sexual representations and typifications operate within specific sites.

Amerjit: Teachers can't see the way that schools make kids act bad. For a lot of blacks, it's the low classes, the non-academic subjects and being pushed into sport that makes them act macho. It's the way that black and white boys having been failed on the school's terms, try to get some status, some self respect. .... At school you only hear of all the great whites. Most teachers don't respect black men, so the kids think they have no choice but to act it out.

Assim: At our school when we started the whites and the Caribbeans were seen as the toughest. But by the fifth year, the Asian gangs were the worst. They were like the Warrior gang in *Young, Gifted and Black.* They formed gangs, smoked, wore the right gear, trainers and tracksuits, watched violent videos and hung around with older kids with fast cars and the music. Things that a lot of white working class pupils do, acting hard all the time. But for the Asians, there is also racism. Outside of school, outside our own area, we are always under suspicion and likely to be attacked from the NF and respectable whites. We know that we get attacked because whites see us as easy targets, as weak. They also knew that the teachers were afraid of the Caribbeans because they saw them as tough. Like at school the teachers would avoid walking through groups of black kids but not Asians.

Stephen: In the last place (secondary school) the blacks were seen as the hardest and most against the teachers. There were only a few of them involved in the main anti-school gang but they were the leaders of the posse, as they called themselves. I think a lot of the teachers stereotyped all blacks as aggressive. And I think some of the kids came to believe this about themselves or thought the teachers believed it, so they may as well act it out as they were going to be picked on anyway.

[...] The black gay students examined the links between the institutional and male peer-group surveillance, regulation and control of female and male gender and sexual reputations. They were surprised at the way in which male teachers and students conflated assumed gay behaviour with femininity in order to traduce the former. The assimilation of masculine non-macho behaviour to feminine behaviour was most evident in relation to the ubiquity of the term 'poof', which in 'denoting lack of guts, suggests femininity-weakness, softness and inferiority' (Lees, 1987, p. 180). (See Cockburn, 1987, p. 41, on the development of the term 'lezzie'.) Furthermore, they linked this form of 'gay-bashing' to that of the use of the term 'Paki' as a form of 'Paki-bashing'. Both these labels, 'poof' and 'Paki' have several meanings, sometimes they are used with a specific sexual or racial connotation; while at other times they are used as general terms of abuse. The notoriety and frequency of these labels acted as major mechanisms of policing gender and sexual boundaries with specific implications for Afro-Caribbean and Asian straight and gay youth.

Rajinder: Nearly all the tough kids, the really hard lads were in the bottom two bands, especially the bottom one. They got their status by fighting the system that they saw abusing them. Some of the toughest ones were the white kids from the estate, always in trouble with the police and teachers. They were obsessed with proving they were real men, like those kids you talked about with their fighting, football and fucking—that was really them ... They hated 'poofs' and 'Pakis' and used to argue with the teachers when they tried to stop fights, say things like, 'Sir, he's only a 'Paki' or a 'poof'. They felt that the teachers agreed with them and in some ways they were right. A lot of the men teachers were really into violence but it was official, so that was okay to them. Anything seen as soft in their terms was despised. Like there was all this sexist talk by teachers. They thought that the best way to control a boy was to say to him, 'Stop acting like a girl'. And they always said it loud so all their friends could hear. You see then outside the class the lads could carry on the sexual bullying that the teachers had set up.

Westwood (1990, p. 59) points out: 'Discourses as registers of masculinity are worked through a variety of spaces.' For the working-class students, territorial imperatives underpinned their inner-city school playgrounds. They constituted a military-like arena in which dominant forms of straight masculinity, physically and symbolically occupied key spatial sites: including the central location of constructed football pitches, smoking areas and school entrances and exits. Within these 'safe' sites, male straight students ascribed the highest status to the toughest gang, projecting a version of working-class masculinity that over-emphasized such traits as physcial toughness, independence and aggression (Tolson, 1977). Fighting was a key signifier, related to a class-specific and gendered use of the body as against the mind (Walkerdine, 1990, p. 178). Joyce Canaan in a paper that examines the construction of white working-class masculinity as highly contradictory and multifaceted, notes that:

> Working-class violence is not something that singularly expresses working-class identity or masculine identity; it is a particular combination of these two, and other factors. In addition, this analysis suggests that male violence is constructed as much through gender as class, it is central to masculinity in general and takes particular forms among distinct groups of working-class young men, which reveals much about their class and gender as well as their sexual orientation and age. (Canaan, 1991, p. 123.)

For the students there was an ethos of physical and symbolic intimidation that pervaded playground life that they were coerced into 'learning to live with'. Most immediately the specific student social hierarchies within this arena were translated into covert and overt dominant forms of straight male violence and abuse (Macdonald *et al.*, 1989).

Stephen: Playgrounds are really cruel places if you're seen as different or weak. In our school the macho gangs treated girls very bad. And they persecuted me and a few friends, calling us poofs and queer and all that because we weren't like them, didn't act hard like them. We survived because we were big and did not show that we were afraid of them.

Vijay: The tough kids were the best at football, could threaten anyone, had the best reputation with a lot of girls, wore the best gear. They bullied younger kids and girls, and any boys who they thought were soft. White kids joined the gang and together the black and white kids abused Asian kids. They were always talking about 'Pakis' and 'batty men' (a derisory homophobic comment).

Assim: Looking back there wasn't probably that many fights but the physical pressure was there all the time. It was all to do with the way you looked. The clothes, hair and most important the way you stood, walked about, how you talked, just little things that signalled whether you were hard or not.

In contrast, to the working-class forms of physical violence, former grammar school students recalled the centrality of verbal violence in serving to police gender and sexual boundaries. The highest peer-group esteem was assigned to those who combined a display of linguistic competence and 'put down' humour. One of the students, Denton Purcell, confided in his best friend that he was confused about his sexuality.

Denton: The next day when some of our mates were around, my friend said, 'Your mom must be proud of you, that means she has two washing powders, Persil (Purcell) and Omo (homosexual)'. They all started laughing. They all got the message, as they already thought I was effeminate. It was one of the worst things that ever happened to me. I felt so violated. Thinking about it since we started talking, I can see it was my friend's way of distancing himself from me, not just for the crowd but also for himself. We were very close, not in a sexual way, more emotionally. Like most straight men, he just couldn't cope.

VISIBILITY OF 'RACE'-INVISIBILITY OF HOMOSEXUALITY OR THE NORMALIZATION OF WHITE HETEROSEXUALITY

One of the major issues that emerged in the research was the question of the visibility of 'race' and the invisibility of 'homosexuality' within the context of the school. In order to more fully understand the absence of lesbians and gays from the curriculum, we need to examine the more general question of the official response to the place of sexuality within schools. Beverley Skeggs (1991, p. 1) has critiqued the way in which 'the discourse on sexuality is either ignored or subsumed within a more general discourse on gender'. Similarly, Wolpe (1988, p. 100) argues that: 'The ideology on sex and sex education, and its relation to the moral order, structure the official way in which sex and sexuality are handled within a school. In spite of these discourses and the tendency for teachers to accept these seemingly unquestioningly, sexual issues are ever present but not necessarily recognized as such by teachers.'

The visibility of the students' secondary schools' racial structuring included: predominantly white staff with majority black student populations, racially stratified curriculum and testing systems, the over-representation of specific ethnic groups in low status subject areas and racial divisions in classrooms and among student peer-groups. More positively at their different schools multi-cultural/anti-racist policies were in operation. Although these official local state interventions, often unwittingly, tended to reproduce reified conceptions of black ethnic cultures, and the accompanying reinforcement of images of 'them' and 'us', they also provided space to contest dominant racial representations. The students pointed out that 'skin colour' is often read as a key signifier of social exclusion. However, as for their parents, it also has positive, productive elements for young blacks positioned within specific racist discourses, thus enabling them collectively to develop positive social identities. [. . .]

The students recalled the invisibility of femininities and subordinated masculinites that the dominant examples of white teachers and student masculinities serves constantly to devalue, marginalize and threaten. Homophobia, compulsory heterosexuality, racism and misogyny circumscribed the boundaries of what constituted 'normal' male and female behaviour. The invisibility of homosexuality at their secondary schools was structured by a 'policy of omission'—it was as if lesbians and gays did not exist. Much important work on the racial and gender structuring of the curriculum has emphasized how discriminatory practices operate against subordinated groups. Here, the students point out that of equal significance is what is excluded in shaping differential curriculum experiences and outcomes.

Raj: It's like you are black, right, and you can accept the white view of blacks or you can reject it and challenge it. But to say I am a black gay, what does it mean? At school they never suggested that there was a history of gay people or any books on gays. They never presented any evidence of black gay people. So, you could think I must be the only one. At school you are totally on your own. It's really bad, you know what I mean? . . . The only times teachers talked about gays was when they talked about AIDS a few times.

As part of the research, I interviewed the students' former and present teachers. Here, I am focusing on white male teachers. Within the context of a broader concern with the question of how schools produce a range of masculinities and femininities, I asked the teachers how they would respond to gay students 'coming out' to them (Mac an Ghaill, 1992). The following interview with a teacher in a senior pastoral care post was illustrative of their responses to the question of black students' sexual identities. Holding on to notions of a unitary self, the teachers were highly defensive in being unable to rationalize the contradictions of their own positions (Henriques, 1984).

Teacher: I don't think a teacher is going to think an Asian or black kid is a homosexual, they just wouldn't. They've got enough problems dealing with being black. Like you wouldn't think of a handicapped person as a homosexual, would you? No, you just wouldn't, would you?

MM: You said earlier that you would advise a student, if he told you he was gay, that he was going through a phase.

Teacher: Yes, definitely. It's part of growing up. Often, these kids would be loners, one-parent families without a father figure, you know?

MM: Is this phase true for all boys?

Teacher: I know, you are going to ask, did I go through it? It depends on what you mean. But, no. I was close to friends, male friends as you are at that age. But I was brought up in a normal family and

all that and I've always known where I stood with the ladies.
MM: But what about most boys?
Teacher: Well, the experts reckon so, don't they?
MM: But wouldn't that include Asian and black boys?
Teacher: You've tricked me. I must say I've never thought of the black kids here like that. Well like a lot of theories they over-generalize. If you saw the big black kids here, you'd see what I mean. We have to pull them away from the girls. The black kids are obsessed with them but to be fair to the lads, the girls do lead them on, hanging around all the time. I could say with certainty, there's no way they've got any homosexual ideas.

The intersection of these homophobic and racist discourses produced contradictions and confusions. On the one hand, in interviews with me, in relation to issues of gay sexuality, the teachers appealed to black parents' religious beliefs as legitimate justification for not taking a positive pedagogical stance towards gay students. On the other hand, as the students stressed, white teachers tended to caricature Asian and Afro-Caribbean male students and their parents as intrinsically more sexist than whites. In class discussions the teachers were pre-occupied with explaining the difficulty of implementing an anti-sexist curriculum which they claimed conflicted with traditional ethnic cultures. Rajinder informed a teacher that he was gay and was most surprised that the teacher responded primarily in racial terms, projecting his own difficulties with the issue of sexuality on to the Asian community.

Rajinder: At school there's no such thing as sexuality, so it seems. Then one day you come out and say you're gay and then you find out that it's the most important thing in the world. The teachers try eveything to change you: It's a phase, you need psychiatric help, it's unnatural, it's against your religion, your parents won't accept you, your friends will reject you, you won't get a job. I've heard it all. I think that teachers feel more threatened by gays than any other group.

WHAT IS HETEROSEXUALITY? OR ARE STRAIGHTS 'BORN' OR 'MADE'?

Lesley Hall (1991, p. 2) in her study of the hidden history of straight men's sexual fears and failures provides much evidence to reveal the 'considerable tensions between the ideals set up and the lived experience of men as they perceived it, and that the "normal" male and male sexuality were more problematic than they are usually assumed to be'. The gay students felt that these tensions took on specific cultural forms for young straight men within the context of secondary schooling that involved the performance of publicly exaggerated modes of masculinity.

Amerjit: If you tell your friends you're gay, they ask you, what's it like? It's
            as if they think that it's totally different from their own sexuality.
            But you know that although they are straight, at least publicly,
            they have a lot of doubts and difficulties about how they feel,
            about relationships, girls, sex. . . . Girls are a lot more honest.
            If you're a man you can't show these doubts—not in public.
            But if you listen, you hear it all; that straights are scared of
            women, unsure about themselves and tired of acting things out.
            It's incredible, you as the gay person are supposed to be the one
            with all the difficulties and they just turn it round. It's probably
            what women have to listen to all the time. And these straights are
            too arrogant to see that they may be afraid of us but they are a
            major cause of gay's and women's problems.

In an earlier paper (Mac an Ghaill, 1991, p. 297) in which some of these
students were involved, I wrote of how the gay students described the
construction of ambiguous and transitional identities in their sexual coming-
of-age. They spoke of:

> . . . the formation of their sexual identity as part of a wider process
> of adolescent development, with all its fluidity, experiments, displace-
> ments and confusions. For them sexuality could not be reduced to the
> conventional perception of a heterosexual—homosexual continuum, on
> which each group's erotic and emotional attachments are demarcated
> clearly and unambiguously. They spoke of the contradictions of the
> public—private worlds that gave them an insight into the complexity
> and confusion of young males' sexual coming-of-age. They have become
> experts at decoding the ambivalent social and sexual meanings of hetero-
> sexual behaviour involved in male bonding and rites of passage.

The black gay students develop their arguments concerning the contextual
contingency and ambiguity of learning to become a man within an overall
rampant school culture of compulsory heterosexuality (Cockburn, 1987, p. 44).
One of the main issues that emerged during the research was the question
of the political and cultural meanings of modern forms of heterosexuality.
For the students, most of whom held a social constructivist perspective,
ambivalent mysogyny, contingent homophobia and racism were contradictory constitutive elements of white male forms of heterosexuality. They
recalled white boys, in learning to be straight men, obsessively distancing
themselves from ascriptions of femininity and homosexuality within themselves and towards others. Hence gender/sexual identities were perceived
as highly unstable categories that their schools, alongside other institutions, attempted to administer, regulate and reify. Most particularly, this
administration, regulation and reification of gender/sexual boundaries was
institutionalized through the interrelated social and discursive practices of

staffroom, classroom and playground cultures. Much work remains to be done on the intersection of the specific social and psycho-dynamics of these processes at the local school level.

PLUSES OF BEING BLACK GAYS

There is much evidence from lesbian and gay literature of the physical, psychological and verbal abuse that lesbian and gay people systematically experience in homophobic and heterosexist societies (Burbage and Walters, 1981). The young men in this paper report similar personal and institutional experiences of such abuse. However, it is important for educationalists in trying to understand the social positioning of these young people, not to adopt a reductionist pedagogical approach that sees gays and lesbians as mere problems or victims. In a *Guardian* article (Simpson, 1992, p. 19) on the experience of young gays in England, two young lesbians suggest a guarded optimism about the future. They claim that '"things are changing", Emily says "But in a confusing way", Rebecca says. Attitudes are becoming more tolerant, but prejudice is responding by becoming more hidden and violent. But if we fight for our rights I believe that we can beat prejudice for good.' The students provided much evidence in the study to support Peter Aggleton's (1987, p. 108) claim that being gay is in many circumstances a positive and creative experience.

Rajinder: Teachers, especially male teachers assume your being gay is a problem but there are a lot of pluses. In fact, I think one of the main reasons that male straights hate us is because they really know that emotionally we are more worked out than them. We can talk about and express our feelings, our emotions in a positive way. They can only express negative feelings like hatred, anger and dominance. Who would like to be like them?

Raj: It's like when you gave that talk at the university about having several identities. I don't think that most people could understand because really everything about them is taken for granted. Their Englishness, their whiteness, their culture, their gender and sexuality—it's just the norm for them. And that's what's really good about being a black gay, you have no choice, you have to question these things. I think what I've learned most in us being together for the last two years, is that the questions can be on our terms not theirs.

Denton: I agree. That's why people like James Baldwin and Langston Hughes are so important for us. Yes, the world is going to hate us but people like them got through and in lots of ways it was worse, much worse for them. And you feel very proud that they are part of our history. . . . They've made me more aware of other outsiders who are oppressed in this society. I used to feel really bad

about being gay and I still get really down at times. But through
being black and gay even if I don't stay gay, I know myself more
than white men, than straights do.

Without reducing black gay masculinity to a unitary category, the students'
analysis finds a resonance in Isaac Julien's (in Bourne, 1991, p. 27) comment that:

Where I see myself different from a number of white activists is that I
think that they are more interested in sex and sexuality as an emphasis.
When I was involved very early on in the Black Lesbian and Gay Group,
we were interested in issues of policing and gender. These kinds of debates
were related to debates around black masculinity and I think that generally this is a debate that takes a far more fundamentally important
position in black politics than it takes in gay politics. I don't know how
a gay political discourse takes on these questions of black masculinity. I
think that black communities are written off as homophobic.

Stephen: I think that gays and lesbians have been really good at working
           through the differences between sex and gender to produce pro-
           gressive politics. And the whole HIV experience and the response
           of the media has put gays, white and black, on the frontline. Now
           there's lots of differences among black gays but maybe we have
           taken a broader agenda; such as issues around gender and the
           treatment of the black community.

Andrew: Reading through this study it shows, yes we are pushed to the
           margins of society as black gays. But that doesn't mean we have to
           accept that position. We can educate ourselves to understand the
           different oppressions. And you can see here that our position can
           be positive in helping us to work out ways forward not just for
           gays and blacks but for others as well because we are questioning
           whiteness and heterosexuality that is usually very hidden.

CONCLUSION

[. . .] At present, young people, collectively and individually are constructing
their identities, at a time of rapid socio-economic and political change, that has
led to a major disruption in the process of coming-of-age in the 'enterprise
culture'. For example, Willis, (1985, p. 6) speaks of how the unemployed now
find themselves in a 'new social condition of suspended animation between
school and work. Many of the old transitions into work, into the cultures
and organizations of work, into being consumers, into independent accommodation—have been frozen or broken . . .'. As the students above demonstrate,
their preparation for these transitions are further structured by an articulation
of complex forms of social differences. Within this new social condition the
young gay students here can be seen as an example of the new generation of
black intellectuals, of whom Mercer (1992, p. 110) writes:

In the hands of this new generation of black diaspora intellectuals rethinking sex ... [they] simultaneously critique the exclusions and absences which previously rendered black lesbian and gay identities invisible, and reconstruct new pluralistic forms of collective belonging and imagined community that broaden the public sphere of multicultural society.

Acknowledgements

A special thanks to the students, who collaborated in the production of the study, and especially to Rajinder. My thanks to the parents and teachers who have taken part. This article has benifited from the comments of Debbie Epstein and Richard Johnson.

Notes

1. In order to maintain the anonymity of those involved, all the names of the students and teachers are pseudonyms.

References

Aggleton, P. (1987) *Deviance*. London: Tavistock.
Bhavnani, K.K. (1991) *Talking Politics: A Psychological Framing for Views from Youth in Britain*. Cambridge: Cambridge University Press.
Bourne, S. (1991) Putting the record straight. *Gay Times*. 155, August.
Bryan, B., Dadzie, S. and Scafe, S. (1985) *The Heart of the Race: Black Women's Lives in Britain*. London: Virago.
Burbage, M. and Walters, J. (1981) (eds) *Breaking the Silence: Gay Teenagers Speak for Themselves*. London: Joint Council for Gay Teenagers.
Canaan, J. (1991) Is 'Doing Nothing' just boys' play?: integrating feminist and cultural studies perspectives on working-class young men's masculinity. In S. Franklin, C. Lury and J. Stacey (eds) *Off-Centre: Feminism and Cultural Studies*. London: HarperCollins.
Carrigan, T., Connell, R.W. and Lee, J. (1985) Hard and heavy phenomena: the sociology of masculinity. *Theory* 14, 551–604.
Cockburn, C. (1987) *Two-Track Training: Sex Inequality and the YTS*. London: Macmillan.
Cohen, P. (1987) Racism and popular culture: a cultural studies approach. Working paper No 9, London, Institute of Education.
Connell, R.W. (1989) Cool guys, swots and wimps: the inter-play of masculinity and education. *Oxford Review of Education* 15, 3, 291–303.
Freire, P. (1985) *The Politics of Education*. London: Macmillan.
Griffin, C. (1987) The eternal adolescent: psychology and the creation of adolescence. Paper presented at the Symposium of the Ideological Impact of Social Psychology, British Psychological Association Conference, Oxford University.
Hall, L. (1991) *Hidden Anxieties: Male Sexuality. 1990–1950*. London: Polity Press.
Henriques, J. (1984) Social Psychology and the politics of racism. In J. Henriques, W. Hollway, C. Urwin, C. Venn and V. Walkerdine (eds) *Changing the Subject: Psychology, Social Regulation and Subjectivity*. London: Methuen.
hooks, b. (1991) *Yearning: Race, Gender and Cultural Politics*. Massachusetts: Turnaround.
Klein,M. (1960) *Our Adult World and its Roots in Infancy*. London: Tavistock.
Lees, S. (1987) The structure of sexual relations in school. In M. Arnot and G. Weiner (eds) *Gender and Politics of Schooling*. Milton Keynes: Open University Press.

Mac an Ghaill, M. (1988) *Young, Gifted and Black: Student—Teacher Relations in the Schooling of Black Youth.* Milton Keynes: Open University Press.
— (1989a) Beyond the white norm: the use of qualitative research in the study of black students' schooling in England. *Qualitative Studies in Education* 2, 3, 175—89.
— (1989b) Coming-of-age in 1980s England: reconceptualizing black students' schooling experience. *British Journal of Sociology of Education* 10, 3, 273—86.
— (1991) Schooling, sexuality and male power; towards an emancipatory curriculum. *Gender and Education* 3, 3, 291—309.
— (1992) *Acting Like Men: Masculinities, Sexualities and Schooling.* Milton Keynes: Open University Press.
— (1994a) The making of Black English masculinities. In H. Brad and M. Kaufman *Theorizing Masculinities.* London: Sage.
Macdonald I., Bhavnani, R., Khan, L. and John, G. (1989) *Murder in the Playground.* London: Longsight Press.
Mama, A. (1992) Black women and the British state: race, class and gender analysis for the 1990s. In P. Braham, A. Rattansi and R. Skellington (eds) *Racism and Antisexism: Inequalities, Opportunities and Policies.* London: Sage/Open University Press.
Mercer, K. (1992) Just looking for trouble: Robert Mapplethorpe and fantasies. In L. Segal and M. McIntosh (eds) *Sex Exposed: Sexuality and the Pornography Debate.* (pp. 92—110). London: Virago.
Mercer, K. and Julien, I. (1988) Race, sexual politics and black masculinity: a dossier. In R. Chapman and J. Ruthford (eds) *Male Order: Unwrapping Masculinities.* London: Lawrence & Wishart.
Miles, R. (1989) *Racism.* London: Routledge.
Nava, M. (1992) *Changing Cultures: Feminism, Youth and Consumerism.* London: Sage.
Paiaczkowska, C. and Young, L. (1992) Racism, representation and psychoanalysis. In J. Donald and A. Rattansi (eds) *'Race', Culture and difference* (pp. 198—219). Milton Keynes: Open University Press/Sage.
Rattansi, A. (1992) Changing the subject? racism, culture and education. In J. Donald and A. Rattansi (eds) *'Race', Culture and Difference.* (pp. 11—48). Milton Keynes: Open University Press/Sage.
Rowbotham, S. (1989) *The Past is Before Us: Feminism in Action Since the 1960s.* Harmondsworth: Penguin.
Rutherford, J. (1990) A place called home: identity and the cultural politics of difference. In J. Rutherford (ed). *Identity: Community, Culture and Difference.* London: Lawrence & Wishart.
Simpson, M. (1992) Out of the closet, into the fire. *Guardian.* 19 August, p. 19.
Skeggs, B. (1991) The cultural production of 'Learning to Labour'. In M. Barker and A. Breezer (eds) *Readings in Culture.* London: Routledge.
Tolson, A. (1977) *The Limits of Masculinity.* London: Tavistock.
Walkerdine, V. (1990) *Schoolgirl Fictions.* London: Verso.
Westwood, S. (1990) Racism, black masculinity and the politics of space. In J. Hearn and D. Morgan (eds) *Men, Masculinities and Social Theory.* London: Hyman.
Willis, P. (1985) Youth unemployment and the new poverty: a summary of local authority review and framework for policy development on youth and youth unemployment. Wolverhampton: Wolverhampton Local Authority.
Wolpe, A.M. (1988) *Within School Walls: The Role of Discipline, Sexuality and the Curriculum.* London: Routledge.

19 PLEASURE, PRESSURE AND POWER: SOME CONTRADICTIONS OF GENDERED SEXUALITY

JANET HOLLAND, CAROLINE RAMAZONOGLU, SUE SHARPE AND RACHEL THOMSON

Problems of how to explain the nature and legitimation of men's power over women lie at the heart of the feminist sociology. While much has been done to identify the mechanisms through which such power is exercised, relatively little is known about the sexual politics of sex at the level of heterosexual practices. Feminist work on sexuality has tended to explore the sexual politics of heterosexuality and lesbianism (Campbell, 1980; Rich, 1983; Conveney et al., 1984; Kitzinger, 1987) which has left the problem of how heterosexual women can experience safer and more positive sexual relations with men less than clear (Hite, 1976; Thompson, 1984; 1990). The tragedy of the AIDS epidemic has now given urgency to questions about the ways in which sexual encounters are constituted as gendered social relationships: how female and male sexual identities are maintained, and what an empowered femininity could mean in bodily encounters. [...]

We have argued elsewhere (Holland et al., 1991a) that women who want to ensure their own sexual safety may have to be socially assertive and so, to some extent at least, unfeminine. Those who wish to control their own sexuality have to be prepared to lose the valued social relationship with a partner or potential partner. [...]

If young women do try to assert their own needs and exert their own agency, they still have to negotiate sexual relationships with men in situations in which there is no convention of positive female sexuality. In this article, we consider two aspects of sexual politics: the pressure to which even assertive young women are exposed in the negotiation of heterosexual encounters, and the ways in which we can begin to think about the empowerment of women in heterosexual relationships.

These related themes of pressure and pleasure are developed through analysis from data from the *Women, Risk and AIDS Project*'s interviews with 150 young women in London and Manchester.[1] From these young women's accounts of their negotiation of sexual relationships, we consider

Source: Abridged from *The Sociological Review* (1992) 40, 4, 645–74.

the pressures on them to define their sexual relationships in terms of men's sexual needs, and how far they can be seen as empowered to define sex as pleasurable for themselves. We argue that a young woman can only assert sexual needs in terms of her own bodily pleasure if she can negotiate sexual boundaries with her partner. She may have to stand up to, if not go against, the boundaries of femininity in sexual relationships, since a positive femininity is a challenge to dominant masculinities. [. . .]

While their willingness and ability to control the ways in which they negotiate sexual boundaries are subject to a variety of pressures, the main pressures on young women come from the men they are with and the meaning and importance they attribute to men's sexual needs and behaviour. The pressures they encounter from men can vary from mild insistence on giving way to intercourse, or to intercourse on his terms, to physical assault and rape. Young women in their interviews gave accounts of situations in which various forms of violence and pressure had played a part and in which they have had to make sense of contradictory pressures in the definition and practice of their own sexuality.

PRESSURE FROM MEN IN SEXUAL ENCOUNTERS

We have classified the pressures that young women experience in sexual encounters in terms of the personal, the social, and pressures coming directly from men. Personal pressures are incorporated into the individual's conception of self and way of organizing and understanding her own sexuality. Social pressures emanate from the variety of cultural and institutional contexts in which the person is located; family, peer group, school, workplace, religion, mass media, culture, sub-culture. It is the different messages from these sources that oblige young women to live with, and make sense of, contradictions in the social construction of feminine sexuality. These pressures, however, are not all treated as equally important. Running through the various sources are pressures which are experienced in terms of expectations of and pressures from men, and it is these that we have concentrated on here.

Feminist studies of male violence have been one of the most successful areas of feminist knowledge, in that women's supposedly private failures as victims, have been reconstructed as the widespread abuse of patriarchal power by men (Wilson, 1983; Hanmer and Saunders, 1984; Hanmer and Maynard, 1987; Rhodes and McNeill, 1985; Stanko, 1985; Kelly, 1988). This is the main area in which arguments for the generality of women's subordination by men can be supported.[2]

While some physical expressions of violence are very obvious, other social pressures for controlling women's sexuality are harder to identify, as the ways in which gender ideologies are embedded in social and economic processes can be very complex (Stanley and Wise, 1983). The sexual pressures which women experience are, in part, enmeshed in loving and caring relationships, and the ideology of male control of sexuality is part of the social constitution of masculinity and femininity. Feminism's contribution here has been to show that violence can be conceived as a range of mechanisms linked to the exercise of power. It is this exercise of power which constitutes a set of interrelated constraints on the empowerment of young women.

Identifying men's treatment of women as part of the exercise of patriarchal power has meant broadening the concept of violence from that of murder, rape and physical assault to include less obvious modes of control and pressure such as flashing and sexual harassment (G. Edwards, 1987). [...]

[...] Definitions of violence are controversial and contested, with feminists seeking to extend definitions against resistance. [...] We do not intend to imply that men's sexual behaviour is always violent nor that women are never violent. If women can exercise power over others, there is always a possibility of abuse (Bhavnani, 1988; Bower, 1986; Cock, 1989; Kelly, 1991). But while individual men need not be violent, male and female sexualities have been socially constituted in Western cultures in ways which make the differences between 'normal heterosexual sex' and 'rape' unclear (Stanko, 1985). What women experience as sexual violence or pressure is not, therefore, simple to categorize, particularly when they blame themselves for the experience.

[...] As violence and sexuality are very closely linked in the social construction of Western sexualities, it was to be expected that young women's accounts of their negotiations of the boundaries of sexual practices, would include accounts of sexual pressures exercised by men. These varied from accounts of reluctant consent to sexual intercourse which they did not want, to an account of a prolonged and violent experience of gang rape.

CONCEPTUALIZING THE EMPOWERMENT OF YOUNG WOMEN

Feminists have conceived the notion of women's empowerment in different ways. These have enabled us to think of women as resisting the pressures of patriarchal societies; as having collective power which gives them agency rather than being the individual victims of patriarchy. The problem with thinking about empowerment in sexual encounters is that these encounters are defined as private. Empowered young women in heterosexual relationships will generally be alone or about to be alone with a man, and will have to exercise their power in a socially constituted dyad in which they are culturally defined as 'other' in relation to the dominant male.

While we can talk of how to empower young women so as to make sex safer or more pleasurable; it is difficult to specify what exactly is meant by empowerment in sexual relations when women are generally subordinate to men. 'It is a good deal harder to de-couple the drives of desire—for sexual pleasure and for power—than appears on the surface' (Janeway, 1977, p. 294). There is no language or model of positive female sexuality for young women (Wilton and Aggleton, 1991). Feminine sexualities as socially constituted in Western cultures are generally disempowering in that they are constructed in subordination to dominant masculine sexualities. [...] Any exercise of women's power in sexual relations is not only unfeminine, but also threatening to men [...]

Feminists have often, as Lepenies has said of the social sciences, 'failed to infuse their enthusiasms with an appropriate spirit of cognitive modesty'.[3] The concept of empowerment which has been invested with tremendous generality needs to be operationalized and made more modestly useful in specific situations. The term is not entirely clear because of the lack of alternative conceptions of power to those of malestream thought. Joan Acker (1989) has pointed out that attempts to make gender visible are constrained by the success of existing sociological paradigms. When we think of empowerment, we have difficulty in extricating our concepts from existing theories of power, even when these theories conceive gender as a form of natural difference.

Envisaging empowerment for young women means defining the power relations which could be changed and defining strategies for tranforming relationships. In the context of sexual encounters, empowering women need not mean women exercising power over men, or behaving like men. We have conceptualized this as 'male model empowerment' and have categorized it as a form of disempowerment for women (Holland *et al.*, 1991b). Whereas the exercise of male power means the subordination and control of women by men, we do not take women's empowerment as the subordination of men. Rather empowerment is both contested, and a process, in which women struggle to negotiate *with* men increasing control over their own sexuality. Effective empowerment could mean: not engaging in sexual activity; not engaging in sexual activity without informed consent; getting men to consent to safer practices; negotiating sexual practices which are pleasurable to women as well as to men.

METHOD OF ANALYSIS

Our method is intended to clarify the constellation of contradictory pressures on women both to become sexually active and not to engage in sexual activity or unsafe sex. In order to identify how processes of negotiation operate in practice, we have used the technique of systemic networks (see Appendix) to clarify the pressures on young women to have sexual intercourse.

The conceptual categories constituting the network can be derived exclusively from theoretical concepts, but in this case we drew on three levels of conceptualization: the terms and meanings used by the young women and explicit in the data; the interviewer's fieldnotes made after the interview, which entail some interpretation of meaning in the interview; team members' discussion, interpretation and coding of these data in the light of feminist and sociological theory.[4] The interaction of these levels of interpretation is built into the categories of the network (see Appendix).

The network gives us a theoretical map of the pressures which can affect young women's sexuality, as interconnected processes. The young women's accounts have been analyzed using the categories of the network.

We have picked out for the purposes of this paper a sub-set of 26% of our sample made up of 39 young women whose accounts indicate experiences in which men had clearly exerted pressure on them to have sexual intercourse.

Numbers have to be viewed with caution as they represent our interpretations of young women's accounts of their experiences. Of the 39 women who gave accounts on pressured sex, 13 reported experiences which we have taken to be rape and 10 said they had had experiences which we have taken to be child sexual abuse. Ten of these 39 young women had experienced more than one form of pressure on different occasions. Women were not pressed to give accounts of violent behaviour where these were distressing to them. [. . .]

We have not attempted to classify young women into static categories of victimised behaviour. We have used the network to identify the pressures on young women as contradictory and contested processes. To illustrate this point we have made some preliminary connections between these violent experiences and empowerment. Here we have looked generally at the problem of operationalizing the process of empowerment and, more specifically, at the young women's sexual pleasure.[5]

YOUNG WOMEN'S RESPONSES TO MALE SEXUAL PRESSURE

The dominance of male sexuality, men's needs and women's compliance, constitutes the social context within which women in London and Manchester negotiate their sexual experience. The possiblity of empowerment for these young women then entails critical consideration of how they can respond to the pressures on them to treat sexual encounters as primarily for fulfilling men's sexual needs. The lack of a positive model of female sexuality means that women have to do a good deal of critical reflecting on their experience in order to gain control of their responses to men.

Women's control over sexual safety is affected by a variety of pressures which they experience as part of their sexual relationships. The explanation of these forms of pressure is not straightforward since women can be pressured by those who love them, and in situations which they could avoid, or in which they could offer social, emotional or physical resistance. Women's lack of resistance requires explanation, as do those cases where women do resist (Bart and O'Brien, 1985; Kelly, 1988). This creates problems for any researcher in interpreting accounts of pressure and violence where the researcher's interpretation differs from that of the young woman's.

Susan Estrich (1987) shows that many men in the US believe that they can force a woman to have sex against her will, but that if the woman knows them and if the man does not use 'violence', then the action does not constitute rape.[6] [...]

The problem that arises from our data is that women in such situations may put themselves under personal pressure in that they share men's perceptions. They may not regard themselves as being raped if the man concerned was known to them, if they were drunk at the time, or if they failed to avoid the situation or to offer effective resistance. Their perceptions then differ from those of researchers who are influenced by feminist perceptions of rape as male violence. [...]

The range of pressures that women are subject to are hard to disentangle in practice, and where women have experienced the more violent and coercive forms of sexual pressure, such as child abuse, rape, assault or threats, these experiences can shape their expectations of men's behaviour in subsequent sexual encounters. In the section which follows we have selected some categories from the network to indicate the complexity of the issue, and the extent to which both male pressure and women's empowerment need to be understood as contested processes rather than as stable categories of young women's experience.

Verbal sexual pressure: persuasion

In some cases women had effectively consented to sex, or to unsafe sex, which they did not want, because of what they felt to be social pressures, or the importance to them of their relationship or potential relationship with a man. Men did not need to take any decisive action in these cases to exert pressure for women to feel that they should submit.

A: I was really like used to blokes treating me really bad. Like I don't think I'd ever really had a bloke as a friend. Like they were all sort of sexually orientated, and not much between us in the way of friendship.

Those young women who stated that they had had sex against their will, often had difficulty in expressing what they meant by this.

A: ... It wasn't sort of physical, I mean, but in a way it was sort of like mental ...
        ... the reason that I think that on these occasions that it's ever happened, is because I haven't been confident enough, you know to sort of stop it. And that's why it's against my will, because in my normal frame of mind, you know ...

One young woman reflecting on her first sexual experience when she was 14 was ambivalent about pressure. The man concerned was 17, and uncertain of his own sexual identity.

Q: And were you pressured into it?
A: Looking back on it now, I would say, yeah, I was a bit. Yeah a little bit. But I don't actually remember having any memory of saying to myself 'this is what I want to do'. I just remember doing it and thinking 'it's not much of a big deal'. .... It just happened. I just accepted it.

This ambiguity is also evident in a comment on an incident of sexual intercourse when the young woman concerned was 16.

A: Well I was young at the time and he was older so like, well not forced me, but pushing me sort of thing. And I just kept saying, 'no, no', because I was too young and everything.

[...]Looking back on their sexual experiences the young women were generally reluctant to describe men's behaviour as violent, or as rape, unless overt force had been used. They usually saw themselves as contributing to the pressure because they had not stopped it.

Verbal sexual pressure: coercion

Verbal persuasion from men could be experienced as coercive not directly because of the man's behaviour, but because of the woman's beliefs about the meaning of men's behaviour and what would happen if intercourse was denied.

A: I was also a little bit worried, but I just tried to brush it off a little bit. But it was obvious that he wasn't going to take no for an answer. I suppose in a way I was scared of what he would do if I said 'no' any more. Because he was really like pushing me. Not pushing me physically, but pushing me in the sense of—'Oh, come on'—you know. I thought,—Oh God I felt guilty, because I thought—'you've led him on—led him on'.

Here the fears of what the man might do were compounded by the woman's conception of male sexuality which made her feel responsible for his state of arousal and its resolution. In another case, the young woman had much more explicit fears about what might happen, based both on expectations in this relationship and on earlier experiences of violence.

A: ... I was very young—I didn't know what was—well I did know what was happening, but he was about five years older than me, and he was very very persuasive and very pushy, and I was so frightened of him at the time that you don't want to say no. If you think—if you say no then they won't want to see you again.

Her account starts with pressure coming from the man in terms of his age, his persuasiveness, but the salient issue for her is her belief that sexual intercourse is the price of a continued relationship. The lack of any pleasure from intercourse makes her realize that this price was not worth it, but she is then caught by her own expectations of men's behaviour:

A: ... At the time, you know—awfully painful—and just kind of lying there and wishing that it'd go away: and that went on for about—I suppose that was about seven or eight times we had sex and I—every time cringing and not—not enjoying it. It—it seems silly—at the time you think, 'well, why can't you say no?'

The reason that she could not say no was obviously difficult for her to articulate in the interview:

A: ... But, as—because I—every—I was very afraid of men at the time because my Dad used to hit me all the time when I was—didn't do something he wanted I'd get hit and I was, like for a long—for three years afterwards I thought that any man would hit me if—if I didn't do what he says, that you—you know, that you have to do. If you say 'no' to somebody then they're going to hit you.

It was only after a period of critical reflection that she was able to connect these events and to make sense of her experience.
[...]

Physical sexual pressure: sex when drunk

Where women had been drunk at the time of unwanted sexual intercourse, they were particularly unwilling to describe themselves as having been raped or physically forced into sex. They felt that they must take some responsibility because they had not been in a state effectively to choose not to have sex.

A: I'd had something to drink, and I started to sober up, very drunk and I started to sober up. And somebody, a friend of this person who was having a party ... We'd had this party, and we'd come back to this person's flat ... just like a friend of a friend. I mean I can't say that I was forced into it or whatever, but I was in that position where I thought, 'God, I don't want to do this, I don't want to do this', and I sobered up a little bit, and I was still slightly tipsy anyway. I thought, 'Oh God, you know, what am I going to say?' Because it was obvious what he was expecting. And really when I was quite drunk I went along with this, not really making the decision to do that ... So I didn't really have a conscious decision to make, but it was obvious, because I had let myself.

For other women though, an experience of having unwanted sexual inter-course could make them more assertive in relation to the man.

A: So, on the second day of me going out with him, I got drunk and he had sex with me and I really regretted it. Like the next day I hated it and I didn't like him. And it seemed that after that, after he'd actually got his sex, it seemed like he thought he could treat me like dirt. He just started speaking to me rudely, just being stupid, you know? So on the fourth day I just told him, I don't want to know. Because he thought because he got it once, he thought he was going to get it every day and I said to him it was a big mistake I made. I really regretted it. I think it was from that point that it made me realize I'm not going to do that again, no way.

Physical sexual pressure: child abuse

Experiencing sexual abuse as a child was profoundly disempowering. The accounts of those who recognized that they had been abused, though, show links between the processes of pressure and of empowerment as young women coming to terms with their sexuality as adults try to understand the impact of their previous experiences.

A: Well, when I was very young I was sexually abused by my uncle. He also abused my two sisters and when it actually happened to me I told my Mum and Dad. It was all hush hush then. It was the time when it was never spoken about and they wouldn't believe me. So since then I decided, 'don't trust anybody, forget all about it', and then somehow I made myself forget. I don't know how I did it, I just made myself forget. And then I started getting close to this lad when I was about 14 and then it just started coming back, sort of in little bits.

Child abuse became a possible source of empowerment when women could look back on their experiences (usually as a result of counselling some years after the abuse), give a name to what had happened, and connect subsequent negative sexual experiences (usually an absence of any enjoyment of sex even in a close relationship) with the abuse. That is, they had to be able to rec-ognize the experience as an abuse of power and to reflect on its impact on them. One young woman (who had been recommended to see a coun-sellor, but had refused because she felt she would break down when recalling the abuse) discussed her first subsequent sexual experience in the following terms. At the time she was 16 and was coming under pressure to have sex with her boyfriend who was a year older and had been her friend since she was 13.

A: And my boyfriend—I was frightened of losing him really, at the time. Now when I think back it wasn't worth having that.

Q: So he put you under quite a lot of pressure, is that what you are
      saying, that you felt you were under pressure?
A: Yes.
Q: And what about when it actually happened, how did you feel about
      that?
A: I felt awful. I remember crying and saying. 'I just can't do it'. It was
      the worst thing, it was awful.

She had reflected a good deal since then on her experiences and also got other
women to discuss the quality of their sexual experiences with her so that she
could compare them with her own. She had had sex with later boyfriends
because it was what they wanted, but in a longer relationship she felt some
pressure from the quality of the relationship itself.

A: It sounds as if I have been used as an innocent victim here. No, I
      wasn't an innocent victim, I went along with it (sexual intercourse)
      because I had been going out with him for a long time and I couldn't
      see us finishing in the future and it wasn't a fling. He wanted it and
      I wanted to make him happy.

At the time of her interview she was 19 and in a much more equal relationship, but the abuse in her childhood still constrained the possibility of
her finding sexual pleasure.

A: He's 23. It's the best relationship I have ever had. . . . he doesn't
      pressurize me into doing anything that I don't want to. If something
      is the matter, he will ask me and make sure that I tell him, and if he
      has any problems, he will tell me. He's fun and he's relaxed, but he
      is also caring. He cares about what I want to do, not just what he
      wants to do.
Q: So it's something you talk about. Is sex something that you feel better
      about now or is it something that you still see as not being a very
      positive part of your life?
A: I don't really enjoy it at all.
Q: Does he know you don't really enjoy it?
A: I think he thinks I am not bothered about it, because I wouldn't like
      to deprive him. I think a lot about him and I am not repulsed by
      sex, I don't think, 'oh God'. I will have sex but I don't think, 'oh
      brilliant' when it's finished, and 'really great'. I would rather get up
      and make a cup of tea or something.
Q: To be blunt, do you have orgasms?
A: No.
Q: Do you think that's an issue?
A: From what I have heard and read, women don't have orgasms a
      lot, like every time and things like that, so I would like to have

an orgasm I suppose, but if I don't it doesn't bother me ... I think it's what has happened in the past really. I would like to enjoy sex.

While this may not seem a very positive example, this young woman has developed some sense of her own needs, has transformed the way in which she relates to a sexual partner, and perceives the possibility of a positive sexuality for women, even if she does not yet know how to achieve it.

Physical sexual pressure: the use of force or the threat of force

While sexual intercourse as a result of the use of threat or force may seem to categorize an incident as clearly violent, women were not necessarily willing to use the term rape when they felt they might somehow have been able to prevent or avoid the situation, or that this was what sex was like.

Q: Did you want to do it at the time?
A: Not really, I think. No it wasn't, because I was like 13, he was 27. He was, know what I mean? He knew that I really liked him. He just sort of like — I didn't want to. He didn't rape me, but I didn't want to, but he just, you know—it's like, 'Oh, come on, come on'—know what I mean? Then it wasn't anything romantic with no clothes on or anything like that. It was just sort of skirt up. Know what I mean, and then by the time he did it, it was all over and done with.

In other cases women were clear that they had been raped. In the following quotation, the definition of rape was clear to the young woman even though she found it difficult not to blame herself for what happened and she already had a relationship with the man concerned.

A: ... I only went out with him for two weeks.
Q: Is he the one that hit you?
A: Yes, but he did rape me as well ... It was a very important thing in my life. It's changed me.
Q: Did you feel guilty about it? Did you feel responsible?
A: Yes I did. I did feel it was my fault, and I still do in a way, but I know it wasn't. I feel angry that I feel that way.
Q: Why did you feel that it was your fault?
A: Well, I was there.

[...] Even where women are empowered to the extent that they recognize that they are being violently treated, they do not always have the power to end a violent relationship decisively.[7]

Q: Is it when he became violent that you finished with him?
A: Yeah. Well, it wasn't exactly straight away. I'd been out with him a year after that. He'd been hitting me for a year.

She states that her first experience of sexual intercourse was when she was 15 and her boy friend was 24. He got her drunk at a party so that she did not know what she was doing. However, she did not experience this as forced sex as she had felt she had enjoyed it. The man had hit her twice with an iron bar in the first year of their subsequent relationship:

Q: Were you scared of him?
A: It wasn't there all the time. The first year it was OK; I enjoyed the relationship, but I was frightened then because in the second year it was either have sex or get battered. It was—it was like every night of the week. Even if I was on my period, he had to have it.

These experiences, need not be taken as wholly negative. The experience of pressured sex was one which contradicted young women's expectations of loving, fulfilling and romatic relationships, and could make them determined not to be used, dominated or controlled in the same way again. [. . .]

While young women cannot always put their positive intentions into practice in every situation, making sense of the pressures in their sexual encounters can be one level of empowerment for them.

PRESSURED PLEASURE: YOUNG WOMEN AND EMPOWERMENT

The problems that women face in negotiating sexual encounters can be clarified by distinguishing between two levels of empowerment. The experience of pressured sex is one possible source of a process of *empowerment at an intellectual level* where young women reflect critically on their knowledge and experience and make decisions about future sexual strategies; they will ask him to use a condom, not let him hit them, not have intercourse just because he is aroused, ensure that they are not at risk of pregnancy, STDs or HIV, make their own sexual needs known. The level of empowerment can be a powerful force in transforming women's consciousness and leading them to work out more positive models of female sexuality. Empowerment at the intellectual level, however, does not mean that young women can achieve empowerment in subsequent sexual encounters, and they are often aware of this.

A: . . . given the same situation again, I'd try, I'd do my utmost not to get myself in the situation anyway, but . . .

If they are to control their own sexuality and to negotiate a positive balance of sexual power with men, young women need to be *empowered at an experiential level*. This level of empowerment means achieving in practice a shift in the male domination of sexual encounters. This level of practice, though, can be extremely unstable. A young woman may be safe with one man, but not with others; assert her needs in one relationship, but not in subsequent ones. Effective empowerment then needs the *integration of the intellectual and experiential levels,* so that the critical consciousness of a positive female sexuality can be negotiated in practice in more than one situation (Holland *et al.*, 1991b).

While we can classify women's experiences by the types of pressure to which they have been subject, their responses to these pressures are variable depending on how they make sense of their experiences. Categories of pressure are not then a static classification, but rather expressions of processes of negotiation in sexual encounters. While some women become more assertive as the result of their experiences of pressured sex, others will settle for unrewarding sexual relationships as adequately fulfilling their expectations. One young woman illustrated in the course of her interview something of the process of moving from intellectual to intellectual/experiential empowerment. She first discussed how she moved from acceptance of a violent relationship to the rejection of it.

A: I went out with someone for six months and it was a really bad relationship, as in he was treating me badly. He was a very spoilt only child. And then for a long while I just accepted it. I was really downtrodden and that sort of thing, and then suddenly I just realized he treated me like rubbish, 'I'm not staying with you, you know, this is no good, this is not a good relationship. You've done a lot of things to upset me'. It was—I read a book called *Women Who Love Too Much* and it was a typical relationship that I read in that; you know, you would do everything to try and please him, and then it doesn't work and you—something wrong with yourself. And I suddenly thought it's not, it's not me, and I got out of it.

Later in the interview she commented on how her expectations at the time of this relationship did not work out in practice.

A: I remember thinking if you had sex with someone you could control him.
Q: You could?
A: Mm. You know, you had that control over them. Because it was something so personal and so special to me, it must be to them, so I could then, you know—if they'd said to me, do this, so I could do it back. But then, you know — you can't, you can't at all.

Empowerment in this young woman's account then comes to mean not her exercising control over men, but being able to exercise control over herself in the negotiation of sexual boundaries.

A: ... now I would sleep with somebody if it pleased me, and if it pleased him, you know, everybody's happy. If it didn't [please him]

I shouldn't think they'd do it. But if I didn't want to, I wouldn't, no matter what.

Although she wanted a relationship with a man and saw mutually pleasurable sex as an important part of any such relationship, she also saw being empowered not to have sex as an important part of her development. [. . .] This decision to avoid unwanted sex illustrates her integration of intellectual and experiential empowerment, and is dependent on her having a positive conception of female sexuality which included the possibility of female sexual pleasure.

Sexual pleasure

It was unusual for young women to discuss sex in terms of their own pleasure, rather than men's needs, or their feelings for a man or a relationship. Sexual pleasure was seen as dependent on the quality of the relationship with a man. Where they were intellectually empowered to the extent of being conscious of women's pleasure then they realized that they needed to be able to communicate with men. One young woman rejected the idea of casual sex because she did not feel she could communicate what she wanted to a stranger.

A: If you don't know them well enough to say what you like—well, I do anyway. Well, if you don't know them at all—say if you go for a one night stand, I think a lad is just out to pleasure himself and not pleasure you, so what is the use of you going to bed with somebody that is only doing it for himself?

Another commented more generally on the problems of communicating her needs to men.

A: . . . I've been out with an awful lot of men, but in saying that, I've had very few relationships, real solid relationships, I think. I've just split up with someone, about three months ago, and that was a wonderful relationship. And after that I haven't actually slept with anyone because I don't want to go through the mechanics without a real solid foundation of feeling there. Because I could discuss anything with my last boyfriend, like 'I get pleasure this way' and he'd say 'oh right' and he'd respond. With some partners you can often feel, 'I'm not really enjoying this', or, 'I'm not feeling as much as I could', but you can't say—'look if you'd just do this' because you don't have the confidence within the relationship.

Another young woman commenting on how confident she felt about asking a sexual partner to use a condom said:

A: . . . I wouldn't ever feel embarrassed. I think if you're embarrassed about sex then you shouldn't actually do it until you're confident about it, because if you—these little—you know—hangups about it, then you're not going to enjoy it.

[. . .] Where women had a notion of their own pleasure to which men would consent, they could negotiate the boundaries of safer sex in ways which were acceptable to men, but also satisfying and effective for women.

Q: Do you see safe sex as meaning using a sheath or are there other sorts of ways of . . .
A: I suppose you . . .
Q: Having sex or . . .
A: Yeah. You don't necessarily have to have intercourse to know. You can just sort of sleep—I don't know—kiss someone or whatever, you know. You don't necessarily have to penetrate, I suppose. Penetrative sex, I don't — yeah, I mean, that—you know, just it's all right just to be with someone isn't it, you know. You don't necessarily have to sleep with them in the full extent, just enjoy being with them. I suppose that's a form of safe sex, not indulging yourself to the full extent.

The rarity of this empowered stance in relation to non-penetrative sex indicates how far there is to go in empowering young women more generally.

CONCLUSION: THE NEGOTIATION OF SEXUAL BOUNDARIES

If women are to be able to negotiate the boundaries of sexual encounters so as to ensure both their safety and their satisfaction, the way in which both men and women are constituted as sexual subjects has to change. Fine (1988, p. 42) argues that 'the missing discourse of desire' which is silenced in US public school sex education effectively treats women as victims of men's sexuality, rather than as female sexual subjects who can negotiate with men. As Tamsin Wilton (1991) states, 'If desire is unavailable to women, then sex can only be something done by men to women'. The cross-cut analysis of our sub-set of data shows that we cannot simply classify women according to men's behaviour towards them, as passive victims of pressured sex. The categories of pressure which we have illustrated indicate something of the complexities of the social context of women's sexual empowerment, and the contradictions of the processes involved.

We have considered empowerment as a process at the level of knowledge and ideas. Achieving intellectual empowerment requires a model of a positive female sexuality which offers women a way of reflecting critically on their experiences of pressured sex. Women are only victims to the extent that their experiences of pressured sex appear to them as isolated personal experiences for which they are responsible, and which they cannot prevent in future (see also Thompson, 1990). Intellectual empowerment is an uneven process of moving away from this position to a more collective sense of women's relationships to men.

Intellectual empowerment, however confident, is insufficient to ensure that women can act effectively on their positive conceptions. Empowerment is also a process of putting into practice ways of negotiating safe and pleasurable sex with men. This experiential level is contested and unstable and to be effective must be integrated with a process of intellectual empowerment. In our analysis we have illustrated some of the many constraints on this level of intellectual/experiential empowerment which come from men's continuing power over women, and women's acceptance of this power.

The concept of empowerment as a contradictory and contested process, is intended as a starting point for considering practical strategies for transforming pressured sexual relationships between women and men.

Empowerment is complicated by the divisions between women such as those of class, race, ethnicity, culture and religion, but women's accounts of their experiences remain a primary source of understanding how these contradictions are dealt with in practice. From their accounts of their experiences, knowledge of a positive female sexuality can be created which perhaps can be developed in ways which can be put into practice by those who need the knowledge (Cain and Finch, 1981).

APPENDIX

The network of pressure in sexual relationships and encounters

A systemic network is an analytic device suitable for the organization and categorization of qualitiative data, preserving and representing some of the original essence of these data. It is an instrument for enabling theory to be tested, translating the language of (in this case) the interview transcript into the language of the theory. This helps with the interpretation of the patterns and meanings in the data (Bliss, Monk and Ogborn,1983). [. . .]

A network of pressure in sexual relationships was developed to categorize the types of pressure experienced by young women in sexual relationships and encounters. Three main types of pressure are identified, personal, social and male pressure. The categories used in the analysis of data, such as verbal pressure or physical pressure to have sexual intercourse, or family/religious pressure not to have sexual intercourse, are not mutually exclusive. More than one category can be used to grasp experience, and a young woman may experience more than one of these pressures on the same or different occasions. Male pressure on young women should be considered in conjunction with the other aspects of personal and social pressure which they experience. It is clear, for example, that internalized social pressures, for example to lose one's virginity, could result from, or be reinforced by, earlier experiences of male pressure, as well as the general forms of peer pressure, the media or other forms of social pressure.

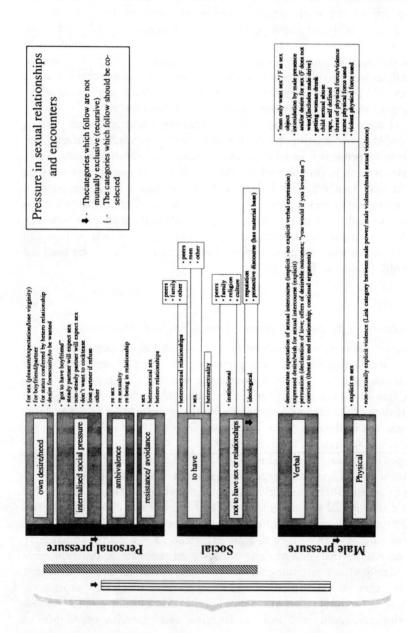

FIGURE 19.1 Pressure in sexual relationships and encounters.

Notes

This article is an edited version of a paper given at the British Sociological Association Annual Conference, Manchester, 1991.

1. The Women, Risk and AIDS Project is staffed by the authors and Sue Scott (Manchester University) working collectively, and has been financed for two years by the ESRC. It has also received grants from Goldsmiths' College Research Fund and the Department of Health. Valuable assistance has been given by Jane Preston, Polly Radcliffe and Janes Ransom. WRAP has used a purposive sample to interview 150 young women aged 16–21 in London and Manchester in depth, and has additional data from 500 questionnaires. A grant for a further year has been given by the Leverhulme Trust for a comparable study of young men.
2. Where male violence towards women is general it is to be expected that there will also be male violence towards other men and children.
3. Cited by Peter Aspden in 'Catalyst College' *THES* 25/1/91.
4. For further discussion of methods see Thomson and Scott (1990) and Ramazanoglu (1990). WRAP working papers are available from the Tufnell Press (47 Dalmeny Road, London N7 0DY, Telephone 071 272 4861).
5. For the further development of this notion of empowerment in relation to safer sex see Holland *et al.* (1991b).
6. In interviews with 141 convicted rapists in a Home Office study, 44% of those who admitted the offence claimed that the woman concerned was not harmed (Grubin and Gunn, 1991). In Scully's study, one third of convicted rapists denied that the act they had committed was rape (Scully, 1990).
7. This is a complex political issue which we do not have space to address here, but our data show a range of coping strategies which are comparable to those found in previous studies, with leaving the violent man as a woman's most effective personal solution (Dobash and Dobash, 1979; Kelly, 1988).

References

Acker. J. (1989) Making gender visible. In R. Wallace (ed.) *Feminism and Sociological Theory*. London: Sage.

Bart, P. and O'Brien, P. (1985) Stopping rape: effective avoidance strategies. *Signs* 10, 83–101.

Bhavnani, K. K. (1988) Is violence masculine? a black feminist perspective. In Grewal *et al.* (eds) *Charting the Journey: Writings by Black and Third World Women*. London: Sheba.

Bliss, J., Monk, M. and Ogborn, J. (eds) (1983) *Qualitative Data Analysis for Educational Research: A Guide to Uses of Systemic Networks*. London: Croom Helm.

Bower, M. (1986) Daring to speak its name: the relationship of women to pornography. *Feminist Review* 24, 40–56.

Cain, M. and Finch. J (1981) Towards a rehabilitation of data. In P. Abrams, R. Deem, J. Finch and P. Rock (eds) *Practice and Progress: British Sociology 1950 – 1980*. London: Allen & Unwin.

Campbell B. (1980) A feminist sexual politics: now you see it now you don't. *Feminist Review*. 5, 1–18.

Cock, J. (1989) *Maids and Madams: Domestic Workers Under Apartheid* (revised edn) London: Women's Press.

Coveney, L., Jackson, M., Jeffreys, S., Kaye, L. and Mahoney, P. (1984) *The Sexuality Papers: Male Sexuality and the Control of Women*. London: Hutchinson.

Dobash, R.E and Dobash, R. (1979) *Violence Against Wives: A Case Against the Patriarchy*. New York: Free Press.

Edwards, A. (1987) Male violence in feminist theory: an analysis of the changing conceptions of sex/gender violence and male dominance. In J. Hanmer and M. Maynard (eds) *Women, Violence and Social Control*. London: Macmillan.

Estrich S. (1987) *Real Rape*. Harvard: Harvard University Press.

Fine, M. (1988) Sexuality, schooling and adolescent females: the missing discourse of desire. *Harvard Educational Review* 58, 1, 29–53.

Grubin, D. and Gunn, J. (1991) *The Imprisoned Rapist and Rape*. London: Home Office.

Hanmer, J. and Maynard, M. (1987) *Women, Violence and Social Control*. London: Macmillan.

Hanmer, J. and Saunders, S. (1984) *Well-Founded Fear: A Community Study of Violence to Women*. London: Hutchinson.

Hite, S. (1976) *The Hite Report*. London: Pandora.

Holland, J., Ramazanoglu, C., Scott, S., Sharpe, S. and Thomson, R. (1991a) Between embarrassment and trust: young women and the diversity of condom use. In P. Aggleton *et al.* (eds) *AIDS: Responses, Interventions and Care*. Brighton: Falmer.

— (1991b) Pressure, resistance, empowerment: young women and the negotiations of safer sex. WRAP Paper 6. London: Tufnell Press.

Janeway, E. (1977) *Man's World, Women's Place*. Harmondsworth: Penguin.

Kelly, L. (1988) *Surviving Sexual Violence*. Cambridge: Polity.

— (1991) Unspeakable Acts: women who abuse. *Trouble and Strife* 21, 13–20.

Kitzinger, C. (1987) *The Social Contruction of Lesbanism*. London: Sage.

Ramazanoglu, C. (1990) Methods of working as a research team. WRAP Paper 3. London: Tufnell Press.

Rhodes, D. and McNeill, S. (1985) *Women Against Violence Against Women*. London: Onlywomen Press.

Rich, A. (1983) Compulsory heterosexuality and lesbian existence. In E. Abel and E. Abel (eds) *Women, Gender and Scholarship: The SIGNS Reader*. Chicago: University of Chicago Press.

Scully, D. (1990) *Understanding Sexual Violence: A Study of Convicted Rapists*. Boston: Unwin Hyman.

Stanko, E. (1985) *Intimate Intrusions: Women's Experience of Male Violence*. London: Routledge & Kegan Paul.

Stanley, L. and Wise, S. (1983) Black into the Personal or: our Attempt to Construct 'Feminist Research'. In G. Bowles and R. Duelli Klein (eds) *Theories of Women's Studies*. London: Routledge & Kegan Paul.

Thomson, R. and Scott, S. (1990) Researching sexuality in the light of AIDS: historical and methodological issues. WRAP paper 5. London: Tufnell Press.

Thompson, S. (1984) Searching for tomorrow: on feminism and the reconstruction of teen romance. In C. Vance (ed.) *Pleasure and Danger: Exploring Female Sexuality*. London: Routledge & Kegan Paul.

—(1990) Putting a big thing into a little hole: teenage girls' accounts of sexual initiation. *Journal of Sex Research* 27, 341–61.

Wilson, E. (1983) *What is to be Done about Violence Against Women?* Harmondsworth: Penguin.

Wilton, T. (1991) Feminism and the erotics of health promotion. Paper given at the Fifth Conference on the Social Aspects of AIDS, London, 1991.

Wilton, T. and Aggleton, P. (1991) Condoms, coercion and control: heterosexuality and the limits to HIV/AIDS education. In P. Aggleton, G. Hart and P. Davies (eds) *AIDS: Responses, Interventions and Care*. London: Falmer.

20 EDUCATION AND THE MUSLIM GIRL

SAEEDA KHANUM

I have come to spend a day at the Bradford Muslim Girls' School. [...]
I am greeted by one of the older girls in a maroon-coloured uniform complete
with *hijab* (headscarf). Over thirty girls attend the private middle school at the
expense of parents who believe their daughters are getting a good education
as well as a strong grounding in Islam. These schools are being set up in this
country in an attempt to reproduce the religous and cultural values of Muslim
home life. The schools act as daytime custodians, ensuring that Muslim girls
do not stray very far from orthodoxy.

The Mulsim Girls' School is staffed by a headmistress and seven part-time
teachers: two Muslims, two Catholics, two Anglicans and one whom the head,
Nighat Mirza, suspects of being an atheist. Costing £100,000 a year to run, the
school raises only £28,000 in fees; some of the rest is made up in donations
from wealthy individuals and from selling school merchandise, like cards and
mugs. The school runs on a large deficit.

After morning assembly the girls disappear to rooms named after the
Prophet's wives and daughters to begin their studies. The classrooms are
spartan, small and decorated with posters showing details of prayer, pil-
grimage and the life of the Prophet. Lack of adequate teaching staff and
equipment, and a narrow range of subjects, indicate that the girls are getting
less than a decent education. Although the school has been open since 1984,
it was only in 1989 that some girls took GCSE exams in Urdu, childcare and
religious studies. In 1990 the curriculum was expanded to include French and
English. In 1991 the girls were promised Maths and Sciences. Although things
may be changing, Mrs Mirza admits that past students have been cheated of an
education: 'Sacrifices have to be made. I'm not sad that those girls left with no
qualifications, but proud; they have the satisfaction of knowing that they did
something for someone else.'

Nighat Mirza says that she too has made sacrifices. She claims that because
of her present job, she will now be regarded as a fanatic by the education
Establishment and will be unable to go back into mainstream teaching. While
feminists eschew the *hijab* and see it as a symbol of oppression, Mrs Mirza says
she feels liberated by it. She claims it makes her feel confident and gives her
freedom to move around in the community: 'No one can see me, I'm private.

Source: Abridged from Saghal, G. and Yuval-Davies, N. (1992), *Refusing Holy Orders:
Women and Fundamentalism in Britain* (pp. 124–40). London: Virago.

I have access to all the world. Although shut off from the rest of the world, I have my own window to it.'

Mrs Mirza's teaching career followed marriage and motherhood. At the school she is interested in passing on the values of Islam as well as the benefits of her own experiences: 'I'd like the girls to be good Muslims and aware of their faith'. She dismisses suggestions that by teaching the girls to be good wives and mothers she is placating the demands of male members of the Muslim community. 'By teaching the girls about Islam we are giving them tools with which to challenge and fight for their rights. Empowering women doesn't frighten men but creates a more stable society,' she says. 'Islam teaches us that men and women are equal but different.' The girls are taught to understand the restrictions of their lives, and that Islam is a preparation for the life hereafter. She denies suggestions that the religious teaching in such separate schools consists of little more than teaching the girls to pray and read the Qur'an in Arabic, something they learn quite early on from their parents: 'In religious studies we teach the girls to question and analyze and to follow the commandments of God.'

Islam is said to pervade the whole of the school's teaching. French is taught by Molly Somerville, a charismatic white woman, dressed in *shalwar-kameez* and wearing earrings in the shape of the continent of Africa. The only presence of Islam in today's lesson is that the walls are covered with press cuttings about the French Muslim Alchaboun sisters Fatima, Samira and Layla, involved in the campaign to allow them to wear *hijab* to school. In the afternoon the same classroom doubles up as a room for religious studies, of which the Christian element is also taught by Molly Somerville. [...]

Mrs Mirza says she wants her ten-year-old daughter to get the best possible education. Will she send her to the school? Yes, but only if things improve. Her daughter, she claims, doesn't need to come to the school to get the good grounding in Islam because, says Mrs Mirza, 'I can provide that at home for her.' If all other parents could do that, wouldn't separate schools like the Muslim Girls' School become redundant? 'Most other parents are failing to do that these days because they don't have the same background as I do,' she says.

Statistics, however, tell a different story. Most Muslim parents don't send their daughters to separate schools but to state schools. Heavy fees may act as a deterrent, but in effect parents still place a value on giving their daughters a good standard of education, if only for the prestige of having an educated daughter in the marriage market.

During the lunch hour, I am surrounded by a sea of maroon uniforms. The majority of the pupils at the Muslim Girls' School have been sent there by their parents and have had little choice in the matter. They are now reluctant to leave, saying they have got used to the school. They agree that they would not be getting an education unless it was compulsory and have reconciled their personal ambitions with the realities of their situation. They say they are educating themselves because they 'might need it one day'. 'If I am lucky I might get married to a man who will let me use my education and get a good job,' says a 15-year-old with thick-rimmed glasses.

What do they like about the school? 'We get to learn all about our religion and can pray when we like. There is no racism here. No one here laughs at the way we dress, because we are all the same,' they say. Few dispute the fact they could get the same religious education by going to an ordinary state school during the day and attending a supplementary school run by the mosque in the evening. They regard the education at the nearby state-run Belle Vue Girls' School with a certain degree of envy and wish they too had more facilities like 'computers, a proper gym and books'. A 16-year-old cannot decide whether she wants to be a doctor or a lawyer, but says it will depend on what her parents allow her to do. This strikes a familiar chord with all of them. 'I want to be a hairdresser', says another. Does she think she will realize her ambition? 'No, because my parents won't let me.'

One tiny 14-year-old with freckles has hopes of being a journalist. I take to her immediately. She does not think her dream will come true because 'Asian parents don't allow their daughters to go into such professions'. A moment of silent confusion follows when I point out that they are talking to such a woman.

At the nearby Belle Vue Girls' School, a Bradford comprehensive where most of the girls are Muslim, there are similar conflicts. A group of about a dozen girls, of differing ages, have given up their lunch hour to talk to me about their hopes and aspirations. On one thing they are all agreed: none of them wishes to go to a 'separate' Muslim School. These girls see themselves as the 'lucky ones', for they have been brought up to regard education as a privilege, not a right. They resent the fact that their brothers are encouraged to get qualifications, whereas they have to fight for them every step of the way. No one is sure of the future. 'We all have our own plans, but we don't actually know what will happen,' says one lively 17-year-old who is about to sit her A levels.

They see education as a means of empowerment: 'If we don't get qualification, then the only alternative is marriage.' These girls see marriage as the end of their individual identity, and some describe it as a form of death. One 18-year-old is getting involved in as many activities as possible before she gets married this summer: 'My in-laws are sexist and won't let me do anything once I'm married.' Yet she doesn't see herself as being oppressed: 'My parents' choice is my choice. My freedom is in my mind.' [. . .]

Community pressure plays an overwhelming role in their lives, and 'mistakes' made by other women in the community result in more restrictions. 'Asian parents don't understand the concept of individuality; we're always judged by someone else's standards, never our own,' says Farrah, a 17-year-old former heavy-metal fan who found her identity at 13 when she became a practising Muslim. Dressed in a *hijab*, she says Islam has taught her her rights,

that she no longer allows people to take advantage of her, and that religion is
the dominant force in her life: 'It answers all my questions, makes sense and
is perfectly logical.' Muslim women, she adds, are oppressed not because of
religion but through a lack of religious education: 'Women have to be educated to use religion as a tool and not leave the interpretation up to men.'

For Asian women teachers, social pressures impose their own particular
restrictions and difficulties. The younger generation of women teachers work
hard to challenge their students' cultural and relgious upbringing and to use
their own experiences as a model and a guide. Saira, aged 29, had been teaching
in a Bradford state school for one year when a colleague reprimanded her for
challenging an Asian girl pupil who said arranged marriages work because there
are hardly any divorces. The white teacher accused Saira of 'arrogance' and
told her to stop confusing the girl and learn to be more 'objective' about cultural concerns. 'As a black teacher in the school ...' began Saira. 'You're not
a black teacher, you're *a* teacher,' came the response.

This incident, says Saira, highlights the complexities and contradictions of
her position: 'As a professional I'm expected to detach myself from the concerns of Asian pupils. However, as an informed insider who has experienced
the intolerable pressures the community brings to bear on girls, I feel I have
a duty to encourage pupils to hope for more from life.'

Some girls assume that because Saira is young, drives a car, wears Western
clothes and teaches a subject other than Urdu, her experiences are completely
different from theirs. To them she's distant and totally 'free'. 'This is just one
step away from seeing me as an Uncle Tom, a mere token,' says Saira. Asian
parents also have different expectations from an Asian teacher. On the one
hand, they welcome the fact that Saira is Asian, but they also expect her to
police their daughters on behalf of the community. 'Tell me straight away
if you see her hanging around with the boys after school, won't you?' they
say. [...]

The education of Muslim girls has less to do with schooling than with the
exercise of control by Muslim men over the lives of women in the family and
wider community. Generally, control is maintained by monitoring the level
and amount of interaction with male relatives and local community. But in
the area of schooling, Muslim parents feel that their grip on their daughters'
lives is weaker. Single-sex education is preferred by Muslim parents, and nearly
always for their daughters only.

While many parents have been content with single-sex state schooling for
their daughters, in recent years there has been a growing demand for 'separate'
schooling—Muslim schools. This demand is now stronger than ever, not least
because of the momentous events of the past decade, such as the *Satanic Verses*
affair and the Gulf War. Muslim schools are seen as the ideal way of maintaining a cultural cohesiveness, but demand for such institutions remained
relatively muted until the *Satanic Verses* affair catapulted British 'Muslims'
into the headlines.

Why did the demand arise in the first place? Was it purely to do with the inadequacies in the state education system, or was there a hidden agenda? If so, whose interest was this serving? The demand for separate Muslim schooling in Bradford in the early 1980s did not occur in a vacuum. The political climate created by the campaign for the provision of *halal* meat in schools and the campaign against headmaster Ray Honeyford for his alleged racist comments provided the perfect breeding-ground for such ideas.

The *halal* meat campaign was fought with the context of debates taking place inside Bradford council as it formulated its multicultural policies. The council's response to discontent among Muslim parents was to construct a multicultural policy based on the special needs of the ethnic minority children. In November 1982 Bradford council circulated a memo to headteachers to promote better relationships with parents of ethnic minority children. The memo outlined plans to provide parents with Asian-language translations of school activities; allow pupils to withdraw from religious assemblies with special arrangements for Muslim prayer; allow pupils to wear clothing in accordance with their faith; and provide segregated physical education and swimming lessons.

These early battles were not fought solely on a Muslim agenda, although the Council for Mosques used them to negotiate reforms with Bradford council. The Council—then recently formed as an umbrella organization and an emergent powerful rallying voice for the community—saw one of its roles as mediating Bradford Muslim demands to the metropolitan authority.

A series of articles in 1983–4 by Ray Honeyford, headmaster of Drummond Middle School, Bradford, published in national newspapers and the right-wing journal *Salisbury Review,* criticized the city's multicultural policies. These articles drew allegations of racism. His writing contained phrases such as: 'A volatile sikh', 'The hysterical political temperament of the Indian subcontinent', 'A figure straight out of Kipling is bearing down on me . . . His English sounds like that of Peter Sellers' Indian doctor on a day off' and 'Pakistan, too, is the heroin capital of the world (a fact which is now reflected in the drug problems of English cities with Asian populations).'

Honeyford claimed that the education of English children was suffering in schools where there were large numbers of Asian children. These views caused outrage in Bradford when he repeated them in the Yorkshire press in June 1984 and, following a sustained campaign, led by Jenny Woodward of the Drummond Parents' Action Committee, he took early retirement in December 1985.

Although the campaign to oust Honeyford was regarded among black people in Bradford as a considerable victory for parents and other anti-racist activists, they nevertheless found themselves facing a backlash from local racists as well as an onslaught from an unsympathetic press, both local and national.

Ian Jack, in his revealing article 'A Severed Head' *(The Sunday Times Magazine,* 15th December, 1985), described how popular racism surfaced at a football match when Bradford's Asian Lord Mayor, Mohammed Ajeeb, went to receive a cheque for money raised for families of victims of the Bradford football stadium fire: 'As his shoes touched the turf a cry broke out. "Honeyford!" shouted a couple of thousand Bradford football enthusiasts, all of them white, "Honeyford, Honeyford, Honeyford!" The Lord Mayor's speech could not be heard. For possibly the first time in British history a football crowd invoked a school headmaster as a hero.'

Another effect of the 'Honeyford affair' was to reinforce the siege mentality of Bradford's Muslim community. The effect of this was paradoxical: faced with institutionalized racism, the community became defensive as it tried to hold on to its culture, but in turn this defensiveness made it internally repressive — as a patriarchal culture, its cohesiveness is threatened when its female members interact with the outside world. The concept of *izzat* (chastity and honour) is central to Islamic culture. However, the burden of upholding the *izzat* of family and community rests solely on the female members, so *izzat* is maintained by controlling women. Methods to control women are different from those that control men. Women's lives are effectively policed—often quite crudely—while for men, preserving honour and chastity is mostly a question of exhortation to self-regulation and 'good' behaviour. The solution of separate schooling preferred by religious fundamentalists finds an echo in the fears of parents who want to hold on to their culture and control their daughters' sexuality.

Asian parents often face conflicting tensions when it comes to making choices over their daughters' education. An educated daughter, particularly one in the socially prized professions such as medicine, law or teaching, is infinitely more marriageable than one who has a poor education or one who is not educated. However, education leads to independent thought, and hence to a desire for actual independence. [. . .]

The idea of Muslim schooling for girls as a radical solution to the perceived deficiencies of state schools had already been on the agenda for a decade. In the 1980s in Bradford the idea never really got off the ground, floundering because the council's education concessions, wrested by community campaigns, proved to satisfy most parental demands. However, in 1983 an abortive attempt to set up separate schools was made by the pressure group the Muslim Parents' Association.

Tensions came to a head in Bradford council when, during the debates about multiculturalism, the Muslim Parents' Association began its bid to take over five state schools with an overwhelming majority of Muslim pupils and run them as volontary-aided Muslim schools. The Muslim Parents' Association wanted to set up Muslim schools at five existing state schools in Bradford: at the Belle Vue Girls' School, Whetley and Green Lane first schools and Drummond and Manningham middle schools. The MPA proposed to run the schools on Islamic lines but would not bar other children. It was estimated that this ambitious scheme would cost about £12 million. Abdullah Patel, a member of the MPA, was reported to have said confidently, 'Money is no problem.' He added that all he had to do was lift a telephone and any of the Muslim states in the Middle East would be willing to help (*Guardian*, 19 February 1983).

Bradford City Council decided to put the proposal to public consultation, claiming that most Muslim parents were opposed to it. At one of the schools earmarked for the change, teachers took matters into their own hands and conducted a ballot among the girls. Pupils at the predominantly Muslim Belle Vue Girls' School overwhelmingly rejected the proposal. All the 50 teachers at Belle Vue, including Muslims, vowed to find other jobs if the plans went ahead. Polls taken later by the Commission for Racial Equality within Bradford schools and the community also found little support for the idea of separate Muslim girls' schools. The then prominent Bradford Asian Youth movement also voiced its objections.

The plans for separate schools (rejected by the education committee in September 1983) forced Bradford to speed up its educational reforms to cater for minority needs and so maintain good race relations. This in turn weakened the Muslim Parents' Association's case for separate schools. Ironically enough, at the time, the Council for Mosques opposed the demand for separate schooling and opted for a compromise, accepting Bradford council's concessions on school dress. In public the Council for Mosques said the proposal had not been thought out properly. Other Asian organizations said the idea smacked of 'educational apartheid'. Privately it was rumoured that the Council for Mosques decided that 'tactically' the time was not right to pursue the campaign because of the atmosphere created by the Honeyford affair.

In all these campaigns the Council for Mosques played a central role in the negotiations, using the tensions between the community and the city council to wrest concessions which fulfilled its agenda too. It supported the state's multicultural banner in the *halal* meat controversy, and flew the anti-facism banner to join in ousting headmaster Ray Honeyford from Drummond Middle school.

After the failed attempt by the Muslim Parents' Association to 'buy' the five schools and run them as voluntary-aided Muslim schools, a short-term compromise was found. The Bradford Muslim Girls' school came into existence in 1984 when the Muslim Association of Bradford bought a former DHSS office in the city centre and converted it into a private school funded by fees and private donations.

Several unsuccessful attempts have been made in the past few years to get voluntary-aided status for the Bradford Muslim Girls' School and other schools like it up and down the country. Surplus places available at the local schools is often the reason given for not awarding voluntary-aided status—as in the case of the Islamia Primary School in the London Borough of Brent and Zakaria Girls' School in Batley, West Yorkshire.

Although far from perfect, the apparent acceptance of state schools today among Bradford Muslim parents and the gains in the city's multicultural poliçies since 1984 have come under attack from renewed demands for separate schooling, perhaps indicating that the issue was never really resolved. In 1984, in an interview [. . .] Liaqat Hussein from the Council for Mosques gave the orthodox Islamic perspective of threat to the community's religious and cultural well-being. The struggle, he said, is between Islam and godlessness, which in the schools takes the form of coeducation, Darwinian theory, female emancipation and 'Muslim girls running away with non-Muslim boys': 'There's no such thing as freedom in religion. You have to tame yourself to a discipline. We want our children to be good Muslims, whereas this society wants children to be independent in their thinking.'

The *Satanic Verses* affair put Muslims on the defensive about their religion and culture, and Muslim men (in particular) on the offensive in their desire to control Muslim women. This in turn has put 'separate' Muslim girls' schools firmly back on the agenda—only this time, in fundamentalist eyes, Rushdie and all he represents has become a symbol of the struggle between Islam and godlessness. Despite his Muslim faith, Rushdie's professed 'godlessness' is unpalatable to most ordinary Muslims. Rushdie has, in effect, become a nightmarish role model from which the Muslim community and its impressionable young women must be protected.

A culture besieged in this way throws up its own notions of what a 'good Muslim woman' is—or should be. Religion becomes a substitute for a kind of cultural conformity. In practice Islam has come to represent what is allowed rather than what is possible. For women the idea of *izzat* has become more blatantly a means of social control, and Musim schools have become the perfect institutions for exercising that control. Similarly, Muslim fundamentalists, like those of other religions, have misappropriated the word 'freedom'. Freedom to explore one's own potential as a human being intellectually, socially and sexually—has come to mean being 'permissive' and therefore morally corruptible.

However, the argument in favour of separate schooling finds strength in its aim of gaining parity with other religious denominations and is in keeping with provisions enshrined in the 1944 Education Act: minority parents should be accorded the same rights under law as Christian and Jewish parents in their demands for voluntary-aided schools under the policy of equal opportunity.

According to Department of Education and Science figures (January 1988) about a third (32%) of all state schools have voluntary status (under the 1902 and 1906 Education Acts) and are denominational. The pupils at these schools account for 23% of all pupils being educated in state schools: there are 4,768 primary and 233 secondary Church of England schools, 1,863 primary and 421 secondary Roman Catholic schools, and 16 primary and 5 secondary Jewish schools. There are also a handful of Methodist schools. Apart from the few Jewish schools, there are no voluntary-aided schools of ethnic minority faiths, although there are a small number of Muslim, Seventh-Day Adventist and Orthodox schools in the private sector.

But the 1988 Education Reform Act has established the dominance of the Christian religion and undermined any notion of sufficiently catering for the religious needs of minority children. It has led to an increase in the popularity of supplementary schools where Muslim and other faiths seek to redress the balance. The overall low achievement rate of black children from some minority groups in state schools strengthens the hand of the separatists, who believe that only in separate schools can pupils get a positive religious and cultural education. This non-racist environment, coupled with higher teacher expectations, should increase pupil confidence and performance.

The counter-argument is that an increase in separate religious schooling will result in racial segregation. The creation of minority-faith schools will undermine multicultural or anti-racist education by absolving other state schools from carrying out such policies. Finally, there is the division along class lines: the creation of Muslim schools will be more attractive to working-class than to middle-class families. Politicians, including the Labour Party leadership, are divided over the issue of separate schooling. Those most vocal in their support for the idea also happens to have a large number of Muslim constituents. Others want to see the abolition of state funding for all separate religious schooling.

While attempts to gain voluntary-aided status for independent Muslim schools [. . .] have failed, religious fundamentalists may have found a way of overcoming that hurdle. The opt-out legislation of the 1988 Education Reform Act gives state schools grant-maintained status and gives parents and governors control over the school. If the majority of these parents and governors in a school are Muslim, then the school can become, in effect, a state-funded Muslim school. At the time of writing, it remains to be seen whether this strategy will succeed.

However, very few have acknowledged the 'hidden agenda' behind the demands of religious fundamentalists: an attempt to stifle dissent and exert absolute control over the lives of women in the community. It is no accident, nor is it an act tinged with racism, that Muslim relgious schools are referred to not as 'Islamic denominational' schools but as 'separate' or 'segregated' by those who have a particular idea of the kind of community they want to foster—both those who want the schools and those who oppose them.

The issue of education and the battle for young minds has become a matter of vote losses or gains in areas where there is a large minority community. The education of Muslim females has become a pawn in a power struggle. Can the self-appointed and often fundamentalist community leaders deliver the much-needed Muslim vote to either Conservative or Labour? Maybe, but only if their religious and cultural demands are met, particularly in the education arena. However, this claim has yet to be put to the test. Where Muslim parents have been forced to express their opinion they have tended to support the existing state school, not the idea of a 'separate' school. For example, in 1991 an attempt to organize an 'opt-out' at Willowbank Primary School in

Glasgow failed amid accusations that campaigners had not made it clear that their aim was to set up a Muslim school ('Signing up for pupil segregation,' *Guardian*, 5 November 1991).

Male Muslim 'leaders' are willing, it seems, to go to any lengths to achieve their goals. In January 1989 Muslim parents in Batley, West Yorkshire, enlisted the help of the right-wing organizational Parental Alliance for Choice in Education. PACE, whose patrons include Baroness Cox and Norris McWhirter, is the offspring of the right-wing pressure group, the Freedom Association. PACE fought and won the court case for the 26 white Deswbury parents (1988) who withdrew their children from a state school where 84% of the pupils were Asian, in order to be allowed to send them to another, predominantly white, school.

Batley Muslim Parents, under the guidance of German convert Sahib Mustaqim Bleher, hope that PACE will win them their battle for state aid for the Zakaria Muslim Girls' School. Bleher has said that the co-operation between PACE and the Muslim parents is an 'interfaith alliance against multiculturalism, as what is at stake is not race but culture and religion'. The alliance, he admitted, is one of convenience, not a political marriage: 'We have different religions but both are preferable to some kind of secularistic mishmash.'

There has been virtual silence from Muslim girls and women over the issue of Muslim schools. In the poll taken in 1983 at the Bradford Belle Vue Girls' School the overwhelming majority of pupils and teachers rejected the proposal to turn the school into a 'separate' Muslim school. Another poll taken at the time by the CRE within Bradford schools showed a similar result. At the time of writing there are no indications that Muslim girls and women are preparing to voice their demands either in support for or in opposition to Muslim schools, but if the movement for separate schools continues at its current pace, or increases, those who object to it will be under increasing pressure to speak out and make their views known.

Note

A version of the first part of this chapter appeared in *New Statesman and Society*, 25 May 1990.

INDEX

— as gendered x, 18, 41, 51-60, 85-8, 96-
7, 99, 101-2, 124, 260
— and identity 85
— and masculinity 96-7, 187
— of medical profession 215
— over children ix, 24-38
— and the personal 108-9
— and post-structuralism 132-5, 137-8
— and postmodernism 117-19, 145
— and race 98, 170-1
— and sexuality 97, 261-2
— and the state 128, 130
pressure, in heterosexual relationships
260-2, 263-5, 274
— and child abuse 268-70
— and coercion 266-7
— and drunkenness 267-8
— and force 270-1
— and persuasion 265-6
— and pleasure 271-4
Prince 193
Pringle, R. 137
production, in Marxism 148
psychoanalysis 143
— and gender 100-1, 110, 111-12, 118, 147
— and lesbianism 225-6
psychology
— relational 196-7
— and relationship in development
194-208
— and studies of masculinity 82-9, 98-
100, 102, 173
puberty *see* adolescence
public/private spheres 41, 93, 96, 108-
9, 154
— and liberal feminism 125-6
— in social sciences 181

Quinby, L. 132

race
— and class 45, 47, 115, 163, 168-9, 170
— and education xii, 41-7, 48, 74-80,
96, 246
— and feminism xi, xii, 48, 93-4, 107,
115-16, 119, 154, 186
— and homosexuality xi-xii, 186-93,
244-58
— and masculinity xi-xii, 41-2, 93-4,
98, 186-7, 248-52
— and pornography 186, 187, 189
— and religion xiii
— as social category 163

racism
— and difference 161-6, 168-9
— in education 253-4, 255, 283, 287
— and ethnicity 162-3
— institutionalised 96, 111, 163, 284
— and masculinity 167, 180, 190, 244-5
— and psychological development 205
— and resistance 163-4
— and sexism 115, 218
— and sport 190-1
Ramazanoglu, C. 167, 260-75
rape
— effects 24, 270
— social construction 262, 265
— studies 83, 86, 264
reason
— and gender 152
— in postmodernism 144-5, 156
rejection, by parents 35-6, 38
relations, social
— and gender relations 123, 146-56,
260
— and identity 170
— and race 163, 166
relationship
— in psychological development xii,
194-208
— and vulnerability 197, 203, 205
religion, and race xiii, 281-8
representation
— and race 190-1, 249, 252
— sexual 186, 187-90, 244
reproduction
— and anatomical difference 151-2
— female control 114, 165
— and oppression 123
research, and invisibility of men 176
resistance
— black 163-4, 166, 191, 248
— by adolescent girls xii, 201, 204, 207-8
— by boys 206-7
— by women 262
— and cultural identity x, 45-6, 74-80,
170-1
— and feminism 117, 167
— lack of 264-5
Rich, A. 47, 114, 157 n.14
Richards, 180, 182, 183
rights, female 115-16, 119
— in liberalism 115-16, 124, 126
risk, in psychological development
194-6, 203-4, 206-7
Robbins report 16, 67, 72-3